FOUND IN TRANSLATION
GREEK DRAMA IN ENGLISH

In considering the practice and theory of translating classical Greek plays into English from a theatrical perspective, *Found in Translation* also addresses the wider issues of transferring any piece of theatre from a source into a target language. The history of translating classical tragedy and comedy, here fully investigated for the first time, demonstrates how through the ages translators have, wittingly or unwittingly, appropriated Greek plays and made them reflect socio-political concerns of their own era. Chapters are devoted to topics including verse and prose, mask and non-verbal language, stage directions and subtext, and translating the comic. Among the plays discussed as 'case studies' are Aeschylus' *Agamemnon*, Sophocles' *Oedipus Tyrannus* and Euripides' *Medea* and *Alcestis*. The book concludes with a consideration of the boundaries between 'translation' and 'adaptation', followed by an appendix of every translation of Greek tragedy and comedy into English from the 1550s to the present day.

J. Michael Walton was a professional actor and director before joining the Drama Department at the University of Hull where he was Director of The Performance Translation Centre and is now Emeritus Professor of Drama. His books on Greek Theatre include *Greek Theatre Practice*, *The Greek Sense of Theatre: Tragedy Reviewed*, *Living Greek Theatre: A Handbook of Classical Performance and Modern Production* and *Menander and the Making of Comedy* (with Peter Arnott). He was Editor for Methuen of *Craig on Theatre* and of the thirteen volumes of Methuen *Classical Greek Dramatists*, and three collections of Greek and Roman plays. He has translated many Greek and Latin plays, several with Marianne McDonald with whom he has collaborated on a number of other publications including *Amid Our Troubles: Irish Versions of Greek Tragedy* and *The Cambridge Companion to Greek and Roman Theatre*.

FOUND IN TRANSLATION

Greek Drama in English

J. MICHAEL WALTON

CAMBRIDGE
UNIVERSITY PRESS

CAMBRIDGE UNIVERSITY PRESS
Cambridge, New York, Melbourne, Madrid, Cape Town, Singapore, São Paulo

Cambridge University Press
The Edinburgh Building, Cambridge CB2 2RU, UK

Published in the United States of America by Cambridge University Press, New York

www.cambridge.org
Information on this title: www.cambridge.org/9780521861106

First published 2006

Printed in the United Kingdom at the University Press, Cambridge

A catalog record for this book is available from the British Library

ISBN-13 978-0-521-86110-6 hardback
ISBN-10 0-521-86110-1 hardback

Contents

Acknowledgements

Formal work on writing this book began during a period as a guest scholar at the J. Paul Getty Museum in Los Angeles in 2002 and has concluded with the assistance of a Leverhulme Emeritus Fellowship from 2004 to 2005. My considerable thanks are due to both institutions for their assistance and, in particular to Mary Hart and Marion True, who was at the time head of the Department of Antiquities, as my hosts at the Getty; also to Kenneth Hamma who first invited me to work as dramaturg on the production of one of my translations in Malibu in 1994.

Individual thanks are due to numerous librarians in Los Angeles, Dublin, London, Oxford, Cambridge and Hull who became enthused by the quest for translators; and to individuals who offered their time, expertise and goodwill, amongst them, Vicki Cooper, Nancy-Jane Rucker, Elizabeth Davey and Rebecca Jones at Cambridge University Press, Katerina Arvaniti and Vicky Madeli (who have also translated one of my books into Greek), Christina Babou-Pagoureli, Peter Burian, Pat Easterling, J. J. Hall, Edith Hall, Tony Harrison, Fiona Macintosh, Christopher Stray (a beaver among researchers), Amanda Wrigley and Jozefina Komporaly (a diligent and patient Research Assistant). My wife Susan has given valuable help in drawing attention to reviews of nineteenth-century translations while involved in her own research into the period.

Colleagues in the Drama Department and the Performance Translation Centre at Hull, past and present, and especially Tony Meech and Carole-Anne Upton, have all contributed over many years to the testing of ideas, as have the long-suffering casts who helped mould rehearsal versions of my own translations into something reasonably presentable.

Translating for the stage is collaborative but such a wealth of creditors begins to resemble the Old Man's list in Ionesco's *The Chairs* who ends up thanking everyone from the joiners who made the chairs to the paper-manufacturers, printers and proof-readers of the programmes.

Nevertheless, I cannot omit offering thanks to fellow-translators, Peter Arnott, Richard Beacham, Robert Cannon, Jeremy Brooks, Kenneth McLeish, Fredric Raphael, Michael Sargent, David Thompson and Don Taylor (some sadly no longer alive), as well as to an inspired and beady-eyed copy editor for Methuen in Georgina Allen, with all of whom I worked as general editor between 1988 and 2003 on the sixteen volumes of Classical Greek Dramatists, a series which has covered the whole of Greek drama and, latterly, some Roman comedy. Of these translators the late Kenneth McLeish must be singled out. He was responsible, either solo or in collaboration, for twenty-nine of the forty-six Methuen Greek translations and was a close ally as well as mentor in the craft of translation.

One name is missing from the above list, that of Marianne McDonald, collaborator in a number of books and translations, several ongoing. Without her prompt and assiduous reading of the manuscript at various stages, inspired suggestions and unflagging support this would be a much poorer book.

Introduction:
'Summon the Presbyterians'

MA UBU: You are married, Mister Ubu?
PA UBU: Too true. To a vile hag.
MA UBU: You mean to a charming lady.
PA UBU: An old horror. She sprouts claws all over, it's impossible to get one's hand
up her anywhere.
MA UBU: You should give her a hand up kindly and gently, honest Mr Ubu, and,
were you to do so you would see that she is just as appealing as Aphrodite.[1]
(Alfred Jarry, *Ubu Rex*, translated by Cyril Connolly)

Most of us wedded to translating Greek tragedy or comedy have experienced Ubu's marital problems. Translating anything from one language and culture into another is tough enough. Translation of drama adds a new dimension of risk; translators of classical plays find claws sprouting wherever they lay a finger. Ubu's wife (who is appropriately enough disguised as a ghost) offers scant consolation to anyone who recalls the fate of most mortals who tried to get their hands up a goddess.

The title of this Introduction reflects the complexity of finding language in a theatre that is becoming ever more cross-cultural, something which, for better or worse, seems to be inevitable. At the XIth International Meeting on Ancient Drama in Delphi in 2002 one of the most exciting productions was a Beijing Opera performance called *Thebais*, based on Aeschylus' *Seven Against Thebes* and Sophocles' *Antigone*. Subtitles were screened in modern Greek and in English. At one point Creon gave an instruction to the Chorus, subtitled into Greek as *Kaleste tous presbuterous*, 'Call the elders'. The English below it read 'Summon the Presbyterians'. Sometimes what looks like the obvious translation is actually the most misleading, a 'false friend' as it is known to translators. When the culture is at least two and a half thousand years old the problems of transference are inevitably magnified. Many of those who have made a study of such issues over the last three hundred years have tended to come up with proposals about Greek drama in English tied only to the nature of language. The performing arts have never been at their most creative when following literary formulae and many productions in the early part of the twentieth century seem to have suffered accordingly. Too many of the kisses proffered in the hope of miraculous transformation have resulted, not in the frog becoming a prince, but in the princess turning into a frog.

It is a matter both of the classics and of drama. Within the translating community those who know Greek and Latin are naturally enough more sympathetic to the special nature of dealing with the classical world. They are frequently the least sympathetic to the tightrope that the translator for performance is constantly walking.

Even the word 'translation' is difficult to pin down, though based on Latin – Latin authors being well versed in translation from the Greek. The English covers a multitude of sins. If you pick up a copy of *The 1811 Dictionary of the Vulgar Tongue*, with its subtitle of *Buckish Slang, University Wit and Pickpocket Elegance*, you will find 'Translators' between 'Tradesmen' (described as 'Thieves'), and 'Transmography or Transmigrify' ('to patch up, vamp or alter'). Translators are defined as 'Sellers of old mended shoes and boots, between coblers [*sic*] and shoemakers'. In the theatre they may lay claim to being a bit more than that: original artists, perhaps, but therein lies a conflict of interests. What is the purpose of translation? What are the function and responsibilities of the translator; and 'the rules of engagement', if any, in transferring a play from one era to another? And why do most of the theories and methods of procedure that can be applied to translation in general prove inadequate for the translation of a stage work? That is what this book is intended to be about.

Most of today's translators from Greek tragedy or comedy for performance are aware of the need to leave open that 'performance door' which much literary and literal translation from the past seems to close. There may be a positive virtue in the fact that so many translations will have dated within ten years, but bring an immediacy which ensures that the plays of the Greeks are accorded the same respect which has for years been taken for granted for plays of the Renaissance: namely, that they reflect both the time *in which* they were first performed, and the time *for which* they are now being revived. There are special questions, in translating as well as in directing plays from the classical period, as to how you cultivate a cultural context into which they will fit both theatrically and historically. How do you find a voice that will speak of centuries before

Christ in tones that the twenty-first century of the Christian era will comprehend? How should an English-speaking Electra sound? Will that be the same in a play by Aeschylus, by Sophocles and by Euripides? And in New York, Dublin or London? As significant, perhaps more so, is the question of how does the contemporary translator tackle all those aspects of the stage play that only come alive through performance: iconography, nuance, subtext, irony? Are there any guidelines or parameters in trying to ensure that Greek plays are made to live for an audience of today? Or is it a free-for-all?

One of the factors that make Greek playwrights difficult to translate is that they were, in their own day, the *avant-garde*. Aeschylus uses coinages which are not found anywhere else in surviving Greek literature.[2] Sophocles incorporates emotional contrasts which have their physical, hence visual, counterparts. Euripides uses a mixture of colloquial and forensic language to make the plays sound as though spoken by fifth-century Athenians, not miscellaneous Greeks from that distanced and unfocused past which was the Greek confluence of myth and history. Aristophanes has gods talking to prominent figures of state, who talk to fictional Athenians, who talk to dogs, clouds and birds, who talk to stage-hands or the audience. Menander makes domestic issues universal as, years later, will Chekhov or Ayckbourn. All of them were breaking new ground, pushing forward the possibilities of the stage. One of the priorities for any translator of Greek plays, surely, is to have such a firm grasp of the playwright's distinctive features, as well as of the broad political and theatrical conditions for which each of them was writing, that their equivalences are anchored solidly in the past before being transmitted into the present. To this may be added the variety of metre used in tragedy and in comedy, from the iambic trimeters of dialogue to the subtle and varied lyrics of choral interlude and formal (probably sung) lament.

Direct translation of Greek plays into English for performance had to wait, with a few exceptions, until the twentieth century.[3] From Gilbert Murray, the professor of Greek who became closely associated with the Vedrenne-Barker management at the Court Theatre, the debate began about what was the 'right' way of rendering these ancient classics into a form that was speakable, playable, and sufficiently faithful to the original work (though not necessarily always with that order of priorities). As you might anticipate, in the collision of academics with critics – never mind with creative artists – the result has been the kind of Babel identified by George Steiner in his study of the history of translation.[4] But maybe a theatrical Babel was what was necessary to free Greek drama from the stranglehold of linguistics, and return it to its rightful position as a performing, rather than a literary art. In Athens theatre was an art form akin to those of sculpture, painting, architecture and music. It was a synthesis of all the arts, statues that move, pictures that change, architecture that frames, music that highlights; amongst which poetry and rhetoric must take their place, but they must take that place alongside music, dance, acting and visual stagecraft. Perhaps on the theatrical tower of Babel the table is a round one where language has to take its seat as an equal among many, instead of demanding to be at the head.

Stage translators are well aware that playwrights make and fashion plays rather than simply rendering them on paper. Menander, as the probably apocryphal story goes, was asked by a friend how he was getting on with his new play and replied in words to the effect of 'Oh, I've finished it. All I have to do now is write it.' A play is an artefact; if it happens also to be a poem, or a piece of fine prose, well and good. It was Arthur Miller, a playwright much influenced by the Greeks, who suggested that there was no need for a great playwright to be a great writer. The Greek canon consists of great poems and pieces of great literature, as does the Jacobethan: all the more reason for translators to search as strenuously for the dramatic qualities as well as the literary, and work with directors at finding a context which may not be wholly dependent on the original. This is what the French critic Patrice Pavis calls 'relativism': the issue, if you like, of 'referential' and 'emotive' meaning. At one level, as Israeli scholar Yurit Naari put it, it adds up to translating the word 'sword' as 'rifle'; at another, it means keeping the *word* 'sword', but giving the actor a rifle. In an essay called 'The play: gateway to cultural dialogue', Gershon Shaked affirmed categorically that:

The past is a closed world unless we translate it into the present. The political regimes, ways of behaviour, transportation, communication, and architecture of the past are all insufficiently understood in the present. Therefore they are reinterpreted: candles become electric lights, swords and bows become rifles and mortars, human labour becomes machines, slave society becomes capitalism.[5]

This may help bring the past into the present. But if the past is a closed world, may not theatre perform an equal service by helping to reveal that closed past? Or absorb it? The stage is a place of metaphor and icon. Greek tragedy and, to a lesser extent comedy, offer a fund of *exempla*.

It doesn't need much imagination in an audience to see that the Trojan War can be any war. You don't need to know that Paris and Alexander are the same person, or that Helen was abducted as the bribe in a beauty competition, to understand that war can degrade both the losers and the winners, or that some people are born survivors. Those are the messages to be found in Euripides' *Trojan Women*. Sometimes the 'local' details are almost peripheral. Medea's personal conflict can be seen today as a war of the sexes, or a class war, or the battle for survival of all those who find themselves classified as outsiders. All such concerns can be found in Euripides' *Medea* of 431 BC.

Klaudyna Rozhin offered an insight when she wrote in an Introduction to her English translation of a Polish play, 'The cultural context of the play is a framework built of objects, processes, institutions, customs and ideas peculiar to one group of people amongst whom the play is set.'[6] She was writing about a Polish play set amongst immigrants in New York, so that for most of the characters, with varying degrees of fluency, the receiving language was itself a secondary and unfamiliar language which she had translated from Polish into Polish/English for a New York production. Does not the translation of an ancient Greek drama today – tragedy or satyr, comedy old or new – deal with similar propositions? Greek plays were created for a specific place, a special occasion, for performance in masks, and so on, a 'framework built of objects, processes, institutions, customs and ideas'.

An encouraging note for the status of the translator was struck by the remarkable writers' agent, Peggy Ramsay, when she described translation as 'a privileged form of conversation with an author'. It is about the nature of that privileged conversation that this book has been written. There is about Greek tragedy and comedy a sense of immediacy which is sometimes difficult to identify and harder to represent. The Greek playwrights had no idea that their work would last. Usually they expected a single performance. *The Oresteia* for Aeschylus was Michelangelo's snowman. The artist Serena de la Hey who works in Somerset creating sculptures from material which cannot last has suggested that 'There's a wonderful sense of freedom in something which is there for a very short time.' Greek playwrights of the fifth and fourth centuries BC did not know they were creating dramatic poems for posterity. They did believe that, if they allowed the attention of the audience to flag for even two minutes, those two minutes were gone, not to be recovered. For the creative artist such impermanence must clarify the mind with all the intensity of approaching death. Except in some areas of performance art, contemporary theatre is insulated from that sort of moment of truth. Capturing a similar momentum is a real challenge for a translator.

In the rest of this book I want to consider three main areas. First of these will be the history and theory of translation of Greek drama into English, and the manner in which many translations have reflected as much the historical period of the translation as the time of the original play. The second will cover specific aspects of Greek tragedy and comedy, including verse and prose, the language of grief, the language of the mask, stage directions, stage action, irony and deception, unfamiliar concepts, subtext and dialogue. The third will deal with the special nature of dramatic translation, the differences between tragedy and comedy, and the variety of plays which claim to be 'versions' or 'adaptations'. Three tragedies are chosen as 'test cases' and other tragedies and comedies (though by no means all) provide examples.

The topic turned out to be far larger than anticipated. A whole thesis could be written comparing eighteenth- and nineteenth-century translations of a single Sophocles play. This is not the place for a detailed analysis of why translation should have proved more popular in certain periods than in others, beyond pointing to the burgeoning movement towards a wider access in education from the middle of the nineteenth century onwards. Certainly the repertoire of the public theatres had precious little to do with it until comparatively recently. Nor is there as much speculation here as I would have liked on why certain plays have proved more attractive to translators than others (over eighty have tackled *Prometheus*, *Agamemnon*, *Antigone* and *Oedipus Tyrannus*), and in some periods rather than others (at least six new translations of *Medea* in the 1860s, twelve of *Alcestis* between 1870 and 1890). The recent publication (2005) of *Greek Tragedy and the English Stage 1660–1914* by Edith Hall and Fiona Macintosh puts flesh on many of the bones I worry at here.

Paring everything down to manageable proportions has resulted in referring to far fewer translations than are available, good, bad and indifferent. Apologies are due to the authors of those many excellent translations which have not been specifically mentioned. I have used only published translations and tried to avoid my own, or those on which I have collaborated. As the prime reason for instigating a new translation has to be a belief that yours will be better than any previous one, I wanted to look at the questions without suggesting there were answers up my sleeve. This is not a search for the 'best' translations. All I can hope is that the book will in some small way illuminate the nature of drama and its relationship to its own time as well as to the contemporary audience.

For the sake of the general reader words and passages in Greek have been transliterated into an English equivalent, though this leads to a number of distortions. The length of 'e's and 'o's, where Greek has two letters, one short, one long, is indicated by the use of a macron over the long vowel. Titles of plays and characters in quotation have been kept as they are to be found in the relevant translations and, as most of these use the latinised versions (e.g., 'Oedipus' rather than 'Oidipous'), that convention has been continued in the main body of the text, though this too involves an unavoidable element of inconsistency.

As for the Appendix of translations (complete works by Aeschylus, Sophocles, Euripides, Aristophanes, Menander and the third-century BC writer of Mimes (*miamboi*), Herodas), this too proved more difficult than anticipated even with the benchmark for inclusion being a fairly rigid adherence to the original (though less so with Aristophanes). This has allowed the inclusion of some turgid historical efforts while ruling out all manner of popular 'versions' of Greek originals from Todhunter to von Hofmannsthal, Cocteau to Jeffers, O'Neill to Paulin. There are some marginal inclusions by fine poets who have no Greek – Seamus Heaney, Brendan Kennelly, Ted Hughes, Blake Morrison amongst them – where reference to their work has been included in the main argument of the book.

A layer of complexity was provided by the absence in many early editions of a formal publisher and sometimes a date, compounded by a certain coyness amongst translators, especially those from 1820 to 1860, over admitting their identity (though seldom their provenance). The prolific 'First-Class Man of Balliol' (who turned out to be Thomas Nash) may have declared in his Preface to *Hecuba* (1869) that his translation 'is not solely as an antidote to the piebald and treacherous version now in use' (that of Theodore Alois Buckley – academic condescension towards the largely self-taught Buckley is not entirely unique in the history of scholarship), but was certainly not inclined to expose himself to similar ridicule; nor were the various 'Graduates' of Oxford, Cambridge, Dublin, or 'One of the Universities', those identified by initials only and the 'Anons' (some of whom are here unmasked). Details of the lives of major translators, Potter, Wodhull, Cumberland, Theobald, Mitchell, Frere, Buckley, Swanwick, Campbell, Way and others have necessarily been reduced to a minimum and must await another book. The large number of comparisons, some as little as a single word, means that identification is sometimes by publisher rather than translator. The Appendix should be used in association with the Index of translators for finding or comparing individual plays discussed in the main text. See also the preamble to the Appendix.

Errors there will be and omissions, for which my apologies, tempered at least by the possibilities that may have been uncovered for further and more reliable research. A number of mistakes have been corrected from the existing data bases, and some translations unearthed that have been overlooked. A few of the recorded translations (especially from Foster, 1918), proved impossible to locate, including some of those listed by the Cambridge publisher, J. Hall and some of the *Kelly's Keys to the Classics*, but I have at least looked at the vast majority. It has been a salutary experience which served to increase my respect for most of those who have shared this elusive craft.

CHAPTER I

Finding Principles, Finding a Theory

> The theorists, like Gibbon's Byzantine heretics, contradict one another at every turn; and what is worse, they show the most lamentable discrepancies between theory and practice.
>
> (Peter Green, 'Some versions of Aeschylus',
> *Essays in Antiquity*, London, 1960)

In a recent book on translation for the stage the Finnish scholar Sirkku Aaltonen made a welcome attempt to show how and why translation theory may meet some of the concerns expressed by Peter Green forty years earlier in his essay about translations of Aeschylus.[1] That translators from the classics should have proved wary of modern theoretical formulae which appeared to offer a general analysis of the processes involved in transferring material from a source into a target language is unsurprising.[2] Just as much suspicion has been accorded by those who translate for the stage who point out, with reason, that the translating of a play is no more than an early station in a progress which ends up, via directors, designers and players, as a new artistic entity. The position of the classical play, a tragedy by Aeschylus, Sophocles or Euripides, or a comedy by Aristophanes or Menander, involves leaps of faith and imagination and a whole new series of definitions. Green's conclusion that 'Translation is not, at any level, an ideal art; it is a crutch for human infirmity' does at least help to focus the mind on what happens in the process of taking the text of a Greek tragedy from the fifth century BC and renewing it for a reader in the twenty-first century AD, never mind for a contemporary audience.[3] A consolation in any search is the fundamental imperative that drove Aeschylus and is shared by today's translator/director/performer. Whatever else can be discovered by scholars and critics in the extant written text, Aeschylus' own priority had to reside in the immediacy of performance before an audience as diverse in experience, intellect and concentration as might be expected in any modern theatre.

9

Aaltonen was not writing exclusively about classical theatre but, in a wide-ranging review of stage translation, she uses classical examples on a number of occasions. She reminds us that 'theatre translation is not necessarily synonymous with drama translation', and that the act of translation is closely involved with theatre praxis. 'Readers are tenants who move into texts and occupy them for a while. In the theatre there are many tenants, and just as many meanings to be taken of texts.'[4] Her subsequent engagement with the various aspects of intercultural theatre and 'cultural collage' illuminates much of the frequently dense but sensitive areas of appropriation thrown up in recent years both by translation and by direction of classic texts.[5]

The brief here being to identify specific questions raised by classical theatre, it may be useful to look at where the theoretical study of dramatic translation currently stands. Where such a study comes from and how is more complicated. A selective, indeed idiosyncratic, trawl through a wide variety of approaches and proposals will result in few rules for the dramatic translator – rules, as Susan Bassnett has pointed out, are no longer appropriate – but may help to draw attention to what is distinctive in Greek tragedy and comedy and what may be worth preserving for the contemporary audience or reader.[6]

After the death of Aeschylus, the proposal that his plays might be revived at a major festival required a decree of state. Such discrimination was short-lived. In the century following the death of Sophocles and Euripides revivals of their work became commonplace alongside new versions of the old myths, influenced by and full of resonances from the works of the masters. The history of the drama bears witness to the process of renewal of an old theme being valued more for its diversion from the original than from its closeness to it.

The extent to which the first Roman tragedies of dramatists such as Livius Andronicus and Ennius of the third century BC were based on actual Greek models is simply unknowable. The influence of Euripides is claimed for Seneca in the first century AD but, whatever his merits or lack of them, as a tragedian little seems to have been bequeathed by Euripides beyond a passing similarity of plot outline. Nothing more survives than the odd fragment from the very early Latin tragedians, enough to make it almost a relief that it is Plautus rather than either of them who supplies the first literature in Latin. Plautus was both original and not original; for his plays and those of Terence we do have some indication of what translation meant for the Romans.

All surviving Roman comedy, twenty full plays of Plautus and six of Terence, was based on Greek comedies from anything between 80 and

150 years before their Latin versions. They come down to us as original works, though that, perhaps, is the point at issue. The fourth century BC in Athens had seen the new vogue in comedy develop away from the fantasy and the politics of Aristophanes to the more polite world of Diphilus, Philemon and Menander. The first two both wrote some plays on mythological themes – a fragment of Philemon appears to be the first known burlesque of the Medea story – but the majority concentrated, as did all the plays of Menander, on domestic issues in an Athenian world that had become ever less significant since the rise of Macedon. Unfortunately, only fragments survive of the plays of either Diphilus or Philemon; the precious little we now have of Menander consists of effectively two whole plays, *The Bad-Tempered Man* or *The Malcontent* (*Dyskolos*) and *The Woman from Samos* (*Samia*), and substantial sections of several others.

Native Italian comedy varied from the kind of stock farce which may have been the forerunner of the *Commedia dell'Arte* to mythological burlesque more akin to the old satyr plays. The more literary forms of Roman comedy survive in the works of Plautus and Terence, played in Rome during the first part of the second century BC and under the genre title of *Comoediae Palliatae*. In a Rome that would refuse to allow the building of a permanent theatre for another hundred years, Plautus and Terence created stage comedies, consciously and confessedly 'adapted' or 'translated' from the Greek originals of such as Diphilus, Philemon and Menander. Their world, then, is a curious blend of Greece and Rome. What parallels there might be and what challenges this affords strike at the heart of what and where the translator stands in relation to cultural transference or translocation.

The notion of 'translation' meant little to the Greeks except as it might affect identification of physical objects encountered in different parts of the barbarian world. No other culture that they knew or cared about had literature which they might wish to share with their contemporaries. With the Romans, things were different. A major proportion of their culture, in its broadest sense, was derived from the Greek and the whole concept of translation was widely addressed. Several different Latin words were used for the act of linguistic translation and several of the words used them-selves had other meanings which spelled out the status of the transaction. *Interpretari* has listed among its other meanings in the Oxford Latin Dictionary 'to expound, explain or interpret'; *transferre* 'to transfer to a new context'; *reddere* 'to give off the smell or flavour of'. For someone looking for a definition of stage translation the second and third of these

'transfer to a new context' and 'to give off the smell or flavour of'
splendidly pin down that realm of latitude within any stage work which
demands that the translator address issues of dramatic rhythm, mood and
tension as well as the words.

The most commonly used Latin words for 'to translate' are *vertere* and
convertere. In one passage Cicero describes the kind of snobbery that he
finds in those who prefer Greek to Latin: 'notwithstanding Sophocles'
Electra being a masterpiece, I still believe Atilius' not very good translation (*male conversam*) well worth reading'.[7] This has a direct bearing on
exactly what it is that Terence was doing when he took a Greek original
and 'converted' it into a Latin play. The ramifications of this will be
considered later (Chapter 9) when considering the rise of social comedy
and its Latin manifestations. The point here is that Terence and Plautus
may well have headed for the Greek repertoire but their originality as
dramatists allowed Terence to criticise one of his rivals as a decent
translator but a poor playwright: to put it literally 'in translating well, he
has written badly and from good Greek plays has made Latin ones that
are not any good'.[8]

This lies at the heart of most of the questions that arise about the
nature of stage translation, and the theories associated with it.[9] The
translation of a poem is a straight transaction or negotiation between
source and target with the translator functioning as broker, midwife, or
whatever metaphor you choose. The dramatic translator is certainly that,
but with the added dimension of performance where every element has to
be honed through all those involved with the production process.

Within the English tradition translation from the Greek was as
sporadic as it was erratic. English versions of Aesop, Aristotle and
Plutarch saw the light of day in the time of Elizabeth I: so did Homer.
Dryden, Pope, Diderot, Cowper and others in the seventeenth and
eighteenth centuries were to make elegant and eloquent observations on
the nature and function of translation. In the nineteenth, Schleiermacher,
Humboldt, Goethe and Nietzsche in Germany; Arnold, Newman and
Browning, reinforced by a growing band of translators of Greek tragedy,
committed to print miscellaneous thoughts about how and why they had
proceeded as they did.

John Dryden, an original playwright as well as essayist, Poet Laureate
and Royal Historiographer, was claimed by Samuel Johnson as the father
of English criticism. Dryden was fortunate in the time into which he was
born. Managing to make his name both for writing his *Heroic Stanzas*
on the death of Cromwell and, barely two years later, for his celebration

of the restoration of the monarchy (*Astrea Redux* of 1660), he was instrumental in introducing heroic drama to the newly liberated English stage, most notably in *All for Love*. By the time of its first performance (1678), he had already been Poet Laureate for ten years. Dryden and Lee's *Oedipus* (1679) contained quotations from Virgil and Horace on the title page of the first published edition. The classics had never been that far away from the mainstream literary tradition, though, as far as the drama was concerned, more through the influence of Seneca than of Aeschylus, Sophocles or Euripides, but here was a writer steeped in the classics, a major body of whose literary work was in the field of translation.

In the Preface to *Sylvae: or the Second Part of Poetical Miscellanies* (1685) Dryden wrote 'For this last half year I have been troubled with the disease (as I may call it) of translation'. He was speaking about translating the Latin poets – Virgil, Lucretius, Theocritus and Horace – but much of what he wrote would appear to have a major significance on the blossoming in the following century of translation as both a craft and as an art in its own right:

Translation is a kind of drawing after the life; where everyone will acknowledge there is a double sort of likeness, a good one and a bad. 'Tis one thing to draw the outlines true, the features like, the proportions exact, the colouring itself perhaps tolerable; and another to make all these graceful, by the posture, the shadowings, and chiefly by the spirit which animated the whole ... What English readers, unacquainted with Greek or Latin, will believe me, or any other man, when we commend those authors, and confess we derive all that is pardonable in us from their fountains, if they take those to the same poets whom our Oglebys have translated?[10] There are many who understand Greek and Latin and yet are ignorant of their mother tongue.[11]

Dryden's own *Aeneid* was a significant advance on any before him, never mind the now forgotten Ogleby. The extensive 'Of dramatic poesy' (1668) discussed at length classical works in the Greek, Latin and French traditions, but it was in his *The Life of Lucian* that he offered the following recipe for translation:

The qualification for a translator worth reading must be a mastery of the language he translates out of, and that he translates into; but if a deficience be to be [*sic*] allowed in either, it is in the original, since if he be master enough of the tongue of his author as to be master of his sense, it is possible for him to express that sense with eloquence in his own, if he have a thorough command of that. But without the latter he can never arrive at the useful and the delightful, without which reading is a penance and a fatigue ... A translator that would write with any force or spirit of an original must never dwell on the words of his author. He ought to possess himself entirely and perfectly comprehend the genius and sense of his author, the nature of the subject, and the terms of the art or subject treated of.[12]

The first systematic exploration of the principles behind translation are to be found in the series of papers delivered to the Royal Society in 1790 by Lord Woodhouselee, Alexander Fraser Tytler. They were published anonymously as *Essay on the Principles of Translation* in 1791 – something that aroused suspicions of plagiarism until Tytler revealed his authorship.[13] The principles he proposed provided groundrules that were to remain influential for at least the next hundred years; indeed many recent books on the theory and practice of translation still take them as a starting-point. Tytler's 'laws of translation' suggest:

1. That the translation should give a complete transcript of the ideas of the original work.
2. That the style and manner of the writing should be of the same character with that of the original.
3. That the translation should have all the ease of original composition.[14]

He proceeded to address translating the classics, though mainly from Latin as his source language rather than Greek. He accused Dryden, not without some justification, of 'the most outrageous bombast' in his translation of Ovid. More contentiously, he found himself uncomfortable with Echard's Plautus for failing to distinguish between 'the familiar and the vulgar' while admitting to his 'true dialect of the streets'.[15] This is an issue for comedy that is not going to go away (see pp. 176 ff).

Tytler put his finger here on why translating classical plays represents a struggle for supremacy between a number of warring factions. Plautus, translating or transferring or transmogrifying some unknown play about *Amphitryon* into his own *Amphitruo*, chose to use Latin that does seem to have reflected the 'true dialect of the streets', not Greek dialect and Greek streets, but Latin dialect and Roman streets. Echard re-dressed this in the argot of the London of his time; and Tytler found himself uncomfortable without being quite sure why. He accused Echard of seeing no distinction between 'the familiar and the vulgar':

By the mackins, I believe Phoebus has been playing the good-fellow and 's asleep too. I'll be hang'd if he ben't in for't, and has took a little too much o' the creature.[16]

This being Sosia's reflection on a night that Jupiter has extended considerably because he is spending it begetting Hercules on Alcmena, it seems restrained if not positively decorous. Tytler returned to the attack on Echard's handling of Terence as 'extremely censurable for his intemperate use of idiomatic phrases', and in a passage of the *Andria* exhibiting 'a strain of vulgar petulance'. Here Tytler did manage to pin down the source of his unease. Making a Greek or a Roman speak as though he were French or English is 'to use a phrase borrowed from painting ... an offence against the *costume*'.[17]

The desire to represent a classical play as contemporary may be a deliberate and unapologetic appropriation but the justification is a simple one. However laudable the desire to do justice to the playwrights of antiquity within their own milieu, a modern performance is for a modern audience. Anything that comes under the broad banner of cultural transference is inevitably writ large when considering Greek tragedy. There is always likely to be a gulf between those whose classical training demands a respect for the play on the page, in the context of the society of ancient Greece, and those for whom text is pretext, no more than a map from which they wish to create a landscape of their own imagination. Later chapters will give some indication, I hope, of how the texts that survive, however imperfectly, have been opened up in recent years to reveal a theatrical awareness on the part of the ancient dramatists that reveals them as profoundly effective makers of plays. It may be as much the responsibility of the translator to address this aspect of their craft as it is to find any linguistic match.

Much of what happened to translation in the nineteenth century will be considered elsewhere by recourse to specific example. If a move forward into the twentieth century seems abrupt at this point, it is justified by the need to address questions of theatre and of translation in terms of the theoretical base that transformed the study of both without, initially, creating any bridge between the two. Lawrence Venuti writing an introduction to theory during the 1960s–1970s identified 'equivalence' as the 'controlling concept' of that time: 'Translating is generally seen as a process of communicating the foreign text by establishing a relationship of identity or analogy with it.'[18]

'Equivalence' rang a bell with those concerned with the dramatic text because of the enthusiasm of that era for both deconstruction of the classics and for renewal by means of cultural borrowings. In fact the continuing search by practitioners of theatre for 'universals' which will give access to what Antonin Artaud called 'the concrete language of the stage' goes back, as does so much of theatrical experiment in the last hundred years, to Vsevolod Meierhold, the dynamic Russian director whose search for artistic innovation took him to all periods and to all the great traditions of theatre. When, as Meierhold was aware, each new director, each new actor, each new designer creates a new version of an original playtext: and when each new audience and each member of that audience provides a new dimension in reception, then the gloves are off in the battle to preserve rather than to exploit the past. In a directors' theatre the role of the translator embodies that of the dramaturg, on tap to answer the odd question about this or that, but seldom expected to contribute in other than an advisory capacity. Translation of a stage work may have a number of functions, but most of them are subordinated to what happens when the translation is relinquished, as was the original play, into the hands of the practitioners. No first production is definitive; a translation, staged or not, implies that a variety of stagings are possible. The whole history of Greek tragedy confirms this. Aeschylus created plays according to a production formula that included himself in most of the creative positions but was still dependent for the outcome on processes of state and private finance. After his death his plays were reproduced, in itself a kind of translation. After their deaths so were the plays of Sophocles and especially Euripides who was the mainstay of the repertoire of the travelling troupes in the post-classical and Hellenistic eras. These plays survive through a flexibility which is both their strength and a potential weakness.

One of the most sympathetic of classical scholars to take up the challenge of dramatic translation of Greek drama as drama in the earlier part of the twentieth century was Edith Hamilton, herself a translator and populariser of sympathy and erudition who took few prisoners when she identified her preferences in translation. 'Browning's Agamemnon', she stated, 'is beyond question one of the worst translations ever made'.[19] On Gilbert Murray she was less brutal than was T. S. Eliot (see p. 50), but no fan. She discussed the relative merits of 'fidelity to the text' and 'fidelity to the spirit' but still concluded that 'so far [1937] there has never been a really great translation of a Greek play'.

The debate was addressed from a variety of perspectives in *The Craft and Context of Translation* edited by William Arrowsmith, one of the most notable translators from the Greek of his era, and Roger Shattuck.[20] Amongst a number of ideas and ideals proposed in this collection, D. S. Carne-Ross made a case for its being a positive help for the translator to think in terms of a stage production. Brave assertion though it may be, this has sometimes proved more of a hindrance than a help. Issues relating to stage directions, dialogue and anachronism will be considered later, but it is worth stressing here how far theatre studies has developed as an independent discipline in the last fifty years and the extent to which putative stage action by the under-experienced may muddy the waters. Carne-Ross suggested that 'true translation is much more a commentary on the original than a substitute for it', advocating somewhat vaguely that 'the translator must be given all the liberty he needs'.[21]

Arrowsmith himself went back to basics, pointing out not only the extreme 'cultural incompatibilities' between classical times and our own, but the conventions whereby Hector, a Trojan, will be expected to speak similar Greek to Agamemnon or Odysseus. This is no sort of a problem in Shakespeare and it led Arrowsmith into a discussion of how to handle the everyday details of living, especially in comedy. All in all he summed up translation as 'the skill of honourable deception', without recognising that this is simply part of the process of stage production at every level from proxemics to semiotics.[22]

If Arrowsmith aimed mainly at practicalities, the publication of George Steiner's *After Babel* in 1975 was a landmark for translation theory for a number of reasons, not least his association of the act of translation with 'initiative trust', 'aggression', 'incorporation' and the 'piston-stroke', and the act of sexual conquest. 'The translator', Steiner insisted, 'invades, extracts and brings home'.[23] In his less fevered moments he used both classics and the theatre as part of his terms of reference.[24] A whistle-stop tour of classical myth on stage since Euripides took in Seneca, Racine, Goethe, Hölderlin, von Hofmannsthal, Brecht, Anouilh and Martha Graham in a chapter on 'The topologies of culture', in which he also established a difference between 'translation proper', 'transmutation' and 'partial transformation'.[25] Steiner posited the importance of Aeschylus as probably 'the first to locate in dialogue the supreme intensities of human conflict'.[26] His familiar identification of the barrier between source and receptor as 'time' led to the major concern about the way in which words alter their meanings over time. Though this is something with which any English-speaking reader or actor of Shakespeare is familiar, the problem is exaggerated in translation, leading each generation to retranslate other people's classics. For Steiner it also suggested that much of our theatre is based in 'lazy translation'. However true this may be, it is in part the result, it might be argued, of ignoring the differences between words as words, and words as they are used in a dramatic context.

For Tytler's three 'laws' of translation, Steiner came up with three 'orders'. The first and simplest involves acquaintance with foreign cultures by transference 'in our own sense' – dramatically, perhaps, the 'lazy' translations he identified earlier; the second, 'appropriation through surrogate', might well describe how Terence treated Menander: 'A native garb is imposed on the alien form'; the third will aim at 'perfect identity between the original text and that of the translation'. It might be objected that this third is less a translation aspiration than a metaphysical concept, and that Steiner moved away from the flexible nature of drama rather than engaging with it.[27] Even Samuel Beckett does not provide the 'perfect' translation of his own work, on occasion varying the meaning between French and English text. The notion of the 'perfect' translation of a play is as alien as the idea of a finished play on the page. But as an apparently definitive production of any classic may be definitive only until social shift makes alternatives viable or inevitable, so it is not a mark of imperfection if a translation needs renewing.

Similarly Umberto Eco in *Mouse or Rat? Translation as Negotiation* elegantly elaborated the nature of engagement between writer and reader.[28] His riddling example of the Italian 'pulling one's nose' which has to be translated into English as 'pulling one's leg' is easily extendable into play translation. But when Eco suggested that 'a translation can be either *source* – or *target-oriented*' he seemed to leave little room for the polysystemic approach.[29] The polysystem focuses less on the solitariness of the source for which an equivalent must be found than on the open-ended possibilities of the target where potentials are legion. The polysystem is bound to be more comfortable for the theatre practitioner if for no other reason than the freshness of each 'new' translation in its wider sense every time a play is produced. A drama has a multiplicity of targets, each a staging-post where horses are changed along the road between rehearsal draft and curtain-call, or, thinking Hollywood, between pitch and Oscar.

The sense of intertextuality in Greek tragedy is easy enough to follow in any reading of the three Electra plays. *Libation-Bearers*, the second play of Aeschylus' *Oresteia* (458), is invoked by both Sophocles and Euripides in their plays from at least thirty years later, both of which similarly cover the return of the grown-up Orestes to his home and the revenge taken on his father's killers.[30] The *Oresteia* was sufficiently familiar in Athens when Euripides presented his *Electra* (variously dated between the 420s and 413) for his Electra, in a direct echo of *Libation-Bearers*, to reject the Aeschylean recognition tokens on the grounds of illogicality (see p. 66–8,

291n). Nor is this a unique example. In *Phoenician Women* Euripides appears similarly to remind his reader/audience of the Messenger who describes the various heroes ranged against the city in Aeschylus' *Seven Against Thebes*, while at the same time the playwright advertises his own more sophisticated dramatic technique. There may have been many more examples in plays which are no longer extant. Euripides frequently offers revisionist versions of his own characters, never mind those of Aeschylus and Sophocles, when introducing Helens, Hecubas or Oresteses.

But Eco suggested that these represent 'the custom of starting from a stimulus text in order to get the ideas for creating one's own text'. To imply further, as Eco did, that Sophocles was 'emulating' or even writing an adaptation of Aeschylus' *Oedipus* in his own *Oedipus* reveals a narrow understanding of the manner in which playwrights of the classical era explored the flexibility of myth rather than being bound by some 'original'.[31]

The number of translation theorists who have seriously entered the field of translation of drama is select but growing. Ortrun Zuber's claim in 1980 that hers was the first book to be devoted exclusively to 'translation problems unique in drama' is evidence in itself of how uncomfortable those working in translation have found themselves with this curious, protean art of the stage play, and how those who practise the art of translation for the stage have been even less comfortable to lay down rules for what they do. Zuber's *The Languages of Theatre* is a series of essays by a variety of writers with very different points of view. Several of the authors address areas of theatre which are resistant to declared strategy.[32] Reba Gostand looks at 'Verbal and non-verbal communication: drama as translation'. The subject is widened with attention drawn to the physical dimension of production and the relationship of that to the translating process. The examples are somewhat random and the same is true of several other contributions where Tennessee Williams can rub shoulders with Monteverdi, and Giraudoux with Heiner Müller. Casting the net wide has a number of advantages, not least in highlighting the sheer range of stage possibilities. This very breadth can lead to generalisations. Franz H. Link, for example, in 'Translation, adaptation and interpretation of dramatic texts', referred to a bizarre hybrid, Eva Hesse's translation of Ezra Pound's translation of Sophocles' *Women of Trachis*. Link's tangling with the classics led him to one of those commonplaces about Greek drama which cannot help but be thoroughly misleading:

Greek drama was written for the whole polis (with the deplorable exception, of course, of its women). Accordingly the theatre in which the Greek playwright could expect to see his play performed was large enough to seat all its citizens. The size of the theatre, for example, influenced not only the acting but the text itself insofar as it did not allow interiors or intimacies to such an extent as they became possible in the drama of later periods.[33]

Leaving aside that the balance of critical opinion from Pickard-Cambridge onwards has been more in favour of women's attendance at the Theatre of Dionysus than against it, there is the implied equation of Greek tragedy and comedy with some organic theory of state.[34] The reality was probably far more subtle than that, but also far simpler. The proportion of the inhabitants of Attica who attended the theatre was probably not much greater than the proportion of Londoners who visited the theatre in Shakespeare's time. Amongst the audience of whatever size, there will have been a cross-section of opinions and attitudes from the war-mongering to the pacifist, from the religious fanatic to the spiritually inquisitive, from the intellectual to the feeble-minded. Yes, the audience will have reflected Athens and have been a reflection of it; the keyword is diversity, with no two plays the same, no two playwrights with identical approaches. The translator of an Aeschylus play, or a Sophocles, or a Euripides, is not faced with the task of trying to home in on some universal of the composite Greek experience. The matter at hand is a play, on a day, before an audience, the then becoming the now. This does not make it easier or harder, just different.

Other essays in Zuber intriguingly consider Ibsen in English (May Brit Akerhold); O'Casey in German (Ute Venneburg); Wilde and Strauss (Marilyn Gaddis Rose); and O'Neill in Cantonese (Vicki C. H. Ooi). André Lefevere, profoundly influential in this field, has two bites at the cherry, considering Soyinka's relationship with Euripides in his *Bacchae*,[35] and a more general essay on 'Translating literature/translated literature: the state of the art'.[36] The latter feeds into the former by rehearsing the notion of 'polysystem', switching emphasis away from what is, for want of a better term, the monosystem of the source language to the poly-system of the target which Lefevere describes as 'a canonised system, which is the leading "fashion" of a given day ... The polysystem also contains countercurrents, which try to displace the canonised system and replace it.'[37] If I understand this correctly, and even if I don't, this is a useful tool for addressing what happens to the translated dramatic text when it blossoms into the multiplicity of possible amplifications and resolutions of a performance, the pragmatics of performance beyond text leading to the whole process of reception.

Zuber's own contribution addresses 'Problems of propriety and authenticity in translating modern drama', usefully reminding the student of literature that most of the greatest dramatists, the Greeks, Shakespeare and Molière among them, wrote for actors. Her conclusion is that:

the task of a translator as well as that of a producer of a modern play should be to transpose the play in such a manner, that the message of the original and the dramatist's intention be adhered to as closely as possible and be rendered, linguistically and artistically, into a form which takes into account the different traditional, cultural and socio-political background of the *recipient* [my italics] country.[38]

If this may seem to beg as many questions as it answers, it does state the case unambiguously for the special nature of a theatre text; and for 'modern' why not also read 'non-modern'?[39]

Susan Bassnett, on the other hand, may be claimed as the first systematically to have addressed issues of stage translation in any period through a series of theoretical models, but with a serious understanding of not only that, but why, a play is so different and why translating a play is different from translating a poem or a novel. Bassnett's contribution to the field is without parallel. It stretches over nearly twenty-five years, with revisions and adjustments that offer ample evidence, as do the theoretical writings of all the best practitioners, of constantly worrying at the bones and never being content with yesterday's discovery. *Translation Studies* was first published in 1980.[40] The virtue of her approach lies in her being at home with all the major issues of translation while being sympathetic to the specifics and practicalities of translating a variety of dramatic material.

The most immediate for the Greek play relates to questions of archaizing. Torn, as it is difficult not to be, between the language of a hundred and more years ago and the kind of street language that so upset Tytler and which will always risk sounding dated within ten years, the translator of the classics is in an invidious position. Ranged on one side are the ghosts of translators past, on the other the free spirits of the present. The uncertain hope that the language of the comparatively recent past, at least as viewed from the perspective of the fifth century BC, will supply a kind of pedigree has a built-in logical flaw. There is no reason why Aeschylus, still less Euripides or Menander, should seem more viable in the sort of language used by translators from the eighteenth century, still less in the never-spoken language of a Gilbert Murray. Greek tragedy does belong in a world of varying translation strategies where the strangeness of the original may be the guiding principle behind a production concept. Bassnett has drawn attention to J. M. Cohen's concern that Victorian translation of the classics, in opting for the 'mock antique', was a part of 'colonizing the past'.[41] She tied this in with Longfellow's assertion that 'The business of the translator is to report what the author says, not to explain what he means.'[42]

Some eighteen years after the first edition of *Translation Studies*, in *Constructing Cultures: Essays on Literary Translation*, edited with Lefevere, Bassnett posited three modes of translation: the Horatian model (keeping faith with the target audience); the Jerome model (which, favouring the source and Jerome being a translator of the Bible, one might call 'keeping faith with the faith'); and the Schleiermacher model (preserving the alterity of the source model for the target audience).[43] These divisions do work relatively comfortably when extrapolated into the world of the drama where the translator is more midwife than pundit, more hermit than hermeneutist.

In an essay later in the same book entitled 'Still trapped in the labyrinth: further reflections on translation and theatre', Bassnett revisited a 1985 essay 'Ways through the labyrinth' for her latest thinking on theatre translation.[44] A central concern here was the 'gestic' text which the actor will be able to decipher, though experience with theories of acting would seem to indicate that the notion of an encrypted inner text which is encoded in the original (and hence needs to be similarly encoded in any translation) simply cannot be quantified. Two statements elsewhere in the same book serve to restore the confidence of the theatre practitioner in the immunity of the discipline to formula. In his Introduction Edwin Gentzler stated:

When I read work by Jacques Derrida, Homi Bhabha, or Edward Said, I am often struck by how naive their ideas about translation sound in comparison with the detailed analysis provided by translation scholars. Bassnett, as ever, is looking to the future and pointing the way to a new interdisciplinary phase.[45]

Her twenty-year sojourn 'within the labyrinth', he suggested, leads her to conclude:

The time has come for translators to stop hunting for deep structures and coded subtexts ... What is left for the translator to do is to engage specifically with the signs of the text: to wrestle with the deictic units, the speech rhythms, the pauses and silences, the shifts of tone or of register, the problems of intonation patterns; the linguistic and paralinguistic aspects of the written text that are decodable and reencodable.[46]

One of the terms against which Bassnett has steadfastly set her face is 'performability'. She has reasonably pointed to the manner in which 'performability' has been used and abused as a term of artistic correctness, and hence closed to reason, much as though it offered the winged sandals and polished shield by which the scholar Perseus may confront the Gorgon 'practitioner'.[47] She has admitted that 'It may, of course, be true, that one translation *works better* (my italics) than another'.[48] 'Performability' may defy definition but so does the word 'works' which she has been prepared to use to distinguish a better translation from a worse. A life spent more in rehearsal rooms than in libraries has given me fewer problems with 'performability' than with most critical terms. 'Love', 'courage', 'pity' and 'fear' seem much more resistant to any form of definition than the ultimate term for theatrical appropriateness, 'It works'. Only a rare playwright, and a rarer translator, will not often have experienced an actor's urge to place an adverb in a different part of a sentence; or who will not have experienced, often, an actor's urge to place an adverb in a different part of a sentence; or who will not have experienced an actor's urge to place an adverb in a different part of a sentence, often. A writer or reader might know which is better English; an actor which can be made more emphatic, or awkward, or glib, or comic.

Hanna Scolnicov and Peter Holland's *The Play out of Context: Transferring Plays from Culture to Culture* picked up on the sensitive issue, for director as well as for translator, of cultural appropriation. The balance between fruitful interculturalism and cultural imperialism had been a matter of concern for a number of years, but, as Edward Said pointed out, appropriation goes all the way back to Aeschylus' *Persians*. The colonialism which Rustam Bharucha found so offensive in the work of Richard Schechner can easily seem to be a form of abuse.[49] The Jean-Claude Carrière/Peter Brook *The Mahabharata* was accused not only of naivety but of 'cultural exploitation of non-western people'.[50] If this is more the province of the director than the translator it becomes significant if a translation is required for a specific concept and as an act of translocation from the classical world into a specific 'other' period.

For the practitioner, if an ancient play is to live again in our own time and speak to a contemporary audience, there must be freedom of interpretation because that is what directing involves. For the practitioner there is no *ur-text*, no primary finished version of the original: there is only the text as Ordnance Survey map from which the director and designers fashion the landscape for the players to inhabit. Interpretation has to be part of the process for director and actor. The extent to which interpretation may be, or cannot help but be, a part of the process for the translator is another matter. The Irish actor Fiona Shaw suggested informally on one occasion that her preference for the translations of Kenneth McLeish was based on their neutrality.[51] In other words, as a translator McLeish left open possibilities within which the production and the actors could breathe, the 'performance door' which much literary theory seems only to close. In the theatre, as Patrice Pavis put it, 'The translator is a dramaturg.' Pavis drew attention to the special nature of translation for the stage in a seminal essay entitled 'Problems of trans-lation for the stage: interculturalism and postmodern theatre'.[52] An examination of some of his general points about translation demonstrates the specificity of dramatic translation while suggesting how the classical play is largely a law unto itself.

Pavis began by asserting the importance of the *mise-en-scène* in any act of theatre translation:

In order to conceptualise the act of theatre translation, we must consult the literary translator *and* the director and actor; we must incorporate their con-tribution and integrate the act of translation into the much broader translation (that is the *mise-en-scène*) of a dramatic text.[53]

He acknowledged that translation arrives via the actors' bodies and what he called 'heterogeneous cultures and situations that are separated in time and space'.[54] He then proceeded to identify those factors that make the act of translation for the stage dramaturgical rather than linguistic: the imperatives of a performance text; the audience; the socio-political image of a culture and so on. He discussed possible solutions to the problems of interculturalism and cultural appropriation, using the Carrière/Brook *Mahabharata* as a test case. All this is such a fundamental review that it offers a code of practice for the whole broad question of translating a play from any period or culture to any other. With plays from the classical repertoire there *are* problems common to all dramatic translation. Pavis is helpful in identifying these.[55] What he cannot do is tackle the specifics of the classical play.

The trouble with the Greeks is that not only is the original the pro-vince of a diminishing few, for none of whom is ancient Greek still a regularly spoken language, but the source language is dominated by a series of linguistic and dramatic propensities whose significance is not generally agreed by those who are meant to know about them, and have no necessary meeting point with contemporary stage practice. The Greeks may have subscribed to a stage language of image, gesture and space but personal academic preference over unrecoverable aspects of stage practice cannot claim the authority of universal theatrical truth. There is no such thing as 'authenticity'.

In translation for the stage there is a real difference between the presentation of the work of the writer in a different language and the *re*-presentation of that work through the artistic intervention of a director. Drama as a collaborative art is frequently concerned with *re*-creation, the *re*-interpretation of a classic text. In fifth-century Athens this was not so, the playwright being unable to guarantee anything more than his single performance on a single occasion. This does make Greek tragedy, and translating Greek tragedy, something of a special case. The challenge in recreating a Greek play today is to make the original live, but through the creative act of a contemporary production. The long history of translating Greek tragedy and comedy into English suggests that the issue has always been one of finding a balance between cultures: for the director it is often a matter of inventing an etiquette. It is to that history that we can now turn.

CHAPTER 2

Historical Perspectives: Lumley
to Lennox

It is useless, then, to read Greek in translations. Translators can but
offer us a vague equivalent; their language is necessarily full of
echoes and associations.

(Virginia Woolf, 1925)[1]

Virginia Woolf's stricture came in her essay 'On not knowing Greek'
where she offered a number of examples of how impossible it is to find
direct equivalents for the density and breadth of the Greek playwrights.
The problem was pinned down to not knowing what Greek tragedy
meant to the Greeks. She wrote of the landscape, the climate and the
cruelty in Greek tragedy 'which is quite unlike our English brutality',
noting that we simply do not know how actors delivered lines or 'where
precisely we ought to laugh'. She also drew attention to the need for
instant impact, unalloyed by time for reflection and unusually open to
the power of the visual as well as the aural. Her examples, Electra and
Clytemnestra from the Sophocles *Electra*, Antigone, Pentheus and
Agamemnon, were chosen to mark the differences between the three
tragedians, their subtlety and their sheer dramatic brilliance. All of which
led her to a sensitivity for the originals which any translator would be
advised to heed. On two choral lines in *Agamemnon* she commented:

The meaning is just on the far side of language. It is the meaning which in
moments of astonishing excitement and stress we perceive in our minds without
words; it is the meaning that Dostoevsky (hampered as he was by prose and as we
are by translation) leads us to by some astonishing run up the scale of emotions
and points at but cannot indicate; the meaning that Shakespeare succeeds in
snaring.

Aeschylus thus will not give, as Sophocles gives, the very words that people might
have spoken, only so arranged that they have in some mysterious way a general
force, a symbolic power, nor like Euripides will he combine incongruities and thus
enlarge his little space, as a small room is enlarged by mirrors in odd corners.[2]

Hence her sad conclusion about the uselessness of reading Greek in translations: sad because what a translator she herself might have made; less sad in that some at least of what she identifies as untranslatable relates to performance as well as to translation and may be accommodated by an alliance between the two. In 1925 this may not have seemed so. Eighty years later the theatre has changed, as the theatre does. The aim of this chapter is to look back to the history of translation of Greek plays before Virginia Woolf's time as a prelude to considering what may have happened since to render her judgement overpessimistic.

Writing some dozen years ago on the revival of Greek plays in English I suggested that the first English-language translation from the Greek was the *Jocasta* of George Gascoigne and Francis Kinwelmershe.[3] That, as was widely acknowledged, was no more than a cousin thrice removed, being derived from an Italian version of a Latin translation of Euripides' *Phoenician Women*. Nevertheless, it appeared to have a fair claim to being the first Greek tragedy in English and gets the credit for it in *The Cambridge Companion to English Renaissance Drama*.[4] I was, I confess, wrong to describe it as the first translation of a Greek play, and can defend myself only by saying that so were Palmer and Lathrop, the bibliographists who wrote the major studies of classics in English, both of whom made similar claims for Gascoigne and Kinwelmershe: as did William J. Harris and Finley Melville Kendall Foster who refers only to Gascoigne and Kinvvelmershe [*sic*].[5]

A sterner search would have revealed the brief but significant output of Lady Jane Lumley, known already to writers of female biography. Amongst Lady Lumley's manuscripts preserved in the British Museum is *The Tragedie of Euripides called Iphigeneia translated out of Greake into Englisshe*, based on the posthumously produced *Iphigeneia at Aulis* of Euripides.[6] Lady Lumley's tentative dates are 1537–1578; it seems more than likely that her *Iphigeneia* was written during the early years of her marriage and thus predates the *Jocasta* of Gascoigne and Kinwelmershe, which was performed at Gray's Inn in 1566 but not published until 1572. Harold H. Child prepared an edition of the Lumley *Iphigeneia* (as *Iphigenia at Aulis*) from manuscript for the Malone Society in 1909. This was only two years before Henrietta Palmer's *List of English Editions and Translations of the Classics Printed before 1641*, which missed or chose to ignore it, perhaps because the Malone Society's was the first formal publication of any of Lady Lumley's work. In 1998 Diane Purkiss brought out *Three Tragedies by Renaissance Women* which included *The Tragedie of Iphigeneia in a version by Lady Jane Lumley*.[7]

Lady Jane is herself still sufficiently shrouded in mystery, to be identified in at least two modern bibliographical digests not as Jane Lumley but as Joanna, an error which it would be pleasing to put down to an excess of television-watching were it not possible to trace the incorrect Christian name back to the *Hays Female Biography* of 1803, and beyond that to Lewis William Brüggemann who identified her as Ioanna in 1797.[8]

Historians of neither the classics nor the drama seem to have paid much heed to the text either before or after its official publication in 1909, until the excellent recent Purkiss edition. It did become the subject of two articles in *The Classical Journal* during the early 1940s, one by David Grene, the other by Frank D. Crane, which took up the issue of whether or not Jane had worked from the original Greek, or from a Latin translation by Erasmus. Neither thought much of her work.[9] It was not until 1997 that the Lumley *Iphigeneia* was first staged, in a production by Stephanie J. Wright for the Brass Farthingale Company at the University of Sunderland, 'as part of a research project designed to investigate the performance dimension of Renaissance drama by women', as she stated in a programme note.[10] Scholarship is indebted to Stephanie Wright and her company for allowing the text to resurface and for demonstrating that, whether or not it is good Euripides, this version has rather more to offer to actors than the dismissive articles in *The Classical Journal* might have suggested.

Lumley Castle, the seat of the family into which Jane married, is in County Durham. The Lumleys had land and connections from the Scottish borders down as far as the North Riding of Yorkshire but Jane was a Fitzalan, elder daughter of the twelfth Earl of Arundel. She was probably born in Sussex and is buried at Cheam. Her father met with disapproval from some members of the Lumley family and clearly spent the majority of Jane's lifetime involved in political intrigue, attempting to gain a political status from which his Catholic background might have been expected to have disqualified him. Jane was also a cousin of Lady Jane Grey, who found herself Queen of England for all of ten days in 1553 and was beheaded on Tower Hill a year later. When the Earl's second wife died, Jane and her husband, Lord John Lumley, went to live at Nonesuch in Sussex. According to the Lumley records 'The Earl had a very bad influence on his more upright but weaker son-in-law, and implicated him in many intrigues connected mainly with Mary, Queen of Scots.'[11]

In such a time the study of the classics looks like the tiniest of oases in a desert of cozenage but Harold Child, editor of the Malone Society edition, refers to an even earlier translation of Euripides by none other than Elizabeth I before she succeeded to the throne, though that may well have been into Latin.[12] Would that it had survived! Henry Fitzalan, the twelfth Earl of Arundel, had encouraged his son and both his daughters to study Greek and Latin. Jane's elder brother, Maltravers, went to Cambridge and became friendly with John Lumley to whom Jane was married when she was only thirteen or fourteen, possibly as young as twelve. John was probably not that much older, three years at most, but at this point even half-reliable chronology grinds to a halt. Though dedicated to her father, *Iphigenia at Aulis* may have been intended by Jane as an adjunct to her husband's translation of Erasmus' *The Institution of a Christian Prince* (1550), Erasmus having translated into Latin both the *Iphigenia* and the *Hecuba* of Euripides.[13] That would appear to suggest that *Iphigenia* was from the same year; and in 1550 Jane was only thirteen. She was eventually to have three children, all of whom died in infancy, but the received view is that her extant writing, which included translations of Isocrates as well as *Iphigenia*, were completed while she was still a child, if a married child. This seeming lack of years has been enough to have had her Euripides disparaged and practically discounted by most of those who have bothered to pay any attention to it.

A closer look may suggest that her work – if no masterpiece doing for Euripides what Chapman did for Homer – has intrinsic worth and displays a sense of decided dramatic form which is all hers. As significantly, Lady Lumley provides a translation of classical Greek into an Elizabethan English, albeit an Elizabethan English as yet unenriched by Shakespeare: an English, though, mercifully unsullied by the romanticism which perverted the classics during the Hellenic revival of the late eighteenth and nineteenth centuries and from which the twenty-first century is linguistically still recovering.

The issue that most exercised the minds and pens of David Grene and Frank Crane in *The Classical Review* was whether she worked from the original Greek or used the Latin translation. The first printed edition of Euripides in Greek was published by Aldus in 1503. The two plays of Euripides, *Hecuba* and *Iphigenia at Aulis,* in the Erasmus translations into Latin, were published in 1506 in Paris and the following year in Venice.[14] At the time there was nothing, even in Latin, with which to compare them. So unusual did these pieces seem that Erasmus was accused of having made them up as original plays, a charge he refuted with some heat: disarmingly, it has to be admitted, as the works were much admired. Possibly he believed that any original work of his would have been rather better. He was dismissive of the construction of Greek tragedy. 'Nowhere in antiquity is there anything that seems to me more stupid than the chorus here', he wrote in his dedication of *Iphigenia*.[15]

Lady Jane may have agreed with him because she left out almost all of the chorus, finding, perhaps, either that it interfered in her opinion with the narrative line, or, less charitably, because it proved too difficult to translate. Her version is substantially shorter than the original which, at 1629 lines, is one of the longest of Greek tragedies. The Chorus is not wholly excised but has only as much to say as the plot requires. The first choral ode, for example, is heralded by Agamemnon's line 'To be born is to be heir to grief'. Jane offers 'for ther is no man to whom all thinges have chaunsed happilye', but continues immediately with the Chorus (whose entrance has not been previously marked) responding 'What is this? me thinkes I see Menelaius striuinge withe Agamemnons seruante'.[16] In Euripides that choral entrance is 140 lines long, ending with the abrupt and unannounced entrance of Menelaus and the Old Man. The other choruses receive similar treatment from Jane with the exception of the one that follows the final exit of Iphigenia of which ten lines are included beginning:

Beholde yonder goethe the uirgine to be sacraficed withe a grete companye of souldiers after hir, whos bewtifull face and faire bodi anone shalbe defiled withe hir owne blode. Yet happie arte thou, o Iphigeneya, that with thy deathe, thou shalte purchase unto the grecians a quiet passage.[17]

Jane includes a number of other cuts, following no precedent set by Erasmus, but there is a pattern to these which suggests that the derogatory tones in which Grene and Crane dismiss her – 'There is no art or method in her compression' (Grene); 'her version succeeds only in reducing high tragedy to a mediocre tale of "troble"' (Crane) – are the product of a conviction that Euripides in his last play was still attempting to write 'high tragedy' and that nothing of much worth could be expected from a mere child. The case for neither such assumption is proved.[18]

Excisions are mainly aimed at reducing the emphasis on mythological background while, at the same time, concentrating on a strong narrative line. Lumley eliminates Greek names and references, to Helen and Orestes, for example, where mention of them does not seem to further a scene. Far from carelessness on her part, one might argue the hand of a good editor here, faced with a play which the author himself never had a chance to revise in rehearsal. As it happens, the presence of the baby

Orestes with Clytemnestra has a strong dramatic purpose throughout which, perhaps, Jane fails to see, but her motives for cutting seem, if anachronistically, to be those of any dramaturg. Her changes are logical and consistent with a search for decorum, clarity and directness.

This is most obvious in the handling of the physical features of the death of Iphigenia. The crueller aspects are played down or removed. She may underestimate the moral paradox Euripides offers in Iphigenia's act of sacrifice but this is no simple bowdlerisation to sanitise the reality of human sacrifice. It is the logical outcome of a shift in the emphasis of the play which owes little or nothing to Erasmus. Iphigenia has a long speech where she resolves the problem faced by Achilles, Clytemnestra and Agamemnon by volunteering to die. In the original Euripides her argument is carefully structured. 'Don't blame Agamemnon; don't expect anything more of Achilles. I must die (1) to save Greek wives from being abducted by foreigners; (2) because I am a Greek and the Greek nation has been insulted; (3) because Artemis is demanding a sacrifice and women are no use in war compared to an Achilles': ending with the lines in the translation by Merwin and Dimock:

> Mother, it is the Greeks
> who must rule the barbarians,
> not the barbarians the Greeks.
> They are born to be slaves;
> we to be free.[19]

The Lumley version introduces a new dimension:

I wolde counsell you therfore to suffer this troble paciently, for I muste nedes die, and will suffer it willinglye. Consider I praie you mother, for what a lawfull cause i shalbe slaine. Dothe not bothe the destruction of Troie *and also the welthe of grece*, [my italics] which is the mooste frutefull countrie of the world hange upon my deathe? ... Again remember how I was not borne for your sake onlie, *but rather for the comodite of my countrie*, [again my italics] thinke you therfore that it is mete, that such a companie of men beinge gathered together to reuenge the greate iniurie, which all grece hathe suffered should be let out of their iournye for my cause.[20]

This emphasis on Iphigenia's sacrifice as a matter of economics looks like a reflection on Elizabethan rather than Euripidean priorities. It is matched by Iphigenia's further injunction to her mother 'not to hate my father for this dede: for he is compelled to do it for the welthe and honor of grece'.[21] There is little justification for any of this talk of 'welthe' or 'comoditie' in Euripides, though a hint in the Latin of Erasmus. As it happens, it does point to the current historical view that the thousand ships were more likely to have been launched to secure trade routes to the Black Sea than to rescue a single face.

Lady Jane deserves some rehabilitation. Much of her *Iphigenia* does read like the work of a sometimes distracted child, but her version is a more mature and a more conscious act of translation than has usually been assumed. Nevertheless, the infelicities have to be acknowledged. She does make a terrible botch-up of one passage where she appears to misread Erasmus and awards Clytemnestra boy triplets, a mistake which it would have been impossible to make had she been working from the Greek, and pretty difficult if she had any but the most perfunctory knowledge of the House of Atreus. Erasmus is responsible for translating Artemis into Diana, Aphrodite into Venus and Odysseus into Ulysses, though such latinisation is to become a commonplace of all Greek scholarship in English, to such an extent that English still tends to use 'c' for 'k' (*kappa*) and 'us' for 'os' in transliteration, writing of Aeschylus for *Aischulos* and *Oedipus Rex* for *Oidipous Turannos*.

Anachronisms such as 'midnighte' or 'candle-lighte', on the other hand, are wholly Jane's and offer an acceptable touch of her own social *mores*, used sparingly, but offering evidence of a sensitivity that others have denied her. Elsewhere, the lack of conciseness which a verse structure might have imposed – she makes no attempt to reflect either the iambics or the lyrics – leads to an excess of words. Up to twenty or, in one instance twenty-seven, may be used for a mere ten in the Greek. In an extreme example a nine-word stichomythic line of Clytemnestra's, *pōs? apeptus', ō geraie, muthon; ou gar eu phroneis* (l. 874), which might comfortably be rendered in eleven words as 'How so? Out with it, old man. You must be mad', comes out from Jane's pen in thirty-five as 'Suerlie I thinke either you be mad to telle such an unlikelie tale, or else, if it be so indeed, Agamemnon to be halfe out of his witte to agree to suche a cruell murther.'[22] Jane may be weak on ellipsis but at least she conveys Clytemnestra's shock at being told that Agamemnon intends to slaughter their daughter. The line is speakable, infinitely more so than Arthur Way's Loeb version of 1912. Way manages the line with eleven words to Euripides' nine and Jane's thirty-five, but 'How? Avaunt the story, ancient! Sure thy wit is all astray' hardly suggests progress in the trans-lator's art over 360 years.[23]

Lady Lumley's translation may show lapses both of judgement and of concentration but, at its best, the sheer simplicity and directness bring their own dramatic power. 'I haue determined the deathe of my daughter', confesses Agamemnon 'under the color of mariage'; 'In all this matter I will be ruled by you', says the shamed Clytemnestra to the equally shamed Achilles, 'wherfore if I obtaine my swte [suit] the thankes shall be yours and not mine'.[24] Clytemnestra's final speech in response to the Messenger's account of the miraculous intervention at the moment of Iphigenia's death hits precisely the right note of scepticism: 'But I am in doughte whether I shulde beleue that thou, O daughter, arte amongst the goddes, or els, that they have fained it to comforte me.'[25]

The issue of whether or not she had access to the Erasmus version seems little more than a distraction. Almost certainly she did. Even if she made extensive use of it; even if she simply translated Erasmus direct from the Latin into English; even if she had no access to the original Greek at all, her *Iphigenia* is still an original and remarkable piece of work. She may not have shown the way to others but she seems to have known where that way might lead.

The qualities of Lady Jane's efforts become all the more welcome in their denial of authority to the Gascoigne and Kinwelmershe *Jocasta* as the first Greek tragedy in English, and thus saving future generations from any perceived obligation to wade through it. George Gascoigne (*aka* Gascoygne) was a little older than Lumley. He left Cambridge without taking his degree but entered Gray's Inn where some of his plays were later performed. Though an original poet of some note and an avid translator from the Italian, he lived a wastrel, if picturesque life, which included a couple of years as an MP and a period of detention under the Spanish in the Low Countries. His more prestigious dramatic efforts involved creating entertainments for the Queen at Kenilworth. Francis Kinwelmershe is a shadowy figure whose line is severally traced in the Dictionary of National Biography from Essex to Cornwall but in such a welter of alternate spellings as to make it likely that he was an otherwise undistinguished student friend of Gascoigne's at Gray's Inn. *Jocasta* is based on Euripides' *Phoenician Women*, reworked from Ludovico Dolce's Italian *Giocasta*, and takes some of Euripides' structure. Clearly too it was intended for performance, as it includes a number of stage directions. The characters enter and the scenes follow one another in more or less the same order as in Euripides. There any resemblance ends.

Phoenician Women was one of Euripides' later plays and appears to be one of those which responded to a dramatic predecessor. Aeschylus' *Seven Against Thebes* covers the same ground, the civil war in Thebes, resolved, if not concluded, by the death in single combat of the sons of Oedipus.

The original Euripides is full of surprises for those who might be expecting a sequel to Sophocles' *Oedipus Tyrannus*. Jocasta opens the play and dominates it, committing suicide eventually on the battlefield over the corpses of her dead sons. There is a review of the troops by Antigone and her Tutor which suggests that Shakespeare knew the scene when writing his *Troilus and Cressida*. Creon's son Menoeceus commits suicide as an act of self-sacrifice required by Teiresias to save the city, and only after the deaths of Jocasta, Eteocles and Polyneices does Oedipus himself appear, a forlorn and broken figure.

   Phoenician Women is a long play, the longest extant Euripides and only marginally shorter than Sophocles' *Oedipus at Colonus*. The Gascoigne and Kinwelmershe *Jocasta* is almost twice as long again: and that is without adding the effect of five 'dumme shewes and Musickes' which precede each act. What these effectively do is establish that, whether or not the authors knew the Euripides in other than the Italian translation, what they are writing is an Elizabethan play. The third of these dumb-shows gives a fair indication of how far they deviate from Euripides:

Before the beginning of this .iii. Act did sound a very dolefull noise of cornettes, during the which there opened and appeared in the stage a great Gulfe. Immediately came in vi gentleme~ in their dublets & hose. bringing upon their shulders baskets full of earth and threwe them into the Gulfe to fill it up, but it would not so close up nor be filled. Then came the ladyes and dames that stoode by, throwing in their chains and jewels, so to cause it to stoppe up and close it selfe: but when it would not be so filled, came in a knight with his sword drawen, armed at all poynts, who walking twice or thrise about it, & perusing it, seeing that it would neither be filled with earth nor with their Jewells and ornaments, after solempne reverence done to the gods, and courteous leave taken of the Ladyes and standers by, sodeinly lepte into the Gulfe, the which did close up immediatly: betokening unto us the love that every worthy person oweth unto his native cou~trie, by the historie of *Curtius*, who for the lyke cause adventured the like in Rome. This done, blinde Tyresias the devine prophete led in by hys daughter, and conducted by *Meneceus* the son of Creon, entreth by the gates *Electrae*, and sayth as followeth. (ACTUS. III. Scena. i)[26]

This is much more an original play than a translation. Translations of Seneca are already by this time familiar if not commonplace but here is at most a 'version' with a passing acknowledgement of Euripides. The Greek context virtually disappears. Though the Chorus is composed of 'Four Thebane dames' and the setting is Thebes, there is no Delphi. The prophecy to Laius that if he had a son that son would kill him arises as a result of Laius' being 'desirous to searche / The hidden secrets of supernall

powers' – a very Senecan touch. The Cadmus chorus in Euripides
(ll. 636–89) and Sphinx chorus (ll. 1018 and 1068) become a brief prayer
and a longer chorus which offers the poetasting folk wisdom:

> Well did the heavens ordeine for our behoofe
> Necessitie, and fates by them alowde,
> That when we see our high mishappes aloofe
> (As though our eyes were muffled with a cloude)
> Our froward will doth shrinke it selfe and shrowde
> From our availe wherwith we runne so far[r]e:
> As none amends can make that we do marre.[27]

While allowance may be made for changes in the fashion of language so
that Tyresias' injunction to the Sacerdos 'With knife then stick ye kid'
may have at the time had less of the flavour of the sacrifice of Isaac in *The
Pitmans' Bible* than might now appear, it is hard to believe a Gray's Inn
audience, even one enthused by Seneca, would be moved to pity by
Jocasta's 'O wretched wretch, Jocasta', or to fear by:

> His servant thus obedient to his hest,
> Up by the heeles did hang this faultless Impe,
> And percing with a knife his tender feete,
> Through both the wounds did drawe the slender twigs...[28]

There is plenty more where that came from. The expository prologue, in
Euripides at 87 lines one of the longest speeches in Greek tragedy, is
expanded by Kinwelmershe to 219 lines in a one-way dialogue to which
Jocasta contributes all but 36. This is known, as are both examples quoted
above, to be the work of the obscure Kinwelmershe (whose name within
the text is also rendered as both Kinwelmersh and Kinwelmarshe),
credited in the text with having 'done' acts 1 and 4.

A fairer comparison may be made by looking at the final speech of
Oedipus. In a modern translation this reads as:

> Mark me, you Thebans! I am Oedipus –
> Oedipus who read the famous riddle,
> Who was the greatest among you.
> Oedipus who was the only one
> Could break the Sphinx's murderous hold on you
> And did it alone! Look at me now!
> Disowned, dishonoured, fit only to be pitied.
> And yet ... pity's no use. Grieving's no use.

> The gods decree and we are mortal.
> There's no appeal
> And we must bear it.[29]

Gascoigne, arriving at the same finishing tape, if in a parallel universe, offers:

> Deare citizens, behold your Lord and King
> That *Thebes* set in quiet government,
> Now as you see neglected of you all,
> And in these ragged, ruthfull weedes bewrapt,
> Ychased from his native countrey soyle,
> Betakes himself (for so this tirant will)
> To everlasting banishment: but why
> Do I lament my lucklesse lot in vaine?
> Since every man must beare with quiet minde,
> The fate that heavens have earst to him assignde.[30]

Take your pick.

After these early examples translation from the Greek repertoire falters, the result, one can only assume, of the glorious outpouring of new plays, tragedies and comedies, that followed hard on the heels of the opening of London's first theatre, The Theater, in 1576, only four years after the first publication of *Jocasta*. If that was Greek tragedy, who needed it when, within twenty years the native repertoire could offer *The Spanish Tragedy*, *Tamburlaine*, *Doctor Faustus*, *Henry VI*, *Romeo and Juliet* and *Richard III*? There was a flirtation with Sophocles in 1615 by Thomas Evans Bach's *Oedipus: Three Cantoes, Wherein is contained: 1. His unfortunate Infancy. 2. His execrable Actions. 3. His lamentable End*, but he was happy enough to admit that 'I thought it as good to follow my owne fancy as the uncertainty of others'.[31]

It was not until after the closing of the theatres in 1642 that further translations from the Greek emerged: and then it was first Sophocles, then Aristophanes, rather than Euripides, who found favour. *Electra* of Sophocles translated into verse by CW [Christopher Wase] was published in 1649. This is a remarkable political document which has few, if any, parallels. The title page declares it to be '*Electra* of Sophocles presented to her highness Lady Elizabeth with an Epilogue shewing the parallel in two poems, the Return and the Restoration'. The Lady Elizabeth was the second daughter of Charles I. She was only thirteen at the time of her father's execution on 30 January 1649. Wase seems to be advising her to take Electra as a role-model but she was herself to die, a prisoner in Carisbrooke Castle, the following year. The play was published in the Hague and contained an endorsement from WC, 'To his learned friend on his ingenious choice and translation of Sophocle's [*sic*] Electra, Representing Allegorically these Times'.

The translation itself has little to recommend it:

ORESTES: O Body wickedly and basely rent!
ELECTRA: I, gentle Stranger, am the same you moan.
ORESTES: O sad, unwedded desolation.
   O me! O me!
   O Doleful course! Ay! Ay!
   O how dismall! Oh me! Oh me!
         (ll. 1181–3)[32]

But the comment on the flyleaf that 'Plays are the mirrours wherein men's actions are reflected to their own view' is more than a passing reflection on the possibilities afforded by the translator's agenda.

Thomas Randolph's *Hey for Honesty, Down with Knavery* appeared in 1651. This, according to Foster, 'contains a translation from the *Plutus*'.[33] Randolph's play will be considered in more detail later but any similarity to Aristophanes' *Plutus* is only about as convincing as are the claims by Gascoigne and Kinwelmershe for their *Jocasta* being from Euripides. These, and the further translation of the *Plutus* by HB (H. H. Burnell) in 1659, represent the sum of Greek, or near-Greek, drama to emerge in the whole of the seventeenth century. Despite a strong, if irregular, tradition in Italy and France, it was not until the eighteenth century, and then for the most part the second half (despite a number of plays which show the influence of Greek originals: see, in particular, Hall and Macintosh, *Greek Tragedy*), that there were any significant translations in English of Aeschylus, Sophocles or Euripides.[34] The Dryden *Oedipus*, to be sure, written in collaboration with Nathaniel Lee, was presented at Dorset Gardens in 1679.[35] It would have been recognised by neither Sophocles nor Seneca, but it had no pretensions to be based on either. The opening stage direction *Enter Alcander, Diocles and Pyracmon* (all from Pierre Corneille's *Oedipe*, produced at the Hôtel de Bourgogne in 1659) leaves the reader under no illusions here. Eurydice and Haemon both put in an appearance before Oedipus turns up with Adrastus, King of Argos, in tow whom he has just defeated in battle. In the next act a stage direction *Oedipus Enters, walking asleep in his shirt, with a Dagger in his right hand, and a Taper in his left* leaves one wondering whether

Dryden was embellishing Davenant's *Macbeth*, rather than rediscovering the classics. Oedipus, awakened by either thunder and Jocasta, or, possibly some combination of the two, surfaces with the line, 'Night, Horrour, Death, Confusion, Hell and Furies!' Still, Betterton played the role to acclaim and the play was revived at least twice. Most of the subplotters, including Creon, get killed off in one frantic scene. This, and Jocasta's stabbing of all her children (bar Oedipus), before being discovered 'stabb'd in many places of her bosom' renders a sequel less likely. Oedipus then commits suicide by throwing himself out of a window onto the stage, a challenge at which even Olivier might have blenched. The epilogue is aimed at the audience and refers to 'weak poets' whose:

> Treat is what your pallats relish most,
> Charm! Song! and Show! a Murder and a Ghost!
> We know not what you can desire or hope,
> To please you more, but burning of a Pope.

The early years of the eighteenth century saw a rash of real Sophocles, initially from the prolific critic Lewis Theobald with three Sophocles translations (as well as two Aristophanes) published between 1714 and 1715. Theobald knew his Greek all right, drawing attention in his notes for *Electra* to the curiosity (never satisfactorily accounted for) of a reference to a living sister called Iphianassa and declining to equate her with Iphigenia. He also apologises for reducing by half the Messenger speech about the 'death' of Orestes which he finds 'too tedious' even though he realises that he may be 'accus'd by the Adorers of *Sophocles*'. Give or take some uneasy rhymes in the choral odes, this is the only serious liberty he takes and he does display a sound enough awareness of Sophocles as a writer for performance for the play wrongly thought to have been staged at Drury Lane after his death (see Chapter 4, note 19). There is more of an odour of the Renaissance than the Restoration in a number of speeches, amongst them Electra's:

> For if my noble Father unreveng'd
> Must moulder into Dust and be forgot;
> Whilst they, triumphant in their happy Guilt,
> Laugh at the lame Revenge that cannot reach 'em:
> Farewell to Virtue; let religious awe
> No more restrain Mankind, but Outrage flourish!
> (Act I, scene 3, 245–50)

Richard Brinsley Sheridan's grandfather added a *Philoctetes* in 1725 and Euripides'*Hecuba*, translated by Richard West, came out in 1726.[36] Three years later the first complete Sophocles was published in two volumes, 'translated into English prose' by George Adams.[37] Adams has a more obviously scholarly mien, offering notes that are 'Historical, Moral and Critical: Wherein several Mistakes of Editors and the old Scholiasts are corrected'. A long Preface makes comparisons with the Precepts of the Gospel and 'our great Prophet *Jesus Christ*'. His translations are both in prose and prosy. Theobald's Electra in the passage quoted above can manage no better than:

> But if the wretched murthered King, who is now but Earth and Nothing, lies miserably abandoned, and they suffer not a Punishment equal to their Crime; Shame is no more on earth, no Piety among Mortals.

Adams' *Electra* offers for Sophocles' *ō pasan keina pleon hamera / elthous' echthista dē moi* (ll. 201–2) only 'O that Day which of all Days was most bitter to me' whereas Theobald uses the splendid 'O Day most hated of the rowling Year!', 'rowling' a word which may be a neologism, but is a real 'actor's word'.

The revival of interest in the world of the Greek dramatists took wing in the second half of the eighteenth century. The relative dearth of native serious drama of merit in the century after the Restoration of the monarchy may have been a contributory factor, combined with an awareness of the influence of the Greeks, as well as of Seneca, on the classical theatre in France. Initially single plays from a severely restricted list, known from Italian translations, were most popular: another *Hecuba* to add to that of Richard West, this time from the Revd Thomas Morell in 1749, and an *Iphigenia in Tauris* to be found in Gilbert West's translation of Pindar (1753). In 1759 the repertoire was suddenly opened up with a translation by Mrs Charlotte Lennox of Father Pierre Brumoy's *Le Théâtre des Grecs*.[38] This is a massive three-volume work, the first ever comprehensive study of Greek drama. Somewhat in the manner of Donaldson's later *Theatre of the Greeks*, Brumoy's work is notable for the addition of translations. Brumoy was a Jesuit priest from Rouen who subsequently lived in Paris where *Le Théâtre des Grecs* was probably first published in 1730.[39] He wrote several plays of his own on sacred subjects as well as being editor of a *History of the Gallican Church*. *Le Théâtre des Grecs* includes a number of Discourses: *Upon the Greek Theatre; Upon the Original of Tragedy; Upon the Parallel of the Theatres* [Greek and French];

Upon Greek Comedy; and an *Annals of the Peloponnesian War*, for its effect on the drama of the time.

The Lennox translation of his *Théâtre des Grecs* is thorough and revealing.[40] In her own introduction she is not uncritical of Brumoy: 'Brumoy is a good critic, and an excellent translator, but he is a bad and tedious writer.'[41] She is also very suspicious of his inclusion of an account of 'Chinese tragedy'. The main body of Brumoy's work revolves around translation of the entire corpus of Greek drama that we now possess (excluding only our recent Menanders). Much of this, however, is partial. The only plays translated in their entirety by Brumoy, and from his French by Lennox, are Sophocles' *Oedipus*, *Electra* and *Philoctetes*, and Euripides' two Iphigenia plays, plus *Hippolytus* and *Alcestis*. All the other 'translations' are selections with linking narrative. Lennox is sanguine enough about the loss: 'Eschylus [based on the French spelling] must have excited aversion rather than admiration, if he had been fully translated'.[42] As far as decorum is concerned, the eclectic approach provides a means of ducking the awkward problems posed by Greek comedy which she passes over to other hands, including Samuel Johnson, though a translation of Aristophanes by Brumoy, with notes by C. A. Wheelwright, was published after Brumoy's death.[43]

Charlotte Lennox's own use or knowledge of the Greek is not clear. When she states that 'He [Brumoy] assures us, that he has avoided every extreme to which too vague or too close translations are liable'[44] it would seem to imply that she is translating solely from the French. The undertaking of such a task could hardly be done blind, one might think, without a thorough knowledge of the original repertoire, but it is surprising to find this as a résumé of the entire plot of *Medea*: 'Medea, abandoned by Jason, kills her rival, and retires to Athens, where she marries Aegeus, ninth king of Athens'.[45] The Lennox/Brumoy *Oedipus* and others will be considered later in more detail (p. 87). What can be said is that the publication of these three volumes introduced a number of Greek works into the English language for the first time and, as importantly, gave prominence to the existence of the whole canon.

All previous attempts must pale into insignificance when compared with the achievements of the Revd Robert Potter. Though Thomas Morell's *Prometheus in Chains* (1773) was the first single Aeschylus, Potter, a schoolmaster and cleric, was the first translator of the whole of Aeschylus into English. He produced all seven surviving plays in 1777 in an edition which was still being regularly reprinted a hundred years later.[46] Two volumes of Euripides followed in 1781 and 1783,[47] and in

1788 the seven plays of Sophocles.[48] Potter's first volume of Euripides, dedicated to Her Grace the Dowager Duchess of Beaufort, Baroness of Botetourt, had quickly to compete with the complete Euripides of Michael Wodhull in 1782,[49] but his Aeschylus remained in a league of its own for many years. Potter marks the belated flowering of classical tragedy in English and his work too will be considered in more detail in the chapters on the *Agamemnon* and *Oedipus Tyrannus*. All this marked a flurry of new translations, mostly prepared for the schoolroom rather than the stage, which formed a significant element in the classical revival of the late eighteenth and nineteenth centuries. Potter failed to make much impression at first in literary circles. Boswell records in his *Life of Johnson* the following journal entry for 9 April 1778, the year after the publication of the Potter *Aeschylus*:

I got into a corner with Johnson, Garrick [the actor David Garrick] and Harris [James Harris of Salisbury]. GARRICK. (to Harris) 'Pray, Sir, have you read Potter's *Aeschylus*?' HARRIS. 'Yes; and I think it pretty.' GARRICK. (to Johnson) 'And what think you, Sir, of it?' JOHNSON. 'I thought what I read of it *verbiage*; but upon Mr Harris's recommendation I will read a play. (to Mr Harris) Don't prescribe two,' Mr Harris suggested one, I don't remember which. JOHNSON. 'We must try its effect as an English poem; that is the way to judge a translation. Translations are, in general, for people who cannot read the original.' I mentioned the vulgar saying that Pope's *Homer* was not a good representation of the original. JOHNSON. 'Sir, it is the greatest work of the kind that was ever produced.' BOSWELL. 'The truth is, it is impossible to translate poetry. In a different language it may be the same tune, but it has not the same tone. Homer plays it on the bassoon, Pope on a flageolet.'[50]

But then the pomposity of Johnson was never more insufferable than when he found himself exposed to a rival for the floor. Potter's work rapidly became the standard against which to judge all other translations and remained so at least up to, and probably past, the rise of the upstart Gilbert Murray. Here, though, the modern age of translation is truly born.

In an essay published for The British Council and the National Book League in 1962, J. M. Cohen wrote compellingly about how each century needed new translations 'to suit the change in standards and taste of new generations' and continued:

The Elizabethan translations ignored their author's style and background, intent only on producing a book for their own times; the 18th century made the Classics conform to their own aristocratic standards, ruthlessly pruning away all complexities and digressions that might cause a gentleman's interest to flag; the Victorians conferred on all works alike the brown varnish of antiquarianism; and our own age, in its scientific devotion to simplicity and accuracy, demands plain versions which sacrifice sound to sense, and verbal idiosyncrasy to the narrative virtues.[51]

Perhaps it was this chameleon quality that ensured that the plays could and would survive on into modern times in other ways than as a spur to the classical world, as a setting for original work. By the end of the nineteenth century the theatre was undergoing a major change and the plays themselves began to return to the repertoire, offering a new and different challenge to translators. Aeschylus' *Agamemnon* offers a case in point.

CHAPTER 3

Aeschylus and the Agamemnon: *Gilding the Lily*

A translator's best hope, I think, and still the hardest to achieve, is Dryden's hope that his author will speak the living language of the day.

(Robert Fagles, Foreword to Aeschylus' *Oresteia*)

In Terence Rattigan's one-act play, *The Browning Version*, there is an early encounter between the schoolmaster, Frank Hunter, and the reluctant classicist pupil John Taplow:

TAPLOW (*protestingly*): I'm extremely interested in science, sir.
FRANK: Are you? I'm not. Not, at least, in the science I have to teach.
TAPLOW: Well, anyway, sir, it's a great deal more exciting than this muck. (*Indicating his book.*)
FRANK: What is this muck?
TAPLOW: Aeschylus, sir. The *Agamemnon*.
FRANK: And your considered view is that the *Agamemnon* of Aeschylus is muck, is it?
TAPLOW: Well, no, sir. I don't think the play is muck – exactly. I suppose, in a way, it's rather a good play, really, a wife murdering her husband and having a lover and all that. I only mean the way it's taught to us – just a lot of Greek words strung together . . .

A little later in the play the teacher of Greek, Andrew Crocker-Harris, during whose final hours at the school the play takes place, begins a translation session with Taplow. Taplow's free rendering of the Chorus's confrontation with Clytemnestra is treated with some scorn by Andrew:

ANDREW: Then why do you invent words that are simply not there?
TAPLOW: I thought they sounded better, sir. More exciting. After all she did kill her husband, sir. (*With relish.*) She's just been revealed with his dead body and Cassandra's weltering in gore –

43

ANDREW: I am delighted at this evidence, Taplow, of your interest
    in the more lurid aspects of dramaturgy, but I feel I must
    remind you that you are supposed to be construing Greek, not
    collaborating with Aeschylus.
TAPLOW (*greatly daring*): Yes, but still, sir, translator's licence, sir – I
    didn't get anything wrong – and after all it *is* a play and not just
    a bit of Greek construe.'

Rattigan's play received its first production at the Phoenix Theatre in
London in 1948. The title comes from a present of the Robert Browning
translation of the *Agamemnon* which Taplow gives to his teacher, a
present dismissed by the bitchy wife as a bribe for promotion. Though
these exchanges reflect an aspect of the teaching of Greek which, it is to
be hoped, is a thing of the past (if remembered vividly by many of us who
could have seen the first production of the Rattigan), there is one phrase
there that cries out from the page, Crocker-Harris's admonition to his
pupil that he is not meant to be 'collaborating with Aeschylus'. Taplow's
tentative suggestion that this is exactly what a translator should be doing
homes in on the main argument already identified about the function of
the translator. By choosing the *Agamemnon* as his example, Rattigan the
playwright does point to the very special nature of Aeschylus and the
unique problems that translating his work raise. For Crocker-Harris the
Agamemnon is 'perhaps the greatest play ever written' and he subsequently
confesses to himself having, in his youth, written a 'very free' translation
in rhyming couplets. The *Agamemnon* is the obvious choice for the first of
the three 'case studies'.

    Most readers and audiences today, and this includes in Greece, must
approach a Greek play through translation. Already that offers one sort of
collaboration with Aeschylus, a collaboration that is augmented in performance by other contributors to what is inevitably a collaborative art. It
always was, even when Aeschylus' own contribution as writer, director,
actor, and possibly composer and choreographer too, made him something of a one-man band. Rattigan knew, if his characters did not, that
any collaboration includes the audience at the point of impact, bringing
to their perception their own historical, political and cultural experience.
In retrospect, what sticks may so differ from the experience of one person
to that of another, that the 'reality' of the performance is no more than an
agglomeration of all the partial recollections of everyone involved as
creators and as audience. Even what the eye sees, neuroscientists now tell
us, is no more than an educated guess by the brain in response to the
stimuli fed to it and previous experience.

Classical theatre as a synthetic art may well have the text as a starting-point, but the text as blueprint, the text as score. A well-constructed play, and most of the surviving Greek plays are constructed well, is as many-faceted as a diamond, with a whole variety of possible interpretations. The same may be true to some extent of any work of literature, but a play has the major dimension of being created for performance: and, therefore, barely fashioned when merely in print. The nature of this malleability, this promiscuity, if you like, is part of the translator's responsibility, included in the relationship of all the features of performance, but especially the balance between translation, production and reception. Aeschylus' *Agamemnon*, and the history of its translation into English, turns out to be a particularly effective way to examine this relationship.

The history of translation of the Greek classics into English may go back, as we have seen, as far as Lady Jane Lumley's *Iphigenia* in the middle of the sixteenth century. No one, it seems, braved Aeschylus in English for another two hundred years until Thomas Morell's *Prometheus in Chains* (1773) and Robert Potter's complete Aeschylus (1777). *The Critical Review* is quoted on the flyleaf of one of the nineteenth-century reprints of Potter's *Aeschylus* as saying 'The translator has happily preserved the dignity of style, that bold and descriptive imagery, for which the author is particularly distinguished'. Potter's eventual, but belated, reward was to be given an appointment as Prebendary of Norwich. Maybe it was this perceived need for a combination of 'dignity of style' and 'bold and descriptive imagery' that had daunted previous translators.

Potter's Aeschylus is principally in iambic pentameters. This includes the first section of Chorus which subsequently remains in iambics but reverts to a mixture of mainly four with some five-feet lines. Any loss of substance from the original Alexandrine and lyric mix is compensated by an increase in overall number of lines from the 1673 of Aeschylus to 1740.[2] Here is a taste of Potter's Aeschylean style, in the opening speech of the Watchman:

> Ye fav'ring gods, relieve me from this toil:
> Fix'd as a dog on Agamemnon's roof
> I watch the live-long year, observing hence
> The host of stars, that in the spangled skies
> Take their bright stations, and to mortals bring
> Winter and summer; radiant rulers, when
> They set, or rising glitter through the night.
> Here now I watch, if haply I may see
> The blazing torch, whose flame brings news from Troy.

The signal of its ruin: these high hopes
My royal mistress, thinking on her lord,
Feeds in her heart.

(ll. 1–12)[3]

This, then, is from 1777. Compare it with Gilbert Murray, who can take the credit for first returning the Greeks to the commercial theatre with his translations for the Vedrenne–Barker management at the Court Theatre in the early years of the twentieth century. Murray, that formidable Australian scholar who was awarded the Chair of Greek at the University of Glasgow at the age of twenty-three and became Regius Professor of Greek at Oxford in 1908, had tackled Euripides, Sophocles and Aristophanes before turning in 1920 to *Agamemnon*. Here is his opening:

This waste of year-long vigil I have prayed
God for some respite, watching elbow-stayed,
As sleuthhounds watch above the Atreidae's hall,
Till well I know yon midnight festival
Of swarming stars, and them that lonely go,
Bearers to man of summer and of snow,
Great lords and shining, throned in heavenly fire.
   And still I await the sign, the beacon pyre
That bears Troy's capture on a voice of flame
Shouting o'erseas. So surely to her aim
Cleaveth a woman's heart, man-passionèd!

(ll. 1–11)[4]

The change in style is startling. The twentieth century Murray seems to have consigned Aeschylus, not to a poetic past pre-Potter, for all that Potter wrote 123 years earlier, but to a dramatic wilderness, a world that never was, a mirage, a figment of his own fevered imagination that bears no resemblance whatsoever to Aeschylus. Yet it is Murray to whom no less a playwright than George Bernard Shaw could write in 1940: 'Though I have lived in the thick of a revolutionary burst of playwriting in London, the only plays that seem to me likely to survive are the old Greek ones in your translations'.[5]

It is interesting to speculate exactly where Murray acquired his style, a style that appears to have enchanted Shaw but is now so hard to stomach. Rattigan may offer the clue. Though none of the Robert Browning version of the *Agamemnon* appears in the play to which it gives a title, Browning's *Agamemnon* does have some of that quality of the old-fashioned which for some typified what Aeschylus really was and for others did no more than condemn him through a diet of self-conscious archaism.

Browning's tangling with the classics was sincere enough. In 1871 he published *Balaustion's Adventure* which included a 'transcript' of Euripides' *Alcestis*. The play was included as a linked narrative within the poem and, odd idea though this might seem, met the approval of the notable historian J. P. Mahaffy in his *History of Greek Literature* (1880): 'By far the best translation of the *Alcestis* is Mr Browning's.' Two years later Browning was translating *Hercules Furens* (Euripides' *Heracles*) which was inserted into *Aristophanes' Apology*. This *Apology* is a curious conceit in which a debate takes place, ostensibly between Aristophanes and Balaustion, about the merits of Euripides as a playwright, whose death in Thrace has recently been announced. The occasion is the evening of Aristophanes' victory at the Lenaea with *Thesmophoriazousae* in 411 BC. As Euripides was still alive and writing for another six years after 411, for some of the time in Thrace, something has gone wrong somewhere with the chronology. Be that as it may, Browning's *The Agamemnon of Aeschylus* appeared after these forays into Euripides, in the autumn of 1877. In the Introduction he set up a kind of challenge:

Should anybody, without need, honour my translation by a comparison with the original, I beg him to observe that, following no editor exclusively, I keep to the earlier readings so long as sense can be made out of them, but disregard, I hope, little of importance in recent criticism so far as I have fallen in with it. Fortunately, the poorest translation, provided it only be faithful – though it produce all the artistic confusion of tenses, moods, and persons, with which the original teems, – will not only suffice to display what an eloquent friend maintains to be the all-in-all of poetry – 'the action of the piece'.[6]

The problem lies, unfortunately, less in 'the action of the piece' than in the 'all-in-all of poetry'. Browning goes in for a tortuous sentence-structure that is in places nigh on impenetrable. Add to this a Germanic enthusiasm for the multiple coinage ('bad-wave-outbreak' is an adjective), and a choice of language that outdoes any Housman parody and you find, in the Warder's prologue alone:

> On the Atreidai's roofs on elbow, – dog-like –
> I know of nightly star-groups the assemblage
> And those that bring to men, winter and summer
> Bright dynasts, as they pride them in the aether
> Stars –, when they wither, and the uprisings of them.

        ... so prevails audacious
        The man's-way-planning hoping heart of woman.
          ...

        And when I sing or chirp a tune I fancy,
        For slumber such song-remedy infusing,
        I wail then, for this house's fortune groaning,
        Not, as of old, after the best ways governed.[7]

The choruses are even more convoluted:

        Flame – medicated with persuasions mild,
        With foul admixture unbeguiled –
        Of holy unguent, from the clotted charism
        Brought from the palace, safe in its abysm.
                          (ll. 94–7)

The dialogue is no less unrecognisable as the English language. News of
the fall of Troy elicits the response from the Choros [*sic*] 'Joy overcreeps
me, calling forth the teardrop' (l. 291), while Klutaimnestra instructs the
Herald:

        This tell my husband –
        To come at soonest to his loving city.
        A faithful wife at home may he find, coming!
        Such an one as he left – the dog o' the household.
                         (ll. 627–30)

Browning is an easy target, but this is more than Victorian extravagance.
Elizabeth Barrett (later) Browning had come up with a far more acceptable *Prometheus Bound* – actually two (see p. 109–10) over forty years
earlier. John Conington, whose translation of *Agamemnon* came out in
1848 asked the question in his Introduction:

How can we be said to give a true copy of a Greek expression when we substitute
for it one made up of English words indeed, but conveying no meaning at all, or
perhaps a harsh meaning to English ears? or how can we flatter ourselves that a
composition which an English reader would regard as oddly-fashioned prose,
with no harmony, is a facsimile of an Aeschylean Chorus?[8]

Even the editor of Browning's *Collected Works*, Sir F. G. Kenyon, was
scathing about this *Agamemnon*: 'it is hard to say much in its favour, and
it is not easy to understand the spirit in which it was produced'.[9] He
criticised Browning's principles of translation 'to be literal at every cost

save that of absolute violence to our language', and accused him of producing something more obscure than the original. Choice of the hendecasyllabic line he finds incomprehensible and concludes 'The greater the reader's admiration for Aeschylus and Browning, the deeper must be his regret that their collocation should have done so little justice to either.'[10]

That an editor should so savage his subject is something over which it might be more tactful to draw a veil, were it not for two things: the first is the debt that Murray might seem, for good or ill, to owe to Browning; and, second, the fact that the Browning version is still a worthy gift to offer to a retiring schoolmaster sixty-nine years after its original publication. Few translators will find themselves so redeemed. Perhaps too it gives some food for thought as to the reasons why Aeschylus remained neglected by translators for so long.

Part of the problem later generations have had with Murray (though less with Browning whose rhymes are confined to the chorus) was his use of rhyming couplets, a predilection which adds little to any tragic work, especially that of the Greeks, beyond strengthening a determination on the part of most actors to fracture the delivery wherever possible so as to deceive the audience into mishearing the text. Equally alarming was Murray's enthusiasm for archaisms as though they awarded authority to the translation of an old play by virtue of sounding nothing other than old. The only consolation for Aeschylus might be that worse disservice was done by Murray to Euripides. The evidence of Murray's translation of Aristophanes' parody of Aeschylus and Euripides in *Frogs* would suggest that any competition between the two tragedians in Hades would have been for the privilege of remaining dead rather than having to return to see their work so mangled.[11]

It is worth comparing at this point the opening lines of two contemporary 'versions' of *Agamemnon* in English by poets from West Yorkshire, each of which figured in a production at the Royal National Theatre in London. From 1981, for the production in masks by Peter Hall, Tony Harrison wrote:

> No end to it all, though all year I've muttered
> my pleas to the gods for a long groped for end.
> Wish it were over, this waiting, this watching,
> twelve weary months, night in and night out,
> crouching and peering like a bloodhound,
> paws propping muzzle, up here on the palace,

the palace belonging the bloodclan of Atreus –
Agamemnon, Menelaus, bloodkin, our clanchiefs.

(ll. 1–8)[12]

Ted Hughes, the first of these mentioned so far not to be working from
the Greek, wrote the version that Katie Mitchell directed at the Cottesloe
Theatre in 1999:

> You Gods in heaven –
> You have watched me here on this tower
> All night, every night, for twelve months,
> Thirteen moons –
> Tethered on the roof of this palace
> Like a dog.
> It is time to release me.
> I've stared long enough into this darkness
> For what never emerges
> I'm tired of the constellations –
> That glittering parade of lofty rulers
> Night after night a little bit earlier
> Withholding the thing I wait for –
> Slow as torture.
>
> (ll. 1–14)[13]

In 1960, before either of these or a host of other more recent *Agamemnons*, Peter Green wrote a thoroughly entertaining essay entitled
'Some versions of Aeschylus'.[14] There he identified over fifty translations
of *Agamemnon*, all of which he had read and most of which he dismissed
as 'a prop on which the scholarly poet *manqué* could peg his own
threadbare Muse'. About Murray as a translator of the Greeks he was
sleekly dismissive, referring his readers instead to the excoriating assault of
T. S. Eliot who concluded an evaluation of Sybil Thorndike's struggles
with Murray's *Medea* with the words 'it is because Professor Murray has
no creative instinct that he leaves Euripides quite dead'.[15] Instead, Green
referred less to the translations themselves than to the effect those
translations had in their own time:

Up and down England there were thousands of innocents who very likely went
to their graves imagining that this was the way that Aeschylus or Euripides
actually wrote. They gave the credit for Professor Murray's poetic sensibility to
the Greek dramatists on whom he modelled himself; and since Aeschylus was
dead, and Professor Murray, with scholarly modesty, refused to take any of the
credit, error crept in and persisted.[16]

Tempting as it is to dwell on examples of the grosser Murray, the real point is that Murray is not a victim of changing language patterns in the way that makes an old French/English phrasebook now seem old-fashioned. Rather, he is a warning to all translators of the inherent dangers of invoking classical authority in the cause of self-promotion. Green's lucid and comprehensive study also queried the assumption, which he claimed was endemic amongst classical scholars, that there was somewhere a single ideal translation of anything classical waiting to be uncovered. 'Nothing', he concluded, 'improves by translation except a bishop'.[17]

That, though, seems simply to overstate the case by consigning anyone who does not have access to the originals to a purgatory from which they may do no more than gaze from afar on the state of the blessed. Might a case not be made for absolution through translation? After all, in France, Germany, Russia, the multiplicity of Shakespeares seems to have done minimal damage to his reputation. Green seems to be endorsing here Virginia Woolf's dismissive 'It is useless, then, to read Greek in transla- tions'.[18] But what both Woolf and Green overlook are the two factors above all that make translation for the stage so different from translation of literature or poetry. Shakespeare, and Aeschylus, Sophocles and Eur- ipides are poets, but more than poets. Their text as language depends on the translation of the words on the page. Their text as drama depends partly on the translation of stage action, partly on the realisation of that action through performance. Perhaps for a theatre work a better word than translation would be transubstantiation: because if one dictionary definition of translation is 'inferring or transmitting the significance', the non-religious meaning of transubstantiation is identified as 'describing a change of substance or essence'.[19]

This issue of writing with performance in mind is the constant factor in this book, not least because those fifty plus translations of *Agamemnon* through which Professor Green waded will have contained such a variety of experience of what the mechanics of the stage might entail. As a counterbalance, all too few translators are likely to have indulged in much heart-searching over whether their responsibility lies with the original text or with their personal slant on that text. The attitude to stage directions can be revealing. Director, designer and theatre reformer Edward Gordon Craig believed that stage directions were nothing to do with the play- wright, never mind with the translator. In the received texts of Aeschylus there are none, none, that is, written in as extra-textual guidance as to what is happening, where and to whom. Much of the stage action can be inferred but it is a rare translator who can resist spelling it out as part of the duty of office. Potter was exemplary in his faithfulness to Aeschylus, offering no more than the characters in each scene and indications in the choral passages of *strophē, antistrophē* and what he calls 'prosode'. There are no entrances or exits marked. Maybe this is a purist vision. A modern translation, it might be argued, should include some stage directions if only to give the uninformed reader an idea of what is meant to be happening. Many translators, indeed, seem to see their task as dictating their own production preferences.

In his *Agamemnon* Murray initially does little more than set the scene: '*The Scene represents a space in front of the Palace of Agamemnon in Argos*' – Not much to argue with there – '*with an Altar to Zeus in the centre and many other altars at the sides. On a high terrace of the roof stands a* WATCHMAN. *It is night*'. Soon, however, we find '*Lights begin to show in the Palace . . . The women's "Ololūgē*", or triumph-cry, is heard again and again further off in the City. Handmaids and Attendants come from the Palace, bearing torches, with which they kindle incense on the altars. Among them comes CLYTEMNESTRA, *who throws herself on her knees at the central Altar in an agony of prayer . . .*'

The Chorus have elaborate directions as to what their odes are all about. When Agamemnon enters '*amid a great procession . . . the chorus make obeisance . . . some of Agamemnon's men have on their shields a White Horse, some a Lion . . . Clytemnestra controls her suspense with difficulty. . . . As he* (Agamemnon) *sets foot on the Tapestries* CLYTEMNESTRA's *women utter again their cry of triumph*.' After the murder of Agamemnon and Cassandra, Aegisthus says a few lines and '*a body of Spearmen from outside, rush in and dominate the stage*'.[20]

Much of this is less descriptive than prescriptive.[21] For the most part, translators now resist the urge to dictate their notional ideal production. Among translations still in use, Vellacott (1956), Fagles (1966), Raphael and McLeish (1991), Meineck (1998) and Hughes (1999) offer few directions; the same holds for John Lewin in his 'free adaptation' for Tyrone Guthrie in 1966. Grene and O'Flaherty within a single volume (1989) present two different translations, one the 'unabridged text', the other an 'acting version', both with minimal directions.[22] The 'acting version' is condensed to a mere thirty-three pages from the fifty-eight of the full text and would make an interesting study in its own right. Ewans acknowledges the stage directions as modern but includes a few of his own such as '*Klytaimestra prostrates herself full length on the ground before him in homage. After a few moments she rises to her feet again*'; later '*Kassandra leaps from the chariot which is then removed by the left parodos*.'

She bursts into agonised, energetic dance and song'.[23] Alan Shapiro and Peter Burian's *The Oresteia* (2003) offers a smaller number of reasonable suggestions as to the stage action, a distinct improvement on the previous translation from Oxford (Collard, 2002).

Louis MacNeice in the Introduction to his *Agamemnon*, published in 1936 when he was only twenty-two and a lecturer in Greek at Birmingham University, asserted 'I have written this translation primarily for the stage ... it is hoped that my play emerges as a play and not as a museum-piece'.[24] MacNeice's stage directions are wholly functional offering to the reader nothing that is not implicit in the lines of Aeschylus. The production, as it happens, was infinitely more imaginative than anything envisaged by Murray. The translation was offered to the London Group Theatre in 1936 and was directed, somewhat reluctantly, at the Westminster Theatre by Rupert Doone in November of that year. The production details traced by Michael Sidnell make often hilarious reading.[25] MacNeice himself thought the production should 'tend towards the statuesque and rather larger-than-life'. At the same time he seems to have accepted, even if not all the reviewers were as happy, a chorus in dinner jackets and masks made of cellophane panels to look like stained glass; Agamemnon in a jester's cap; and Aegisthus' soldiers offering a Nazi salute. 'Classical Greek dress ... to be avoided ... Best to create your own costume with hints from the Mycenean age', he told Doone. What he got, according to *Time and Tide* was 'more slaves dressed like the Klu Klux Clan, Cassandra as an Arab from the shores of the Euphrates, with an Elizabethan ruff, and lastly Aegisthus in a Christmas cracker helmet and black evening cape'.[26]

Other 'translations' have raised other issues. Robert Lowell, the American poet who died in 1977, confessed to having written his *The Oresteia* from existing translations. It was not published until after Lowell's death but contained a frontispiece in which he had written:

I do not want to cry down my translation of Aeschylus but to say what I've tried to do and not tried. ... No version of the *Oresteia*, even a great one such as Marlowe or Milton might have written, can be anything like what was first performed in Athens with music, dance, masks and an audience of thirty thousand or more – an event we cannot recover and something no doubt grander than any play we can *see*.[27]

Here, of course, is the rub. A translation of a piece of literature, or of a poem, is a finished product. A translation of a play, unless it is strictly for publication, is barely the start. There are a number of imperatives for the translator which range from some kind of duty to the original so as not to flout the Trades' Descriptions Act, to the need to free directors, designers and actors from the straitjacket of archaeology. There is, in fact, a world of difference between translating a classical text for a production that the translator will direct and offering a text as a block of stone from which the processes of production will fashion a finished sculpture the translator may hardly recognise. MacNeice and Tony Harrison, as both poets and playwrights, would, no doubt, agree. MacNeice, indeed, was substantially to revise his *Agamemnon*, post-Doone, before sending it to Faber and Faber.

Aeschylus' *Agamemnon* is a play which presents a number of unusual features when viewed in isolation. To begin with it is only the first play of a group of four, two others of which we have, the three usually performed together as the only extant trilogy. Without the satyr play, *Proteus*, our *Oresteia* is incomplete. Knowing *Libation-Bearers* and *Furies* makes it much harder to recreate the impact of the play at that first performance. Obvious though it may be, Aeschylus wrote *Agamemnon* for an audience who may have known the bare bones of Agamemnon's return from Troy but had no idea how he would develop the action in the other two, or three, plays.

The overall structure has few dramatic parallels. The choral ode that immediately follows the departure of the Watchman is the longest in surviving Greek drama. After a scene of fewer than 100 lines with Clytemnestra, there is another chorus. In the first 500 lines – almost a third of the play – all but 116 are allocated to the Chorus. Agamemnon, the title character, has 84 lines, only 20 more than the marginal Aegisthus, one third fewer than the Herald and less than half of Cassandra's. This is not unusual – Aeschylus frequently places greater emphasis on the Chorus than do Sophocles or Euripides – but there are questions to be addressed about it as dramatic narrative. Greek plays contain what they contain; exposition for a Greek playwright was as much about ruling out possible intrusions from the myths as it was about explaining what was included. Agamemnon's allies have been dispersed, possibly fatally in a storm. Does this make his entrance a grand one or a rather bedraggled affair? Cassandra is mentioned by name only once, and that is by Clytemnestra. How does Clytemnestra know who Cassandra is, and when does she know, and does it matter? And why does Clytemnestra introduce the carpet of scarlet drapes?

All of these are inevitably production issues. They may all be solved by the nature of the production which could treat them as irrelevant, or explained through presentation, or flamboyant theatrical gesture, which is probably a mixture of the other two. It may well be as unnecessary to explain them as to explain why Orestes' footprints in *Libation-Bearers* should appear the same size as his sister's, or why his hair should be of the same colour and texture.[28] These are, of course, precisely the questions that Euripides' Electra, as a character, will be asking in the same theatre some forty years after the *Oresteia*. The problems are not insurmountable but they do invite the translator to be as aware as the director that there is a need to create a whole context in which the play is possible.

The scene in Aeschylus' *Agamemnon* which most clearly exemplifies the balance between text and stage action, between linguistic and performance values, is the 'carpet' scene. The two productions at the Royal National Theatre, Peter Hall's in 1981 and Katie Mitchell's in 1999, relied on substantially different translations. Here is Tony Harrison's for the sequence where Clytemnestra tempts her husband to walk on the red drapes (*Ag.* 905–57):

CLYTEMNESTRA
> Now, my great manlord, come down from your warcar.
> But don't let those feet that have trampled Troy under
> step on mere earth.
> *To SLAVES*
>   Why are you waiting?
> Carry out my commands for strewing the pavestones,
> drag the dark dye-flow right down from the doorway.
> Let bloodright, true bloodright be the king's escort.
> No sleeping for me till the gods get their pleasure.
> The she-gods of life-lot, I'll be their she-kin,
> the female enforcer of all they have fated.

A battle of wills ensues at the end of which Agamemnon concedes:

AGAMEMNON
> If it means so much ...
> *To SLAVES*
>   here help get these boots off.
> Campaign comrades, loyal old leathers.
> Keep godgrudge off me as I tread on this sea-red.
> I'll feel that I'm walking the women who wove it.
> Mounds of rich silver went into its making.

So much for me . . .
Indicates CASSANDRA
        This stranger needs looking after.
    The gods like some kindness from those who have triumphed.
    Be kind. Nobody wants to end up in bondage.
    Pick of the booty, the Trojan spoil loot-pearl,
    the girl's the men's gift to grace their commander.
    Well, since I've yielded, I'll do what you ask me,
    and tread on your red path into my palace.

AGAMEMNON begins walking on the cloth towards the palace doors.[29] (pp. 27–9)

Here is Ted Hughes for the same passage:

CLYTEMNESTRA
    Agamemnon, step down from your chariot.
    But this bare earth is too poor
    For the foot that trod on the neck of Troy.
    Hurry – the long carpet of crimson.
    Unroll the embroidery
    Of vermilion and purple.
    The richest silks of Argos are prostrated
    To honour the King's tread at his homecoming,
    And cushion every footfall of his triumph.
    Justice herself shall kiss his instep
    And lead him step by step into the home
    He never hoped to see.
    After this, everything that thinking,
    Night after harrowing night,
    Hacked out of the darkness,
    Everything shall follow
    As the immortals have planned. (p. 43)

In the Greek Aeschylus has a mere six lines here for Clytemnestra, compared to the nine of Harrison and seventeen of Hughes, though Hughes's are shorter. And Agamemnon's submission in Hughes:

AGAMEMNON
    How determined you are.
    Here – unlace these leathers
    That have trampled the walls of Troy.
    When I tread this ocean purple
    As if the glory were mine
    Let no god resent it, or be offended,
    As it offends me
    To trample such richness under my unwashed feet.

Woven fibres, costly as wire of silver.
This heaped-up, spilled-out wealth of my own house.
Do I make too much of it?
This is Cassandra.
Let her be cared for.
The gods reward a conqueror's mercy.
Her house is ashes,
And she is now a slave. Treat her as mine.
The jewel of Troy, my army's gift to me.
And now since you have conquered me in this matter
Of treading the crimson path –
Let me enter my house at last.
He goes in.[30] (pp. 46–7)

For this last speech Aeschylus has fourteen lines, Harrison twelve, Hughes twenty, amongst which are several where he clearly identifies Cassandra whom Agamemnon calls only 'the stranger' or 'guest' '*tēn xenēn*' (l. 950). The very ambiguity of the word *xenos*, which in Greek can mean both 'stranger' and 'guest' and in addition 'friend' or 'mercenary', highlights the need for decisions.

The difference in the playing of this scene in different productions can be startling. There are visual records, though adjusted to the requirements of the camera, of the productions of both Peter Stein in 1980, performed first at the Schaubühne in Berlin as part of the Antiquity Project,[31] and Peter Hall's for the National Theatre in 1981.[32] Hall's, with all the characters masked, offers formality rather than tension: Stein's is a sequence of agonising suspense as Agamemnon stumbles just before he reaches the palace door and Clytemnestra instinctively puts out a hand to steady him.

Oliver Taplin considered this sequence in considerable detail in *The Stagecraft of Aeschylus*, coming to the conclusion that 'the scene has several meanings, all interconnected in various ways. Some are explicit, some are implicit, some are clear at the time, some emerge clearly only later in the trilogy'.[33] There is little to argue with there except, perhaps, to suggest that for a director any questions about why Clytemnestra should set up this scene come down less to tempting Agamemnon into contributing to his own downfall through an act of *hubris* than to the promotion of a sequence of pure imagery, the past, the present and the future, the massacre of an innocent, the rivers of blood ten years long, and generations back, the pathway to his crimson bath. Here is the transubstantiation, the substance, the essence, the word made flesh.

Translating such a scene into stage action is only marginally the province of the translator at all because Aeschylus effectively suspends words and lets action take over. It is the production team who decide the details.[34] Clytemnestra invites the servants *stornunai petasmasin* (lit. 'to strew with things spread out', l. 909); and speaks of *porfurostrōtos poros* (a purple path, l. 910); Agamemnon refers to *heimasi* ('with garments', l. 921) as does Clytemnestra (l. 962);[35] Agamemnon exits, *porphuras patōn* (his last two words, 'treading on purple', l. 957). Various stagings offer varying solutions, each of which becomes *ipso facto*, a statement of interpretation. Peter Hall's was an ornate and sumptuous red cloth. Peter Stein's 'pathway' was created not from a single 'carpet' but from a mass of folded cloths.

For Katie Mitchell, on the other hand, in the intimate Cottesloe Theatre, the theatrical imperative resided in Aeschylus' initial visual shock, the red carpet. Taking her cue, perhaps, from Martha Graham's 1958 dance-drama, *Agamemnon*, Mitchell included in *The Home Guard* – her, but not Hughes's, title for *Agamemnon* – the ghost of Iphigeneia, a gagged and desperate creature who flitted in and out of the action as though trying to account for her brief life.[36] Her presence made Clytemnestra's murderous plans towards her husband seem driven primarily by the loss of her daughter.

When Agamemnon and Cassandra made their initial entrance, the traverse staging emphasised the engagement of wills between Agamemnon and Clytemnestra. When she called for the servants to 'unroll the embroidery of vermilion and purple' they started to lay out a tapestry from the foot of the 'chariot' up to the palace. So far, as you would expect: except that it suddenly became clear that this was not a tapestry but a patchwork, a patchwork made up of a hundred little girl's dresses; Iphigenia's dresses, all in different shades of red, the obsessive recoverings or remakings of a dead child's wardrobe. The effect was all the more powerful for Agamemnon's never appearing to notice what he was walking over as he strode to his death.

None of this, it hardly needs emphasising, was predicated on or invited by Hughes's text on the page, which offered no stage direction of any kind between '*Enter Agamemnon with Cassandra, in chariot. Clytemnestra comes out from the palace to greet him*' and '*He* [Agamemnon] *goes in.*' The full impact had to wait until after the display of the dead bodies of Agamemnon and Cassandra (Hughes: '*Corpses revealed*'), when, after first confronting her mother, the little ghost of Iphigeneia moved to lie down and become, as it seemed, absorbed into her dead father: only for

Agamemnon to rise himself and leave the tableau to take up a position as resident ghost for the play that was to follow, *Libation-Bearers* run together with *Furies* as *The Daughters of Darkness*.

Contact, context and concept are not really the translator's affair. They are what take over when the imagination of the performers, including under such an umbrella designers, choreographer, composer and director, enter the equation. This is not to suggest that translators need not be aware of the theatrical elements within a scene. The next chapter will pick up the argument about performance writing in Sophocles and Euripides and the extent to which guidelines can be offered to identify the dramatic action.

Hughes's final speech for Cassandra in the Mitchell production was very deliberately chalked as a message on the floor and shown in video closeup on a screen above the palace facade:

> This was life.
> The luckiest hours
> Like scribbles in chalk
> On a slate in a classroom.
> We stare
> And try to understand them.
> Then luck turns its back –
> And everything's wiped out.
> Joy was not less pathetic
> Than the worst grief.
>   (p. 65, *Ag.* 1327–30)

This is Hughes, elaborated from the Greek, and free, compared with Robert Fagles (1966):

> Oh men, your destiny.
> When all is well a shadow can overturn it.
> When trouble comes a stroke of the wet sponge,
> and the picture's blotted out. And that,
> I think that breaks the heart.

Shapiro and Burian (2003):

> Alas for men and their vicissitudes!
> In good times one may say they're like a shadow;
> in bad times like a picture that a wet sponge
> brushing against it lightly wipes away.
> And these I pity so much more than those.

Harrison (1981):

> Man's life! Luck's blotted out by the slenderest shadow.
> Trouble – a wet sponge wipes the slate empty.
> That pain's also nothing makes life a heartbreak.

Raphael and McLeish (1991):

> Human success is but a shadow,
> Our grief a chalk drawing
> Cancelled by a damp sponge.
> I'm sadder for mortal fate
> Than ever for my own.

Potter (1777):

> This is the state of man: in prosperous fortune
> A shadow, passing light, throws to the ground
> Joy's baseless fabric; in adversity
> Comes malice with a sponge moisten'd in gall,
> And wipes each beauteous character away:
> More than the first this melts my soul to pity.

In the other two plays Hughes's 'version' is similarly erratic (see also Chapter 10, p. 188) as a representation of 'pure' Aeschylus but, equally, offered a challenge to Mitchell which she met with a series of theatrical strokes providing, as do the greatest directors, superb moments, single flashes of scarlet which, when linked, make a patchwork more telling than the sum of the parts.

Of translation, direction and reception, the latter may be the most capricious. In the theatre everything is, indeed, in a state of flux. Aeschylus may have created a play for a single performance but he surely understood that his *Agamemnon* would not be the final word on the subject. A multiplicity of translations of *Agamemnon* from the last 200 years is no guarantee that any of them will be any good, or, that even if they are, for one production, in one place, in one year, they will still hold their authority over a period of time. There is certainly an argument that the shade of Aeschylus is better off in the translating hands of a poet than of an academic. Shapiro and Burian combine the two in a joint translation. There is an equally strong argument that the Greeks are better served by a playwright than by a poet. In the case of Fredric Raphael and Kenneth McLeish, both had claims to be both.[37] One thing only is sure.

No translator is without prejudice. The great productions add something special to the original, sometimes in their entirety, often in their tiniest detail. They can 'improve' a play, because of, and despite, the translation, as Stein did with his Russian *Oresteia*, renewing it in a contemporary context. In doing this the translator may have a major role.

Plato was wary of theatrical performance for being an imitation of an imitation. Seen on video the Stein *Agamemnon* is not even that. It is at best an interpretation (by the viewer), of an interpretation (by the video director), of an interpretation by a stage director (Stein), at one stage in his creative life (twenty years ago), of an interpretation by the translator (Greek into German and thence into surtitle), of an interpretation (via a combination of manuscripts), of an interpretation (in the original production), of what may have been Aeschylus' own work. The translator may have an important relationship with a dead playwright. How far that relationship is reflected in what a living audience eventually sees or hears is a very different matter.

CHAPTER 4

Translating the Mask:
the Non-Verbal Language

We began before words, and we will end beyond them.
(Ben Okri, 'Beyond words', lecture delivered in
Trinity College Chapel, Cambridge, June 1993)

In his *Mouse or Rat? Translation as Negotiation* Umberto Eco suggested
that 'only by being *literally unfaithful* can a translator be truly faithful to
the source text'.[1] If this sounds like some sort of literary equivalent of
a libertine's charter it reaches positively Casanovate proportions when
applied first to drama, and, beyond that, to Greek drama. Eco's argument
is not new. It had received a clear exposition in Hilaire Belloc's 1931
Taylorian Lecture 'On translation'. Belloc offered a number of formulae
relating to knowledge of the source and target languages before coining a
particularly useful phrase:

what must also be remarked and what is equally important when one is
attempting the rendering of any great matter – great through its literary form or
its message – is the atmosphere of the word.[2]

This was echoed by Theodore Savory when he pointed out in *The Art of
Translation* that more than half of what had been written about translation (1957) concerned turning Greek and Latin into English and
reminded his readers of the two distinct camps, the 'Hellenizers' and the
'Modernizers'.[3]

Controversy over Greek tragedy and comedy is largely lodged within
these three positions, finding a means of 'negotiation', to use the word as
Eco does, between the stylisations demanded by a text for masked actors
and the range of dramatic devices which these first playwrights were in the
process of investigating; translating Belloc's 'atmosphere of the word';
and Savory's 'Hellenizing' or 'Modernizing'. In this chapter I wish to
look at four modes of expression and their implications, namely mask

language, inbuilt stage directions, expressions of grief and non-verbal 'language'.

In a recent paper given at the American Philological Association in San Francisco Eric Dugdale drew attention to deictic language and what he described as a 'recognition formula' in Sophocles' *Electra*. All three Electra plays of Greek tragedy are dominated by recognitions, focusing as they do on the return home of an unrecognised or unrecognisable Orestes. Some basic recognition turns up in one guise or another in every surviving Greek tragedy and comedy, even if it is no more than a realisation of the reality of a situation; indeed it is difficult to think of a single play from any period which fails to make use of the dramatic device first formally acknowledged by Aristotle as *anagnorisis*. Harnessed with *peripeteia*, these two, 'recognition' and 'reversal', are rightly identified by Aristotle as the very stuff of drama. When a narrow meaning of each is extended to 'recognition of the truth' and 'reversal of expectation' for spectator as well as for character, then there can be little arguing with Aristotle's definition of them as 'conjuring the souls of audiences'.[4]

Dugdale's analysis of Sophocles' *Electra* traced no fewer than twelve occasions where attention is drawn to the act of recognition. These include the introduction of Orestes to the landmarks of the city he left when still a baby; the false description by the Tutor to Clytemnestra and Electra of the death of Orestes in the chariot race; Chrysothemis' assumption of her brother's return because of the offerings at Agamemnon's tomb, accurate but dismissed by Electra; Orestes' presentation of the urn of ashes, so affectingly received by Electra that he finds himself forced to reveal his real identity; Orestes' introduction to his sister of the Tutor; the deception off-stage of Clytemnestra and on-stage of Aegisthus, whose discovery that the body beneath the sheet is that of his wife not her son leads rapidly to the play's conclusion. Dugdale's point about all this was to show a pattern of simple and repetitive language in such revelations. At such moments the words used for identification are almost always deictic, 'this man' or 'this thing' (*hode, houtos, tode*) or 'that man' or 'that thing' (*keinos, ekeinos, ekeino*). Such repetition is difficult for the translator into English for whom mere repetition can appear monotonous.

What lies behind this apparent simplicity, I would argue, is the language of the mask. 'This' and 'that' are demonstration words, redolent of expression through gesture, the *cheironomia* ('language of gesture') so easy to overlook when addressing a text on the page which was written for masked performance. The Tutor at the beginning of the play points out to Orestes the agora of Apollo, the temple of Hera and the palace of Pelops: hardly actual locations in Athens, as Jebb over-literally suggested, but different places conjured by gesture into the *theatron*.[5] Later in the play when Chrysothemis believes (correctly) that she has found evidence of Orestes' return she says (translating literally): 'But that man is present among us' (*all' ekeinon hōs paronta nōn*, l. 882), a gesture away from the stage followed by one inwards toward the characters who are present. Modern translators have variously addressed these lines as 'We have him here again' (Loeb, 1913); 'He is here in person with us' (Chicago, 1957); 'He is here among us' (Oxford, 1962); 'Orestes is back' (Methuen, 1990); 'Orestes is here! Near us now!' (Smith and Kraus, 2000); 'He's here, I tell you' (Hern, 2004). The translators have unanimously chosen to overlook the contrast between 'that man' and 'present among us' in favour of the verbal emphasis on his being 'here'.

If this seems a somewhat abstruse point, it is reinforced by the widely discussed urn, supposedly filled with Orestes' ashes. The scene is constructed around a similar pattern of attention through gesture – to the urn, perhaps to Pylades who may have been carrying it, to Orestes himself and to Electra. The reuniting of brother and sister suggests similar shifts of focus, a technique that would appear more filmic than theatrical were it not for the manner in which Sophocles ensures that the stage property becomes the centre of attention. Again, this is basically a mask technique as Orestes draws Electra's attention away from her fixation with the dead urn and onto the living brother.

So is the final scene with Aegisthus confronting the sheeted body he has been told is Orestes. He calls for Clytemnestra only for Orestes to reply (literally) 'This same woman is close to you; do not look elsewhere.' (*hautē pelas sou; mēket' allose skopei*, l. 1474), translated as 'She's near you; look not anywhere but here –' (Lewis Theobald, 1714); 'She is beside thee; look not otherwhere.' (Loeb, 1913); 'She is near you now, / Not far to seek.' (Penguin, 1953); 'She is near you. You need not look elsewhere.' (Chicago, 1957); 'She is not far away; look straight before you.' (Oxford, 1962); 'There is no need to fetch her. She is here.' (Methuen, 1990); 'She's near you now. No need to look.' (Smith and Kraus, 2000); 'She's close enough. No need to look elsewhere.' (Hern, 2004).

Aegisthus draws back the sheet expecting to see Orestes and uncovers the dead Clytemnestra, only to realise it must be Orestes who has brought him the news. Sophocles' *Electra* – and in no scene more than this final one – is an object lesson in writing and underwriting stage action. In Greek tragedy words are often used for the action they imply rather than as dialogue. Those translators who seem not to take account of this contrast between two forms of stage communication (akin, perhaps, to that between the music and the words in opera) may miss a dimension of Greek tragedy by confining the dramatic action to the word.

A look at how the recognition scene between brother and sister is handled by Aeschylus and Euripides reveals very different dramatic methods, the latter inspired by and, it is difficult not to believe, in reaction to how the plot had been handled by other playwrights, including Sophocles. All three use a similar 'mask' language, and an alternation of word and action by employing the simplest of speech when the main purpose of the words is to identify or reinforce a stage action. In Aeschylus' *Libation-Bearers* the recognition-tokens by which Electra identifies her brother are, in order, the lock or locks of hair that Orestes has placed at the base of the tomb (on the steps leading up to it if any credence can be placed on the several vase-paintings which appear to reproduce the scene); footprints; and a piece of woven cloth. To see the hair which Orestes has cut and put on his father's tomb, Electra must identify a moment of 'recognition' – the masked actor reacts before putting the reaction into words. A literal translation might go as follows:

CHORUS: Then is this [*tode*] a secret gift of Orestes?
ELECTRA: It most resembles that man's [*ekeinou*] hair.
CHORUS: And how has that man [*ekeinos*] dared to come here [*deuro*]?

(ll. 177–9)

The hair is identified simply as 'this thing', Orestes as 'that man', some off-stage presence who, Electra gradually realises, may be not 'there' but 'here'.[6] The presentational nature of the exchange is brought out with varying degrees of success in different translations: 'Can it then be that Orestes offered it in secret here? / 'Tis *his* curling locks that it most resembles. / But how did *he* venture to come hither?' (Loeb, 1926); 'Can it then be a secret gift from Orestes? / It seems that it must be nobody's hair but his. / Did Orestes dare to come back here?' (Chicago, 1953); 'Orestes . . . he brought a gift in secret? It's *his* – I can see his curls. / And how could he risk the journey here?' (Penguin, 1976); 'You mean Orestes? Orestes here in Argos? / Whose curls are these but his? / Orestes! How could he dare come here?' (Methuen, 1991); 'Could it be a secret gift from Orestes? / It does look very like his hair. / But how would he dare to come here?' (Dent, 1995); 'You mean Orestes? A secret gift from him? / It does seem like this. Who else could it be from? / How in the world could he have risked returning?' (Oxford, 2003); 'Orestes! Orestes has sent us this secret sign. / It can only be his hair, if it's not mine. / Orestes in Argos? Too risky if that's what you meant.' (Collings, 1981). This last, by Tony Harrison, is the only one that was prepared for a masked production; it is described as 'a version' on the outside cover but 'a translation' on the flyleaf. One incidental point of interest from the above is that eighteen words in the Greek come out as more than twenty in all of the translations, with three having as many as twenty-eight. The difficulty of rendering the elliptical nature of much Greek tragedy and comedy is a recurring headache for the translator.

The second means of recognition are the footprints on the ground close to the tomb. Electra 'sees' them, then walks across to find two sets of imprints, those of Pylades and of Orestes. She tries her own feet against one set and takes their similarity as a second proof. This is one of the nudges offered to the audience by Euripides in his later version.

Most of the above translators of Aeschylus try to make it seem as plausible as possible, with Harrison apparently sufficiently uncomfortable for the lines to be cut from the first published text. Robert Lowell (1978) not only removed the footprints but, bizarrely, substituted for the lock of hair 'a knot of eagle feathers'. Within a masked tradition there should be less problem with the token as a token, the only stage requirement being for Electra to duplicate the exact position on stage where her brother was previously standing. Euripides' concern about the relative sizes of men's and women's feet, or associated questions about whether Orestes has travelled all the way from Phocis without any shoes on, are subsumed in the act and process of effecting a reunion between the siblings. Aeschylus again signals that this is happening by making the language direct and appropriate for describing her physical action – in a literal translation 'And indeed here are tracks, a second proof, of feet, fitting each other and like mine ...', the built-in stage direction matched cleverly to Electra's mounting excitement in the Oxford translation of Shapiro and Burian by an erratic sequence of line endings:

> Wait! Look! Another sign,
> these footprints, see? they match each other, and
> they look like mine. Two outlines, yes, two pairs,
> his own and a companion's. The heel and the
> ball of the foot, and the arch, too. Oh god,
> this is unbearable, I don't know what to think.
> (ll. 237–43)[7]

This may largely be a product of layout on the page but it gives a clear signal to the actor of what Aeschylus is about.

Orestes and Pylades now confront Electra. As she holds back, suddenly needing to be certain, Orestes rehearses her previous reactions to the lock of hair, showing from where on his head/mask he cut it, and pointing to the prints before offering her the final proof, in a literal translation: 'See [*idou*] this woven garment, work of your hand, the marks of the weaver's blade and the wild beasts in the design. Be inside [*endon genou*; i.e. 'control yourself'] and don't lose your mind from joy' (ll. 231–3). The mix of physical action and emotional upheaval is so beautifully and so economically rendered in the original as almost to defy translation. The two words *endon genou* are a supreme challenge, met, without too much conviction by anyone. 'Control thyself' (Loeb); 'Contain yourself (University of California Press); 'No, no.' (Everyman); 'No, no, control yourself' (Chicago and Penguin); 'Be steady now' (Mentor); 'Now careful' (Oxford); 'Easy! Still!' (Collins); 'Electra, Electra, not yet' (Methuen). Aeschylus' own choice of two words that are so slight, and which might well never be heard in the moment of Electra's emotional release, might suggest that they are best represented by the least literal of the versions.

Euripides, whose dialogue is frequently racy by comparison with that of either Aeschylus or Sophocles, has a field day with the recognition scene. Orestes and Pylades are inside Electra's husband's farm when the Old Man arrives and suggests hair, footprints and some woven garment as possible reasons for thinking that Orestes may have returned. Electra scathingly rejects all three. When Orestes emerges from the house, the Old Man spots a scar on his brow and a seemingly reluctant sister at last acknowledges an even more reluctant brother. The context seems at least to hint that Orestes and Electra would never have been reunited but for the interference of the Old Man.

The translator's challenge here is how to deal with what appears to be an uncomfortable reunion. A literal translation is almost impossible but the sense is as follows:

OLD MAN: Then are you waiting to fall upon your loved ones?
ELECTRA: No longer, old man. I am persuaded in my heart by your signs [*sumbolois*]. You appear after a long time. I hold you unexpectedly.
ORESTES: A long time for me too.
ELECTRA: Never expected.

ORESTES: I never hoped.
ELECTRA: Are you that man? [*ekeinos*]
(ll. 576–81)

Most translators allow for the ambiguities and even the possibility that
the scene borders on comedy. Euripides' language is so spare as to render
the professed joy of Electra and her brother minimalist. As in so much of
Euripides there is that neutrality in the dialogue which permits the
playing of a subtext. The new 1998 Loeb translation by David Kovacs
seems least to allow for this:

ELECTRA: O brother long in coming, I embrace you though I no
    longer hoped to ...
ORESTES: And at long last I too embrace you!
ELECTRA: ... and never thought this would happen!
ORESTES: No, for not even I had hope.
ELECTRA: Are you the very man?

Others offer more to director and actors.
Chicago:

ELECTRA: O Brother so delayed by time, I hold you against hope –
ORESTES: Time hid you long from me.
ELECTRA: I never promised myself –
ORESTES: I had abandoned hope.
ELECTRA: And are you he?

Penguin:

ELECTRA: At last I hold you close.
ORESTES: At last you are in my arms.
ELECTRA: I had despaired.
ORESTES: I too.
ELECTRA: You really are Orestes?

Methuen:

ELECTRA: O Orestes, after all these years ... I never dared
    hope ...
ORESTES: Hold me ...
ELECTRA: After all these years,
ORESTES: I never dared hope.
ELECTRA: You're really Orestes?

Aris and Phillips:

> ELECTRA: O at long last
> you appear; I hold you as I never hoped to . . .
> ORESTES: And are held by me too at long last!
> ELECTRA: When I never expected it . . .
> ORESTES: Nor did I hope for it either.
> ELECTRA: You are truly he?

Hern:

> ELECTRA: It seemed so long. I'd almost given up hope.
> ORESTES: It seemed so long for me too.
> ELECTRA: I never expected . . .
> ORESTES: Neither did I . . .
> ELECTRA: Can it really be you?

It is worth noting again that what Euripides accomplishes in twenty words takes the most literal translator more than forty.

What seems to be shown from these few examples is that tragic playwrights simplified the language that they were using at points in the play when the focus of attention was demonstrated by physical action and stage picture. Attention has been drawn to the relationship between actor and property and between actor and space by a number of recent critics, notably J. R. Green, David Wiles and Rush Rehm.[8] An awareness of such factors in the reading of the original text is, it would appear, of major importance to the translator who wishes to do justice to the plays' potential for action.

It is now possible to return to the broader issue of stage directions raised in the previous chapter with reference to Aeschylus' *Agamemnon*. The surviving Greek manuscripts have virtually no stage directions. Aeschylus' *Furies* has the word *mugmos*, 'muttering' and *oigmos*, 'whining', both twice, followed by *mugmos diplous oxus*, 'shrill muttering twice', referring to the sleeping Furies who are proving oblivious to Clytemnestra's harangue over their dereliction of duty.[9] There is a single reference to the playing of a pipe in Aristophanes' *Frogs* (l. 1263) and several indications of omitted choral interludes by insertion of the word *chorou* in late Aristophanes and in Menander. A number of notes by scholiasts give suggestions, some of which make theatrical sense but none of which offers definitive authority for how the plays were originally performed. The last twenty-five years have seen a blossoming of scholarship devoted to production and presentation. The texts have been

mined for indications of a developing awareness on the part of tragedians
and comedians of the part played in dramatic performance by such
dramatic devices as metatheatre, semiology, proxemics, group dynamics
and reception. Plays that seemed rich only in their literary and linguistic
intricacies have proved to be 'wrought' by playwrights with a sophisticated understanding of entrances and exits, of actors and objects,
movement, mask, space and stage picture.

Some early translators appear to have become aware of elements of
stagecraft even before they were translating with stage performance in
mind. What tended to happen, though, was that their understanding of
theatrical, as opposed to literary, values was rooted in the theatre of their
own time. Just as the shade of Shakespeare found his plays, little more
than fifty years after his bodily death, presented in Restoration fig with
full-bottomed wigs and adjustments of the text to suit a moral of the
times, so the first translations of Greek tragedy tended to ape the manners
of the translator's time.[10] Sophocles' *Electra*, in the strict verse translation
by Lewis Theobald (1714) opens with Orestes and his Governor (*Paida-
gōgos*) making plans:

> Mean while, as the great Lycian God injoin'd,
> We, with Oblations and devoted Hair,
> Will please my Father's Shade, and crown his Tomb.
> That done, here let us meet; and in our Hands
> Bear to th' incestuous Court the brazen Urn,
> Which lies conceal'd in yonder verdant Thickets:[11]

The scene concludes with the stage direction '*Exeunt* Orestes *and* Pylades
at one Door, Governor and Attendants at another', a nice example of the
outdoor theatre of Sophocles being domesticated in the direction of the
proscenium arch in print, without an expectation of the play taking its
place in the public theatre. Amateur theatricals were a different matter, of
course, and it may well be that in the eighteenth century some of the
country house theatres, where characters could enter or leave the stage by
the proscenium doors, did get to host Sophocles or Euripides on stage.
Theobald for the most part indicates only entrances and exits but, as part
of an imposed five-act structure, begins *Electra* V.4 with the direction
'*SCENE opening discovers the body of* Clytemnestra *cover'd*; Orestes,
Pylades, *and Attendants round it*, Aegysthus, Electra and Chorus'. A
'discovery' at the beginning of a scene in the theatre with which Theobald
was familiar implies shutters or a curtain.

The prolific Robert Potter was so discreet as seldom to mention an entrance or an exit but he did divide plays into scenes, as might be expected in the eighteenth century, identifying each by a character list. Subsequent translators were similarly circumspect, ignoring matters of staging or leaving them to the imagination. The beginning of the twentieth century shows a sea change with the Vedrenne/Barker management at the Court Theatre commissioning a series of translations from Gilbert Murray and stimulating his long and prolific career in this field. The first of these, *Hippolytus*, was published in 1902, preceding its production which had to wait till 26 May 1904, at the Lyric Theatre before being revived at the Court in October. There followed further Euripides productions by Granville Barker of Murray's *The Trojan Women* (1905), *Electra* (1906), *Medea* (1907), and *Iphigenia in Tauris* (1912). The dictatorial style of Murray's *Agamemnon* referred to earlier (see p. 52) is left more open in his other printed translations.[12]

Amongst more modern translators the tendency to give authority to preconceived notions of the original staging can be helpful but is more often dogmatic than stimulating. This is especially noticeable in plays such as *Prometheus Bound*, *Ajax*, *Oedipus at Colonus*, *Bacchae* or *Rhesus* where the identification of specific locations (the seashore or the grove of the Furies), or stage actions (earthquakes, suicide, darkness), seems often to confuse what may well be better left to the imagination of designers and directors. The downside of the translator's aids to the reader is a closing of what may well be open questions.

Some specific examples may be helpful. Long entrances and exits in Greek plays can be identified by the length of warning given between the sighting of new characters and their arrival into the scene. What is appropriate in a vast open-air theatre, where the distance between *parodos* and a central entrance in the *skēnē* may be twenty metres or more, can sound clumsy or unnecessary in an indoor theatre, particularly some of the small spaces in which much of Euripides has been presented in recent years. It may be significant that two of the plays referred to above, *Prometheus Bound* and *Rhesus*, are considered by many critics to be of doubtful provenance. Without opening this can of worms at this point, there is no disputing that they are plays which have a place within the classical canon and are therefore as useful examples (arguably more so) for staging practice as any of the accepted work of Aeschylus, Sophocles or Euripides. A brief look at both these plays may establish some patterns.

By the middle of the nineteenth century *Prometheus Bound*, Aeschylus or not – and nobody then had any doubts – had been more frequently translated into English than any other Aeschylus play (see Appendix). As a piece of theatre it appears to have staging problems, though none that have not been adequately overcome in several modern revivals. Soon after the opening Prometheus is chained to a rock somewhere in the Caucasus. He is visited by a number of characters who include a chorus of the daughters of Oceanus, and subsequently their father, all of whom, if the words in the text are a literal guide, appear to have taken an aerial route. Eventually Hermes warns the Chorus to withdraw 'lest the inexorable roar of thunder overwhelm your senses' (ll. 1061–2). Prometheus then describes in graphic terms a storm which engulfs him (1080–93), and the play ends; which, of course, is not enough, in that Greek plays like any other need some sort of indication of closure for the clearing of the stage.

Morell, Aeschylus' first English translator (1773), has the chorus describe their entry as 'sailing on eager wings'. At the end they heed the warning of Mercury and Morell has them exit with the god before the final speech of Prometheus. Potter (1779) pays no attention to the staging issues. Morshead (1881) offers '*Enter the* CHORUS OF OCEANIDES, *in winged cars*', from which they '*alight*' just before the entrance of Oceanus, '*Mounted on a griffin*'. At the end '*The rocks are rent with fire and earthquake, and fall, burying* PROMETHEUS *in the ruins.*' The Loeb translation of 1922 offers '*a winged car*' and '*winged steed*', concluding somewhat mystically with '*Amid thunder and lightning Prometheus vanishes from sight; and with him disappear the daughters of Oceanus*', not a great deal of help either to the would-be scholars of theatre history nor to the contemporary director. Not until the Chicago translation of 1942 is as much as lip-service paid to actual staging. David Grene describes the entry of the Chorus, '*the members wearing some formalized representation of wings, so that their general appearance is birdlike*'. Such a practical disavowal of the likelihood of twelve chorus-members being flown in cars is thrown into perspective by the entry of their father '*riding on a hippocamp, or sea-monster*'. In the last hundred lines Grene gives not a single stage direction. The Chorus are '*in a winged ship or carriage*' (Penguin) which they leave and '*group themselves on the ground*' as Oceanus arrives '*seated on a winged four-feeted creature*'. After Prometheus' last line 'The rock collapses and disappears, as the CHORUS scatters in all directions.'

E. A. Havelock (Beacon Press, 1951) became almost as carried away as Prometheus insisting that 'During Prometheus' second song the catastrophe intensifies, the rocky terrain begins to shake, violent gusts assault the stage, and the darkness becomes total until, at his concluding apostrophe to the cosmos, some blinding flashes from the rear outline the collapsing scene.'

Raphael and McLeish (Methuen, 1991) wisely leave everything as bare 'entries' with a footnote about the improbability of getting the entire chorus onto the *mēchanē*. They also hint at the possibility afforded by dance without going so far as to suggest that this would be a plausible way of staging the ending. They too leave the final scene without stage direction, perhaps preferably to the Dent *'Exeunt Prometheus and the daughters of Okeanos, buried underground'*.

Richard Emil Braun in the Introduction to his Sophocles' *Antigone* defended imaginative practice: 'But it is surely preferable that a good stage direction should be provided by the translator than that the reader should be left to his own devices in visualizing action, gesture, and spectacle.'[13] 'Good' being the operative word here, it remains a moot point whether a translator should be trying to solve staging problems rather than offering designers and directors a blank cheque in the name of, but not signed by, the original author.

Another 'stage earthquake' occurs in Euripides' *Bacchae* when Dionysus escapes from the prison into which Pentheus has thrown him. As this play was performed posthumously in 405 BC, it is not unreasonable to assume that staging possibilities and expectations were far different from what they had been in earlier times. This may not be a translation point at all but it does affect any reading of what happens when the palace of Pentheus is apparently destroyed. After Dionysus is led off to prison there is a choral ode, at the conclusion of which the voice of Dionysus is heard off-stage calling to the Bacchants. They respond and the off-stage voice calls at line 585 *<seie> pedon chthonos, Ennosi potniai.*[14] Kovacs, accepting this reading in the new Loeb (2002), translates as '<Shake> the level earth, O Goddess of Earthquake'. The Chorus then bear witness to the collapse of the palace: 'See here on the columns the stone lintels / are falling apart!' (ll. 591–2). Dionysus summons lightning to 'burn up the palace of Pentheus' (594–5) and the Chorus respond 'Ah, ah, / do you not see, not mark the fire / about Semele's tomb <here>, / the flame left behind / by Zeus' lightning?'

As has often been noted by critics uncomfortable about what is really meant to be happening here, when Dionysus and soon after him Pentheus return to the stage, neither mentions the apparent destruction of the palace. There are only three explanations for this. The first is that the palace does collapse but once that has happened, the consequences are no longer relevant; the second is that the suggestible Chorus react to

what Dionysus says and *believe* that the palace has collapsed, demonstrating it in the choreography of their behaviour when Dionysus finds
them lying on the ground; the third possibility is that the text is
unrevised or otherwise untrustworthy as a guide to the actual staging.
Many translators have seen it as their job to define what happens.
Kovacs offers no stage directions until just before the entrance of
Dionysus at line 604 where he has '*They* [the Chorus] *prostrate themselves on the ground. Enter from the skene* DIONYSUS'. This is far more
circumspect than the original Loeb of A. S. Way (1912) who included (in
what was intended as a literal translation) two directions of '*earthquake*'
and another that reads '*A great blaze of light enwraps the palace and the
monument of Semele.*' Murray (1906) was similarly 'literal' over an
earthquake which '*suddenly shakes the pillars of the palace*'. Arrowsmith
(1959) informed his readers that '*A blast of lightning flares across the
façade of the palace and tongues of flame spurt up from the tomb of Semele.
Then a great crash of thunder*', and a few lines later '*The Chorus falls to
the ground in oriental fashion, bowing their heads in the direction of the
palace. A hush; then Dionysus appears, lightly picking his way among the
rubble. Calm and smiling still, he speaks to the Chorus with a solicitude
approaching banter.*' Pentheus enters soon after '*stamping heavily, from
the ruined palace*'.

But, as Edith Hall notes in a penetrating introduction to a recent
translation, Dionysus 'proves that human perceptions of reality are fun-
damentally unreliable and that the truth can sometimes be better discovered through the illusion available in the theatre than by strict
empirical inspection of the strictly observable world'.[15] The intelligent
reader may well be better served by leaving the ambiguity of the Euripides
text we have. There is a difference between guiding the reader and dictating what may over-interpret an ambivalent action.

A similar exercise can be carried out on the entry of Ajax in the
Sophocles play, when he has left the stage and returns to a different
location on the shore before committing suicide. George Adams (1729)
has a footnote on his return (at ll. 814–15), but this deals only with Ajax's
state of mind. Francklin (1759) confines himself to recording the beginning of a new Act (IV.I) and later pointing to the precise moment when
Ajax falls on his sword. Sir George Young (1888) identifies that '*The scene
changes to a lonely part of the sea-shore. Enter* AJAX *who fixes his sword in
the ground.*' Storr's Loeb (1913) passes without explanation from the exit
of the Chorus to 'AJAX *alone on the sea-shore*'. The Chicago translation

(Moore, 1957) is far more elaborate. After line 814 we find:

Tecmessa leaves Eurysaces with the attendants and goes hurriedly out. Meanwhile the Chorus divides into two equal semichoruses and exits through the side entrances.
    SCENE: *An empty place by the seashore. No scenery need be indicated except some bushes, behind which Ajax' body will fall. His preparations, though, should be largely visible to the audience. Enter Ajax.*
Ajax (carefully fixes the sword in place, tamps down the ground, and feels the edge of the blade): He's firm in the ground, my Slayer.

Too elaborate, some might think, though less prescriptive than Mueller and Krajewska-Wieczorek (2000):

The Chorus splits into two groups. Tekmessa, the Leader, the Messenger, all the Servants, and both parts of the Chorus rush off through the right and left exits, as the double doors slowly open and the ekkyklēma moves forward into full view. The scene is now an isolated grove of trees near the seashore, represented perhaps by a single tree on the ekkyklēma on which Aias is discovered crouched down, planting the haft of his sword in the earth.

In either example there is a strong case for offering some possible staging, if only to make the reader aware that something out of the ordinary is taking place. A change of location in mid-action is as unusual as an on-stage death in Greek tragedy, though neither is without parallel.
    Whether such liberty can be accorded to the same translators' *Oedipus at Kolonos* is another matter. Scholarly/theatrical argument in this play is usually confined to the appropriate location of Oedipus' place of sanctuary and whether he goes to meet his final resting-place through the sacred grove (i.e. into the *skēnē*) or away from the setting (down one of the *parodoi*).
    Mueller and Krajewska-Wieczorek, whose directions are particularly busy for all of this play, have a vivid and extensive description of the storm effects. After line 1461 when Oedipus speaks of (literally) 'the winged thunder of Zeus [which] will lead me to Hades', their stage direction reads:

The growing storm now flashes with searing bolts of lightning that shake the earth and light the sky as the atmosphere grows increasingly darker. The Chorus in a state of terror darts about the stage.

Ten lines later:

The storm's display ceases momentarily, leaving in its place a silence heavy with portent. The Chorus cowers in fear. From here to his exit, Oedipus' anxiety, slowly at first, is progressively but quite visibly transformed into a resignation that betokens calm, security, and spiritual authority – but it is never less than total simplicity.

Another forty-four lines and Oedipus is ready for his final speech which they frame as follows:

His apotheosis complete, Oedipus rises, unaided from his rocky seat, though Antigonē and Ismenē [sic] rush to help him; but seeing the physical power of his renewed strength, they retreat a few steps. Oedipus, led by a profound inner force, with slow but secure steps, at first makes his way toward the left exit, beckoning the others on, though no one moves but himself. He turns several times, slowly, suddenly not sure of his direction, then gradually seeks out the center of the orchestra. Again he turns, head raised as if listening to an unheard voice. The darkness of the storm passes rapidly and sunlight breaks through.
    OEDIPUS: Children . . .
      . . . Forever new!
Music fades in and continues to the end of the play as Oedipus turns upstage once more toward the Sacred Grove and slowly goes straight into its center in the direction of the skēnē: the Brazen-Floored Threshold of Earth, whose doors slowly open to admit him. He is followed at a distance by Antigonē and Ismenē, Thēseus behind them, and behind him an Attendant. When all have entered the Chorus reassembles.[16]

A reader believing this was what Sophocles was prescribing might be seriously misled.

The 1889 translation of *Ion* by H. B. L. (Henry Barrett Lennard) appends to the title the legend 'now first translated into English, in its original metres, and supplied with stage directions suggesting how it may have been performed on the Athenian stage'. This implies some dissatisfaction, or, at the least, perceived deficiency in previous *Ion*s (of which there had been a number: see Appendix A). Though the original metres can hardly be said to give much impression of the stageworthiness of the play, the stage directions are elaborate and frequently fanciful. During Ion's initial peroration, for example, H. B. L. offers in fairly rapid succession the following:

Here, as an eagle flies towards the temple, he [Ion] *starts up* (after l. 192).
He strings and adjusts his bow (after l. 155).
He shoots, the eagle falls, and a swan appears, chirruping (after l. 160).
Having killed the swan, he espies a swallow (after l. 169).
He shoots and misses his aim (after l. 173).
Hawks, storks and herons appearing he scares them away by discharging
  repeated volleys of arrows (after l. 177).

His bag may suggest we have here no Heracles or Philoctetes. An orni-
thological invasion worthy of Aristophanes, if not Hitchcock, does imply
a level of imagination by the stage-management team, or an even greater
one on the part of the audience, that evidence for Greek theatre in
practice suggests would be hard put to sustain. Creousa, according to
H. B. L. has a special 'weeping mask', as well she might, being accompanied at her entrance not only by the chorus but also by a band of
trumpeters, a group of bearers of the Athenian standard of the Grass-
hopper, and a guard of honour. Xouthus has his own trumpeters and
guards and in no time at all the stage is invaded by:

sundry adult and juvenile therapes bearing censers, candelabra and urns of gold and
silver, also images and attributes of Apollōn, under canopies: musicians with horns,
trumpets and pipes: men and boy choristers: the five 'hosioi', attended, and followed
by priests and pages: the prophetess accompanied by priestesses and virgins in a solemn
dance: the 'hieros' . . . attired as Apollōn-Mousagētes . . . a gilded car . . . four white
horses . . . a train of boys and girls in white dresses, and crowned with
roses . . . incense, accompanied by vocal and instrumental music.[17]

Vellacott offered for the same scene. *Enter Ion.*

Rhesus is a nice curiosity, less because of the scholarly wrangling over its
authenticity than because, whoever wrote it and when, it offers an entire
play taking place at night. Several Greek plays, *Agamemnon, Ajax, Iphi-*
genia in Aulis and *Clouds* amongst them, open at night. At the end of
Rhesus dawn is about to break. The various reminders to the audience are
carefully planted, sometimes by the use of lamps or torches, at others by
the way in which the actors play their restricted vision. In one scene
Odysseus and Diomedes, who have slipped into the Trojan camp and
assassinated Rhesus, arrive on stage with the chorus of guards in hot
pursuit. A combination of the darkness and Odysseus' cunning help them
to escape. It is one of the rare scenes in Greek drama where the lines are
actually unimportant except for how they point up stage business. The

dialogue need only indicate confusion and a reminder of the reason for the confusion.

Michael Wodhull, the first English translator of the play (1782) was reluctant to abandon his iambic pentameters so that lines 675–91 read:

CHOR: Come on, strike, strike, destroy. Who marches yonder?
        Look, look, 'tis him I mean! these are the robbers
        Who in the dead of night alarmed our host.
        Hither, my friends, haste hither; I have seized them.
        What answer mak'st thou? tell me whence thou cam'st,
        And who thou art.
ULY:[18]   No right hast thou to know;
        Insult me, and this instant thou shalt die.
CHOR: Wilt though not, ere this lance transpierce thy breast,
        Repeat the watch-word?
ULY: That thou soon shalt hear;
        Be satisfy'd.
1ST SEMICHOR: Come on, my friends, strike! strike!
2ND SEMICHOR: Hast thou slain Rhesus?
ULY: I have slain the man
        Who would have murder'd thee: forbear.
1ST SEMICHOR: I will not.
2ND SEMICHOR: Forbear to slay a friend.
1ST SEMICHOR: Pronounce the watchword.
ULY: Apollo.
2ND SEMICHOR: Thou art right; let not a spear
        Be lifted up against him.
1ST SEMICHOR: Know'st thou whither
        Those men are gone?
2ND SEMICHOR: We saw not.
1ST SEMICHOR: Follow close
        Their steps, or we must call aloud for aid.
2ND SEMICHOR: Yet were it most unseemly to disturb
        Our valiant comrades with our nightly fears.
                    Exeunt ULYSSES *and* DIOMEDE.[19]

The Greek manuscripts lacking the identification of speakers, allied by some uncertain lines, all contribute to the muddle. Murray (1913) opted to attribute bits, not to the chorus, but to Voices: 'Ha! Ha! – At them! After them! Down with them! – Where are they?' and to others identified as 'Captain' and 'A Man'. He has Odysseus accuse the Captain of murdering Rhesus and ends the sequence with Odysseus saying 'We saw them running, somewhere here', soon after which '*He makes off into the darkness.* DIOMEDE *follows and some Thracians'.* This is all effective enough, though Murray cannot resist gilding the lily so that Odysseus and Diomede are presently seen '*crossing at the back in a different direction'.*

Chicago (1958), with soldiers identified as 'First' through 'Seventh' and references to 'shooting' and 'regiments', adds a contemporary touch, as does Methuen (1997), more obviously comic and staccato with more of the lines given to Odysseus:

ODYSSEUS: Was it you killed Rhesus?
CHORUS: You're the assassin, I think.
ODYSSEUS: Calm down, will you? Look, come over here.
CHORUS: Put a knife in him. Kill him. Kill the pair of them.
ODYSSEUS: Hold on a minute . . .

The Greek text is equally fractured. Wodhull's formal version suggests far less confusion than does the original. The first lines of the Chorus (ll. 675–7) read as:

eä, eä
bale, bale, bale, thene, thene, <thene>
tis anēr?

Bale means 'strike': so does *thene*. *Tis anêr?* is, literally, 'Who's that man?': *eä* is just an exclamation. Greek plays are full of such non-words that are sound indicators of anything from surprise to scorn to grief to a sort of cough to draw attention. Such expressions, especially those relating to mourning or outrage merit special attention and it is to those that we may now turn.

In a paper delivered at Northwestern University in 1994 and subsequently published as an article called 'Screaming in Translation', Anne Carson pointed to the presence in Greek drama of 'outbursts of sound expressing strong emotion'.[20] She identified fourteen different such 'bones of sound' in Sophocles' *Electra* alone, a few of which also contain recognisable words such as *talaina* and *moi dustēnos* but where the literal meanings 'wretched' or 'unhappy me' are a challenge for the translator.

Greek tragedy is, of course, stuffed with short expressions of grief, such as *iō, pheu, aiai* and some more prolonged such as *otototototoi* or *pappa-pappapai*, most of which serve to represent the 'scream' reduced to written form. English has a more restricted vocabulary of pain. The difference in

Sophocles between expressions of physical discomfort as experienced by male characters such as Oedipus, Philoctetes or Heracles is hardly distinguishable from their corresponding mental anguish, or the pure distress of bereavement of Electra, Antigone or Tecmessa. The keening of sympathetic witnesses might show some differentiation, but for the most part these are all noises, outbursts of sound when words will no longer serve and, as often happens, when chorus as well as characters move into lyric mode. Usually these expressions have similar vowel formations, reflecting the reduction of reason to the primal below grief. Some appear to suggest the epsilon, the short 'e' but many are diphthongs or a repeating refrain.

Cataloguing how translators of Greek tragedy over the years have addressed the problem could prove a sterile exercise, though it may be worth recalling that much of the unease felt over staging and playing the Greeks in translation does come down to a low tolerance threshold amongst contemporary audiences for extreme emotion, however expressed. The translator has to do something. F. A. Stilwell Freeland, in his 1876 translation of *Hippolytus* opted for 'Oh dear' for the Greek *pheu* which is accordingly the response of Phaedra, the Nurse, Hippolytus and Theseus to the various revelations, outdone only by the Chorus' 'Oh dear. Oh dear'. More Modern versions have come up with a variety of noises from Aiiiiiiiiiiiiiiiiiiiiiiiiii (that is 26 'i' s in case anyone was counting – why 26?) from an agonised Philoctetes to 'No!' (which could just as well have 26 'o's) as Agave recognises her son's head in *Bacchae*.

Laurence Olivier's scream as Oedipus, in the W. B. Yeats 'version' directed by Michel Saint-Denis at the New Theatre in 1945 left no critic unharrowed, contemporary reports imply.[21] Olivier had the actor's interest in the technicality and the effect. In his autobiography *Confessions of an Actor* he recorded:

The detail most remarked upon in this performance was the cry Oedipus might give when the whole truth of the message, in this case conveyed by an old shepherd, is revealed to him. 'Oh, Oh' is given in most editions. After going through all the vowel sounds, I hit upon 'Er'. This felt more agonised and the originality of it made the audience a ready partner in this feeling. Apart from this, the acting secret lay, as usual, in the timing, which was heightened by the spontaneity contained in the length of the pause before the cry.[22]

'I never hoped for so vast an anguish ...' wrote Kenneth Tynan. 'The two cries were torn from beyond tears or shame or guilt.'[23]

Yeats actually opted on the page for 'O! O!' as a response to Sophocles' *iou iou*. Let nobody doubt that Sophocles was aware of what he was inviting from his actor.

An alternative used by some recent translators has been to leave these exclamations of grief as simple transliterations from the Greek, offering both the original sound and the challenge of transforming this into performance without having the words get in the way of the emotion. Surely it will not only be the actor invited to confront the intolerable realisation by Theseus that he has wrongly condemned his son who might prefer the freedom of *oee moee* (Raphael and McLeish, Methuen, 1997) to express his anguish at the end of *Hippolytus* rather than 'Alas' (Chicago), 'Woe is me' (Bantam, 1960) or 'Oh woe' (Loeb, 1997).

If dealing with such part-verbal expressions is something that may be dictated by broader considerations than the linguistic, without much deviation from the spirit of the original, there is another, though more limited, series of non-verbal formations in the texts. The significance of these is that they seem to have been inserted as a means of indicating some change or realignment of the dramatic focus of the scene. The first worth noting is conspicuous because it uses precisely the same 'words' as are to be found in Sophocles' *Oedipus Tyrannus* whose delivery by Olivier so excited his audiences in 1945.

Sophocles used *iou, iou* to express Oedipus' final realisation of the truth. The *Oresteia* opens with the disgruntled Watchman on the roof of the palace at Mycenae waiting for news about Troy. What should he say when at last the beacon shines out to signify the Greek victory? *Iou iou*, he calls (l. 1214) – 'What ho!' in one translation it might be unkind to identify. The exclamation is exactly echoed in *Agamemnon* by Cassandra at the beginning of her fated prophetic speech to the Chorus; and by the Servant who reveals the murder of Aegisthus in *Libation-Bearers* (l. 881); also by the Herald in Aeschylus' *Suppliants* in an attempt to frighten the women out of sanctuary (l. 851). In *Philoctetes* it is the register of repulsion with which Neoptolemus reacts on discovering Philoctetes' disgusting bandages (l. 38). More surprisingly *iou iou* is how the chorus of satyrs in *Cyclops* gleefully greet Odysseus' news that he intends to 'twirl my twig in his socket and recycle the Cyclops' (l. 464); and how the Cyclops himself reacts to his first swig of Odysseus' unadulterated wine. Any translation depends less on a meaning for the word *iou*, than its context.

A more emphatic change of direction is marked in the *Oresteia* at the moment when Orestes is celebrating his success against the usurpers and planning his visit of supplication to Apollo at Delphi. The Chorus herald his achievement but Orestes breaks off with the terse *a, a* (outside the iambic trimeters between ll. 1047 and 1048). It marks his awareness, as sudden as a stroke, of the approach of the Furies. The same terse *a, a* is used by Io, followed by *e, e* in *Prometheus Bound* to announce the arrival of the tormenting gadfly (l. 567).

Euripides uses the even less defined exclamation *eä* in almost every play to register surprise. In *Helen eä* is Teucer's reaction to catching sight of the 'real' Helen and Helen's 'take' on recognising Menelaus (l. 71), though not the 'double take' when the Servant catches sight of the Helen he has been trying to explain to Menelaus evaporated in a puff of smoke (l. 541). In *Ion eä, eä* is what Ion calls out to scare off the birds which keep landing on the temple of Apollo (ll. 153 and 170). Only 71 lines later a single *eä* is how Ion reacts when, after a formal and polite greeting to Creusa, she turns away in tears, in Vellacott's translation:

Whoever you are, my lady, I can see at once you are noble both in birth and nature. Royal blood shows in the face and bearing. – What? [*eä*] Oh, my lady, what is the matter? Why do you hide your eyes? Your cheeks are wet! The sight of Apollo's oracle has made you weep! What can be making you so unhappy?[24]

The earliest translators such as Wodhull chose to ignore such exclamations, judging, perhaps, that they are unhelpful on the page. Nevertheless, on the page they are, and they nearly always mark a strong theatrical, as opposed to dramatic moment. Willetts (Chicago) identifies it in *Ion* with 'But? – You surprise me – ...'; McLeish an elliptical 'I – What is it?' (Methuen, 1997); Kovacs 'But what is this?' (Loeb, 1999).

Two especially emphatic turning-points in Euripides are to be found in the two posthumously produced plays, *Iphigenia in Aulis* and *Bacchae*. One is an *eä*, one a simple *a*. In *Iphigenia in Aulis* there are a number of such shifts of tempo. Agamemnon changes his mind about killing his daughter and sends a letter telling her not to come. The Old Man entrusted with delivering it is intercepted by Menelaus who forcibly takes it from him. Hearing a commotion outside his tent Agamemnon enters with the word *eä* (l. 317) 'Ha!' (Loeb, 1912); 'Ah, ah!' (Loeb, 2002); 'What is this –' (Chicago, 1958); 'Here, what's all this?' (Penguin, 1972); 'Hey there ...' (Methuen, 1991).

When Iphigenia, having arrived in Aulis to marry Achilles as she believes, greets her father he welcomes her affectionately, then, overcome by the horror of what he is planning, seems to rebuff her. Iphigeneia's *eä* is how she responds to his sudden rejection, followed by *hōs ou blepeis hekēlon asmenos m'idōn* (l. 644), a neat line being both pithy and childlike, contrasting his pleasure at seeing her, *asmenos*, with his disquiet, *hekēlon*. Potter (1781) with 'A gloom hangs on thee midst thy joy to see me' seems to have failed to understand the moment. The young Jane Lumley's instinctive sympathy for Iphigenia (*c.*1555) is more pronounced in her puzzled 'What is the cause father, that you seame to be so sadde, seinge you saye, you are so ioyfull at our comminge?' Amongst more modern translations the Oxford (1978) 'How troubled your eyes look, yet you say you are happy to see me' and the Methuen (1990) 'What . . . ? / Why look at me like that, if you're so glad to see me?' both offer something to the actor though only the latter finds a verbal equivalent for Euripides' *eä*.

In *Bacchae* Euripides conceals the turning-point of the play in a single *a*. During the second confrontation between Pentheus and Dionysus, the god offers to bring back the women to Thebes. Pentheus responds by calling for his weapons and ordering Dionysus to be quiet. Dionysus responds with *a. / boulē sph' en oresi sugkathēmenas idein?* (ll. 809–10), literally 'A! Do you wish to see them sitting in the mountains?'[25] It is a potent moment, combining stage direction, change of mood and transfer of status. Pentheus' line to his servant is both forceful and a 'travelling' line, an apparent false exit (a move away from Dionysus and another back towards him). Dionysus' timed response seems to show the precise moment when he begins to exert his power to distort Pentheus' judgement, as he already has with the Chorus and will continue to do with Agave and her sisters. Dionysus, the god, chooses to 'befuddle his [Pentheus'] wits, / Make him mad. Never in his right mind / Would he put on a dress. Possessed he will' (ll. 845–50).

Translators could hardly have failed to recognise the significance but have reacted in different ways. Milman (1888) with

> PE: Bring out mine armour! Thou, have done thy speech!
> DI: Ha! wouldst thou see them . . . ?
> displays little dramatic sense.

Murray (1906) elaborated:

> DIONYSUS: (*after regarding him fixedly, speaks with resignation*).
> Ah! – Have then thy will!
> (*He fixes his eyes upon* PENTHEUS *again while the armourers bring out his armour; then speaks in a tone of command.*)
> Man, thou wouldst fain behold them on the hill
> Praying!

The second Loeb (2002):

> PENTHEUS: Servants, my armor from the palace! And you, shut your mouth!
> DIONYSUS: (*with imperious authority, countermanding Pentheus' orders*) Stop! Do you want to see them sitting together on the mountains?
> PENTHEUS: (*as if under a spell*) Yes, indeed: I'd give much gold to do so.

Less magisterial responses, but more aware include:

> DI: [*With an authoritative shout*]:
> Wait! [*Then quietly*] Do you want to see ... ? (Penguin, 1954)
> (*Pentheus strides towards the left, but when he is almost offstage, Dionysus calls imperiously to him*).
>
> DI: *Wait!* Would you like to *see* ...? (Chicago, 1959)
>
> DI: One thing more. You would like to watch ...? (Methuen, 1988)
>
> DI: Sss. / D'you want to see them at it ...? (Hern, 1998)
> and, reading the scene differently, perhaps:
>
> PE: You – we're through talking.
> DI: Are we! Would you like to see ...? (Applause, 1978)
>
> PE: Quick, I must go –
> DI: Ahhhhhh, I see / You want to see them ...? (Oberon Books, 2002).[26]

All these exclamations are simply pointers for reader, actor or director, just as they are, but presumably were not intended to be, for the translator. Their value to the translator is to give authority for interpreting the stage action in terms of scene construction and dramatic rhythm. A more detailed study of a single play, *Oedipus Tyrannus* of Sophocles, may help to show how translators have chosen to interpret that dramatic rhythm.

CHAPTER 5

Sophocles' Oedipus Tyrannus:
Words and Concepts

> While a poet's words endure in his own language, even the greatest
> translation is destined to become part of the growth of its own
> language and eventually to be absorbed by its renewal.
>
> (Walter Benjamin, 'The task of the translator',
> in *Illuminations*, trans. H. Zohn (London, 1970))

Of the surviving Greek plays only Sophocles' *Oedipus* contains a major
translation issue in the title. Most Greek tragedies are identified either
through a direct transliteration, *Hepta epi Thēbas, Trachiniai, Hiketides*;
or through a latinised version *Septem contra Thebas, Trachiniae, Supplices*;
or anglicised to *Seven Against Thebes, Women of Trachis* (or *Trachinians*),
Suppliant Women (or *Suppliants*). The comedies are much more variable
with *Ekklesiazousai* known variously as *Ecclesiazusae, Congresswomen,
Women in Parliament, The Assemblywomen, The Women in the Assembly,
Women in Charge* and *Women in Power*.

The Greek title for the Sophocles play is *Oidipous Turannos*, which
appears in various translations as *Oedipus Tyrannus, Oedipus Rex, Oedipus
the King* and *Oedipus King of Thebes*. It is the word *turannos* that is in
question here. It can mean both more and less than 'king' or *rex*. It does
imply 'tyrant', though not necessarily in a pejorative sense. A tyrant could
be simply someone with absolute power, or part of the ruling family, or
someone who had achieved the power of an absolute monarch by other
than succession. Medea uses the word in the feminine to describe the
princess whom Jason is going to marry without suggesting that Jason will
end up as a henpecked husband. Hecuba in *Hecuba* (*Hekabē*) contrasts
her present status as a *doulē*, a slave, with her previous life as a *turannos*, a
queen (l. 809). Prometheus may have more of a statement to make when
he describes Zeus as the '*turannos* of the gods' in *Prometheus* (l. 936), but
when the Chorus of clouds do the same in *Clouds* they are not implying
any oppression. The Chorus in *Women of Trachis* invoke Apollo as the

'*turannos* of my mind' and seem quite happy about it. On the other hands, Euripides uses the word figuratively to describe *Erōs*, the god of love, as 'tyrant of both gods and men' (Fragment 136). When, in Sophocles' *Electra*, the Tutor arrives with his faked story of the death of Orestes, he uses the word twice in successive sentences, first when he assumes that this must be the palace of the *turannos* Aegisthus, then pretending to identify Clytemnestra 'because she looks like a *turannos*' (ll. 661 and 664). As he knows perfectly well who Clytemnestra is, and that this is the palace where Aegisthus now rules, it is difficult not to believe that Sophocles is using the word ironically.

Oedipus both is and is not a tyrant. He is the legitimate heir to the previous king, Laius, but believes he is not. Nor does he hold absolute power if any sense is to be made of the exchange with Creon when Oedipus accuses him of plotting against him:

> CREON: Why then: are you not married to my sister?
> OEDIPUS: I am indeed: it cannot be denied.
> CREON: You share with her the sovereignty of Thebes? [lit. 'do you
>   not rule?']
> OEDIPUS: She need but ask, and anything is hers.
> CREON: And am I not myself conjoined with you?
> OEDIPUS: You are; not rebel, therefore, but a traitor!
> CREON: Not so, if you will reason with yourself.
>   As I with you. This first: would any man,
>   To gain no increase of authority,
>   Choose kingship [*turannon*], with its fears and sleepless nights?
>   Not I. What I desire, what every man
>   Desires, if he has wisdom, is to take
>   The substance not the show of royalty.
>   [*turanna dran*, lit. 'to do tyrannical things']
>   For now, through you, I have both power and ease,
>   But were I king [lit. 'if I ruled'] I'd be oppressed with cares.
>   Not so: while I have ample sovereignty
>   And rule in peace, why should I want the crown [*turannis*]?¹

The nature of Oedipus' authority seems deliberately to be made vague. As Kitto translated in the above passage Thebes is ruled by a triumvirate. Creon rejects sole rule because this way he gets the power without responsibility.² In the eighteenth century power and its exercise appeared as a major theme within the play. George Adams in the first complete translation of Sophocles into English (1729) seems to change the emphasis where Kitto has 'sovereignty' and Sophocles has the simple *archeis*

(l. 579): 'And is it not true that you divide with her the supreme Power?' to which Oedipus replies 'She hath an absolute Power over me, and I grant her whatsoever her wish can form'. Creon's defence is to ask whether there is:

any Man in the World, who would rather be a King with all those Fears and Terrors which accompany a Kingdom, than to live in the Bosom of Rest, with all the Surety of the Condition of a Person, which by another Name possesseth Power?[3]

The rest of his speech, reasonably literal translation though it is, reads like a debate between 'ambition' and 'power'. Oedipus' reaction to the suggestion that Jocasta is on equal footing to his own, *han ē thelousa pant' emou komizetai* (l. 580) is considered by some to be an evasion. Thomas Gould suggested that Oedipus is actually correcting Creon, translating the line with the evasive 'She gets from me whatever she desires'.[4] Back in the eighteenth century Charlotte Lennox had Creon ask directly 'Does she not share with you the sovereign power?' to which Oedipus replies 'She does; and my respect and tenderness for her are boundless.' Creon's defence against the charge of 'treachery' is:

I enjoy what monarchs taste not, security and quiet. What madness to forfeit these advantages for the fears, the anxieties, that surround a throne! Say can there be room for choice in such unequal blessings? Born without ambition, I prefer the title of subject to that of king.[5]

Lennox appears to have appended a footnote: 'This moral, and consequently this defence of Creon's, will not be admitted in our time; but in Greece a crown was not what it is with us.' But this footnote, as others alongside the translations, are from the original author, Pierre Brumoy who had published *Le Théâtre des Grecs* in Paris in 1730, not from Mrs Lennox, and is consequently a comment on Louis XV, not the England of 1759 where George, prince of Wales, to whom Lennox dedicated her three volumes, was about to become the first English Hanoverian as George III, and hoping to restore some of the power of the monarch lost in the Civil War.

The word *turannos*, used directly or in cognate form, occurs a dozen times within the first two thirds of Sophocles' *Oedipus Tyrannus* (using the bastardised form of the title), but not subsequently.[6] It is up to the translator to decide how to represent this in English, but there is clearly some ambiguity, or slack, in what is being implied, and in what sort of way, that is oblique to the main themes of the play. The late nineteenth-century scholar Richard Jebb drew special attention to the choral ode whose second stanza begins *hubris phuteuei turannon* (l. 873). In a note to his 1887 edition he pointed to the rebuke that the Chorus are making as a result of Oedipus' reaction to Creon.[7] Jebb wrote of *turannon* 'here not "a prince," – nor even in the normal Greek sense, an unconstitutionally absolute ruler (bad or good), – but in our sense, "a tyrant"', quoting two parallel instances in Plato.[8] It may be more than just a response to a single scene. The Chorus is prepared to back Oedipus as their *turannos* but there comes a point in the play where loyalty to the *turannos* conflicts with their belief in Apollo and the oracle, and in Teiresias. In this choral ode, it seems, one kind of *turannos* has reached the point of looking alarmingly like another sort of *turannos*, the one who is created out of *hubris*.

The concern over who may be responsible for the plague and why, does turn into a test of loyalty which Oedipus as a good *turannos* feels he must cope with even if, in the process, he shows himself to be someone who will be disqualified from being their *turannos* at all. This choral ode is a turning-point. As far as the Chorus are concerned, in a confrontation between human sympathy and a divine thumbs-down, there is no contest. They will side with Apollo.

The ode comes immediately after the scene in which Jocasta has revealed all that is known about the death of Laius, and Oedipus has responded by telling her of his reasons for consulting Apollo's oracle, the oracle's ominous response and Oedipus' fatal encounter with a group of men on the road away from Delphi. Everything now comes down to whether or not Laius was killed by a band of men, as the survivor reported, or by only one. Jocasta sends for the man and leaves with Oedipus. The first *strophē* contains words like *moira* (destiny), *nomoi* (laws) and promotes the enduring rulings of Olympus. Then the line '*hubris* gives birth to the *turannos*'. Lewis Theobald, in the earliest translation into English (1715), used rhyme for the choruses and his *antistrophē* reads:

> The Tyrant and illegal Man
> From Pride and rash Contempt began,
> Pride and Contempt that lift him high
> O'er mountains of Impiety;
> Till plac'd aloft he dazled grows,
> And in his Fear his Hold foregoes.
> O! may the City's Cares succeed,
> Nor envying Fates their Search mislead.

> With ardent humble Pray'rs the Gods I'll move;
> The Gods shall still my kind Protectors prove![9]

Adams (1729) who, despite translating lyrics into prose, did identify *strophai* and *antistrophai*, was straight to the point in his best moralistic and pedantic style:

Insolence begets tyranny: Insolence when it adds Crime to Crime, and having raised Men to the highest Precipice, it throws them down into fatal Necessity, then their Fortunes forsake them and they fall from that Grandeur to which their Injustice raised them. But I beseech the Gods never to deprive the City of that Happiness of which Oedipus was the Author for I still put myself under the Protection of the Gods.[10]

Mellifluous it isn't, but you get the point. You also get a passing credit for Oedipus which is pure Adams unless you can read all that about 'the Happiness of which Oedipus was the Author' into the single word *palaisma* which means 'a wrestling-match'.[11] The difference in these various translations does come down to whether the *turannos* is made specific, and thus refers to Oedipus, or whether the Chorus are making some generalised comment which has little or nothing to do with the present dramatic situation. Thomas Francklin, for instance (1759), in an ABBA rhyming pattern in iambic dimeters offered:

> Pride first gave birth to tyranny:
>   That hateful vice, insulting pride.
>   When every human power defied,
> She lifts to glory's height her votary.[12]

The prosy Lennox tried to raise her game with:

Tyranny is the offspring of pride. Pride, when it has accumulated evils upon evils, reaches at length its summit, and, giddy, with the heighth, precipitates itself into an abyss of miseries.[13]

Neither seems germane to the situation.

The Revd Thomas Maurice published what he described as 'a free translation' amongst a set of poems in 1779. In erratic dimeters he seems to heap more blame than is warranted upon Oedipus without actually mentioning him:

> 'Twas insolence first drench'd in blood
> The tyrant's hand; but when elate with pride

> He spurns at right, and dares the gods deride.
> From the proud precipice where late he stood,
> That insolence shall dash him headlong down.[14]

Potter was also using rhyming verse, of a kind, by the time he tackled Sophocles (1788):

> The tyrant Pride engenders. Pride
> With wealth o'erfilled, with greatness vain,
> Mounting with outrage at her side,
> The splendid summit if she gain.[15]

George Somers Clarke opted two years later for prose 'undertaken at the suggestion of a friend who was of the opinion that such a version of the Greek tragedies would possess obvious advantages over the metrical translation', but offered an alliterative and self-conscious 'Pride is the parent of impiety in princes'.[16]

If the issue of the play's title has been laboured here it is because, in the earliest translations, the political dimension seemed as important as any other. Power and the exercise of power were linked to the arbitrariness of Fate and the uncertainty of human existence. The final lines of the Sophocles play come from the chorus, in Fagles' slightly free translation:

> People of Thebes, my countrymen, look on Oedipus.
> He solved the famous riddle with his brilliance,
> he rose to power, a man beyond all power.
> Who could behold his greatness without envy?
> Now what a black sea of terror has overwhelmed him.
> Now as we keep our watch and wait the final day,
> count no man happy till he dies, free of pain at last.[17]

Dryden, for all that he had to say about translation, as we have seen, chose to write his own version with Nathaniel Lee, concluding with a homily from Teiresias:

> Let none, tho' ne're so Vertuous, great and High
> Be judg'd entirely blest before they Dye.[18]

Greek tragedy often ends with such capsules; four separate plays of Euripides conclude with exactly the same four lines which muse on the uncertainty of life. A defining feature of Greek myth is its Protean capacity to take on the shape of each period in which it resurfaces. One reason for resurrecting Greek tragedy at all is its capacity to speak anew to each generation and different generations have certainly responded differently. For the political flavour of sixteenth- and seventeenth-century Oedipuses, the nineteenth offers his renaissance, subject to the manifold and rapid changes that moved from romanticism into the age of industry. The manner in which the nineteenth century colonised classical civilisation has been comprehensively chronicled by Richard Jenkyns in *The Victorians and Ancient Greece*.[19] Amongst the wealth of social and cultural adjustments that used Athens as a platform, Jenkyns pointed in particular to the recreation of Greek society as though it conferred a moral authority which happened to suit the temper of its own time. For Matthew Arnold Greek tragedy offered 'a lofty sense of the mastery of the human spirit' which leads to 'a sentiment of sublime acquiescence in the course of fate, and in the dispensation of human life'.[20] Jenkyns continued by pointing to Arnold's 'translating' the *Oedipus Tyrannus* 'into a kind of scriptural language: "Oh! that my lot may lead me in the path of holy innocence of word and deed ... The power of God is mighty ... and groweth not old".'[21]

If such appropriation has met with short shrift in more recent times, it is only one of a conflicting mass of new attitudes and stances too complex to catalogue here without gross over-simplification. Amongst them, though, the reason for having translations at all was addressed while the rash of new translators met with solid and sometimes spiteful resistance amongst reviewers. When Sir Francis Doyle in 1849 produced his *Oedipus, King of Thebes*, he was at pains to explain *why* he was translating the play at all:

The plays of the Athenian dramatists, in spite of their great celebrity, are but little known in this country, except to those who can understand them in the original Greek.[22]

His aim, therefore, was to attract:

some of those whom circumstances have shut out from a classical education ... I have made my translation on the whole as literal as I could: paraphrases are, no doubt, much easier to execute, and flow more smoothly, but it is not so desirable to preserve, not only the thoughts, but also the style of the author unchanged, that no word, small or great, should, I think, be left out of any version without an attempt to bring it in.[23]

This didn't prevent Doyle from falling into doggerel with his rhyming choruses:

> The pride of life breeds tyrant will
> And pride, if gorged beyond its fill
> With joys that oft recur in vain
> And suits not with our mortal strain.[24]

A few years later in 1856 a critique in *The Saturday Review* of William Blew's translation of the *Agamemnon* began:

> It is to be regretted that English scholars so seldom employ themselves in the work of translation, which is therefore abandoned to the lowest class of labourers in the field of literature – booksellers' serfs, who have neither the knowledge nor the skill requisite for the task ... Our scholars may, indeed, urge in excuse that translation is a thankless task .... They may plead that the learned reader, acquainted with the original, is prone to dwell only on the inevitable inferiority of the modern version; while the unlearned reader, not dreaming of the difficulties to be mastered, is incapable of appreciating the translator's manifestation of skill and power.[25]

The anonymous reviewer of Henry Williams' *The Medea, Alcestis and Hippolytus of Euripides* offered a general attack on those translators 'who have deservedly gone to their own place, the butterman's counter', lambasting 'verse translations which combine so many sins against rhyme, right interpretation, and good taste as to deserve notice only by way of warning'.[26]

One surprising response of this scathing critic was to level against translators, amongst their other sins, that of being 'undramatic'. Few of the translations of the time *were* dramatic but few of them were aimed at performance. It was a production of *Oedipus Tyrannus* that was to bring into the consciousness of the age at long last something of the potential of Greek tragedy for performance on the professional stage. And it was in France. The production was at the Théâtre Français in 1858 in a rhyming translation by Jules Lacroix: it kept being revived over the next forty years, latterly with Jean Mounet-Sully in the leading role.[27] The stranglehold of stage censorship in Britain would ensure that it would be over fifty years before a professional production of *Oedipus Tyrannus* was to be permitted on the English stage, and then in the marbled tones of Gilbert Murray via the diversion of Reinhardt's spectacular production at Covent Garden in 1912. There were some unlicensed productions in Britain, mostly amateur and associated with universities in England and

Scotland. The history of such revivals has been charted as part of continuing work by Fiona Macintosh, drawing attention to the hesitant manner in which the plays themselves, as opposed to new plays based on them, returned to the stage.[28] Scholarship still turned mostly on linguistic and metrical issues and in the public schools this is how the works of Aeschylus, Sophocles and Euripides were still taught.

The latter part of the nineteenth century saw publication of translations of *Oedipus Tyrannus* by Edward Hayes Plumptre in 1865, Lewis Campbell in 1874, Benjamin Hall Kennedy in 1882, Robert Whitelaw in 1883,[29] E. D. A. Morshead in 1885,[30] and Richard Claverhouse Jebb in 1887 alongside the Greek text which was used in the Cambridge production in Greek of that year.[31] Three other translations were published in the same year, by Edward Conybeare, George Young, and Thomas Nash: Edward Coleridge followed in 1893.

Campbell certainly saw the Mounet-Sully performance, having lamented in his *A Guide to Greek Tragedy for English Readers* (1891) that such was not possible in England. Mounet-Sully's performance, as might be expected of a major nineteenth-century actor, was focused on Oedipus the man rather than Oedipus the king, and his responsibility, or otherwise, for the situation he found himself facing. The extent of Oedipus' contribution to his own downfall is far from fixed. Aristotle's enthusiasm for *Oedipus Tyrannus* comes down to his belief that 'pity' and 'fear' are evoked neither by witnessing a good man 'falling from happiness to misery' nor by the same happening to a bad man. He is left with:

> . . . the sort of man who is not especially virtuous and just, someone whose fall is not the result of viciousness or depravity, but rather from some error of judgement (*hamartia*), someone who enjoys prosperity and status, like Oedipus and Thyestes or from famous families like theirs.[32]

Oedipus as a victim of hostile gods, or of an indifferent Fate, may just about accord with Aristotle's requirements, but is Oedipus, as the Chorus claim at the end of the play, nothing more than a warning 'to call no man happy till the day he dies'?

At least part of an answer does depend on a translation issue. At the height of the confrontation with Teiresias Oedipus says to the blind prophet:

> *mias trephei pros nuktos, hōste mēt' eme*
> *mēt' allon, hostis phōs hora, blapsai pot'an.*
> (ll. 374–5)

Literally this runs 'You are nourished by darkness, so as to be unable to harm me or anyone else who can see the light', or, rather more elegantly from Constantine Trypanis:

> Blind slave of an endless night!
> You cannot hurt me nor anyone who sees the sun.

Teiresias responds:

> *ou gar se moira pros g'emou pesein, epei*
> *hikanos Apollōn, hō tad' ekpraxai melei.*
> (ll. 376–7)

This runs literally: 'It is not my fate to make you fall, since Apollo is enough, to whom it is a care to bring this to pass', and in Trypanis:

> I will not be your downfall. Apollo is enough.
> He will work it out.

The implication seems clear. Teiresias is telling Oedipus that he, Teiresias, has no need to bring Oedipus down because Apollo will do that, and, indeed, wants to. Other translations of Teiresias' lines include:

> No, not from me proceeds thy fall; the God
> Who cares for this is able to perform it.
> (Lewis Campbell, 1874)

> It is not fate that I shall be your ruin,
> Apollo is enough; it is his care
> to work this out.
> (Grene, 1942)

No. It is not at my hand that you are destined to fall, since Apollo, who has it in mind to bring this about, will be sufficient. (Hugh Lloyd-Jones, 1994)

> It is not for me to take you down.
> Apollo has that well in hand.
> (Mueller and Krajewska-Wieczorek, 2000)

> That's true,
> as it happens – it's not me who'll destroy you.
> The gods have already decided that.
> (Morrison, 2003)

There seems to be little alternative here but to accept that the oracle of Apollo is a curse; before he was born, Oedipus was cursed, for reasons unknown, by the God, the gods or Fate (the Greek refers to both *moira* – 'destiny' or 'one's portion' or 'measure in life' – and to Apollo), and that Apollo intends to make sure that the curse is fulfilled. Free will does not exist. Oedipus is the victim. Even Jebb, a commentator to whom most classical scholars still defer, feels only a qualm, suggesting that *ekpraxai* should mean 'accomplish' rather than 'exact' and that *tade*, 'these things' that Apollo is going to 'accomplish ... has a mysterious vagueness'. But where does this leave Aristotle and *hamartia*? What is Oedipus' 'fatal mistake'? Trying to avoid the oracle? Killing an old man when he has been warned he will kill his father? Marrying an older woman when he has been warned he will marry his mother? *Hamartia* is an unconscious transgression, 'an offence committed in ignorance'[33] but the issue of cause as opposed to effect is still a live one. As Bernard Knox emphasised, the codices don't say:

> *ou gar se moira pros g'emou pesein, epei*
> *hikanos Apollōn, hō tad' ekpraxai melei.*
> (ll. 376–7)

but

> *ou gar me moira pros ge sou pesein, epei* ...[34]

As Knox translates the line which appears in all the manuscripts Teiresias is not saying:

> It is not destiny that *you* should fall at *my* hands [my italics]
> since Apollo is enough for that, and it is his affair.

Rather:

> It is not destiny that *I* should fall at *your* hands [my italics]
> since Apollo is enough, and it is his affair.[35]

Gilbert Murray, for his published text (1911) and for the first production in English (1912), preferred the old reading, if in language obfuscated by the demands of strict rhyme:

> OEDIPUS: Thou spawn of Night, not I nor any free
>   And seeing man would hurt a thing like thee.
> TEIRESIAS: God is enough. – 'Tis not my doom to fall

Gould (1970) followed this original reading in his translation (TEIRESIAS: It's not my fate to be struck down by you), and appended a footnote which pointed to the ambiguity of the original, with the timely warning that 'of course no interpretation of a play should depend upon a line that is a scholar's conjecture'.[36]

If in the eighteenth century the fall of Oedipus was tied to ambition and its comeuppance, the early nineteenth preferred a romantic view of him as the victim of his fate (with or without a capital 'f'), rather than its master, with a soul condemned of which he has never been captain. For Jebb, writing and translating at the end of the nineteenth century, the most interesting aspects of the *Oedipus Tyrannus* involved 'the intellectual position of Oedipus and Jocasta towards that divine power of which the hand is laid so heavily upon both'.[37] When he interprets the play as some sort of a warning to Athens and Greece he may be in effect pointing to a less immediate, but more comprehensive, warning contained in the dramatic situation. The immediate and long-term reactions of various people to various prophecies, and to their interpreter *extra cathedram*, Teiresias, address a raft of human errors in trying to second-guess Apollo. These are compounded by the very human reactions through which the real situation is exposed: the herdsman who rescued the baby through pity; the foster-parents whose concealment made it possible for a drunk in Corinth to deride Oedipus as bastard; the sole survivor of the encounter where the three roads meet who couldn't admit that a single man had routed them.

Such smaller issues began to surface not only when the Greek plays were at last beginning to become subject to the scrutiny of performers (though *Oedipus* in England was still only in Greek) but when the theatre was undergoing two major developments. The first of these was the flourishing of Naturalism, a movement with separate but complementary dimensions. Zola's *Naturalism in the Theatre* (1881) demanded a new seriousness in the theatre and a drama to match the truthfulness of his own novels. Dramatic texts, from the earlier plays of Ibsen, Strindberg and Hauptmann, exemplified the slogan of 'Art for truth's sake' to use James A. Herne's rallying cry. Such a movement in the content of the drama was matched by a more long-lasting renewal of its form which affected all aspects of design and presentation. New means of using electric light made it possible to give some impression (relatively) of real life happening on stage, bolstered by the work of André Antoine, Otto Brahm and Konstantin Stanislavski who founded the Moscow Arts Theatre with Vladimir Nemirovich-Danchenko in 1897, a theatre dedicated to such principles.

The rise of the director as an independent functionary in the theatre can be attributed to a number of social and artistic factors. As potent as any was the new subjection of old plays to the kind of scrutiny which opens the door to interpretation and re-interpretation. After generations when Shakespeare was distorted and garbled to suit the sensibilities of the time or the vagaries of star actors, more or less complete texts were returning to the stage. Intellectual and scientific revolutions demanded that the relationship between man and god, and between man and the inner self be drastically revised.[38] Inherited characteristics, environmental influences, childhood experiences, all became subject to scientific investigation and scientific explanation. The way people behaved became in its own right the target for literature and for drama.

The classics were in a strange position here. Nobody's feeling about the ancient world was going to be exploded by the questioning of a Christian creation myth. On the other hand, suggestions that Orestes, Antigone or Pentheus might be driven by subconscious as well as conscious motives was a real Pandora's box. Oedipus and Electra were up for grabs. If a new concern for women's rights in the nineteenth century might already have externalised Medea's act of infanticide into a metaphorical statement about the circumstances of despair, so the development of psychological theory turned the story of Oedipus inwards to the subconscious, in the fracture of taboos to which we might all be heirs. Such a change of emphasis from the general to the specific does not seem to have been greatly affected by Nietzsche's determined assertion in 1886 that 'The Greeks simply *could* not suffer individuals on the tragic stage', an attitude to which contemporary production simply *could* not subscribe.[39]

Freud did see the Mounet-Sully *Oedipus*. He may not have considered his application of the Oedipus complex as having anything to do with the play (as opposed to the myth) but he did suggest that Sophocles had written a 'tragedy of fate' whose:

tragic effect depends on the conflict between the all-powerful gods and the vain efforts of human beings threatened with disaster; resignation to the divine will, and the perception of one's own impotence is the lesson which the deeply moved spectator is supposed to learn from the tragedy.[40]

The reaction of a number of critics to this is most clearly expressed by Knox in his offer of alternative reactions to Apollo's oracles as *fiat* or *fiet*. *Fiat*, 'let it be', is the threat; *fiet*, 'it will be' is the warning, or as near as is possible to a warning from a god whose notions of time are not bounded

by mortal linearity.[41] The spine of Oedipus' life as parricide and husband
to his mother, is fixed, for Apollo as much as it is for the playwright
writing the story anew. Free will resides for the playwright, as it does for
Oedipus, in the manner in which he reacts to the story. Apollo does not
forecast the blinding, nor Jocasta's suicide.[42]

   It is at this point that the translator comes in again. Murray's translation, as shown above, opted for the old and largely discredited reading
according to which Teiresias does not tell Oedipus that Apollo is
'working out' Oedipus' destruction. An echo of this moment comes after
Jocasta has killed herself and Oedipus has put out his eyes. In a *kommos*
Murray has the Chorus leader ask at the end of the first *antistrophē*:

>   O fearful sufferer, and could'st thou kill
>   Thy living orbs? What God made blind thy will?

and Oedipus reply at the beginning of the second *strophē*:

>   Tis Apollo; all is Apollo.
>   'O ye that love me, 'tis he long time hath planned
>   These things upon me, evilly, evilly,
>   Dark things and full of blood.
>   I knew not; I did but follow
>   His way; but mine the hand
>   And mine the anguish. What were mine eyes to me
>   When naught to be seen was good?
>   (ll. 1327–35)

One of Murray's uglier passages ('evilly, evilly'), this has nonetheless an
Oedipus unequivocal about where to place the blame, even if he retracts
when answering the question from the Chorus. The Greek literally has
the Chorus leader ask not 'what God?' but 'which of the *daimones*?' The
word *daimōn* is one of several used within this play and elsewhere to
indicate some form of single controlling power. It poses particular problems for the translator. In the second speech of *Oedipus Tyrannus* the
Priest, as spokesman for the suppliants, appeals to Oedipus, not as a god
but as the first among men at coping with 'life's crises' (*sumphorais biou*)
and in 'dealings with *daimonōn*' (ll. 33–4). Oedipus describes himself
(l. 816) as *echthrodaimōn*, a *hapax* (found nowhere else in Greek literature), usually taken to mean 'hated by the gods', which could just as
easily, and more probably in the context, mean 'with a hostile *daimōn*'.

Twelve lines later in the same speech Oedipus asks:

Would not he be right in whose judgement some cruel *daimōn* [*ōmou . . . daimonos tis*] had brought these things upon me [lit. 'on this man']? (l. 828)[43]

The Chorus anticipate their concern for Oedipus in the choral ode which precedes this final scene, lamenting, in the Lloyd-Jones translation:

Ah, generations of men, how close to nothingness I estimate your life to be! What man, what man wins more of happiness [genitive *'eudaimonias'*] than enough to seem, and after seeming to decline? With your fate [accusative *'daimona'*] as my example, your fate [*'daimona'* is not repeated in the original], unhappy Oedipus, I say that nothing pertaining to mankind is enviable. (ll. 1197–207)[44]

The Messenger describing Oedipus breaking in to find Jocasta speaks of him as 'though guided by one of the *daimones*' (*daimonōn deiknusi tis*, l. 1258). The Chorus use the word again when Oedipus first emerges, blinded:

O grief terrible for men to see, O grief most terrible of any I have yet encountered! What madness has come upon you, unhappy one? Who is the god [*daimōn*] that with a leap longer than the longest has sprung upon your miserable fate [dative *dusdaimoni moira*] (ll. 1297–302)

Oedipus responds:

Alas, alas, miserable am I! Where am I being carried in my sorrow? Where is my voice borne on the wings of the air? Ah, god [vocative *daimon*] how far have you leaped? (ll. 1308–11)

Stilted as this may seem, it must be an improvement on the first Loeb's 'On, on the demon goads' (l. 1311), 'demon' offering an ecclesiastical overtone which surely comes in the theorist's category of 'false friend'.

Daimōn is one of those difficult Greek words with so many shades of meaning. In *Oedipus at Colonus* the Stranger tells Oedipus he looks noble enough *'plēn tou daimonos'* (l. 76), 'apart from what your life has thrown at you'; later in the play Polyneices responds to Antigone's profession of grief over losing her brother 'Whether I live or not lies with the *daimōn*' (l. 1443); the Chorus in *Birds* pledge themselves to Peithetairos *'kata daimona'*, 'come what may'. It may be used in a generalised sense of 'the Divinity' but has more of the sense of 'destiny', the controlling feature of one's life. Frequently to invoke the *daimōn* is to offer the equivalent of averting the evil eye or, in Christian societies, crossing yourself. The context dictates the nuance but, notwithstanding Murray's translation 'What God ...' to which Oedipus replies "Twas Apollo, all is Apollo', one of the things the *daimōn* is unlikely to refer to here is Apollo.

Gould pointed to the difficulties of finding any equivalent to *daimōn* in contemporary English and the subtlety of the variations in this play alone when he wrote as a note to his own translation:

The title *daimōn* is the natural one for a superhuman being that is not quite worthy of the full standing of a god, and for this reason is fitting for the Sphinx, who is referred to in 36 [line 36 carries on from this reference at line 34 to how to deal with *daimonōn*]. *Daimones* in this sense were more often benevolent than hateful beings in the fifth century, although eventually the word came to be used almost exclusively of sinister beings.

He continued with the possible use of the word as a synonym for *theos*, 'god', and concluded that:

reference to a man's *daimōn* could be a reference to his luck, his character, to his immortal self, or to his guiding divinity – depending on what one's philosophical or religious views were .... One may still enquire of an unhappy man: should he be despised for having a bad *daimōn*, or was the *daimōn* an independent deity who did not undo the man because the man deserved to fail?[45]

If, for the second time, considerable emphasis has been placed on translating a single word, it is simply because no other Greek tragedy is so defined by concepts. The words *turannos* and *daimōn* underpin the play's meaning, its characterisation and its dramatic rhythm. It may well be that there have been perfectly adequate translations which have found a single solution to neither but a comparison from those available in previous centuries suggests that they have more often contributed to confusion than illumination.

Adams made a clear statement and for the 'cruel *daimōn*' (l. 828) offered:

Cannot one say with Justice, that all this is the Curse of cruel Fortune resolved to persecute me?

Oedipus blinded blames 'Fortune', but when asked by the Chorus 'What angry God [*tis daimonōn*] lent you his aid?' replies 'It was Apollo, my

Friend, who is the only Author of my Miseries; none ever lent me his aid.' Potter resorted to a 'remorseless Demon' (l. 828)[46] but also had the Chorus ask 'What god enforced this rage?' (l. 1328);[47] Francklin 'This must be the work of some malignant power' (l. 828) and 'What madness drove thee to the desperate deed? What god inspired?' (l. 1328). Jebb was much more vague 'Then would he not speak aright of Oedipus, who judged these things sent by some cruel power above man?' (ll. 828–9) and 'What more than human power urged thee?' (l. 1328). Jebb was, in fact, most reluctant to offer any specific authority to the *daimōn*, coming up elsewhere with 'more than man' (l. 34), 'a power above man' (l. 1258) and 'The unearthly foe that, with a bound of more than mortal range, hath made thine ill-starred life his prey' (ll. 1300–02). Amongst contemporary translators Gregory McCart's decision to leave the word *daimōn* as 'daimon' makes excellent sense, used consistently so that the reader/ audience member's attention is drawn to the word, though there is more of a problem with cognate words which define the nature of the *daimōn*.[48] Kitto used a variety of words according to circumstance, asterisking them to point to the original. Others have used a number of words indis- criminately and interchangeably, 'God', 'god', 'gods', 'divinity', 'deity', 'spirit', 'fortune', 'fiend', 'power', 'curse of my life', 'Fury', 'premonition' and, somewhat eccentrically, 'someone'.

Though any play must rewrite itself to attract attention in each new age, *Oedipus Tyrannus* seems tied more than any other from the Greek repertoire to the religious mood of the time. So too its translations and translators. *Prometheus, Antigone, Bacchae* can all adjust their viewpoint to contemporary socio-political circumstance. Oedipus is a different kind of archetype. Gilbert Murray was initially resistant to it at all. When W. B. Yeats invited him to provide a translation at the beginning of 1905 for an Abbey Theatre which had been open only a month, Murray's reply was extraordinary:

> O Man
> I will not translate the *Oedipus Rex* for the Irish Theatre, because it is a play with nothing Irish about it: no religion, not one beautiful action, hardly a stroke of poetry. Even the good things that have to be done in order to make the plot work are done through mere loss of temper. The spiritual tragedy is never faced or understood: all the stress is laid on the mere external uncleanliness.[49]

David R. Clark and James B. McGuire, in their restoration of the extended processes and varying draft texts of Yeats's own version, covered the likely reasons which lay behind Murray's attitude. There was also a hazily supported suggestion that he was being invited to provide no more than a 'literal', Yeats acknowledging that his own smattering of Greek was insufficient for him to provide a 'real' translation. Yeats's enthusiasm for doing the play in Dublin appears to have waned a few years later once the censor removed his objections to the play's performance in England. There were serious discussions about *Oedipus* between him and Edward Gordon Craig in 1910 but Craig was preoccupied at the time with his designs for the Stanislavski *Hamlet* which opened in Moscow at the beginning of 1912. It took more than twenty years before the Abbey production on 7 December 1926, which led to the publication of Yeats's *Sophocles' King Oedipus: A Version for the Modern Stage.*[50]

Murray's resistance to the play was certainly overcome by the time he started to work on it in 1910, though he was still uncomfortable with what seemed to him to be the play's standpoint. In the Introduction to his published edition (1911 and pre-production) he wrote of:

the remarkable absence from the play of any criticism of life or any definite moral judgement. I know that some commentators have found in it a 'humble and unquestioning piety', but I cannot help suspecting that what they saw was only a reflection from their own pious and unsuspecting minds. Man is indeed a 'Plaything of Gods', but of Gods strangely and incomprehensibly malignant, whose ways there is no way to explain or justify.[51]

Beyond his work as a classicist, Murray's dramatic world was the world of Ibsen, Granville Barker, William Archer, William Poel and, George Bernard Shaw (who paid him the compliment of reproducing him on stage as Adolphus Cusins in *Major Barbara*). Archer, in correspondence with Murray, declared that:

Greek tragedy demands to be clothed in a formal, decorative beauty scarcely obtainable in English without the aid of rhyme. A very great poet might attain it in blank verse; but that noble measure is so intimately associated with Elizabethan drama as to bring with it, when applied to Attic tragedy, a wholly incongruous atmosphere. What one requires in the theatre is, so to speak, a certain pressure of pleasurable sensation to the square inch – or rather to the minute. In Greek tragedy we can seldom expect to receive this pleasure from the rapid and bustling action, the swift interchange of cut-and-thrust dialogue, to which we are accustomed on the modern stage. Except for the brief passages of 'stichomythy', character is portrayed and emotion uttered in long speeches, the dramatic effect of which required in Greek, and requires in English, the reinforcement of highly wrought and continuous verbal beauty.[52]

Few comments better illustrate the manner in which Oedipus has somehow taken hold as a representative of man faced with the vicissitudes of life in whatever century he has been located, including the twenty-first.

Less attention has been paid here to 'continual verbal beauty' in Sophocles than to considering ways in which individual words or ideas may be recovered or renewed. It seems only fair to give the last word on Oedipus to the poets, and for that to turn not to *Oedipus Tyrannus* but to *Oedipus at Colonus*. The Chorus in that play produce the most Beckettian of statements on human life to be found in Greek tragedy, and it comes at a strange time. Theseus has just seen off Creon and given active proof of his support for the blind man. Oedipus has his daughters back and is assured of a position of honour at his death. But Oedipus has unfinished business. Polyneices is asking to see him to enlist help for his invasion of Thebes. As Antigone and her father await his entrance, the Chorus sing the ode whose first *antistrophē* begins:

> *mē phunai ton hapanta ni-*
> *ką logon; to d', epei phanę,*
> *bēnai keithen hothen per hē-*
> *kei polu deuteron hōs tachista.*
>   (ll. 1224–7)

A few variant readings are suggested but there's no doubting what is being said:

(literally) Not to be born (*phunai*) beats every reckoning. But, once appearing (*phanę*), second-best is to go back where you came from as soon as possible.

They are lines to judge the translator by. Ultimately, we each prefer in a translation what we prefer, according to our various priorities. I offer no comment on the following selection, picked not entirely at random, but in chronological sequence:

Not to be born at all, overcomes all Arguments for Life. But since he is born to return thither whence he came as soon as possible, merits the second Praise. (George Adams, 1729)

> Not to be born is heav'n's first grace:
> If born, extinguish'd soon the vital flame,
>   Back to return whence late he came,
> Is heav'n's next blessing to man's wretched race.
>   (Robert Potter, 1788)

Not to be born at all is superior to every view of the question; and this, when one may have seen the light, to return thence whence he came as quickly as possible, is far the next best. (The Oxford Translation, 1823)

> Not to be born is the first boon of Heaven;
> If born, that life may quickly reach its bourne
> And fate resume the vital spark so given
> And end the being wretched and forlorn.
> > (John Benson Rose's revision of Potter
> > 'with a fulsome apology', 1867)

> Never to have been born is much the best;
> > And the next best, by far,
> To return thence, by the way speediest
> > Where our beginnings are.
> > > (Sir George Young, 1888)

Not to be born is, past all prizing, best; but when a man hath seen the light, this is next best by far, that with all speed he should go thither, whence he hath come. (Sir Richard Jebb, 1888)

> Ah! Not to be born, that beats
> > all man's reckoning; once appeared
> Back there, whence he hath come, to go,
> > for the best left of him is, quick as may be.
> > > (Arthur Compton Auchmuty in
> > > 'An experiment in metre', 1894)

Never to have lived is best, ancient writers say;
Never to have drawn the breath of life, never to have looked into the light of day;
The second best's a gay goodnight and quickly turn away.
> > (W. B. Yeats working from translations by Monck,
> Whitelaw, Lewis Campbell and Roscoe Mongan, perhaps others, 1928)

> Say what you will, the greatest boon is not to be;
> But, life begun, soonest to end is best.
> > (E. F. Watling, 1947)

> Not to be born, by all acclaim,
> > Were best; but once that gate be passed,
> To hasten thither whence he came
> > Is man's next prize – and fast, Oh fast!
> > > (Gilbert Murray, 1948)

Not to be born is best
when all is reckoned in, but once a man has seen the light
    the next best thing, by far, is to go back
back where he came from, quickly as he can.
                              (Robert Fagles, 1982)

            The best is never to be born.
            But if a man has seen the light,
            Then it is good to return at once
            To the land from where he came.
                              (Constantine Trypanis, 1986)

– Not to be born is best. And then,
second, to hurry whence he came.
                    (Carl R. Mueller and Anna
                    Krajewska-Wieczorek, 2000)

            Never to have been born is best,
            But once you've entered the world,
            Return as quickly as possible
            To the place from where you came.
                              (Marianne McDonald, 2004)

CHAPTER 6

Text and Subtext: From
Bad to Verse

The translator of prose is the slave of the author and the translator of
poetry is his rival.

(Andreï Makine, *Le Testament Français*,
translated by Geoffrey Strachan, 1997)

When Aristophanes talks about playwriting in *Frogs* the word he uses for
playwright is *poiētēs*. Because it has the same root as 'poet' it belongs with
what translators call 'false friends', homonyms which sound as though
they will transfer smoothly from source to target but have rather different
meanings. Steiner's example is the French *habit* and the English 'habit'.[1]
Greek and Latin are full of such words if only because so much of the
English language (and indeed the language of translation theory) is rooted
in the classical languages. *Poiētēs* is something of a special case. All Greek
drama is in verse. The dialogue of tragedy and comedy is for the most
part in iambic trimeters, the twelve-syllable Alexandrine. This is the
standard speech rhythm with a progression to greater flexibility of reso-
lution as the fifth century proceeds, two short syllables being used for a
single long.

The lyric metres used in choral odes, or in formal passages such as a
kommos, are varied and almost impenetrably intricate. They involve the
regular use of trochee, anapaest, dactyl, spondee and dochmiac, amongst
others, with a complexity that would be impossible to replicate in
translation, even were it desirable. In a not untypical Introduction to his
edition of the *Oedipus Tyrannus* (1887) Richard Jebb devoted no fewer
than thirty-three pages out of ninety-five to metrical analysis. The pulse is
based on quantity, every syllable being either long or short according to
its vowel. Some vowels being neutral (alpha, iota, upsilon) the quantity of
the syllable is dictated by the number or nature of the consonants which
follow the vowel. Composed for musical accompaniment the variations
seem almost endless. There are some moments when the rhythmic

structure may seem to break down, during expressions of grief or
dramatic interchanges such as the first confrontation between Chorus and
Oedipus in *Oedipus at Colonus*, but it is always possible to find *some*
pattern and metrical structure (if not always the same pattern and
structure from rival metrical critics). But patterns there are and it is
frequently on metrical grounds that scholars suggest dates for individual
tragedies or reject as spurious lines, scenes or entire texts.[2] As we have
seen, most (though by no means all) translators have chosen to highlight
this major difference between passages of dramatic action and reflection
by a contrast in the structure and language they afford to each.

What makes *poiētēs* different is that it does actually carry the con-
notation of 'maker' as, in English, a 'playwright' is a 'maker' or 'fashioner'
of plays. The need to find a balance between the strict verse of the original
and the priorities of the 'made' play are the first that need to be faced in
the search for an appropriate language for either tragedy or comedy.
Though all the Greek dramatists wrote in verse there is an inexorable
move, as the fifth century progresses, towards the language of everyday, at
least in the dialogue. Menander's plays are still in verse though the
choruses have disappeared entirely from the text and the manner in which
characters address one another more resembles actual conversation than
anything formal. The steady tread of the standard iambic is often in
comedy so resolved as to challenge analysis. *Frogs* includes the first dramatic criticism to find its way into print when the stage Euripides con-
demns the stage Aeschylus for what in Barrett's (prose) translation comes
out as 'a torrent of verbiage, stiff with superlatives, and padded out with
pretentious polysyllables', this last in one of Aristophanes' wonderful
coinages *kompophakelorrēmona*.[3] He goes on to describe an Aeschylean
speech as 'a dozen galumphing phrases, fearsome things with crest and
shaggy eyebrows. Magnificent. Nobody knew what they meant, of
course.'[4]

Aeschylus' reaction is predictable. It is Euripides who is responsible for
lowering the tone of tragedy and encouraging decadence. Euripides offers
one of his choruses (*Phlatto-thratto-phlatto-thrat*) to which Aeschylus
responds that he must be getting his inspiration from the brothel or the
drinking-club; 'His lyrics are full of the rhythms of the dance-floor, the
dirge-like wailings of these Carian trumpeters.'[5] Beyond the enormous
difference in poetic style between these two playwrights, who must at
least have met one another, lies the enormity of the translator's problem
over what to do with the verse. The temptation to opt wholly for prose is

understandable. The title of the present book reflects the whole subject, with its echo of Robert Frost's 'Poetry is what is lost in translation. It is also what is lost in interpretation.'[6]

William Frost, in a commentary on Dryden, looked at the tendency for scholars of the past to favour prose translations for poetry and put it down to the primacy of the word. The issue goes back easily as far as Dryden himself who in his 'Of dramatic poesy: an essay' (1668) wrote of his preference for blank verse to rhyme:

First, then, I am of opinion that rhyme is unnatural in a play, because dialogue there is presented as the effect of a sudden thought. For a play is the imitation of nature and since no man without premeditation speaks in rhyme, neither ought he to do it on the stage.[7]

Apart from being an interesting reflection on the art of the Restoration actor, Dryden was talking only of translation from the Latin, as he does in his letter to Roger, Earl of Orrery (1694) entitled 'Rhyme and blank verse'. Dryden was, of course, a considerable poet and a prolific translator of Virgil and Juvenal amongst others but, as far as he was concerned, translation of Greek plays had not yet happened. Alexander Fraser Tytler, in his extended *Essay on the Principles of Translation* a hundred years on, was somewhat wary of Dryden's freedom in translation, concerned about a descent into paraphrase. He devoted a whole chapter, albeit a brief one, to whether poetry can be translated into prose (though translating drama is not uppermost in his mind), concluding that translating verse into prose is 'the most absurd of all undertakings ... it is impossible to do complete justice to any species of poetical composition in a prose translation; in other words none but a poet can translate a poet'.[8]

A majority of the earliest translations of tragedy into English (though not the Lumley *Iphigenia*) were in verse. Thomas Morell's *Prometheus in Chains* (1773), the first Aeschylus, is frequently staccato in style but uses for the most part the iambic pentameter with choruses in rhyme. Morell shows some awareness of the theatre, if only in his dedication: 'The translation of this the *first* play extant' is dedicated to David Garrick 'indisputably the first actor in this (perhaps in any) age.'[9] Potter opted for the same in his complete Aeschylus (1777) rather than the Greek Alexandrine, with simple but variable rhyming patterns for the choruses. This is more effective in his Aeschylus and Sophocles than it is in his Euripides whose more homely exchanges tend to leave him in limbo.

Poking fun at easy targets is an unworthy game which has not always been easy to resist, but it does not require an actor's ear, or even – one would have hoped – a cleric's, to see that a line such as this from the Farmer on his second entrance in Euripides' *Electra* will not do: 'Ha! who these strangers, whom before my doors / I see?' (l. 341). On the other hand Orestes' celebrated greeting of the Old Man (*chair', ō geraie, tou pot, Ēlektra, tode palaion andros leipsanon philōn kurei?* (ll. 553–4)), variously rendered in more modern translations as 'Greeting, old man. / Electra, whose friend is this antique relic here?' (Penguin, 1963); 'Greetings, old man – Electra, to which of your friends is this ancient remnant of a man attached?' (Aris and Phillips, 1988); 'Good morning, old man. / (*Aside to* ELEKTRA.) Who's this old relic? / Who's side is he on?' (Methuen, 1997); 'Ah, hello, old man. / Electra, where did you find this decrepit old wreck?' (Hern, 2004), emerges in Potter 'Hail, hoary sire! Electra, of what friend / Doth chance present us the revered remains?': which at least treads the line between anxiety and scorn.

Amongst the earlier translations of Sophocles, Theobald (1714) opted for iambic pentameters and rhymed chorus; so did Francklin (1759) and Maurice (1779). Adams (1729) is in prose throughout; as is Charlotte Lennox (1759) translating from the Greek via French, in her mix of translation and résumé with quoted passages from the whole canon.

For Euripides, whose work lends itself more easily to prose, Lumley (c. 1555) settled for it exclusively in her *Iphigenia*, but cut most of the choral odes. Wodhull, in the first complete Euripides (1782), used iambic pentameters routinely, and in the choruses opted for variations of iambic in between three and five feet; as did Bannister (1780).

In the nineteenth century prose features in many more of the translations, the obvious exceptions being amongst established poets. Elizabeth Barrett in the earlier version of her *Prometheus Bound* (1833) presents a strict metric structure for the entry of the Oceanids, still dominated by the rhyming couplet:

> I mourn thy ruin'd destinies,
> Prometheus! From my tender eyes
> A tear-distilling stream doth break,
> With humid fount to dew my cheek;
> Because Saturnius, cruel still,
> Ruling by his proper will,
> Doth the royal sceptre bear,
> Subversive of the gods who were.[10]

Seventeen years later (1850), now a wife and mother, her new version reads:

> I behold thee, Prometheus – yet now, yet now,
> A terrible cloud whose rain is tears
> Sweeps over mine eyes that witness how
> Thy body appears
> Hung awaste on the rocks by infrangible chains!
> For new is the Hand and the rudder that steers
> The ship of Olympus through surge and wind –
> And of old things passed, no track is behind.[11]

So startling is the change that it is tempting to spend more time on these two translations from a single hand than their dramatic value merits. In her Introduction to the 1833 version Barrett claims that the present age 'says it has no need of translations from classic authors. It is, or would be, an original age.' Certainly there is no inkling that either of the Barrett versions might be staged: still less, Robert Browning's eccentric and unwieldy translation of *Agamemnon* (1877) which carries one of the more destructive introductions you are likely to find, from Sir F. G. Kenyon in his edition of the complete works of Browning already referred to in Chapter 3 (see p. 48–9):

An additional, and particularly unintelligible, perversity is shown in the metre chosen to represent the Greek iambic. Why Browning should have regarded an eleven-syllable line, – a blank verse with a superfluous syllable at the end of each line – as a better counterpart of the Greek metre of six iambic feet (or their equivalent) than ordinary blank verse passes comprehension. The result is peculiarly unfortunate, and gives a monotony to the non-choric passages which is neither fair to the original nor pleasing in itself.[12]

The issue of verse or prose exercised many of those whose pronouncements on translation in general have been the most enlightening during the twentieth century. Hilaire Belloc offered the injunction 'to translate *as a rule* [his italics] verse into prose and not into verse', but this may be seen, at least as far as translation for the stage is concerned, as an extension of his search not for the exact word in the receiving language but for 'the atmosphere of the word'.[13] D. S. Carne-Ross addressed the matter more directly in Arrowsmith and Shattuck's *The Craft and Context of Translation* (1961) where he stated that the translation of bits of Euripides' *Iphigenia in Aulis* by HD (Hilda Doolittle, 1919):

suggested certain elements in the Greek lyric better than they have ever been suggested before or since. She leaves out an enormous amount. She is not interested in the syntax, in the elaborate weave of the Greek lyric; and she shows little dramatic feeling.[14]

This might appear to satisfy absolutely nobody, but what Carne-Ross was impressed by was the sense of 'image'. Perhaps, then, the issue of translating verse is indeed the issue of translating 'metaphor' and stage metaphor is as much a matter of stage image as of language. Carne-Ross went on to identify the dangers inherent in turning a non-native English metre (such as the unrhymed dodecasyllable of the iambic trimeter) into 'not metre at all'.

William Arrowsmith in his own essay in the same book looked at comedy, pointing out that Aristophanes 'is a poet who goes through more metres in a single play than most English poets get round to in a lifetime'.[15] His priority, though, was elsewhere than in the verse (as will become clear in later chapters on comedy), when he pointed out that 'No translator of an Aristophanic comedy could possibly translate a page of trimeter dialogue without realizing that his dialogue must be essentially colloquial; that it cannot afford the full flood of traditional rhetoric.'[16]

In the search for an appropriate language for Greek drama the issue of verse or prose may be a red herring. Consider the following two translations of a speech of Phaedra in Euripides' *Hippolytus* (ll. 375–83):

> I have at times lain long awake in the night,
> Thinking how other lives than mine
> Have been shattered;
> And I believe that such misfortune
> Does not arise from inborn folly,
> Since often those who suffer are wise and good.
> But this is how we should regard the matter:
> We know and see what is right,
> Yet fail to carry it out. Some fail through sloth,
> Others through valuing some pleasure more than goodness;
> And life offers us many pleasures.

And the second:

How often, sleepless in the night, I've wondered why mortals wreck their lives. We're evil by nature? I don't believe it. No lack of decent people. So: we learn what's right, we know it – and how many choose to live it? Can't be bothered! This pleasure, that, beats what's right. Plenty to choose from.

Irrespective of which is the closer to Euripides, more graceful, or can offer more to the actor, these two passages have, in fact, been re-set by me.[17]

The first is prose by Philip Vellacott in the published edition, continuous without the initial capitals:

I have at times lain long awake in the night, thinking how other lives than mine have been shattered; and I believe that such misfortune does not arise from inborn folly, since often those who suffer are wise and good. But this is how we should regard the matter: we know and see what is right, yet fail to carry it out. Some fail through sloth, others through valuing some pleasure more than goodness; and life offers us many pleasures.

The second is in free verse by Frederic Raphael and Kenneth McLeish, the lines arranged on the page:

> How often, sleepless in the night,
> I've wondered why mortals wreck their lives.
> We're evil by nature? I don't believe it.
> No lack of decent people. So:
> We learn what's right, we know it –
> And how many choose to live it?
> Can't be bothered! This pleasure, that,
> Beats what's right. Plenty to choose from.

The most prominent contemporary Greek translator of Shakespeare, Christina Babou-Pagoureli, is revealing:

Can Shakespeare be translated in verse? This is a question that every translator has to answer, I think, in his own language. In Greek the ten or eleven syllables of Shakespearian poetry are – in my opinion – impossible to achieve. The Greek language is more analytic than the English, so more syllables are needed. And the corresponding fifteen syllables of Greek popular poetry sound very old-fashioned and fake today. In our days the form of writing drama has changed. Even the form of writing poetry has changed. So you have to decide if you want to translate a play in a form that no longer exists.

    I think to count syllables is a very dangerous trap. Knowing that the English and the Greek language are similar in syntax, the best solution is to translate the meaning – of course – and keep the structure but not the form. Keep the poetic metre and the internal rhythm of the text and the rhyming in monologues or at the end of a scene. In this way the text sounds almost modern, while it keeps its charming classic distance. The style of the text is not destroyed.[18]

Babou-Pagoureli is a professional translator of plays and novels from English into Greek, whose expertise in tackling a range of dramatic material from Sheridan to Caryl Churchill is comprehensive. What she has never undertaken, rather surprisingly, is translation from ancient Greek into modern Greek, something that was not attempted in Greece until 1903 and led to rioting in the streets of Athens which left several people dead.

It helps in putting the process of stage translation into perspective to remind oneself again that having a single Shakespeare is not the common experience in Europe. With Greek tragedy and comedy the plays are no longer in anyone's native tongue. To take a play that is more than 2400 years old and create a translation which may have dated within twenty is not something to feel ashamed about. On employing verse at all for Greek plays, as opposed to dramatic prose or very free verse, Michael Alexander offered a personal stance in an article in 1988 entitled 'Homer, sweet Homer' where he spelled out the unpalatable truth that without translation the classics will simply die. He confessed that 'I once wrote, over 20 years ago when I was not an academic, that I could not see the point of translating verse into anything but verse. Much have I travelled in the realms of lead since then, and am happy to prefer good prose to bad verse.'[19] His suggestion was that ideally there should be *two* translations of anything so that they might be compared one against the other. For a play, many directors would agree you also need two translations. The difference is that today's director will often want a 'literal' to provide the basic information from which the director, or a playwright with no knowledge of the original, may fashion whatever seems best for the particular production.[20] The resistance to the 'literal' by professional translators is understandable but may be the result of a consistent failure in some translators, especially of the Greeks, to appreciate the requirements of the performance text.

If a performance text is the major priority for the translator, the search for a subtext has become as significant in the recovery of Greek tragedy. Comedy will be considered in later chapters, presenting as it does entirely different stage dynamics where the quality that is of most use to the translator is probably having a dirty mind. In tragedy there are two aspects of subtext to look at. The first is the simple act of deception, where a character will make some pronouncement which he or she does not mean, the refinement being whether or not the audience is let into the secret and how far other characters are convinced. The second aspect of subtext is the unearthing of stage dynamics in a broad sense, anything from irony to implied action, a development which grew more sophisticated in the Athenian drama as the playwrights some of whose work has survived, and, presumably, the work of those who haven't, systematically pushed back the boundaries and investigated more and more how a play may be a unique means of combining public debate and private conflict.

One of the prime achievements of Euripides was to create evasive dialogue. Much of the comic technique of Menander is based on characters *not* saying what they mean. The translation issue comes down to identifying where this is happening and then to providing a suitable form of words to indicate as much to the audience without too obvious a signal that a character is being economical with the truth. Within our limited resources – the percentage of produced Greek plays that have survived is miniscule and those that can be dated even smaller – something of this progress can be charted.

In Aeschylus' *Persians*, the first surviving Greek tragedy, nobody deceives anybody about anything. The Messenger who brings news of the defeat at Salamis makes no attempt to play down the scale of the disaster; the defeated king Xerxes hides nothing and makes no pretence. *Seven Against Thebes* offers nothing more subtle than the rhetoric of a general under attack; *Suppliants* a debate between opposing viewpoints; *Prometheus* a secret which the protagonist refuses to reveal. Not until the *Oresteia* does active deceit take its place in the dramatic armoury. *Agamemnon* had a new dramatic structure, at least amongst the extant plays, when one character first withheld information from another, or from the Chorus, sometimes from the audience too. The prime mover in this is Clytemnestra who pretends to be the loyal wife while having already plotted her husband's murder before he arrives. She needs to divert his suspicion in order to get him inside the palace and into his bath. Her first words to the Chorus are a half-truth, when she applauds the victory of the Greek army against Troy but fails to mention the implications. Her message for the Herald to take to Agamemnon about finding a faithful wife at home is part of the plot against her husband's life. Her first words to her husband when he finally makes his entrance are a false expression of love in a long dissembling speech which concludes with an act of deception when she has the tapestries laid out for him to walk on.

The extent to which the actor reveals the dishonesty is of course dictated by the style of performance. If Aeschylus gives away no indication that she is lying, the translator is hardly obliged to do so. But Clytemnestra's initial deceit establishes a pattern for the rest of the trilogy. Orestes returns in *Libation-Bearers* and sets out to avenge his father. His plot involves Electra, while he will disguise himself as a foreigner (*xenō gar eikōs*); both he and Pylades will 'put on the accent of Parnassus, imitating the dialect of Phocis' (*amphō de phōnēn hēsomen Parnēsida,/ glōssēs autēn Phōkidos mimoumenō*). Now such an accent might exercise a director, and possibly a translator, but Aeschylus gives no indication in the Greek text that Orestes *does* modify his speech when he first addresses Clytemnestra with the words 'I am a Daulian from Phocis', or that Pylades, in his three brief lines, when the deception is no longer significant, reveals that he speaks in a natural Phocian dialect.[21] What Orestes does have to do is *convince* his mother: that is all.

The Chorus subsequently join in the plot when they tell the Nurse that she must alter Clytemnestra's message to Aegisthus, an unusual intervention, at least from what we know of Aeschylus' other plays. They compound this by playing dumb when Aegisthus does arrive by himself, without a guard. In very little of this does the translator need to make any interpretative decisions.

The trial in *Eumenides* is again without deception, as both parties or their advocates believe they are in the right.

In Sophocles duplicity is much more prominent and, as a result, the pressure on the translator to make decisions about how much to reveal that much greater. Each of the seven plays has its major deceivers or deceptions. Lichas in *Women of Trachis* has a yarn to spin about what Heracles has been up to and who Iole is. Antigone and Creon in *Antigone* are frank enough about their attitudes, but Ismene is more complicated. At one point she untruthfully confesses herself implicated in Antigone's act of defiance, while Teiresias is thrown into his usual position during stage appearances, of knowing exactly what is going on but being able to divulge no more than a part of what he foresees. He finds himself in a more compromising position in *Oedipus Tyrannus*, but there it is the old Shepherd who took pity on the baby he was meant to expose who has to try and wriggle out of his responsibility until the truth is forced out of him. The posthumously performed *Oedipus at Colonus* has an interesting and ambivalent scene in which Polyneices attempts, unsuccessfully, to ingratiate himself with his father. In *Electra* the Tutor proves himself sufficiently steely to indulge in the long and complex, fictional description of a chariot-race in which Orestes is meant to have lost his life.[22] Orestes himself, pretending to be only a messenger bringing back the ashes, has his resolve overwhelmed by Electra's grief and blows his cover. No such frailty gets in the way when he confronts Aegisthus with the body of his mother under the sheet. *Ajax* includes a dramatically sophisticated scene where the hero has decided to kill himself but has to convince those around him that all is well.

Philoctetes, a play given over to tricking a gullible and vulnerable castaway, was performed in 409 BC when Sophocles had had nearly sixty years to refine his dramatic technique, and Euripides had presented all but a handful of the plays which survive him. Examples of how different translators have handled the varying deceptions could be taken from any of the plays but one from *Philoctetes* is noteworthy. The play is unique in extant tragedy in having an all-male cast, with only five main characters, the Greeks Neoptolemus and Odysseus, who need to persuade Philoctetes to come to Troy if they are to win the war, the lame Philoctetes, abandoned on the desert island, and Heracles who appears *ex machina*. The fifth character appears after Neoptolemus has succeeded in gaining Philoctetes' confidence and is about to accompany him into Philoctetes' cave home. Neoptolemus has already duped Philoctetes into believing that he doesn't know Philoctetes' history and has informed him that he, Neoptolemus, has fallen out with Agamemnon and Menelaus.

The Chorus of Greek sailors, who are also part of the plot, suddenly see two men approaching: 'Wait, let's find out. Two men are coming, one from your ship, the other a stranger; you should find out what they have to say, then go inside' (ll. 539–41). It is the 'stranger' who speaks. He identifies himself as a trader who has heard that Phoenix and the sons of Theseus are pursuing Neoptolemus and that Odysseus is searching for someone else. Before revealing the object of Odysseus' quest this 'trader' asks Philoctetes to whisper the identity of the ragged figure beside him. Only when Neoptolemus 'introduces' Philoctetes does the trader reveal that Philoctetes is the man sought by Odysseus who wants to take him to Troy, by force if necessary, because the Greeks need him and his bow.

Even on the page, where there is the opportunity to backtrack and see who knows what and when, this is an extraordinarily complicated scenario. There is no means of knowing whether or not the Chorus are present from the opening or only enter once Odysseus has first come and gone. If they enter at the beginning, they know everything that Odysseus and Philoctetes have planned: if later, a limited version of it. This clearly affects what they say and the slant of what they say. There is the additional issue, equally unclear, of whether only the bow is needed at Troy or whether Philoctetes has to be with it. Many critics and commentators have drawn attention to these complications, summed up by David Seale in *Vision and Stagecraft in Sophocles*:

One quickly realises the range of possible combinations and contradictions. It is impossible to unravel one thread to which the audience can cling. The design is deliberately ambiguous and complex so that they may be led this way and that, never quite sure of the exact nature of the mission nor of the method which is eventually to be successful.[23]

Then there is the identity and purpose of the Trader, also translated as the 'Merchant' and as the 'Spy'. In the Oxford text he is described in the cast-list as *Skopos hōs Emporos*, 'a Spy as a Trader'. Odysseus has already said that if negotiations seem to be taking too long he will send Neoptolemus' attendant from the beginning of the play 'disguised as a sailor so as to be unrecognisable' (l. 129). The nature of the disguise may have more to do with the director and designer than the translator but it is certainly a scene that needs some accounting for. What is the point of the disguise? There is no reason why Philoctetes should recognise one of Neoptolemus' sailors, unless, perhaps, they have some sort of uniform. George Adams (1729) identified this man as 'One of the Chorus, one disguised like a Merchant sent by Ulysses'.[24] Potter (1788) offers a footnote to the effect that 'This stranger, this pretend Merchant of Peparethus, is the attendant whom Ulysses had promised to send back habited as the master of some bark (143). His tale is artful indeed.'[25] Sophocles seems to indicate as much though there has even been a suggestion that this is meant to be Odysseus in disguise, just checking that everything is going to plan.

As several critics have pointed out, the intervention of the Trader or Merchant at this point confuses the issue rather than clarifying it. Part of what he reveals is true – Odysseus is coming looking for Philoctetes; part is false – other Greek leaders are after Neoptolemus. The questions in all this are how much the translator should be giving away and what is the tone of the scene. Sophocles offers a pointer when he has the Trader hesitate before speaking in front of Philoctetes. A comparison between an eighteenth-century translation and one from the twentieth century shows the possible differences of approach:

NEO: But wherefore then
    Came not Ulysses? Did his courage fail?
SPY:[26] He, ere I left the camp, with Diomede
    On some important embassy sailed forth
    In search –
NEO: Of whom?
SPY: There was a man – but stay,
    Who is thy friend here, tell me, but speak softly.
    [*Whispering him*]
NEO: The famous Philoctetes.

SPY: Ha! begone then!
    Ask me no more – away, immediately!
PHIL: What do these dark mysterious whispers mean?
    Concern they me, my son?

                                        (ll. 868–79)
                                (Thomas Francklin, 1759)

The Penguin translation spells everything out with a liberal use of stage
directions and a kind of mock heartiness to indicate how uncomfortable
Neoptolemus is finding the whole charade:

NEO: Strange that Odysseus was not willing to sail on the errand
    himself. What kept him back? Fear, eh?
MERCHANT: No, he and the son of Tydeus are gone in pursuit of
    someone else. They were setting out as I weighed anchor.
NEO: Whom were they after?
MER: A certain person – (*pretending to spy Philoctetes for the first
    time*). But who's that yonder?
NEO: That –
MER: Speak low, sir.
NEO (*still for Philoctetes to hear*): That is none other than the famous
    Philoctetes.
MER (*feigning alarm*): Say no more, sir! Quick! Out of this country
    as soon as you can!
PHIL (*having by now dragged himself closer*): What is it son? What
    bargain is he making with you behind my back?

                                        (E. F. Watling, 1953)

While the more modern translation clearly suggests a comic touch here –
and this is a plausible reading of Sophocles' original – it does not offer
much of an alternative should the reader and/or the director decide that
Neoptolemus' moral confusion is not at this moment a subject for
mockery. Combining clarity with options may be the essential difference
between translating for actors and translating for readers.

Deception and deceit represent one of the major advances in dramatic
technique between the earliest surviving plays of Greek tragedy and the
latest. The characters of Euripides grew more clever as the lawyers,
politicians and philosophers in Athens grew more clever. The persuasive
powers of oratory, developed under the democratic system of Assembly
and Council, seem to have fed into the dramatic method of the tragedians. The wily Odysseus of *Philoctetes*, who prefers guile to persuasive
argument or brute strength, is a creature of the latter years of the fifth

century. So too are a range of evasive, slippery men and women who dominate the Euripidean stage, with various degrees of justification for the ways in which they choose to behave. Characters like Admetus, Medea, Odysseus, Hecuba, Electra, Agamemnon and Dionysus himself set out to get their own way by whatever manipulation of the truth they find most effective. Some are punished for it, more get away with it.

Euripides seems more complex because of the inevitable modern temptation to speculate on the state of mind which induces such behaviour. Agamemnon's encounters with Clytemnestra in *Iphigenia at Aulis* are a vastly different proposition for the translator from the confrontations between the two, if in rather different circumstances, in Aeschylus' *Agamemnon*. The presence of Iphigenia and of the baby Orestes in the Euripides adds new dimensions to the stage picture and tensions which are subtle. The dynamics of the scenes are led, if not dictated by, the manner in which the exchanges reveal or conceal what the various principle characters are feeling. Agamemnon has tricked his wife into bringing his daughter to Aulis on the pretence of marrying Achilles but actually to be a human sacrifice. He is bound to be found out. It is only a matter of time. When Clytemnestra confronts him, he blusters, then confesses in what most translators treat as an aside, *apōlomestha*; *prodedotai ta krupta mou* (l. 1140): 'Alas, I am trobled more and more, for all my secret councell is now openlie declared.' (Lumley, c. 1555); 'Oh heaven, I am betrayed!' (Lennox, 1759); 'Ruined! my secret out!' (Edward P. Coleridge, 1891); 'I am lost. Someone has betrayed me' (Merwin and Dimock, 1978); 'No hope now. Someone has betrayed me; it's all known.' (Vellacott, 1972); 'I'm finished . . . no chance . . . they know everything' (Taylor, 1990); 'I am lost! My secret is betrayed.' (Kovacs, 2002). I would invite the reader, even the Greekless reader, to try speaking the Greek line out loud to find the sense. *Apōlomestha* ('We are destroyed', but in a single word, short, long, short, long, short); *prodedotai ta krupta mou* ('My secret things are betrayed', but with the verb leading, three shorts and a long, then the noun, short long short, and the final possessive pronoun, the long monosyllable *mou*, 'of me'). Lennox is pithy but the melodramatic response from Coleridge may well seem to get closer than the others here, even if it reads as a stock aside from a Victorian melodrama.

Euripides specialises in characters who are renowned for their tricksy nature or have something to hide, one of the factors that makes him so at home on the contemporary stage. The three Euripidean Odysseuses of *Cyclops*, *Rhesus* and *Hecuba*, and the Sophoclean pair from *Ajax* and

Philoctetes, speak differently (if not in different accents) while demonstrating recognisable aspects of the same man. Odysseus was renowned for getting himself into awkward situations and using his craftiness to get him out again. In other words he says whatever needs to be said in order to save his skin. Much earlier Greek tragedy reveals character from what characters may say, rather than through the way in which they say it. They tend not to have speech mannerisms or a specific and privileged vocabulary. By the time of the later Sophocles and in most Euripides this kind of dramatic writing has arrived. In *Rhesus* the characters sound and behave like soldiers whether they are discussing tactics, bragging, or grumbling like the sentries on watch who feel they should have been relieved of duty:

> Where's that spy got to
> the one Hektor sent to the ships?
> I don't like to think. He's been a while.
> Ambushed, do you think and killed? We'll find out soon enough.
> I vote we wake the Lykians.
> They're fifth watch.
> We've all done our stint
>
> (ll. 556–64)

They talk like professionals about horses, booty or defensive positions. In one curious scene Athene pretends to be Aphrodite to fool Paris and speaks the way that Paris would expect Aphrodite to speak. If such complexity seems more pronounced in this play than elsewhere it may indeed be circumstantial evidence of the play's lateness: alternatively, it may be sound evidence of Euripidean finesse. Hector is blunt and less diplomatic than Aeneas. Rhesus is supercilious, Odysseus cunning enough to get himself out of trouble when he and Diomedes nearly get caught by the guards but also quick to ensure that it is Diomedes who takes the real risks.

The question for the translator is how far to translate up to and beyond fairly tenuous indications of character. What may be legitimate in *Cyclops* as a satyr play, and meant to be funny, may be inappropriate in one of the notional tragedies such as *Helen* or *Ion*. In *Helen* Menelaus arrives in Egypt at the palace of Theoclymenus after being shipwrecked. He calls out to the gatekeeper (*pulōros*), and is confronted by an old woman who tells him to go away because he is a Greek and Greeks are not welcome. He speaks Greek. But then so does she, indeed so do all the characters in the play, Greek or Egyptian. There is no indication in the text that

Menelaus is speaking in any way differently from the Porteress. His clothes are in rags, as we are told some seven times in the play, but it doesn't seem to be his costume that gives him away. No matter. Director's problem. Menelaus is offended by how she speaks to him. She threatens to throw him out *biā*, 'by force'. When he asks her to announce him to the master of the house she interrupts. He insists. She tells him again that he will be thrown out *biā* . Menelaus then has the line *aiai; ta kleina pou esti moi strateumata?* (453), literally 'Alas; where are my famous expeditions' or 'armies?'

It is difficult not to think of this as a comic sequence – 'below the dignity of tragedy' says Lennox, tartly. There is the situation. The Helen of the title never went to Troy. Hera fashioned a double, an *eidōlon empnon*, a 'breathing image' to go to Troy and cause the war while the real Helen was translated to Egypt to live chastely hoping for the return of her husband. Now Menelaus has come but has been shipwrecked along with his crew and the *eidōlon* Helen; things are not working out for him. It is like an actor's nightmare. He's lost; he has this terrible costume; and now he has been sent packing by the stage doorman, who, to add insult to injury, is a stage doorwoman. 'Alas, alas! Where are my valiant troops?' (Wodhull, 1782) gets something of the sense of frustration. Arthur Way, 130 years later (1912) falls into hopeless archaism 'Ah me! – where now my glorious war-array?'; Vellacott's 'Ah! If only I had my army here!' (1954) achieves something of the impotence of a bad dream and in the same number of words as Euripides. Lattimore (1956) 'Ah, where are all my armies now, which won such fame?' and Kovacs (2002) 'Ah me! My famous military campaigns, where are they now?' seem reluctant to treat the line as comic. Taylor (1990), writing for a television production, 'God, my glorious army, if only I had them here ... !' most clearly declares the temper of the line as he sees it.

It is in moments like this that the translator who remains neutral, far from assisting the actors, may betray them in a failure to decide the tone. Because a literal translation, such as that of Kovacs in the Loeb alongside the Greek text, serves only one of a number of possible functions, the reader is left not so much uncertain of how Euripides is treating the scene as unable to keep open the option of the ironic or comic. There are another dozen or more such moments in *Helen* alone, several of which involve Menelaus' costume, or lack of it. The translator for a particular production may need to ask for a brief from the director, or prepare more than one version of key scenes, before deciding what the scene needs to mean *on this occasion*.

There are numerous lines or passages of dialogue in Euripides which can or could be interpreted as comic. Hecuba in *Trojan Women* urges Menelaus not to forgive Helen. Menelaus ignores her plea and Hecuba responds:

> HECUBA: Don't take her on the same ship with you!
> MENELAUS: Why not? Put on weight, has she?
>
> (ll. 1049–50, McDonald, 2005)

Ion in *Ion* appears to react towards the sudden embrace of Xuthus (who has just been told by the oracle at Delphi that the first person he meets outside will be his son) as though he is being propositioned:

> XUTHUS: Let me kiss you and embrace you!
> ION: Sir, are you in your right mind, or has some god sent you mad?
> XUTHUS: I have found what I longed for. Is it mad to show my love?
> ION: Stop! Take your hands away – you'll break my wreath.
>
> (ll. 519–22, Vellacott, 1954)

Iphigenia, intent on escape from the Tauric Chersonese, persuades the gullible Thoas in *Iphigenia in Tauris* that the statue of Artemis has given her a sign and that is why she has brought it out of doors:

> IPHIGENIA: They're unclean. Your prisoners, lord.
> THOAS: Who told you?
> IPHIGENIA: The statue moved.
> THOAS: Was there an earthquake?
> IPHIGENIA: It moved by itself (*automaton*). It shut its eyes.
>
> (ll. 1163–7, McLeish, Methuen 1997)

However much the translator wants to leave options open, the one option which is unacceptable for a performance text, notwithstanding Fiona Shaw's approval of 'neutrality', is the one that fails to give the actor *any* guideline about how or why a character is saying what she is saying, or what he is saying. A Messenger speech, being pure narrative, may allow the playing as uncomprehending, distressed, angry, disgusted, shocked or in shock. A section of *stichomuthia* (line-for-line dialogue, the essence of dramatic debate in Greek tragedy), which fails to give some indication to the actors about the nature of the discussion, status, rightness or even 'cool', risks ending up as a slanging match. The Greeks were skilled in forensic dispute. Verbal conflict was a way of life.

Consistency helps. In other words what is to be translated is whole scenes, a whole play, not simply a part of it. For this the translator armed with a knowledge of source and target languages may indeed be less equipped to handle the classics than someone versed in the translation beyond translation, the translation from language into drama; it is this secondary form of translation which may on occasions sacrifice an aspect of the original to the overall shape of the play. This has less to do with subtext than with supertext.

There are intriguing questions of interpretation raised in most Euripides plays, part of their continuing fascination. In *Electra*, the issue of Orestes' reluctance to inform his sister that he happens to be her brother is central to the whole first half of the play, arguably to all of it. In *Phoenician Women* Jocasta is more affectionate to Polyneices, her younger son who has been living in exile, than she is to his elder brother Eteocles. But how much more affectionate? It is the translator's choice. Euripides' images are not necessarily more emotional than those of Aeschylus or Sophocles; they seem more wide-ranging and sympathetic to today's audiences. Such modernity was part of what intrigued and dismayed his original audiences. When Orestes has murdered his mother in *Orestes* Tyndareos wants to know why he failed to invoke the law of the land. Orestes and Pylades appear before the *ekklētoi*, those who have the final decision in affairs of state, as did members of the *ekklēsia* in Euripides' Athens. This is a society that has means of dealing with criminal behaviour as did the Athenians of the time when the play was written. All the Greek tragedians place their audience in just such a stage world as Shakespeare creates where the Egypt of Cleopatra, or the Athens of Timon and Theseus, are presented in whatever Renaissance socio-cultural framework the playwright has devised. So part of the dilemma for the translator is in finding the original stage culture, not the historical culture, and seeing how *that* may be transformed into something which the director can renew in a contemporary stage culture. It may be a useful working method for the translator who aims at translation for publication, as do most of those who translate classical texts.[27]

The nature of a Euripides play is that it does create echoes of the everyday life of the very first audience and this immediacy transmits itself in how the characters speak and react. Translating that immediacy is nothing if not seductive. In a review of *Agamemnon's Children*, a composite of *Electra*, *Orestes* and *Iphigenia in Tauris* performed at the Gate Theatre in 1995, Tabard, an anonymous columnist for *The Stage*, welcomed Kenneth McLeish's translation as 'dramatic, to the point and

exceptionally witty'.[28] Michael Coveney in *The Observer* suggested that
'Kenneth McLeish's spring-heeled, colloquial translation reaffirms Euripides as a thoroughly modern author.'[29] In that translation the Farmer
who is married to Electra says at one point:

> As soon as it's light, I'll harness the oxen,
> Get on with the harrowing.
> Fine words butter no parsnips
> It's honest toil that makes an honest penny
>   (ll. 78–81)

Orestes (l. 370) asserts that 'Moral pigmies can breed giants', but advises
wariness of posers in public life who turn out to be 'pricked balloons'
(l. 389).

Strictly speaking these are anachronisms, but why should that be significant or unwelcome? The issue is how far translators may want to
distance themselves from the original playwright, and how far they may
impose or personalise the translation. This can be better considered in the
next chapter by a more detailed study relating to *Medea* but one example
from *Bacchae* may be helpful. In a play that is a comprehensive study of
illusion and of the theatre as illusion, Dionysus, incognito, persuades
Pentheus to dress as a woman. Dionysus throughout uses subtext or
double entendre and engages the audience in an act of complicity, if not
conspiracy. He wins the debate, as even Pentheus can see, when he
accuses him of *sophismatōn kakōn* (l. 489), 'disgusting sophistry'. Once
Pentheus has fallen under his mesmeric influence and 'lost his reason'
Dionysus taunts him:

> DIONYSOS: *pheromenos hēxeis . . .*
> PENTHEUS: *habrotēt' emēn legeis.*
> DIONYSOS: *en chersi mētros.*
> PENTHEUS: *kai truphan m'anagkaseis.*
> DIONYSOS: *truphas ge toiasd'.*
> PENTHEUS: *axiōn men haptomai.*
>   (ll. 967–9)

Literal translation: D: You will come, carried . . . / P: You speak of splendour. /
D: in your mother's arms. / P: You force luxury on me. / D: Such luxuries. / P:
Deserving, then, I take them.

The ironies mount crowned by the word *truphan*, which Dionysos
returns to Pentheus in the plural *truphas*.

Most of the earlier translators were uncomfortable with this play, this scene above all others. Lennox saw the comedy all too well but wondered 'How was it possible for Pagans to endure such a representation?' Dean Milman's translation (1865) offers D: Aloft shalt thou be borne / P: O the soft carriage! / D: In thy mother's hands. / P: Wilt make me thus luxurious? / D: Strange luxury, indeed! / P: 'Tis my desert. Murray (1906) has D: Thou shalt be borne on high! / P: That were like pride! / D: Thy mother's hands shall share thy carrying. / P: Nay; I need not such soft care! / D: So soft? / P: Whate'r it be, I have earned it well![30]

Several recent translators have turned the *truphan/truphas* exchange into a pun: 'You will spoil me.' / 'I mean to spoil you.' / 'I go to my reward.' (Chicago); 'You insist that I be spoiled.' / 'One kind of spoiling.' / 'Yet I win what I deserve.' (Penguin); 'She'll spoil me so.' / 'Spoiled you shall be.' / 'My destiny!' (Hern); 'You are determined actually to spoil me.' / 'Yes, spoil you after my fashion.' / 'It's only what I deserve.' (new Loeb). Methuen ignores the repetition in favour of 'You will ruin me.' / 'You could say that.' / 'Not that I don't deserve it.' In Aris and Phillips 'You will compel me to be pampered even.' / 'Pampering in my fashion.' / 'I am taking hold of what I deserve.' picks up the repetition though the double meaning is less effective. Two others are more verbose: 'You'll pamper me to pieces. You'll make me tender by force.' / 'I will indeed.' / 'I will have what I deserve.' (Hackett) and 'You'll make me go all to pieces.' / 'I'd have it no other way.' / 'Then I'll have what I deserve.' (Applause Books).

It is a comic moment, but one to freeze the blood, as Lennox perceived. Which of the above best creates the 'atmosphere of the words' will be a matter of personal choice. Actors know a punch line when they see one and an exit line when they see one. Here we have both. Often it seems, it is in their entrance and exit lines that translators best show their merit.

CHAPTER 7

Euripides' Medea and Alcestis: From Sex to Sentiment

We need an eye which can see the past in its place with its definite
differences from the present, and yet so lively that it shall be present
to us at the present.

(T. S. Eliot, *Selected Essays*, 1932)

The stage history of Medea has been charted in detail in *Medea in Performance* where the variations on the myth in opera, on film and on the
public stage have been meticulously detailed.[1] There and elsewhere Edith
Hall, Fiona Macintosh and Marianne McDonald have traced the manner
in which the portrayal of Medea reflects the social changes of the
seventeenth, eighteenth, nineteenth and twentieth centuries, Macintosh
pointing in particular to the significance of the Divorce and Matrimonial
Causes Act of 1857.[2] Lorna Hardwick in her *Translating Words, Translating Cultures* devotes a central chapter to 'Reverence and subversion in
nineteenth-century translation' and homes in on Greek tragedy in her
'Theatres of the mind: Greek tragedy in women's writing in English in
the nineteenth century'.[3]

It seems hardly coincidental that there were six translations of *Medea*
published in the ten years following the passing of the Divorce Act of
1857, with Augusta Webster's to follow in 1868. As influential in the
enthusiasm for the theme was the taste for sensation literature with the act
of infanticide claiming a classical pedigree. Much of the ground that
might be covered in a chapter devoted to the translation of Euripides'
Medea has already been treated. For this reason, and because so much
more Euripides survives, this case study will look not only at *Medea* but
also at *Alcestis*, another early play amongst the survivors, but one whose
tone and mood have been hotly debated. As it happens, the second half of
the nineteenth century saw more translations of *Alcestis* than of *Medea*, a
case, perhaps, of 'Return of the paragon'.

Medea, the character, has turned up over the years in at least fifty-three operas (McDonald, *Sing Sorrow*, 2001); in several comic versions and in all sorts of guises and manifestations from George Buchanan to Dario Fo, never mind in several novels from Henry Treece to Christa Wolf to Robert Holdstock.[4] The original play, the baby in all this bathwater, hasn't been washed down the plughole – there have been several new translations of the Euripides in English in the last fifteen years – but it has from time to time got lost among the rubber ducks. What is special about Euripides' *Medea* is its malleability. A mother who willingly murders her children can still affront the sensibilities in a theatre which has become accustomed to Sarah Kane, Neil Lebute and Martin McDonagh. There are several scenes and sequences where the sheer modernity of the situation invites dialogue, if not of the school of Kane and McDonagh, at least of the contemporary world. One simple example stands out.

Medea has two scenes with Jason in the Euripides play. In the first she voices her fury for his betrayal and desertion; in the second she is apparently submissive, lulling him into a false sense of security so that she can ensure her lethal present is delivered to Jason's new wife. When Jason first appears it is after her scene with Creon where she discovers the extent of the king's animosity, but has won from him the concession of one day before she must go into exile. She and Jason have here fewer than 200 lines. Jason vents his anger on her for her condemnation of the royal family but wants to secure the future for his two sons. Medea reacts with hostility claiming that his success as a hero is all due to her, her assault moving from bitterness to sarcasm. Jason responds coolly, and apparently rationally, about the advantages to all of them from his new marriage. The long speeches give way to more compact dialogue. Jason's exasperation leads to Medea's final lines before he leaves. Of special interest here is a single word. Jason's assertion that Medea will make things worse if she rejects her friends is greeted by her *chōrei*, followed by three complete lines before Jason exits. *Chōrei* has been variously translated as 'Away!'; 'Go'; 'Go in'; 'Be on your way!'; 'Go quickly' (in Robinson Jeffers' extremely free but popular 1946 version for Judith Anderson); 'Begone' (after a stage direction which indicates that he has already left); 'Off with you!'; 'Just go away, Jason'; and, rather improbably in one nineteenth-century text 'Go away, please'. All these are 'translations'. Brendan Kennelly in his *Euripides' Medea: A New Version* opts for 'Get out of my sight'[5]; Liz Lochhead 'after Euripides' has
'Go on   you're hot for her   go mount the cow'.[6]
[layout as in the published text]

Now *chōrei* is an imperative and it does mean 'Go'. It is also a disyllable dismissal, a snarl, an expletive. It is an explosive ejaculation of impotence and fury. There is an argument for its being translated today as 'Fuck off!', not for the term's obscenity – direct sexual abuse is seldom part of the Greek vocabulary – but for its demonstration of extreme emotion.[7] Euripides is a playwright of passion and none of his plays is more passionate than *Medea*.

Medea's first words to Jason are *ō pagkakiste*, variously translated in the eighteenth century as 'Thou worst of villains'; in the nineteenth as 'Thou craven villain'; in the twentieth as 'Caitiff of caitiffs', 'O coward in every way', 'O worst of the very worst', 'You vile coward', 'Who could be worse than you?', 'Unutterably evil man', 'You vile worm, maggot on the rotting carcass of your vows',[8] 'You evil creature', 'You filthy coward', 'Vilest of knaves' (1994!); and in the twenty-first as 'You bastard! Coward!'

The same extreme is used by Sophocles' Creon of his son Haemon, in *Antigone*:

CREON: He sides with a woman, apparently.
HAEMON: If that's what you are, a woman. I'm on your side.
CREON: *ō pagkakiste*. Right to cross your father, is it?
(ll. 740–2)

The eighteenth century's 'Vile youth'; the nineteenth's 'Shameless'; the twentieth's 'Oh reprobate', 'So', 'Outrageous', 'Villain', and even 'You damned, impertinent devil', lack the enthusiasm for invective in Sophocles that Euripides inspires. The word *pagkakiste* is a double superlative, *pan* 'all', *kakistos* the natural superlative of *kakos* 'bad'. Medea uses *pagkakōs*, 'all-badly' when she asks the Messenger to describe the death of the Princess and of Creon: 'How were they killed? I'll enjoy it twice as much if they died *pagkakōs*' (ll. 1134–5). There is a viciousness here that is difficult to resist.

The question for the contemporary translator is how far to come to meet this violent world. Different ages appropriate Euripides and probably have done ever since he died. If he has the gift of seeming 'modern' to every age, then, every age has an argument for renewing him in its own vernacular, far more so than would be true for Aeschylus or Sophocles. The act of translation here may simply be a matter of cultural adjustment as though Euripides were our contemporary and that the prime search is for cultural substitutes.

Translation of a contemporary play written in English into a host language tends to involve this sort of cultural adjustment anyway, of the sort that Plautus and Terence brought to their treatment of the Greek world. The outcome for them was a cunning mix of Greek and Latin cultures parading behaviour which would have been unacceptable in the host society, but licensed by collusion with the guest audience. So when the slave Olympio in Richard Beacham's translation of Plautus' *Casina* scorns his master's life with his wife as 'day and night with a baying bloodhound' (l. 380), or Kenneth McLeish's soldier Thraso in Terence's *Eunuch* boasts of seeing off someone poking fun at him with ' "Look sonny", I said "I've heard of putting all my eggs in one basket, but you seem to be crossing your bridges before you come to 'em" '(ll. 424–5), the associations have been lifted wholesale into the modern context.[9] Comedy is different from tragedy but it has already been suggested that much late Euripides is on the cusp and can tolerate cultural ambiguity.

The possibility that the wrong word may be the right word is, of course, the thin end of the wedge, and is used as an *apologia* by those who believe that a knowledge of the source language is immaterial when translating Greek tragedy or comedy.[10] Nevertheless, many translators have consciously sought to use an anachronistic word because the situation invites it. The Tutor in the opening scene of *Medea* tells the Nurse of his concern for Medea's future because of the gossip he has overheard in the town from the old men (*palaiteroi*) as he approached the *pessous* (l. 68). *Pessos* is the Greek for an oval disk used in a game; or the game itself, which Liddell and Scott describe as like draughts or backgammon; or, as here, the place where the game is played. Translations include 'the gaming tables', 'backgammon', 'draughts', rather bizarrely, 'the old stone seats' and 'by the laundry-stones', 'dominoes' and 'dice', this last in Potter (1781), Wodhull (1782) and McLeish (1994).

Eight lines later the same character reflects on marital unfaithfulness with *palaia kainōn leipetai kēdeumatōn*, an awkward phrase which reads like an aphorism and means literally 'old things are left for new marriage-alliances'.[11] Wodhull here has 'By new connections are all former ties dissolved'; McLeish 'Old loves are dropped when new ones come'. Murray turned it into a maxim 'Old love burneth low / When new love burns, men say'. What a mouthful compared with three nineteenth-century versions from a period that loved its moral homily, 'Old ties are now outrun by newer loves' (Lee, 1841); 'Former ties are disregarded for the new' (Mongan, 1865); 'Old ties give way to new' (Coleridge, 1891): or one recent one, the Methuen (2000) 'New shoes run quicker than old'.

Then there are the references to sex, handled with decorum by Aeschylus and Sophocles even when dealing with adultery and incest.

This was nothing to do with audience squeamishness as any reading of Aristophanes will testify. No satyr play survives apart from one Euripides where who did what to Helen after the Trojan War, and how often, is about all that interests the chorus of satyrs. Aeschylus did have the reputation for writing filthier satyr plays than anyone, so this restraint should be put down to what is appropriate to the occasion. The stage Aeschylus of *Frogs* is particularly incensed by Euripides' introduction of dissolute women into his plays and it seems to have been the graphic expression by Phaedra of her lust for her stepson that led to the suppression of the first *Hippolytus*. The difference in *Medea* is that *Medea* is not about sex in the same way as *Hippolytus* is about sex, though Jason assumes that it is. It is certainly not a subject that is hidden or taboo within the play. Medea raises it in her very first on-stage speech when she laments the lot of women who have to buy a husband and then cannot divorce him. Other aspects of marriage are raised by Euripides and, unsurprisingly, treated sedately by E. P. Coleridge (1891) as:

Next must the wife, coming as she does to ways and customs new, since she hath not learned the custom in her home, have a diviner's eye to see how best to treat the partner of her life. (ll. 238–40)

In McLeish this has become the racier:

> Set down with strangers, with ways and laws
> She never knew at home, a wife must learn
> Every trick she can to please the man
> Whose bed she shares.

When Jason tries to justify his new marriage he turns on Medea, in McLeish:

> Oh, women are all alike:
> If they're happy in bed, they're happy everywhere.
> If that goes wrong, then offer them the Moon,
> They throw it at your head. Sex!
> We need another way to get us sons. No women then –
> That way all human misery would end.
>
> (ll. 569–75)

This is pretty unequivocal, though the 'Moon' metaphor may seem uncomfortable and is not in the original. The speech has been a challenge to translators of other times. Most seem to have opted for something so tortuous that the sense disappears. Murray, at his most quaint:

> Not thine own self would say it, couldst thou still
> One hour thy jealous flesh. − 'Tis ever so!
> Who looks for more in women? When the flow
> Of love runs plain, why, all the world is fair:
> But, once there fall some ill chance anywhere
> To baulk that thirst, down in swift hate are trod
> Men's dearest aims and noblest. Would to God
> We mortals by some other seed could raise
> Our fruits, and no blind women block our ways!
> Then had there been no curse to wreck mankind.

If, verbose as it is, this makes it sound as though Jason has a problem not with his wife but with his allotment, it is a marginal improvement on the earlier Edwards (1821):

By no means would'st thou say so, if thy bed did not gall thee. But ye women have come to that-way-of-thinking, that if your bed be safe, ye imagine ye have everything.

or Lee (1841):

> Ah! thoud'st confess,
> Did not this marriage sting thee. Such a pass
> Hath woman reach'd, that if her spouse be true,
> She smiles content; but if misfortune touch
> Her jealousy, she scowls in blinded rage
> In wisdom, prudence, magnanimity.

It could hardly be worse than Way (1912):

> But ye − ye women − so unreasoning are
> That wedlock-rights untrespassed-on, all's well;
> But if once your sole tenure be infringed,
> With the best, fairest lot are ye at feud
> Most bitter.

By the middle of the twentieth century it was less necessary to be so coy. Rex Warner (1944) was straightforward, if dull:

> But you women have got into such a state of mind
> That, if your life at night is good, you think you have

Everything; but if in that quarter things go wrong,
You will consider your best and truest interests
Most hateful.

Vellacott (1963) was one of the first to use the word 'sex' and offered a mix of the frank and the clumsy:

Even you would approve
If you could govern your sex-jealousy. But you women
Have reached a state where, if all's well with your sex-life,
You've everything you wish for; but when *that* goes wrong.
At once all that is best and noblest turns to gall.

The Greek uses two words here implying 'sex', both literally 'bed', *lechos*, (a word also used for 'wife') and *eunē*, but that is the extent of the marital and extra-marital vocabulary.

At least, *pace* Murray, it is clear what Jason is on about. It is less obvious in the Aegeus scene where the translator is faced with an important decision over how seriously the character is to be taken. Aegeus' convenient arrival, just at the moment when Medea is running out of options to secure her escape, was put down to poor dramaturgy by Aristotle who called it *alogon*, 'irrational', though probably not by anyone with a clear idea of the play's shape and structure. Aegeus does turn up opportunely, but, notwithstanding the largely spurious 'Unities' for which Aristotle is blamed, Greek tragedy's narrative depends on stage time, rather than the sun's. Aegeus is an ambivalent figure. Already in the play Medea has been seen to be a consummate actress who is adept at working out how to manipulate those whose assistance she requires. Her servants, the Chorus, Creon, are all won round to doing what she wants: as is Aegeus and later will be Jason.

Aegeus is king of Athens and, according to the myth, Medea will later have a child or children by him. He reaches Corinth on his way from Delphi where he has been inquiring about his childlessness. Medea asks him whether he has a wife. The exchange is in *stichomuthia*, Medea saying, in a literal translation:

MEDEA: By the gods, you have stretched your life so far, childless?
AEGEUS: We are childless, by the fate (*tuchē*) of some (*daimōn*) deity.
MEDEA: With a wife, or inexperienced of the bed (*lechos*)?
AEGEUS: We are not unlinked in a marriage of the bed.
MEDEA: What then did Phoebus say about children for you?

AEGEUS: Words too wise for a man to understand.
MEDEA: Is it right for us to know the oracle of a god?
AEGEUS: Yes, since there is need of a clever mind.
MEDEA: What then did he prophesy? Tell me, if you think it right to
    hear.
AEGEUS: 'Do not loose the wineskin's projecting foot.'
MEDEA: Before doing what or reaching what land?
AEGEUS: Before I reach my ancestral hearth.

                                                              (ll. 670–81)

This is a peculiar exchange, not least for its comic potential. Is Medea really asking the King of Athens if he doesn't know how to do it? Enigmatic oracles were not unusual but this one is more than commonly weird. What does it mean? That Aegeus should quit drinking? Or not have sex until he gets home? Aegeus certainly doesn't know. In fact he has stopped in at Corinth on his way to consult one of his friends who is cleverer than he is. Medea doesn't tell him what she thinks the oracle is referring to. She does tell him she can make him a father. And so she extracts from him an oath of protection and, as soon as it is given, packs him off unceremoniously, possibly straight to Athens. She has got what she wants from him.

This oracular utterance which is too clever for Aegeus has proved uncomfortable for translators too. For the most part the older the translation the more easily has the line been absorbed. 'The projected foot / Thou of the vessel must not dare to loose' sounds convoluted in Wodhull and there is no trace of humour about it. Edwards' 'That I must not loose the bladder's projected foot', apart from offering a possible medical dimension to Aegeus' little difficulty, supplies no clarification. Lee sets up the scene:

MEDEA: What said the power? Speak if the god permit.
AEGEUS: No, such a crafty mind might aid me know.

But then Lee cut the 'wineskin' lines without explanation, finding them, perhaps, too near the knuckle. Jebb offered: 'He bade me "not loose the wineskin's pendent neck"'. Murray took off on a completely new tack with 'Not to spill life's wine nor seek for more . . . / Until? / Until I tread the hearthskin of my sires of yore' which out-Apollo's Apollo and no mistake. Townsend (1966) certainly saw the scene as comic and down-graded the oracle to 'Something about not opening my wineskin'. Wilner (1998) declared she knows what it is all about with 'Do not untie the

wineskin's long, extended spout.' Kennelly included the exchange and
came up with a beautifully neat 'I was advised not to let my best wine
flow ... Until I returned in safety to my home.' Kennelly's Aegeus is a
simple man, gullible but sincere.

Perhaps it is in a scene like this where the translator may legitimately
look to the brief before making decisions. If the translation is for production then the director's and/or actor's interpretation of Aegeus does
allow for translation up to that interpretation. As we have seen above, and
in the previous chapter, there are other such scenes in Euripides where a
single line has consequences for the translation of a whole series of lines.
One of these relates most closely to the manner in which Medea has
reverberated over the centuries, her demonisation as an infanticide, never
mind as a regicide, often soft-pedalled or justified when a woman's act of
desperation may seem the result of male oppression. In the Euripides she
reflects the plight of the aging wife and of the foreigner. During the first
of the two scenes with Jason, Medea makes a crucial comment on her
relationship with her husband and her status in Greece.

In Charlotte Lennox's digest of 1759, she translated no more than a
selection of speeches, including the Messenger's description of the death
of Creon and his daughter, though quoting substantially from Brumoy's
French. She did include Medea's reaction to Jason's claim that he was
acting in her interest, *ou touto s'eichen, alla barbaron lechos / pros gēras ouk
eudoxon exebaine soi* (ll. 591–2). Lennox offered the first rendering in
English of Medea's reply: 'my interest was not thy motive; thou despisest
a foreign wife, and one who is in the decline of age'.[12] Wodhull in the first
full published translation, twenty-three years later in 1782, had a different
emphasis: 'Thy real motive was not what thou sayest, / But a Barbarian
wife, in *thy* old age [my italics], / Might have appeared to tarnish thy
renown.' Lee (1841) raised the question of Jason's honour in the most
stilted of language 'That stay thee! No, 'Twas I, a foreign spouse /
Threat'ning dishonour to thy hoary hairs.' Coleridge (1891) offered a
slightly different reaction: 'but thine eye was turned towards old age, and
a foreign wife began to appear discreditable to thee'. Murray got completely carried away and vouchsafed 'Thine old barbarian bride, / The dog
out of the East who loved thee sore, / She grew grey-haired, she served thy
pride no more', which must have gone down really well with the not-that-
old Sybil Thorndike who played the role for him. Amongst recent
translations the elliptical 'you're getting old. / Your "foreigner" embar-
rasses you' (Hern, 1994), Medea's sudden revelation in 'That's not it, is it?
As time went on / You found it inconvenient to have a foreign wife'

(Methuen, 2000), and the sarcastic 'You thought, / As you grew older, it didn't look quite right / To have a foreign wife' (Cambridge, 2000), all seem more subtle than the Chandler (1966) which ignores the age issue in favour of relying on the race card: 'Why not admit you didn't like the thought of being married to someone of my race, / To a barbarian, to a non-Greek?'

If the Victorians seemed fascinated by the dangerous and subversive Medea at a time when their own womenfolk were asserting a new authority, they were also quick to resurrect an alternative wife in the 'ideal' of Alcestis who died that her husband might live.[13] Euripides' earliest surviving play, *Alcestis*, is built around King Admetus and the boon offered by Apollo that, when his time comes to die, he can offer Death a substitute. Alcestis agrees to die instead of her husband. When Heracles arrives soon after her death, Admetus refuses to admit to Heracles that it is his wife who has died. The reason that he does lies somewhere in the territory between shame, pride and not wanting to interfere with his reputation as a good host. When Heracles finds out about Alcestis and brings her back from her grave after wrestling Death himself, he tricks Admetus by offering him a veiled woman, a benevolent subterfuge that leads to her restoration in the family home.

Medea may come down to the partitioning of sympathies between the wronged wife and the obtuse husband. *Alcestis* is something milder, but more contentious. Alcestis acquiesces in her own death, not without some recrimination, and demands an absolute promise that Admetus will never remarry and subject her children to a stepmother. Admetus' inability to find any alternative to Alcestis to die on his behalf is subjected to uncomfortable scrutiny, literally over her dead body. When his father Pheres comes to the funeral to pay his respects he is sent away with a flea in his ear, though not before inflicting some bites of his own. Heracles, when he discovers how he has been misled over Alcestis' death, is dismayed about the way his friend has behaved: as indeed are the Chorus of local townsmen and the servants of the household.

The play may be the earliest Euripides that survives (438) but it is one of the most enigmatic, neither tragedy nor satyr – it was apparently performed in the fourth slot usually reserved for the satyr play – and with several awkward questions asked about the nature and execution of Apollo's gift of a second life. The play has the ambivalence and 'hospitable vagueness', to use Jonathan Miller's term, of a Shakespeare, with Euripides seeming to anticipate the mood of the late romances.[14] The translation issue is the familiar one of the extent to which the family relationships and the customs of hospitality should follow a fifth-century BC Greek or a twenty-first century AD social code. Here it is exaggerated by the world of moral ambiguity that Euripides invokes. Euripides uses as a dramatic method the recreation of a mythical story within the moral structure of his own time, as so often does Shakespeare. In the Athens of 438 there must have been quite enough members of the audience to ask the tricky questions about Admetus' state of mind when asking all these people to die on his behalf without finding anyone who would, except his wife; who would think that lying to an old friend about the death of your wife is a worse infringement of hospitality than allowing him to stay believing nothing important has happened to the family; who would wonder how much Admetus deserves Alcestis back. How can we know this? Because such questions are specifically asked by his family, by the Chorus, by servants and, most of all, by Heracles. And yet – translator's problem, as ever – whose morality are we subjecting to scrutiny, that of the characters, of the first audience, of today's audience?[15]

Alcestis is one of those plays which has taken on different aspects in different ages. Never popular in Roman times – the Romans, it might be thought, would have little notion of what all the fuss was about – it had its heyday in the latter part of the nineteenth century and was the first production performed in the Greek Theatre at Bradfield School in 1881, though in Greek, not English. There had been numerous operatic versions since the sixteenth century, but the Euripides returned to the consciousness of readers as one of the earliest of Greek dramas to be turned into English. It is one of only a few that Charlotte Lennox found in the *Théâtre des Grecs* and that she translated in its entirety.[16] Lennox/ Brumoy had no doubt about its nature and in a brief introduction stated:

The design of this tragedy is to shew, that conjugal love, and a due regard to hospitality, are never unrewarded. Both these virtues were held sacred among the Greeks, and formed the general basis of their government; as the respect of children for their parents does among the Chinese.

The issue of father dying for son clearly exercised Brumoy who was uncomfortable with the Pheres exchange more than with anything else and could only invite the reader to remember that:

this polished Greece, whose taste is incontestible by its beautiful antiquities, was so deficient in judgement, as to admire what was absurd and ridiculous ... If therefore we find ourselves shocked by any passage in this play, we must allow that either Euripides should have reformed his ideas to please us, or that we should change ours to relish him.[17]

In the extraordinary scene over the corpse of Alcestis when Admetus refuses to have his father mourn his daughter-in-law because he refused to die instead, part of the Lennox exchange goes as follows:

> PHERES: How! Darest thou load a guiltless father with horrible imprecations!
> ADMETUS: No; I on the contrary subscribe to thy own wishes. Do'st thou most desire a long train of years?
> PHERES: This is thy wish rather, and this corps too plainly proves it.
> ADMETUS: This corps proclaims thy baseness.
> PHERES: At least, it cannot proclaim that I sacrificed this victim for myself.
> ADMETUS: Ah, that thou in thy turn needed the sacrifice of a son's life to save thee.
> PHERES: Do thou act wiser, and take one wife after another to multiply thy years.[18]

Potter picked up on the last line as 'Wed many wives that more may die for thee', Greek: *mnēsteue pollas, ōs thanōsi pleiones* (l. 720). Euripides here again has found a short phrase, five words only, the essence of dramatic dialogue. The fourteen words of Lennox were never intended as a spoken line but without some sense of verbal tennis even on the page the dramatic exchange is stone dead. Potter is an improvement, though the line limps to a close: as does Coleridge with 'Woo many wives, that there may be the more to die.' Murray, in verse, came up with 'Woo more wives that more may die', but finding himself three syllables short of a pentameter, added at the beginning an utterly meaningless 'Go forward'. Way's 'Woo many women that the more may die' was an improvement, Aldington's 'Woo many women that more may die for you' (1930) hardly cuts to the quick, but the deficiency lies to a great extent with the English language. 'Woo', 'wed', 'court' are weak monosyllables: 'marry' as in 'Marry many women so that more may die' (Routledge) cannot get round the two short syllables to start the line, which is rather like the golfer with a bogey at the first. The Penguin is something of an improvement with 'Marry wife after wife, let them all die for you' while the blunt Methuen offers 'The more you marry, the more you can kill off.'

What even the weaker translations cannot disguise is that this is one of Euripides' best slanging matches, the equal, perhaps to that between

Andromache and Hermione in *Andromache*. The stage picture and the circumstances of the funeral procession contribute to the scene's theatricality, but the possible comic dimension arises from Pheres being able to say to Admetus what the audience have been thinking but that other characters can only hint at. This is not so much interpretation as acknowledgement of the direction in which the playwright is pulling the plot. The priority for the translator is not to decide whose side to be on, father's or son's, but to make it a battle royal.

Pheres appears in only the one scene, a crucial one for deciding who and what the play is about, but not the only feature of *Alcestis* to engage the translator. Death is personified and, uniquely for extant Greek drama, appears in a prologue debating with Apollo. This is a curious exposition where the relative power of the two deities is difficult to gauge, not least when Apollo, having apparently lost the debate, reveals that 'someone' will come [Heracles] and provide a happy ending. Heracles himself is seen as drunken buffoon and heroic saviour in successive scenes. Alcestis, who has volunteered to die on behalf of her husband, has an unusual deathbed scene. The translator is faced with a play which either demonstrates attitudes from Euripides' time which are alien, though no more alien, perhaps, than those to be found in *Taming of the Shrew* or *The Merchant of Venice*: or it is a play where the playwright at his iconoclastic best is using myth to investigate male attitudes and the nature of family relationships in a manner that still reverberates. The problem is, then, not so far removed from that of *Medea*, each play reflecting its own time, but uncomfortable for any audience from any period.

It is the nature of the relationship between husband and wife that has most intrigued interpreters. Brumoy, via Lennox, concluded his translation with a series of 'observations upon the tragedy of *Alcestis*'. A number of factors made him uneasy, high among them the 'coarsness of the persons' and the 'little tinct of familiarity ... which, in our eye, has more of comic airiness than tragic dignity'. Brumoy, brought up on the 'tragic dignity' of Racine and Corneille cannot conceive of this being a tragicomedy, 'a wildness of design unknown to the ancients'. The result is that he is forced to defend Admetus as being unable to circumvent avoiding death, a notion to which Pheres does not subscribe. As for the encounter between father and son:

If there are things in this scene shocking to the reason of any age whatever, so sensible and polite a people as the Greeks would not have approved them. But, if the Greeks found nothing to condemn in those passages which appear indecent and horrible to us, it follows, that they are not altogether such as we imagine them to be: in a word their ideas in this respect were not the same as ours are now.[19]

Brumoy simply cannot accept that Admetus should have invited other members of his family to die for him. Indeed he apologises for him at every turn. Everyone is to blame rather than Admetus, it being Heracles' (here Hercules') fault for not discovering that it is Alcestis who has died. He translates accordingly.

There is an important matter of dramatic emphasis here which does relate to the structure of Greek society and modern society, and to the questions of kinship which underpin so many tragedies and comedies. Medea kills her children because in her perception of the world in which she lives the father/son bond is the most significant and its fracture the most painful she can inflict. In *Hippolytus* it is possible to treat the death of Phaedra as an act whose tragic significance at the time of the first production would have been less for her situation than as a catalyst for Theseus causing the death of his son. Sophocles' *Women of Trachis* can be read in a similar way, and his *Antigone*. Menander's *The Woman from Samos* investigates the relationship of father and son over and against that between the father and the woman he loves and lives with. Brumoy's main concerns over *Alcestis* are less to do with Admetus and Alcestis than Admetus and Pheres. From the nineteenth century onwards such an approach ceased to be acceptable. When the plays of Euripides returned to the stage it was easy enough for most of them to become vehicles for female star actors rather than male.

For the translator in any period, it may be argued, the concern is not so much to unearth the emotional balance of the original play in its own time as to consider the possibilities afforded within the original structure and promote those which will provide the strongest dramatic effect on the page, or the stage of the new age. This would at least account for the enthusiasm for wholesale rewriting, not of the myths which have per-ennial statements to decode, but of the plays themselves if they prove to say something that the author of a 'version' may not want them to say. The tendency today may be to domesticate tragedy. But if this is a process, it is a process which Euripides began. *Alcestis* can be viewed (and translated) as a story about marriage, or as a story about *a* marriage. It can equally be a story about family upheaval where a father's best intentions are almost undermined by mistrust. It is still a fable and little purpose is served by scrutinising the mechanics whereby, for example, Death knows who the substitute for Admetus is, or Heracles how to defeat him.[20] But emotionally Euripides' conscious modernism invites social and linguistic transmission into other times in a way that Aeschylus, Sophocles and Aristophanes do not.

All of which makes *Alcestis* a good translator's test alongside *Medea*, the 'good' wife and the 'bad'. Alcestis is introduced in detail before she appears. The Chorus who enter immediately after the prologue think she is 'to me and to all people the best (*aristē*) wife a man ever had' (ll. 82–4). The Chorus have arrived, uncertain what is happening and a messenger in the form of a Maidservant makes an early entry to enlighten them. Alcestis' sacrifice is adjudged the best possible way of honouring her husband, but she is not going without regret. The domestic detail of her farewell to house and children offers no masking of her passionate distress. This is no Iphigenia or Evadne, welcoming death with equanimity, for all her 'wasting with disease'. She is now carried in accompanied by her husband and their two children. This rare family scene lasts for some 160 lines (233–393) during which she alternates lyric speech with iambics from Admetus, as she 'sees' Charon's boat and winged Hades coming for her. When Admetus finally joins in her lyrics, she moves abruptly into iambics in a rational and sustained forty-five lines during which she outlines her feelings about her death and what she wants to happen to the children. These dying remarks are directed less to Admetus as a loved and loving husband, than at Admetus as widower-in-waiting. After exacting his promise never to remarry she fades into death in stichomythic dialogue with her husband.

The extent of her lucidity, and concern for her family rather than for her husband, are differently evaluated in different periods. Lennox/Brumoy, in strict prose throughout, offers a tender deathbed scene. The editing in otherwise overlong passages is marked by four dots:

> ADMETUS: Yield not to thy weakness, dear Alcestis; oh do not, do not leave me. Implore the Gods for mercy; they can succour us . . . .
>
> Oh, my Alcestis, into what gulph of miseries are we fallen?
> ALCESTIS: Ah, Admetus, they drag me, they drag me to the infernal court. It is Pluto himself who hovers over me – he fixes his horrid looks upon me . . .
> ADMETUS: Good heaven! why, why am I forced to hear these words? They tear my heart: a thousand deaths are not so cruel! Oh, Alcestis! I conjure thee, in the name of the Gods, do not abandon me, abandon not thyself. Thy Admetus dies, if thou

diest: my life is in thy hands. Oh, my Alcestis, live, live and
preserve thy husband.[21]

(ll. 250–79)

These delicate sentiments, which would not have seemed out of place in
Mrs Henry Wood and are echoed in her contemporaries, translators
such as Nash, Nevins and Lennard, are less obvious in the Greek. In
Euripides husband and wife never address one another by name
throughout the sequence quoted above. Admetus once calls her *talaina*
('poor woman'). Alcestis does address the light of the sun, the clouds,
the land where she lives, her house and *unmarried* bed in Iolcos,
Charon, Hades, her attendants (probably) and her children, especially
the daughter: but her husband not once. Wife and husband can hardly
be described as conversing with one another at all, Alcestis singing, if as
is generally believed lyric metre implies musical accompaniment,
Admetus 'speaking' until his final lines. It is only when she becomes
practical and introduces family business that she addresses her husband.
There may, of course, be no great significance in this, but Brumoy or
Lennox, or both, knew what they wanted to find there and made sure
they did find it.

Compare the same lines with Aldington's translation (1930), with the
same cuts as are listed above:

ADMETUS: Rouse up, O unhappy one, and do not leave me!
Call upon the mighty Gods to pity . . . .
Oh my unhappy one, how we suffer!
ALCESTIS: (Shrieking in terror, and clinging to Admetus)
He drags me, he drags me away –
Do you not see? –
To the House of the Dead,
The Winged One
Glaring under dark brows,
Hades! . . . .
ADMETUS: (Declaimed to the flute) Alas! I hear this unhappy
speech, and for me it is worse than all death. Ah! By the Gods,
do not abandon me. Ah! By our children, whom you leave
motherless, take heart! If you die, I become as nothing; in you
we have our life and death; we revere your love.

(*Fluteplayer ceases*)[22]

Most translations, especially those in prose, insist on a real dialogue
between husband and wife, and veer towards the sentimental, though
Vellacott clearly indicated the difference between the first Alcestis, 'in a

sort of trance or delirium', and the bemused Admetus:

> ADMETUS: Lift yourself up, Alcestis! Do not give in, but pray! The
> gods are powerful, and may be merciful . . .
> Oh, what are we to do?
> ALCESTIS: I feel a hand grasping my hand and leading me –
> Do you see? Let me go, down to the house of the dead!
> Death frowns at me; his eyes glow dark under his wings.
> [*To* ADMETUS: *who clasps her*] What are you doing? . . . .
> ADMETUS: O gods! To hear you say farewell
> Is torture worse than death. I plead with you –
> How can you bear to leave me, in God's name,
> To leave your children? Courage! Rise and live!
> How can I live when you are dead? For me
> Living and dying are in you alone.
> Your love claims more than love. I worship you![23]

When it comes to the rational Alcestis the practical tone is set early and maintained from beginning to end: but again an eighteenth-century fondness for the poignant proves hard to resist. Lennox continued where the previous section left off:

My dear Admetus, I am dying. Draw near and listen to my last words, which I reserve for thee. My affection for a husband, whom I loved better far than life, brings me this day to the tomb. Yes, my dear Admetus, I die for thee. I might have lived, thou knowest it, and have reigned happily. Which of the Thessalian princes, on whom I would have deigned to fix my choice, but would have given me his hand, to share my crown? . . .

I resolved to die for thee, and I do not repent this sacrifice. But, in reward for such a benefit as life, I require of thee a return of tenderness not equal (for what can equal the sacrifice of life?) but at least so just, so lawful, that thou canst not refuse to give it. Thy natural rectitude, and thy love for these children, secure the grant of my request. Suffer them not, my dear Admetus, to know any other master but thyself in their paternal dwelling . . . give them no envious stepmother . . .

Ah, death knows no delays; he waits not till the following day, nor to the third of the month. The fatal period is arrived; yet a moment longer, and I am numbered with the dead. Adieu, Admetus; adieu my children; be happy all of you: and thou, my dearest husband, live, and enjoy the glory of having once possessed a wife so faithful, and you, my children, boast that you had Alcestis for a mother. (ll. 280–325)[24]

Aldington is more brusque:

> ALCESTIS: (Recovering herself and sitting upright). Admetus, you
> see the things I suffer; and now before I die I mean to tell you

what I wish. To show you honour and – at the cost of my life – that you may still behold the light, I die; and yet I might have lived and wedded any in Thessalia I chose, and dwelt with happiness in a royal home .... .
(With solemn adjuration) Well! Do not forget this gift, for I shall ask – not a recompense for nothing is more precious than life, but – only what is just, as you yourself will say, since if you have not lost your senses you must love these children no less than I. (Appealingly) Let them be masters in my house; marry not again, and set a stepmother over them .... .
And I must die. Not to-morrow, nor to-morrow's morrow comes this misfortune on me, but even now I shall be named with those that are no more. Farewell! Live happy! You, my husband may boast you had the best of wives; and you, my children, that you lost the best of mothers! (She falls back)

Vellacott is even more aware of the equivocal background to a speech where a dying woman heralds an oath from her husband never to remarry with a deposition about how easy it would have been for her to find a new husband if the boot had been on the other foot:

Admetus, you see that I am dying. Before I go I must tell you what my wishes are. I have chosen that you should live rather than I, because I honour you as my husband. It would have been easy for me to refuse: as a widow I could have married whom I chose in Thessaly, and been rich and ruled a king's palace. Instead, I am dying .... .

Your part, then, is to remember what I have done for you. Since life is a more costly gift than any other, I do not ask you for an equal return; but what I ask, you will allow, is just. You are a man and love your children not less than I: keep them inheritors of my house; give them no stepmother .... .

I must die. Not tomorrow or after two days' grace, but this very hour I shall be spoken of as a woman who once lived.[25]

Goodbye! Be happy! You may be proud, Admetus, that you chose a good wife: and you, my children, that you had a good mother.[26]

Critics may be divided on the virtue, or lack of it, of Admetus.[27] A production has plenty of scope for taking a point of view either way. All that is required of the translator, perhaps, is to be as ambivalent as is Euripides, while homing in on the key exchanges. Two lines stand out, the second a delayed echo of the first:

1. SERVANT: *oupō tod' oide despotēs, prin an pathē* (145), literally 'The master does not yet know this, before he suffers.'

2. ADMETUS: *arti manthanō* (940), 'Now I understand.'

LENNOX/BRUMOY: 'Unhappy prince, he foresaw not this misfortune!'

The second line is cut.

POTTER: 'Nor knows our lord his suffering ere it comes.'
'Late taught what sorrow is.'

COLERIDGE: 'He did not know his loss until the blow fell on him.'
'I know it now.'

WAY: (Loeb, 1912) 'His depth of loss he knows not ere it comes.'
'I know it now.'

KOVACS: (Loeb, 1994) 'My master will not know his loss until it happens.'[28]
'Now I understand.'

MURRAY: 'He never knew her worth. He will know it now.'
'I have learned my lesson at the last.'

ALDINGTON: 'The King will not know his loss till he suffers it.'
'Only now do I perceive it.'

CHICAGO: 'The master does not see it and he will not see it, till it happens.'
'I see it now'.

PENGUIN: 'Noble she is indeed. But Admetus is blind to that. He will see the truth when he has lost her.'
'Too late I know that my life will be a sorry thing.'

METHUEN: 'He doesn't realise yet, nor will till he has suffered.'
'Till now I never realised, never knew till now.'

ROUTLEDGE: 'Not yet does the master understand this, not until he suffers it.'
'I have just learned this.'

Any of these helps to chart Admetus' emotional progress as a central theme of the play.[29] However the play is translated that emotional journey comes over as its spine, leading to Heracles' return from his battle with Death and testing of Admetus before revealing his wife to him. To be true to Euripides sentimentality may be inappropriate; sentiment is unavoidable.

CHAPTER 8

The Comic Tradition

> There is much more art required to make a play actable than a book readable.
>
> (J. R. Planché, *The Extravaganzas*, vol. III, London, 1879)

Translators claim a lot more leeway in the translating of comedy than is usually accorded to the translation of tragedy; accordingly, generalisations about translating comedy are that much more suspect. The problem still comes down, as it always does in any act of cultural transference, to the balance to be struck between source and target, but with some major differences.

In this chapter I want to consider what the Greeks may have understood by the comic in their theatre, and how this has affected translation of plays that were intended to make Athenian audiences laugh. The comic will include the satyr play that was performed alongside tragedy, and old comedy in the earliest translations of Aristophanes. All of these have to have, as do all translations, an element of modernisation, but updating of comedy is a divisive issue and will be considered in the second of these two chapters, alongside Greek New Comedy and the first ever dramatic 'translations' we have, namely the New Comedy adaptations from Greek originals into Latin by Plautus and Terence. Hopefully this will give some handles to grip when confronting the final question of when a 'translation' is or is not a 'translation'.

What distinguishes translating Greek comedy from translating tragedy is the manner in which humour travels. Aristophanes' or Menander's themes may be still topical. Their characters may be recognisable types. The terms of reference, social, political and cultural are not the same, and the translator's task is to address the conflicting patterns of behaviour and attitudes then and now. Two examples pinpoint the issue. The first is from what is almost certainly the oldest translation of Aristophanes into English, Thomas Randolph's *Hey for Honesty, Down with Knavery*. This is a real curiosity, if for no other reason than that it was first printed in 1651, plumb in the middle of the Interregnum when the public theatres were closed. Randolph's play is inordinately long and contains as an Introduction a conversation between Aristophanes and the Translator about what sort of comedy is proper where 'three-quarters of the city are Roundheads' who 'of all the languages of Babylon think it a heresy to understand any but their native English'. W. Carew Hazlitt, who provided his own preface to a reprint in 1875, describes it as:

This very scarce and curious adaptation (for translation it is not) .... Some authorities, who cannot have read *Hey for Honesty*, describe it as little more than a translation from Aristophanes; whereas, in truth, it is an original production with nothing but the name of the Greek poet and his satire put in the forefront.[1]

Randolph was Ben Jonson's adopted son and this, like much of his work, was originally published posthumously with additional notes from FJ (probably Francis Jaques).

Here is the nub of the problem. We are presented with a play which the author clearly based on Aristophanes' *Plutus* but is awash with references to the Doomsday Book (*sic*), the gunpowder plot – 'Garnet and Digby, and Faux', Prester John, Gargantua, Pope Joan, football and the ghost of Hamlet's father. Where in Aristophanes would you find anything approximating to Stiff's remonstration to Clip-Latin who is suggesting that they 'leave the Common Prayer':

God forbid, master ficar! why, twas writ in David's time; and Thomas Sternhold and John Hopkins joined it to the Psalms in those days and turned it into such an excellent metre, that I can sleep by it as well as any in the parish.[2]

Or Higgen, the grand orator, even if it were possible to understand what on earth he is talking about:

> By these good stampers, upper and nether duds;
> I'll nip from ruffman's of the harmanbeck,
> Though glimmered in the sambles, I cly the chates:[3]

This for 1651 is 'modernisation', a topic to revisit.

The second example is from Aristophanes' *Birds*, a play whose utopian nature has given it a perennial appeal in a variety of different shapes and contexts. To begin with there is the question of the names and identities of the two central characters. In most periods of European comedy major characters are labelled. The aspirations of the aristocracy are identified in Sir Politick Would-Be, Sir Tunbelly Clumsy, My Lady Cockwood or Lady Gay Spanker, while the lower orders are closely defined if their names are Androgyno, Gnatbrain or even Doolittle. When Shakespeare does the same with Pandarus, Perdita or Hippolyta he plays with his characters' trade, circumstance or classical origins. For the Greeks names had the power of myth and aspiration. Oedipus may have acquired his name from a physical condition but his decision to call one of his sons Polyneices, 'much given to strife', has the quality of family nickname. For most the names themselves have a self-defining quality allied to the return again and again to the same myths for plots and themes.

In Aristophanic comedy Socrates, Heracles or Dionysus bring their own comic baggage with them. The ordinary citizens – if anyone in Aristophanes can be called ordinary – provide with their names an indication of their personality and function within the play. In *Acharnians* the leading character is Dicaiopolis, 'Just Citizen'; Bdelycleon and Philocleon in *Wasps* are 'Despiser' and 'Adorer' of Cleon; Lysistrata is 'Disbander of', or 'Freer from, the Army'. *Birds* opens with two Athenians trying to escape from the rigours of city life. The one who appears to be taking the lead is Euelpides, 'Son of Optimist'; the name of his companion is less sure. It is either Pisthetaerus or Pisthetairos (which the manuscripts have on the one occasion when the name is given, line 644), Peisthetairos, Peithetairos or Peisetairos. The first two mean 'Faithful Companion'; the other three are variations on 'Persuader of his Companions'. Which of these the translator chooses to use does make a difference: the difference between seeing the takeover of the state as a benevolent and a threatening act. Not only was the Sicilian Expedition about to get going in earnest when *Birds* was produced at the Great Dionysia of 414 BC, but a revolution which temporarily overthrew democracy was only three years in the future. 'Persuader' finds favour with most commentators though not the Oxford text of Hall and Geldhart.[4] B. H. Kennedy, Regius Professor of Greek at the time of the Cambridge production in Greek in 1883 had no doubts when he recorded, as included in the Cambridge archive of the production, that:

The person who wrote the notice of the first representation of the *Birds* at Cambridge has thought proper to call the protagonist in that play Peisthetairos although the Greek text and the translation adopted by the Committee [Kennedy's own published with the Greek text used in the production] .... give the name Peithetairos. Why the writer should thus step out of his way to exhibit his own deficient scholarship, is best known himself.

In more recent times, both Kenneth Dover and William Arrowsmith have made much of the significance of these names, Dover's preferred name being Peisetairos which I shall use below. Dover emphasised additionally that Basileia (Sovereignty), whose hand in marriage Prometheus suggests that Peisetairos demand, weds him to the acquisition of supreme power.[5] Add to that the significance of the two Athenians acquiring wings as the way to further their political ambitions, and the overtaking of the Optimist by the Persuader, and you have a political parable that builds on itself for any age.

This is an issue of overall interpretation; a passage of dialogue from the same play highlights a simple comic routine. The brief engagement is part of a double act between Peisetairos (or Peisthetaerus, Pisthetairos, Peisthetairos or Peithetairos) and a messenger who has brought news that the construction work on the new city is now complete. The plot is temporarily put on ice while one character feeds as the straightman and the other plays the punchlines. Similar sequences occur regularly in Aristophanes, and in comedy since Aristophanes, often with one of the leads 'giving the scene' to one of the comics. The geographical exchange about Luce between the Syracusan Dromio and Antipholus in *Comedy of Errors* (based on Plautus' *Menaechmi*, itself based on a Greek play by Posidippus) offers a similar comic structure. In *Birds* (ll. 1141–7) news has come that the city of Cloudcuckooland has been completed.[6] Peisetairos wants to know which bird contributed what to the building process. Who carried up the mortar and how? 'Herons' says the Messenger, using their feet like shovels: to which Peisetairos responds *ti dēta podes an ouk apergasaiato?*, literally 'Is there anything that feet cannot do?' This arcane response is explained by a scholiast in a side note in one of the manuscripts where he says that there was a proverb at the time 'Is there anything that hands cannot do?' with the word *cheires* for *podes*. Comedy doesn't always travel well.

The earliest English language translation of *Birds* (1812), by 'A Member of One of the Universities', in a 'sort of comico-prosaic style', left the line to fend for itself:

PISTHETAERUS: And how did they apply the mortar to the stonework?

FIRST MESSENGER: This, my good fellow, was cleverly contrived: the geese made shovels of their feet, and, after having minced up the mortar, loaded the hods.
PISTHETAERUS: Wonderful! what use cannot feet be applied to?

John Hookham Frere (1839), in the first verse translation, made a better attempt at the wordplay but put the context of the gag into stage directions of his own before coming up with a pun:

PEISETAIROS: [*in a fuss which he endeavours to conceal.*]
    Yes! yes! But after all, to load your hods,
    How did you manage that?
MESS: Oh, capitally,
    I promise you. There were the geese, all barefoot
    Trampling the mortar, and, when all was ready,
    They handed it into the hods, so cleverly,
    With their flat feet!
PEIS: (*a bad joke, as a vent for irritation*): They *footed* it you mean –
    Come; it was handily done though, I confess.[7]

More recent translations have been rather more ingenious in turning the gag into a pun: and, indeed, according to modern taste, funnier. William Arrowsmith (1961) opted for:

PISTHETAIROS: But how was the mortar heaped in the hods?
MESS: Gods, now *that* was a triumph of engineering skill!
    Geese burrowed their feet like shovels beneath and heaved it
    over their heads to the hods.
PISTH: They did?
    Ah Feet! Ah Feet! O incredible feat!
    What can compare with a pair of feet?

But that is a reader's gag. You can't make the point by *speaking* it, at least not without elaborate 'signposting'. Kenneth McLeish (1993) used the same pun, but turned it into an actor's gag:

PEITHETAIROS: And how did they fill those hods?
MESS: You'd have liked that.
    Geese stuck in their feet like this, and shuffled it.
PEITH: What a feat.

Paul Muldoon (1999) was pithier still, but he too appreciated what an audience needs to work it out:

PEISETAIROS: But how did they get the mortar into the hods?
MESSENGER: That was done by the geese. They shovelled it in with
    their feet.
PEISETAIROS: No mean feat.

The philosophies behind translating comedy are exemplified by these approaches to *Plutus* and to *Birds*. *Plutus* is recreated in the political circumstances of the translator; *Birds* variously invokes the seriousness behind the original comedy and invites the translator to search for a target gag whenever there is a source one.

What made the Greeks laugh requires a more major study than can be attempted here. Fortunately there are enough examples from ancient literature to show that for the most part we can at least understand some of what they found funny. In Book VIII of the *Odyssey* the bard Demodocus, having unwittingly chosen a tactless subject first time round, opts instead to tell the story of the loves of Ares and Aphrodite. When Aphrodite's husband Hephaestus finds out she is being unfaithful with Ares he manufactures an invisible net to trap the lovers *in flagrante*. He then summons the other Olympians to witness their *erga gelasta kai ouk epieikta*, 'comic and intolerable deeds'.[8] The other gods laugh at Hephaestus' cleverness and laugh even more when Hermes agrees with Apollo that it would be worth being caught in the net just to be in bed with Aphrodite. What is funny in this tale is the mixture of cunning, incongruity and discomfort; *schadenfreude* – Sabatini's description of Scaramouche as born 'with a gift of laughter and a sense that the world was mad' juxtaposed with Barry Humphries' Dame Edna Everage proudly announcing that 'I was born with the precious gift of being able to laugh at the misfortunes of others.'

In drama of the classical period both tragedy and comedy were located in a consciously stage world, a cocoon of masks, which nobody expected to resemble real life except in the broadest of outlines. One of the principles of the satyr play was that a stage action, even a potentially gruesome or tragic one, could be rendered comic by the way in which the Chorus reacted to it. Comedy is frequently callous but was a way of looking at life and surviving it, a middle finger to the Medusa as opposed to Nietzsche's deflecting mirror of tragedy. Aristophanes invited a shared awareness with his audience of the frailty of existence by creating a fantasy world of real problems where ever more improbable solutions are proposed for the difficulties of life in Athens. Heroic figures could be cut down to size by the insignificant; the gods threatened more with banana skins than with thunderbolts; seriousness was not a matter of death but a matter of life. The plays of Aristophanes offer castlists of mortals, immortals, animals, prominent citizens in lampoon form and fictional Athenians who might take on and beat the system. By the time of Menander, a hundred years later, all but the ordinary men and women had disappeared, give or take the odd prologue: but this was still a comedy of masks but with domesticity and moralising taking centre stage.

In each and every play that has survived, however divorced from the absolute realities of day-to-day living, the Greek playwrights, tragic and comic, tuned into a political, historical, philosophical, socio-cultural framework that was part of the world they shared with the generic entity of their audiences. That is the translator's dilemma. Whatever else can be recreated in translation that shared experience cannot. The further you go back the more complex that task becomes, less because of the spoken language than because of this cultural context. And yet it is precisely that cultural context, or the variety of cultural contexts, that make the comedy of the classical period so fascinating. As Edith Hamilton noted, Voltaire had Aristophanes in mind when he suggested that 'True comedy is the speaking picture of the follies and foibles of a nation.'[9] For that reason, if for no other, there need to be some translations of Greek comedy around that do actually offer a faithful rendition of the received texts. That they may need to be padded out with commentary and footnotes relieves the pressure on the translator to search for anything but accuracy.

For an audience, of course, such a translation is absolutely hopeless. Few things beyond the cry of 'Fire' will clear a theatre faster than a joke that needs a programme note to explain it. The licence that this gives to translators renders it difficult to make any proper comparisons between their work: hence the decision here to devote two chapters to comedy without a detailed study of any single play. In no two translations of any Aristophanes play is it possible to compare like with like.

The gap between comedy as social history and comedy as a living theatrical entity may be hard to close. A case can be made for the futility of even trying. The stage comedy of ancient Greece is difficult to pin down. Old Comedy, contemporary with the work of Sophocles and Euripides, is represented exclusively by Aristophanes: so is Middle Comedy (his two late plays). New Comedy comprises a couple of almost complete plays of Menander, together with fragmentary scenes of a few others, and a number of later Roman comedies of Plautus and Terence based on lost Greek originals. In addition there are comic moments to be found in every Greek tragedy, frequently enough in Euripides for plays

such as *Helen, Iphigenia in Tauris* and *Ion* sometimes to be identified as
'comedies', with *Alcestis*, often being referred to as 'protosatyric', because
it was played fourth, in the normal position for the satyr play. Represented by the single play to survive in its entirety, Euripides' *Cyclops*, the
satyr play gives an entirely different impression of what 'comedy' might
have involved for the Greeks: it also poses a particular problem for the
translator.

In Book III of the *Republic* (394–5) Plato offers the celebrated exchange
between Adeimantus and Socrates:

> 'I presume,' he [Adeimantus] said, 'that the subject at issue is whether we
> should accept tragedy and comedy into our state, or not.'
> 'Perhaps', I replied, 'or, perhaps, something more radical still. I do not really
> know myself. Wherever the argument takes us, there we must go.'
> 'Right', he said.
> 'Well, then, Adeimantus, should our guardian class be versatile performers
> [*mimētikoi*], or not? Or is it a consequence of what we have already said that
> each man can only do one job properly, not several? If he attempts several and is
> a Jack-of-all-trades, he will be master of none?'
> 'What other conclusion can there be?'
> 'Is it the same for representation [*mimēsis*], that a man cannot play many roles
> as well as he can a single one?'
> 'It must be so.'
> 'Then he will hardly be able to do anything properly if he can imitate many
> things and be a versatile performer, since the same man is incapable of working
> as productively [*hama eu*, lit. 'at the same time, well'] on two forms of imitation
> [*mimēmata*] as close as the writing of tragedy and comedy. You did call them
> forms of imitation, did you not?'
> 'I did. It is true. The same man cannot do both.'
> 'Nor be a rhapsode and an actor.'
> 'No.'
> 'Or actor in comedy and tragedy? These are all forms of imitation, I presume.'
> 'Certainly, forms of imitation.'
> 'And, refining human nature further, Adeimantus, it is impossible to "act" a
> number of things well, or to do well in real life those things of which the acting is
> an imitation.'
> 'Very true', he replied.[10]

Overlooking the circumstances of this exchange, and its significance as a
step in a philosophical argument rather than a comment on theatre
history, it seems to be readily understood, albeit by the gullible Adeimantus, that in the Athens of Socrates' time – Socrates was executed in
399, only six years after the deaths of Euripides and Sophocles – the same

playwright could not write both tragedy and comedy effectively, and that the same actor could not play as well in tragedy and comedy. The same playwrights did write tragedy and satyr plays and the same actors performed in them, so the implication is that the satyr play was not considered to be 'comedy', for all it was a burlesque of tragic performance, but as an aspect of tragedy. Were this not clear enough from the *Republic*, at the end of Plato's *Symposium*, Socrates is reported as trying to convince anyone who was still awake at the end of the drinking-party that the same man *would* be capable of writing tragedies and comedies.[11]

In classical Athens comedy was what was written by Aristophanes and his ilk, satyr plays were written by tragedians. The difference could be neatly defined if all Old Comedy was on contemporary themes, as are all the extant plays of Aristophanes, set in and around the Athens of the day even when they are filtered through a fantastic vision which can take political figures and ordinary Athenians to stage heavens and hells, or points between. The list of titles of old comedies that survive suggests that this was not necessarily so and that figures from the world of myth could not only make the odd entrance, as do gods and heroes in surviving Aristophanes, but feature as principals.[12] Though the likelihood of today's audience getting hung up over such concerns is remote, the difference between the satyr play and what Plato recognised as comedy does pose an unexpected problem for the translator when looking at either genre, or both.

The satyr play at the conclusion of each set of three tragedies was usually, though not invariably, from the hand of the same tragic playwright. Pratinas, a contemporary of Aeschylus, wrote more satyr plays than tragedies, though nothing of his work has survived. The same actors and chorus appeared in any group of four plays, the chorus now dressed as, and behaving like, the drunken and lecherous animalistic attendants of Dionysus who chase Maenads round the drinking-cups and vases of the period. The principal characters tend to encounter the satyrs in scenes from myth that are adjacent to those in the tragedies, any pretensions to heroism being pricked, sometimes literally, by the company they find themselves keeping. In other words, it was deemed fitting not so much to conclude a set of tragedies with a farce, but to include a farcical element to complete any group of tragedies, whether or not on a connected theme. Aeschylus wrote at least seventeen satyr plays, amongst them, a *Sphinx* to go with his *Oedipodeia*; *Proteus* (to follow the *Oresteia*); a *Circe*; two about Sisyphus; and at least one about Prometheus, thought not as the coda to his Prometheus trilogy but to the group which opened with *Persians*. None of Aeschylus' satyr plays is extant.

There are twenty titles of Sophoclean satyr plays. Half of one of them, *Trackers* (*Ichneutae*) has survived, best known on stage via Tony Harrison's *The Trackers of Oxyrhynchus*, a clever and funny play which creates the circumstances of the discovery of the text of *Ichneutae* in Egypt by Hunt and Grenfell at the beginning of the twentieth century before moving on to a performance based on the play itself.[13]

Titles of Euripides' satyr plays amount to fewer than ten but they too include a *Sisyphus*, and also a *Eurystheus* (presumably involving Heracles), an *Autolycus*, and the one and only complete text, *Cyclops*. Far from being simply a knockabout farce, *Cyclops* turns out, much of it, to be written in the language of tragedy, at least as put into the mouths of Odysseus and Polyphemus. The play is comic and contains slapstick scenes of the kind illustrated on many Athenian and especially southern Italian vases, but it is more sophisticated than it first looks. Much of it appears as tragic parody or pastiche, confirming the notion that for the Greeks the satyr play was not an alternative form of comedy, but an alternative form of tragedy.

Historically, one concern for the translator has arisen over the 'no-go' areas within the field of tragedy and comedy. In Britain the office of the Lord Chamberlain as censor of plays ensured that in the early part of the twentieth century British audiences were spared the corrupting influences of *Ghosts, Miss Julie, Six Characters in Search of an Author* and even translations of *Oedipus Tyrannus* until Gilbert Murray's for Reinhardt at Covent Garden in 1912. The grounds for this protection were related usually to what was perceived as sexual transgression – *Oedipus Tyrannus* is 'about' incest. Blasphemy, excessive violence and the inclusion of living people were all grounds for refusing to licence a text for production. There were vaguer categories too. The stage licence for Gilbert and Sullivan's *The Mikado* was withdrawn in 1907 when the Crown Prince of Japan was making a visit to London. If this seems to be no more than a hangover of Victorian propriety, let it be remembered that, at the time of the Falklands War, *Carry On Up the Khyber* was one of a number of proscribed films on British television on the grounds that it portrayed the British soldier in a demeaning manner.

Comedy may offend in different ways. Matters of decorum form a more flexible part of the social fabric in comedy than they ever do in tragedy. Such sensitivity is a matter of fashion. Current concerns over attitudes to people of colour, to disablement, sexism or cultural stereotyping are every bit as coercive as were references to obscenity or profanity a hundred years ago. Marc Connelly's Pulitzer Prize-winning *Green Pastures* of 1929 is a case in point. Though broadcast, filmed and televised in America, it was still banned on the British stage thirty years later on the grounds that one of the main characters is God. That was enough for the Lord Chamberlain: no licence. But not only is a leading figure God, but he is God portrayed as an old black man in an all-black, revivalist history of the Old Testament. Today the banning of a stage play on such grounds might seem absurd: but what would we make of a published edition, such as the first of *Green Pastures* by Penguin in 1941, which describes the play as 'a delightful and daring portrayal of Negro religion. The stories of childhood live again in the naive beliefs of these coloured Christians'?

Greek literature in general, but especially its comic drama, has often fallen victim to the morality of the time.[14] In *Cyclops* there are a number of *double entendres* apparently referring to stage business with the phallus. One sequence is more blatant. The Cyclops, becoming rapidly drunk from Odysseus' special wine, takes a fancy to Silenus and gives an unabashed, if not especially graphic, account of how he wants him as his Ganymede. Silenus is none too keen on the idea.

In the Loeb translation in rhyming verse first published in 1912, Arthur Way made little attempt to conceal what the Cyclops intends to do with Silenus, even if his expression was somewhat coy:

> CYCLOPS: No, I won't kiss you! – that's the naughty Graces
> Tempting me. Ganymede will do for me. (*seizes* SIL.)
> I've got him here; and, by the Graces three,
> I'll have a lovely time with him: I care
> Never a straw for all the female fair.
> SILENUS: What? What? Are you Zeus, and I Ganymede?
> CYCLOPS (*catching him up*): Yes – up from Troy I snatch you – yes indeed!
> SILENUS: Boys! murder! help! I'm in an awful plight!
> CHORUS: What? – snub him 'cause he's tight?
> SILENUS: This wine is bitter beer! – O cursèd spite!
> (*Cyclops staggers into cave, with Silenus under his arm.*)[15]

Way noted that the only existing verse translations at the time were those of Wodhull (1782) and Shelley (1819). Subsequent reprintings of the Loeb fail to amend this to include Sheppard's for the Cambridge edition of 1923 'freely translated and adapted for performance in English'. One might add 'and sanitised'. The expectation of male rape disappears as the whole fifteen lines of Euripides are reduced to:

> CYCLOPS: ... And the pretty Graces, courting me for kisses – Get along with you, hussies! Why – Here's Ganymede. (*He seizes Silenus.*)

SILENUS: Oh dear, he'll eat me next! Oh dear. Oh dear!
CYCLOPS: Good gracious, no! My Ganymede divine
    Shall wait on me and fill my cups with wine!
    (*He staggers off into the cave with Silenus.*)[16]

The bowdlerisation (despite the wholly unconscious implication of oral sex) may bear witness to both the sensitivity and the naivety of a Cambridge audience eighty years ago, but is a recognition too of what the censor still would and would not permit to be spoken in public.

    The first English translation of any of *Cyclops* is by Dr Grainger in Charlotte Lennox's *The Greek Theatre of Father Brumoy* in 1759. Her reliance on a different hand may have been the result of personal distaste but Grainger's selections are partial and harmless. In this particular scene all is reduced to:

Here follow some theatric tricks, which, though farcical, are, however, not entirely to be contemned ... till Polyphemus, being quite tired with these mummeries, commands Ulysses to be his cup-bearer.[17]

Wodhull (1782) offered, with a masterly attempt at obfuscation (and in a text that seems to have ostracised question marks):

POLYPHEMUS [Cyclops]: Were all the Graces to solicit me,
    I would not kiss them: Ganymede himself
    Appears in matchless beauty.
SILENUS: I, oh Cyclops,
    Am Jove's own Ganymede.
POL.:   By heaven thou art!
    Whom from the realms of Dardanus I bore. (*Exit Polypheme*)
SILENUS: Ruin awaits me.
CHORUS: Dost though loathe him now.
SILENUS: Ah me! I from this sleep shall soon behold
    The most accursed effects.   (*Exit Silenus*)[18]

Shelley, on the other hand (1819) appears to opt for complicity:

CYCLOPS: Now if the Graces tempted me to kiss
    I would not, for the loveliest of them all,
    I would not leave this Ganymede.
SILENUS: Polypheme,
    I am the Ganymede of Jupiter.
CYCLOPS: By Jove you are; I bore you off from Dardanus.

A tactful row of dots follows.[19]

The first Penguin translation, by Roger Lancelyn Green (1957), is demure but clear: 'I'm done for, boys. I'm in for something bad', though ends rather tamely 'At last I see the vile effects of the wine' (*pikrotaton oinon opsomai tacha*). Green, in his Introduction, pointed out that the Shelley was 'quite unsuitable for presentation'. He claimed of his own that he was far closer to Euripides than was Sheppard: 'mine, though free, is still a translation rather than an adaptation; it is a version "of" not "after" Euripides: accurate if not literal'.[20] The Methuen (1991) opted for 'He's going to do unmentionable things to me ... This is going to leave a nasty taste in the mouth.'

To confine a comparison of versions of *Cyclops* to one sequence of the rude bits is not to imply that obscenity dominates the play. Far from it; what emerges from a reading of the older translations of *Cyclops* is that, though they appear stilted, confined by language and attitude to their own time, the heroic diction does shine through alongside the burlesque.

In *Cyclops* the tragic is inverted, providing for Odysseus a sense of the picaresque similarly balanced as in the telling of the same incident in the *Odyssey*. The philosophy of life offered by the Cyclops 'The clever man's god is money. Everything else is wind and words .... The biggest of my gods is my stomach. Eat lots and drink lots, that's Zeus for the discerning' (ll. 316–17 and 336–7) is not so different from Heracles in *Alcestis*: 'Here's my philosophy. Enjoy yourself. Live in the present. Live from day to day and let Fate take care of the rest' (789–91).[21] Plato's sense of compartmentalising tragedy and comedy may not attune with the dramatic labelling of later centuries but it does suggest that in satyr play and old comedy the translator may be looking for different sets of guidelines.

The translator of Aristophanes is faced with a kind of dramatic piece for which we have no parallel. Aristophanes' fondness for anachronism, for absurdity, for the fantastic, gives licence to a similar freedom in all but the most literal of translations. But where does the translator stand in looking both for the spirit of the original and for the jokes? There is an argument which says that, if Aristophanes played fast and loose with the conventions of the stage of his own day, then it is surely more true to him today to do likewise. Some examples show the size of the problem.

In *Peace*, when Trygaeus is flying up to heaven to find what has happened to the goddess of Peace, he travels on the back of a dung beetle he has fattened specially for the purpose, describing it as his Pegasus. During his flight there are several lines where he tells the dung beetle to stop getting distracted by the smell of shit from the public lavatories.

Finally he calls out in a lilting resolved line: *ō mēchanopoie, proseche ton noun ōs eme* (l. 174), 'You on the crane, keep your mind on me.'

So, within the same speech we have a reference to a mythological winged horse that a sizeable proportion of a contemporary audience may never have heard of; a reference to an insect which many people may never have seen; some geographical details about the location of brothels in the Piraeus – interesting to some but seriously out of date; and a metatheatrical appeal to the flyman off-stage not to shake the actor off the *mēchanē*.

A second example: at the end of *Frogs* the god Dionysus decides to return from the underworld to Athens with Aeschylus, whose political advice about Alcibiades has proved the more promising at such a time of crisis. Within the last sixty lines we have several quotations from Greek tragedies; some byplay with the audience; references to contemporary politicians including the devout hope that they will be on their way down below as soon as maybe; comments on the Peloponnesian War which is nearing its end; and a journey back from Hades to Athens.

Example three: *Knights* has only five speaking characters, three of whom are slaves in the house of a fourth. The householder is Demos, whose name means the Athenian people. Two of the slaves are Nicias and Demosthenes, both of whom were Athenian generals in 424 BC. The third is called the Paphlagonian, a thinly veiled portrait of the politician Cleon, who had had Aristophanes prosecuted only two years earlier for 'ridiculing the state in the presence of outsiders'. Cleon was from Paphlagonia on the southern shore of the Black Sea. After public criticism of the two generals, Nicias and Demosthenes, in a campaign over Sphacteria, he accepted a challenge to do better: somewhat luckily, he liberated a number of prisoners within the twenty days he claimed it was all it would take, and returned to Athens in triumph. Aristophanes was not impressed and his *Knights* makes no secret of his continuing hostility. The story has it that the maskmakers were too afraid to make a portrait mask of Cleon for *Knights* which suggests, at the very least, that the actors playing Nicias and Demosthenes did wear portrait masks. *Knights* revolves around attempts to defeat the Paphlagonian by finding a political opponent who is even more coarse and disgusting than he is.

The challenges confronting the translator of Aristophanes involve most of those which the translator of the tragedies face: gods; a background of myth; geography; cultural norms and etiquette; an understanding of the difference between the world of the play and the world of the audience; an appreciation of stage conventions including music and dance; an awareness of the sense of occasion; the built-in bank of recent theatrical presentation, with all its novelty and shortcuts. For Aristophanes, add immediacy, in-jokes, local gossip, the current hot issues, verbal abuse and innuendo, stage business, puns and wordplay, together with a sense of the absurd, any and all of which is difficult to replicate.

The earliest translations of Aristophanes into English are concentrated on two plays, *Wealth* (*Plutus*) and *Clouds*. The version of *Plutus* attributed to Thomas Randolph dates from 1651, H. H. Burnell's (under the initials HB) from only eight years later. The first *Clouds* was included, rather incongruously, in Thomas Stanley's *History of Philosophy*, first published in 1655 and reprinted in 1701, while Lewis Theobald's *Plutus; or the World's Idol* and *Clouds* were published separately in 1715, the same year as his *Oedipus, King of Thebes*. Henry Fielding and William Young produced a *Plutus*, first published in 1742: J. White a *Clouds* in 1759.[22] For many years these were the only two of Aristophanes plays regarded as translatable. In the Advertisement to *Comedies of Aristophanes, Four Plays Translated into English* (1812), the anonymous editors claim that their volume:

contains translations of the only plays of Aristophanes, that have ever been attempted in English. Duplicate versions of the *Clouds* and *Plutus* have been made by White and Theobald; and this, if we mistake not, is all that we have of Aristophanes in our language.[23]

They then continue by saying that they have for many years been trying to persuade Richard Cumberland to follow up his *Clouds* of 1793 with a translation of the whole of Aristophanes, but that he had declined on the grounds that 'the generality of the plays would not admit of an English version'. Cumberland was, however, working on yet another *Plutus* at the time of his death.[24]

The edition published in 1812 consists of reprints of Cumberland's *Clouds* (with an extended *apologia* to his unnamed patron for Aristophanes' apparent attack on philosophers in general and Socrates in particular); and the Fielding and Young *Plutus* of 1742 (*with large notes, explanatory and critical*); and Charles Dunster's *Frogs* (1785), which, notwithstanding the apparent disavowal above, had already been published at Oxford, probably in 1780.[25] The last play of the four is the first English translation of *Birds*, the anonymous author of which makes no attempt at versification even for the choruses in 'a sort of comico-prosaic style ... the style which suits best the language of English farce'.[26] The English translation is based firmly on the Brunck text, with regular reference to Beck, Bentley and Porson.

As a translation this *Birds* has merits. Once one has got used to such phrases as 'Pox take thee', 'Marry, well said', and 'Pshaw!', it is possible to live with a conclusion from the chorus which runs 'Huzza! Io! Paeon! Hurra for the wedding! Hail! thou that surpassed all the gods in greatness.' Any cleansing relates to homosexual inference rather than sexuality *per se*. So the friend who might reprove Peisetairos for meeting his son on the way from the baths 'You met the boy coming home from the baths and never fondled him, never even kissed him or tickled his balls' (William Arrowsmith's translation of lines 140–2), finds the son has become 'a pretty wench' over whom 'you were proof to all temptation, though you knew you might have jostled with my daughter at random in the dark'. But this is a recognisable Athens and a real introduction to the play, if not one that ever could be used as a production script.

J. R. Planché's extravaganza *'The Birds' of Aristophanes*, was the first even loose stage production of the play in modern times.[27] Planché, despite his name, was a Londoner who became a costume designer, a concert manager, a scholar of heraldry and founder member of the Garrick Club. He was, of course, best known as a playwright. No fewer than 181 stage pieces are credited to him. These include burlesques, burlettas, pantomimes, extravaganzas, melodramas and operas: and a number of parodies of Greek myths, a vogue which he fostered with enthusiasm. Many of his stage pieces were translations, or adaptations – that blessedly and cursedly protean term – of anything from Scribe to *The Magic Flute*.

'The Birds' of Aristophanes was produced at the Theatre Royal, Haymarket in 1846. The likelihood of real Aristophanes escaping the censor in 1846 when *Oedipus Tyrannus* was unable to do so fifty years later, is, of course, remote, but Planché smelled theatre in the Greek comedian and that was enough for him. The leading characters were transformed from Peisetairos and Euelpides to Jackanoxides and Tomostyleseron. Planché's text, a mere twenty-one printed pages in rhyming couplets, is severely condensed and extremely respectable. There are references to 'caviare', 'Easter', an 'opera-box' and other such cultural updatings, the most disconcerting (not least for its rhyme) being when the Chorus ask:

> Why should not the fowls in the air build a palace,
> When there's hope of a submarine railway to Calais?

The biggest difference comes at the end when a disguised Jupiter reveals himself to ensure that Jackanoxides suffers an almost Luciferian fall for daring to oppose the gods of Olympus. In his Preface to the published version Planché declared himself amused that he had been taken for a classical scholar on the strength of this play and his earlier burlesque, *The Golden Fleece*, which offers the story of Jason, leading into a comic and doggerel version of Euripides' *Medea*. Planché claimed no more than adaptation, or 'paraphrase' of Aristophanes' *Birds*. He expressed surprise and partial disappointment that one critic should have been shocked at the introduction of Jupiter where the language 'was far too earnest; too literal; it was no longer burlesque; it was no less than the voice of offended Heaven'. Planché's defence was that he never contemplated burlesque, this being fable or allegory. The moral, however trite, was a serious one:

> What dire confusion in the world twould breed,
> If fools *could* follow whither knaves *would* lead.

Much then comes down to the level of ambition, the function of the translation, the translator's purpose. Translation of Aristophanes for publication is likely to be for something which is sufficiently faithful to represent the original text but virile enough to convey in the reading the playwright's *joie de vivre*. How problematic this may be was summed up by publisher Nick Hern when he wrote of being reminded by a production he had seen:

how very difficult it is in the case of Aristophanes to follow the Drama Classics brief [the series he initiated] and provide an uncut and uncluttered translation of the original. If you put the whole thing in much of it is incomprehensible (and it goes without saying mountainously unfunny) yet the series doesn't allow you explicatory footnotes.[28]

Perhaps it is the clutter to which rendering Aristophanes in English boils down.

A different set of priorities is set with a text prepared for a production where the translator is in collusion with the production process, from casting to opening, attending all rehearsals and with a comprehensive role in the whole process. From collaboration there can emerge not one translation but a series where the various interests are represented and balanced leading, if the interchange works well, to a finalised production script. It is tempting to believe that this was what happened in the original productions but is no more a recipe for success than any other in the curiously unpredictable world of theatre. It is to this which we can now turn.

CHAPTER 9

Modernising Comedy

> Translation is a quite specific job, to make a version which is true to
> the original and doesn't bore the tits off everyone.
>
> (Pam Gems, 1990)

Until comparatively recently all translations of Aristophanes were adaptations or condensed versions, if not always as extreme as the Thomas Randolph *Plutus* (see p. 145–6). William Arrowsmith, perhaps the most enduring of all twentieth-century translators of both comedy and tragedy, identified why this should be so in an essay entitled 'The lively conventions of translation' in the series of essays on stage translation which he edited with Roger Shattuck in 1961.[1] He pointed to what he described as 'the hard facts of culture', complex enough in Greek tragedy but multiplied in comedy because:

> comedy dumps into the translator's lap an intolerable profusion of *things* – odd
> bits of clothing, alien cuisine, unidentifiable objects, pots and pans and utensils
> of bewildering variety and function, unfamiliar currency, etc .... What the devil
> can a translator do with a culture in which women, for esthetic reasons, depilate
> their pubic hairs, or with a comedian who can build a whole recognition scene
> on the fact?[2]

Mercifully, he provided an answer to his own question a little later, speaking for any translator of Aristophanes when he asserted that 'Incongruity and craft make the obscene more obscene, *truly* obscene. And this is what the translator wants.'[3]

Sir Kenneth Dover picked out a more fundamental issue that relates to reception:

> the audience of tragedy tolerates a certain degree of obscurity and mystification,
> but an audience that has been told that Aristophanes is funny and therefore
> expects to be amused is less tolerant.[4]

It is here that Hilaire Belloc's injunction to pick out 'the atmosphere of the word' acquires the force of mantra which any and all translators should daily rehearse. The atmosphere of a word may well translate into a completely different word from its literal meaning. In comedy there is a real case for a much more radical reappraisal.

Comedy differs from tragedy in this regard. The very distance imposed by the formality of tragedies from Potter or Wodhull makes a production of such translations feasible even if they were never driven initially by any thought of stage presentation. The same cannot be claimed for any area of Greek comedy. Translations that are still regarded as classics in the classroom, those of Dudley Fitts, for example, have dated beyond levels of acceptability for most audiences. Kenneth McLeish, who translated all eleven Aristophanes plays, spoke of the translator of comedy needing to play a more aggressive role to 'unlock' the texts, pointing out that it was even more important in comedy than in tragedy to have the translator present in the rehearsal room.[5] His experience extended to the translation of plays by Plautus and Terence, Molière, Holberg and Feydeau, maintaining not only that the approach needed to be different in each case, but also what he identified as 'the debate'.

In Aristophanes questions arise, not of updating so much as reinventing in the present. The issue, in a nutshell, boils down to what you do about his contemporary references, the significance of which is largely lost on a modern audience. Do you, as Stephen Sondheim chose to do, change the Aeschylus and Euripides of *Frogs* to Shakespeare and Shaw? Clearly this is part of a larger argument about cultures and their specifics. William Arrowsmith set his mind against what he called '*total* cultural translation'. Paradoxically, when talking about comedy he picked out a tragedy as his bad example, the translation of *Women of Trachis* by Ezra Pound, which, inexplicably, still finds its adherents even among the most text-based of classicists. Arrowsmith's grievance was the same as that levelled above against Gilbert Murray (see p. 50):

The Greek characters in Ezra Pound's shabby *Women of Trachis*, for instance, manage to persuade us that they are neither Greek nor American nor English by employing a bastard argot never spoken by anybody except Pound, and in consequence, the whole convention founders.[6]

It must be highly doubtful if Pound ever *spoke* like this either, thereby making it acutely difficult for any actor. It tends to be those who understand the classics mostly as literature who champion Pound. Whatever the virtues in demystifying a classical text for today's reader or audience, drama, and especially Aristophanes, is seldom served by abolishing central features in favour of the instant gag. Arrowsmith rightly points to the heavy-handedness of translating Cleon into Joseph McCarthy or Nicias into Eisenhower – this, remember, was published in 1961:

It is not, of course, topicality that is wrong of itself . . . What is wrong is the heavy and insistent topicality which asserts that Athens not merely resembles America but *is* America.[7]

If this returns to the major question of the delicate balance between translator and director, it does suggest that the translator's task is really one of bridging cultures not absorbing one into another. With few exceptions – Sondheim's *Frogs* with Shakespeare and Shaw may be one – the transfer of an Aristophanic character into some modern parallel may work for a single individual or situation, but plays havoc with the bulk of the play which limps along lamed by the weight attached to its tail. Revitalising is not simply a matter of inventing a succession of jokes: it is finding a stage culture within which the whole play can breathe. Translator, director and designer have to work in tandem. A thoroughly modern production may be dressed in ancient Greek costume, a thoroughly stilted one in jeans and army fatigues. The sixties and seventies saw a vogue amongst the more naive of directors to foist parallels onto audiences as though such audiences had no will of their own. Productions of *Trojan Women* or *Mother Courage* would be presented to a background of slides of the Korean or Vietnam Wars. Euripides and Brecht are subtler than that and had greater belief that their audiences could make their own parallels through visions of Troy or the Thirty Years War.

Comedy is flexible but comedy with a purpose, as is that of Aristophanes, can only be narrowed if it is tied to a defined rather than an open metaphor. This is as true for the broad scope of a play as it is for the detail. Everything comes down to the marriage of script and performance. Comedy, more than tragedy, needs a script of performance potential rather than something finished. The absence of landmark productions of Aristophanes in English is evidence enough of how difficult it has proved to get the balance right. The relationship between translator and director may be of far greater importance than in tragedy; it is also far trickier to negotiate. The commissioned translator for a new production of an Aristophanes is surely entitled as a minimum to an appropriate brief. One recent example of what happens without such proves salutary.

The 2002 production of *Birds* at the Lyttelton Theatre in London appeared to have the potential to satisfy both purist and the demands of an audience, as did Peter Brook's celebrated *A Midsummer Night's Dream* of 1970, and through similar theatrical inspiration. In a collaboration with Mamaloucos Circus this *Birds* was set within a series of trapezes with the roles of the birds played by aerialists. The concept sounds fine but the production was widely deemed to have relied too heavily on this single dominant idea of a circus environment. The translator on this occasion was Sean O'Brien, a poet of repute, with a commissioned 'version' in rhyming couplets which takes some liberties but on the page maintains the Aristophanic spirit without resorting to obvious anachronism. The production was by Kathryn Hunter, an actor well known for her work with innovative companies such as Théâtre de Complicité and The Wrestling School.

Somehow translation and production failed to make contact. O'Brien, who based the dialogue of the two leading characters on English television double-acts, says that he found out only at the first rehearsal that one of the two did not speak English and that a woman had been cast as the other. His lines simply did not fit. Spectacular though the flying effects were, as most critics were to agree, translation and concept were unable failed to gel. Nicholas de Jongh damned both director and translator in his search for the cause:

Classic Greek tragedy still speaks loud, clear and significant to us today. But I doubt whether ancient Greek comedy has this timeless capacity. Certainly Kathryn Hunter's almost mirth-free production of Aristophanes' *The Birds*, presented in association with Mamaloucos Circus, is an object lesson in dumbed-down desperation. Its use of trapezes and trampolines, and a version of the original text from Sean O'Brien that consists of embarrassingly inept couplets, hashed up in contemporary yob-speak, contributes little. By her efforts, Hunter betrays a conviction that Aristophanes must be spectacularly decorated rather than played .... Aristophanes' comedy you vaguely discern through the dank, straggling undergrowth of O'Brien's doggerel, has serious comic intent.[8]

Others among the London critics were equally vituperative in their response, without showing much comprehension of the original with its mix of fantasy and hard-edged politics. Benedict Nightingale in *The Times* picked up the Melos reference;[9] a couple of others referred hesitantly to the Sicilian Expedition.[10] One of the strongest responses was shared by almost all; the transformation of the leading character into a dictator by the end of the play was seen as a travesty of Aristophanes which could only be justified in a modern treatment if the satire on utopianism were to be specifically focused.

However justified in their dislike of the production, it is the critics who seem here on uncertain ground. To Aristophanes scholars such a reading of the ending of the play will hardly be a surprise, and to many of them not even contentious. *Birds* as a warning against the power of the demagogue is a perfectly viable interpretation, and hardly original as a production slant on the play. Aristophanes may have been a comedian but he was also a political playwright whose freewheeling approach does invite a matching inspiration, but only as long as the finished article can meet with contemporary theatrical criteria. An Aristophanes needs not only a concept, but a point of view. Hunter's production failed this test, perhaps, but will it ever be possible for a translator to accommodate the need for spectacle, comic routines, hard politics and fantasy that Aristophanes demands; or find this elusive Aristophanic spirit which invites an audience into a world of pure imagination?[11]

There seems to be little objection to creating a contemporary metaphor for an Aristophanes play, as opposed to a specific parallel, but the translator's imperative has to be to locate the theatrical language rather than just a linguistic equivalent. There are jokes in Aristophanes, but the plays are freewheeling in time and space: the jokes tend to be subordinate to the situations, the business, the gags; and gags belong to the players and the director. They are part of that broad stage world where the shape of a line is important for the actor but the context of the words is what supplies the comic impetus. Translation for the page is a wholly different animal from translation for performance where translator and the performing company really need to work in tandem. If, after his death, possibly even during his latter years, Aristophanes was played regularly outside Athens and as far away as Sicily, as Oliver Taplin seems conclusively to have shown, then it is a fair conjecture that his plays received an early translation of culture before a translation of language became necessary.[12] With the exception of some productions in Greek by Karolos Koun and a couple of moderately successful, if watered-down versions of *Lysistrata*, the marriage of Aristophanes and a contemporary audience probably needs the added dimension that a Stoppard might bring to it.

The linguistic translation of Aristophanes has had a chequered history outside of Greek communities, partly because of his perceived indecency, partly because of his parochialism and partly because later generations simply did not like him. He was never to the taste of the Roman audience. It was Menander rather who enchanted the intelligentsia of republican Rome. Plutarch writing his *Moralia* sometime at the beginning of the second century AD was unequivocal in his comparison of Aristophanes and Menander:

Coarse language, theatrical and tradesmen's talk are a feature of Aristophanes but never of Menander. The uneducated and the commoner will be delighted by what Aristophanes has to say, but not the man of refinement. I am referring to antitheses, rhymes and puns. Menander does use this type of wordplay but sparingly, deeming such things devices to be employed with caution. Not so Aristophanes who uses them all the time, inappropriately and pointlessly. He wins applause for 'drenching bankers like tankers': or 'blowing a north wind and an ill wind . . .' [*there follows a selection of unwieldy and virtually untranslatable examples of wordplay*]. And his language includes the tragic, the comic, the pompous, the pedestrian, the obscure, the mundane, the elevated, the gossipy and all manner of sickening rubbish, And with all this variety he cannot manage to get the appropriate differences of speech for the right people: dignity for a king, eloquence for an orator, shrewdness for a woman, common speech for a common man, slang for the streetwise. He doles out whatever language turns up to any character as though handing it out by lot. There is no way of telling whether someone is a father or a son from what they say, a yokel or a god, an old woman or a hero.[13] (10.853)

The translation of Menander began in the most limited way because of the total absence of complete plays until 1958. F. M. K. Foster's erratic but valuable survey of English translations from the Greek (1918) refers as the first, and only, entry under Menander to the Unus Multorum edition of the recently discovered Fragments in 1909.[14] There had been a number of desultory translations of quotations, this being for the most part the source of Menander's reputation, and a number of scenes, including one from *The Arbitration* in *Blackwood's Magazine* in 1908. The first Loeb edition was by Francis G. Allinson in 1921 with a revised edition in 1930. Allinson apologised, somewhat unnecessarily, for juxtaposing verse and prose, hardly surprising when so much of what he was dealing with was fragmentary. He also offered that he did not feel at liberty to make the English 'more racy' by introducing colloquialisms that 'would obscure the *milieu* of Menander'.[15]

Gilbert Murray wrote his own versions of *Perikeiromenē* (*The Rape of the Locks*, 1942) and *Epitrepontes* (*The Arbitration*, 1945), both Menander plays of which only enough survives to provide the broadest of outlines. Murray was a highly experienced translator with sales of over 300,000 of his various translations of Greek tragedy, and one comedy, *Frogs*, by the time he wrote *The Rape of the Locks*. In the introduction he diffidently admitted that 'I was unable to resist the temptation to patch up by conjecture', something which was forced upon him with barely half of the original available. *The Arbitration* followed three years later where he wrote of 'my earlier attempt, of whose faults I am more conscious now than when I made it'. He confessed to finding *The Arbitration* 'more serious and more mature', implying that this was an aspect of Menander which he had underestimated. He offered as a reason for missing this previously his failure to appreciate that Menander was writing what he described as a 'Nativity Play, celebrating the annual discovery . . . of that renewal of life which we think of as the New Year or the Spring.'[16] Right as he was about the seriousness of Menander, his retreat into the schema of the Cambridge anthropologists was less likely to be the cause than a failure to appreciate Menander's dramatic method. In that he has not been alone.

When first *The Bad-Tempered Man* (*Dyskolos*) in 1958, and then *The Woman from Samos* (*Samia*) in 1969 appeared as though at the wave of a magic wand, translators fell over one another to make up for lost time. Despite a pleasant radio version by Philip Vellacott (commissioned by the BBC and broadcast as *The Bad-Tempered Man* on the Third Programme in 1959), a certain disillusion set in. Was this really the Menander that Plutarch was talking about? Apologists for *Dyskolos* suggested it was fledgling work. What of *Samia*, undated, but at least from the mature period? The manuscript has gaps which mean that we still have no more than 85 per cent, and no choruses (marked by stage directions) scripted or implied. Apart from Plutarch, most critics found the scripts of Menander simplistic and, after Aristophanes, small beer indeed.

When W. G. Arnott took on the challenge of updating the Loeb, in three volumes now that so much more was available, he described his own translation as 'attempting the impossible'. Noting that Menander's style does indeed include the 'colloquialisms' of his day, he aimed for accuracy rather than the literal in the hope that this would prove 'speakable'. As Murray and Arnott came to appreciate, translating Menander is less simple than it seems. There is something lurking beneath the surface of apparently innocuous dialogue that is far more dramatically complex than many of his critics have recognised. I have elsewhere suggested that Menander's work is akin to that of Chekhov.[17] Certainly the more successful translations are those which show an awareness of ambiguity and subtext.

One example from *Samia* (*The Woman from Samos*) will serve as an example of Menander's delicacy. In the crucial scene where Demeas, suspecting – wrongly – that Chrysis has had a baby by his own son, throws her out of his house, the dramatic tension and the emotional effect come from neither knowing why the other is acting as he/she is. Demeas refuses to put his suspicions into words. Chrysis is trying to hide from Demeas that his son *is* a father but that the mother is the respectable girl who lives next door. Demeas abuses Chrysis and tells her to leave his house, but without saying what it is he believes she has done. Chrysis, being innocent, does not know how to defend herself without implicating Demeas' son. The scene is complicated by the presence of a third person, a nosy cook who tries to mediate.[18] This is a scene which was available when Allinson did his translation in 1921:

DEMEAS: ... I'll stop you, though,
     I think
CHRYSIS: From doing what?
DEMEAS (*checking himself*):   Oh, nothing. But you have
     The child; the crone. Off with you to perdition! Quick!
CHRYSIS: Because of his adoption?
DEMEAS: That, and –
CHRYSIS: Well, why "and"?
DEMEAS: Yes, that. 'Twas some such thing amiss, I know it well:
     You knew not how to live in clover.

There was no way that Allinson could at that time have known the real situation. He misread the context offering 'adoption' for what is quite the reverse, keeping the child. And because lines are not attributed in the manuscripts, he had the Cook exit before the above exchange, a decision that distorts the scene. The full text makes it clear that the line given by Allinson to Demeas 'Twas some such thing amiss, I know it well' is actually an aside of the Cook's whose presence as a third, and interfering, party alters the structure of the scene. It is the Cook who disarms Demeas' cruelty by his intervention.

     The first full translation of the play in the Penguin edition (Vellacott, 1967) again failed to read the involvement of the Cook:

CHRYSIS: Is this because I kept the baby?
DEMEAS: Because of that, yes; and –
CHRYSIS: And what?
DEMEAS: Just that. That started everything.
CHRYSIS: I don't understand.
DEMEAS: You had no notion how to live in style.[19]
                        (ll. 371–6)

In a rare lapse in someone who did much to drag the translation of classical drama into the present era, Vellacott introduced the Cook and gave him the line 'I'll stand here out of the way' (l. 368), and then completely forgot about him.

W. G. Arnott, in the new Loeb, correctly, had the Cook present:

DEMEAS: I believe
              I'll stop you –
CHRYSIS: Doing what?
DEMEAS: Oh, nothing – but you've got
              The baby, the old woman. Go to hell and quick!
CHRYSIS: Because I kept this baby?
DEMEAS: Through that, and –
CHRYSIS: What else?
DEMEAS: Through that!
COOK (*from the background*): So that's what caused the trouble! [Now]
              I understand.
DEMEAS: You never knew how to enjoy
              Our wealth.[20]

Arnott also included the no fewer than five further interruptions by the Cook which complete the comic scene. He managed Menander's elliptical exchange from CHRYSIS: 'Because I kept ... DEMEAS: Through that' in twelve words. (l. 374–5)

For the same sequence D. M. Bain, in his critical edition with a translation attached (1983), used eighteen words:

KHRYSIS: Just because I did not get rid of the baby?
DEMEAS: Because of this and –
KHRYSIS: And?
DEMEAS: Because of this.[21]

Bain also correctly identified the Cook and included his additional lines 'That's what the trouble is. I understand now'; 'It's some outburst of anger. I'd better approach them ... Sir, consider ...'; 'Don't bite my head off!'; 'What does he mean?'; 'He's not biting yet. Even so –'; and 'You're quite right. Look! I'm off inside.'

The second Penguin edition (Norma Miller) got the central exchange down to sixteen words:

CHRYSIS: Is it because I kept the baby?
DEMEAS: Yes, and because ...

CHRYSIS: Because what?
DEMEAS: Just because of that.[22]

Lionel Casson has the same, the Methuen reduced it to fifteen. Richard Elman in the Penn Greek Drama Series managed to get it down to thirteen:

CHRYSIS: Is it because I kept the baby?
DEMEAS: Yes, and . . . .
CHRYSIS: What ?
DEMEAS: That's bad enough.[23]

The brilliant Menander manages it in ten:[24]

CHRYSIS: *hoti tout' apeilomēn?*
DEMEAS: *dia touto kai*
CHRYSIS: *ti 'kai'?*
DEMEAS: *dia touto*
(ll. 374–5)

The translator's real challenge is to hit the note of bafflement and pain that both the characters feel, kept within bounds for the audience only by the presence of the Cook. Indeed, this is not a three-hander scene but a four-hander, Chrysis carrying the baby with her, as shown in the Menander mosaic reproduced on the cover of the second Penguin translation.

Perhaps this is not Chekhov country – the characters have comparatively undeveloped lives even if Menander does offer an unsentimental picture of their pasts and their possible futures. It *is* Alan Ayckbourn territory and the line between pathos and the ridiculous is as finely drawn in both. Demeas' dismissal of the hapless Chrysis is in one of those phrases which has to find a new frame of reference: *es korukas ēdē* (lit. 'to the crows already'). Solutions to this vary from 'Straight to the crows' to 'To hell and lose no time', 'Get the hell out of here', 'To hell. This minute'; 'You can go to hell as far as I'm concerned'; 'To hell – Right now!' and 'Go to the Devil'.

Even were the oldest complete Menander in English not from less than fifty years ago, his everyday characters and situations would seem to demand English colloquialism for Greek colloquialism. The sense of modernising becomes more of a translation issue in the manner in which people speak to one another than in the use of the simple iambic trimeter.

Menander's reputation survived when his plays failed to do so because he was so quotable. His own characters make reference to a variety of sources, often other lost plays. There is, as Netta Zagagi pointed out, a recurring link to tragedy and what appears almost as tragic parody.[25] One of her examples is an outburst by Demeas who greets his apparent confirmation of his son's deplorable behaviour with (in Bain's translation):

O Citadel of Kecrops' land! O thin-spread aither! O – Why are you shouting Demeas? Why are you shouting, you fool? Restrain yourself. Bear up! ... (*Samia*, ll. 325–7)

She comments 'he immediately becomes aware of the pathetic exaggeration of his heroic stance. Consequently he lowers his voice to its normal level, and the overdone emotional outburst inevitably gives way to self-irony.'[26] Nothing wrong with Bain's reading of the scene, nor his translation. But, in Michael Hackett's production of my own (with apologies) translation at the J. Paul Getty Museum in 1994, Jay Bell playing Demeas faced with 'Oh citadel of Cecrops' land / Outstretched expanse of Heaven's band / What are you on about, Demeas? You're raving' insisted that he could do nothing with a line from some Greek tragedy that the audience wouldn't recognise, a lost one at that and by an unknown author. His suggestion instead was to substitute from *King Lear*:

> 'Blow winds and crack your cheeks.
> Rage! Blow!'
> What are you on about, Demeas? You're raving ...

And that is what was used in the production, and that is what appeared in the revised translation (Methuen, 2002).[27]

With a stage play for today's audience, the crux resides in what David Constantine referred to as 'extolling the Spirit over the Letter'.[28] This is all the more true in Menander because of his fondness for the quotable line or maxim.[29] Chaereas, the parasite, in *Dyskolos* shares with the audience his method when abducting a *hetaira*, justifying himself with the difficult cliché *en tō tacheōs d'enesti pausasthai tachu* (l. 63), a line which defies literal translation but means something like 'in a matter of speed resides ending speedily': it has the tone of street philosophy, crying out for something pithy in English. Translations have not always done it much justice: 'if he enjoys her soon he soon gets over it' (Vellacott, Oxford, 1960 and

Penguin, 1967) has the sense, but not the style; the same for Casson's 'if it's done quickly there's a chance he'll get over it quickly'. 'Quick action produces / brings quick relief' (Penguin, 1987 and Aris and Phillips, 1995); Methuen 'Soonest gratified, soonest pacified'; and the Loeb 'Brisk starts mean brisk conclusions' all address the sense of aphorism by emphasising the repetition of *tacheōs/tachu*.

Both Menander and Aristophanes are at their most tricky when treading the tightrope between comedy and farce, and at their most challenging when moving from the comic into the serious. Any such balance between high and low comedy was underestimated by Umberto Eco when he discussed the different forms of interpretation:

Now, suppose that I am following a play in a language that I do not know well enough. When an actor utters something, I notice that the other people on stage (and probably people in the audience) are laughing, so I infer that the actor said something funny. These laughs act as an interpretant of the first actor's utterance, telling me that he told a joke; but they do not tell me what the joke was about.[30]

For the practitioner this is an absurd reduction suggesting that something is only funny if, and because, it is spoken. On stage, a situation, a reaction, an engagement with an object, a facial expression, a piece of business, a walk, a trip, all manner of cheironomic detail from the shrug to dismay, to delight, to fury, may be physically comic, transcending language or the understanding of what is being said. Jokes may need to be translated but so does 'the comic'. The implications for the translator of comedy are significant if only because any updating invites the supposition of a replacement theatrical and dramatic grammar as consistent and developed as the original. Aristophanes sometimes gives the impression of being anarchic in his violation of the rules of time, place, logic, space, action and consequence. On the contrary, his alternate universes have their own protocols and proprieties waiting to leap to stage life in the actions of the performers. So, in more subtle ways does the stage life of Menander. It hardly needs someone on stage to laugh in any comedy to cue audience laughter. Aristophanes may have some jokes; Menander has very few, his plays being a conscious blend of the farcical and the comedy of manners.

Negotiating the changes in style takes some doing. Sikon, the cook in *Dyskolos*, tries to borrow a pan from the bad-tempered Knemon and meets with a storm of abuse. Knemon departs and Sikon's response is *kalōs ge me bebōlokopēken* (l. 514). It's a farming metaphor from breaking up clods of earth, as Ireland points out in his edition, translating, accordingly, 'a fine pounding he's given me'.[31] Alternatives vary from 'He's furrowed me into strips of sod' to 'Yes, he's ploughed me nicely', 'Well, he's forked me over properly', 'He just about tore me to pieces', 'He's given me a pretty pounding' and 'I feel rotivated.'

Just as important, or more so, in Menander are the moralising speeches, the effect of which is less to encapsulate some humanistic message than to identify how the characters have grown through their experiences. These are serious comedies about human nature, as Aristophanes is serious about the politics of his wartorn city. To deny one element at the expense of the other betrays Menander as much as it does Aristophanes. Knemon believes he can live his life without depending on other people. The events of the play prove him wrong and make him recant. Knemon has a remarkable sixty-line speech which shows he has become aware of his mortality and uncovered a vein of self-knowledge, but is still unrepentant, because for him there is no other way. It is certainly a speech worthy of Molière and is crafted with an actor's instinct. Too long to compare in its entirety with one translation against another, a single truthful moment must represent the whole when comedy and sentiment meet in a dramatic world which transcends period. Knemon offers to adopt Gorgias and asks him to find a husband for his daughter, the one person for whom he has consistently shown concern and affection and whom he realises he must lose. A literal translation might run:

> I appoint you as guardian of my daughter here. And find her a
> Husband. Even if I do get better, I could never track
> One down. Nobody will ever satisfy *me*.
>
> (ll. 734–5)

Many a father may feel a twinge at this last line *ou gar aresei moi pote / oude heis*, translated variously as 'the man doesn't exist who would satisfy me', 'I'll never find anyone I approve of' and 'Nobody will ever be good enough for her'. Champagne and real pain, that's Menander, the most underrated of ancient playwrights, and a subtle challenge to the translator.

The twenty plays of Plautus and six of Terence, were based on Greek originals, none of which survives in its entirety (see pp. 11–12). In a Rome that would refuse to allow the building of a permanent theatre for another hundred years, Plautus and Terence created comedies, consciously and confessedly 'adapted' or 'translated' from the Greek originals of such as Diphilus, Philemon and Menander. Their stage world, then, is a curious blend of Greece and Rome. What parallels there might be and what challenges this affords strikes at the heart of what and where the translator stands in relation to cultural transference or what I prefer to identify as 'translocation'. The conditions of performance were widely different too, with the Greek new comedians apparently writing for performance at the same festivals for which Aristophanes had created his political comedies. The performance location was also the same, though the Theatre of Dionysus in Athens had been rebuilt in stone under the direction of Lycurgus when Menander was a child. The theatre of Plautus and Terence had by law to be impermanent, and though some later temporary theatres were elaborate, nothing in the texts that survive suggests anything more than a fairly rudimentary fairground theatre.[32] Writing for a known space is an aspect of the playwright's craft and that in itself can affect a play's identity.

The plays of Terence caused considerable controversy in their own time, at least in part as a result of differing responses to his treatment of the originals from which he was working. A defence of his approach is lodged firmly in the prologues of four, arguably five, of his six plays. All deal with the accusation of plagiarism. In his first play, *The Girl from Andros* (*Andria*), the actor delivering the prologue records that Menander wrote two plays which were very similar and that he [Terence] has made a single play from the two. He has been roundly criticised for this but maintains that Naevius, Plautus and Ennius before him went in for the same practice.

In *The Mother-in-Law* (*Hecyra*) a director/manager, Lucius Ambivius Turpio, delivers the prologue, claiming that it is thanks to his revivals that the plays of Caecilius are now so popular. He hopes similarly to benefit Terence. Not much here about how this play was written, but in the subsequent *Self-Tormentor* (*Heauton Timoroumenos*) the same Ambivius is defending Terence for changing a Greek original into a play with a double plot. He also responds to the accusation that Terence has 'contaminated' (the verb *contaminasse*) many Greek plays to make a small number of Latin ones. The *Eunuch* (*Eunuchus*) prologue is largely the attack on another playwright who is accused, despite being reasonable at translation (*vortendo*), of turning a good Menander play into a bad Latin one by poor construction (see p. 12). Terence had reason to dislike this other playwright, Luscius Lanuvinus, who had been so incensed by what Terence was up to as to have interrupted a rehearsal of the *Eunuch* by shouting out that the author was not a playwright but a thief. Terence offers, within his *Eunuch*, or at least as a prelude to it, a complicated defence based on where he claimed certain characters originated.

The prologue of *Phormio* is another attack on Lanuvinus, though a comparatively muted one, but in the last play, *Brothers* (*Adelphi*), Terence is back, all guns blazing, defending himself against having 'stolen' a scene from a Diphilus play which Plautus had left out in his Latin version of the Diphilus original. He prefers to consider what he had done, not as 'plagiarism' but as 'recovery' (*reprensum*).[33]

So what does this add up to, apart from revealing that the Roman theatre scene was as much of a bear garden as most? What it does seem to show is that the process of using Greek originals was virtually a requirement, a guarantee of quality, but that such material was in short supply. On the other hand, there was more than simple translation involved here. In Terence, as in Plautus, the setting is Greek – Athens or Attica; the characters are Greek; and the air of morality is Greek. Sons in second century BC Rome did not spend their time deceiving their fathers: still less did slaves go around making fools of their owners. Then again there is a strong sense of this being a Roman world – Greek cities ruled by Roman officials; in-jokes about what you can get away with in Athens that would be frowned upon in a Rome whose watchwords were *pietas* and *gravitas*. Terence and Plautus may well have headed for the Greek repertoire but their originality as dramatists allows for the criticism by Terence of his rival as a decent translator but a poor playwright: to put it literally 'in translating well, he has written badly and from good Greek plays has made Latin ones that are not any good'.[34]

For the modern translator of Terence this is still the challenge, and a matter of debate over priorities. The 'good' translator, in the manner in which Terence seems to use the term, may turn a good play into a bad play. There is not a lot of arguing with that. But how important is it to consider another possibility that the translator turns a good classical comedy into a good play, but bad Aristophanes, Menander, Plautus or Terence? And does it matter to anyone except the classical scholar? Roman comedy is a subtle and contrived blending of two stage worlds, one a relocation of the real life of Hellenistic Athens in the late fourth and early third centuries BC, the other a bastardisation of this into republican Rome where the nature of the piece and the changes that have been made in it do offer comment, however veiled, on Roman society of the play-wright's time. The personal and immediate nature of the prologues, echoed if less obviously vindictively in Plautus, offers social insights that have no parallel. Should there, at the very least, be some attempt made in any modern version of Plautus and Terence to home in on that inside world of bickering and backstabbing? Might the translator not be justified, for example, in setting up the play-within-a-play world of *The Taming of the Shrew*; or – a more interesting parallel – treat Plautus as Shakespeare did in *The Comedy of Errors*, where he created for the Epidamnus of *Menaechmi* the darker world of Ephesus, in which twice the twins quadrupled the opportunities for comic mistaken identity but where a man's life depends on exorcising the enchanted centre of ancient witchcraft? A better equivalent to Terence might be offered by Tom Stoppard's rewriting of Schnitzler (*Undiscovered Country* from *Das weite Land*) or Nestroy (*On the Razzle*, an adaptation of *Einen Jux will er sich machen*).

If not rules, are there at least guidelines? Translators of comedy will find their own. Definitive versions are rare in the world of translation, especially in comedy. Every production of a play, every performance by an actor, is some sort of translation. With the Greeks, performers, audiences and readers need translators less as mothers, as Kenneth McLeish suggested, than as midwives. If a play is to be renegotiated in another language and another culture, maybe it comes down, not to any pseudo-Aristotelian unities of place, time and action, but to an equivalence of the senses: the smell or flavour, the feel, sight and sound. Here there can be room for the pace and the silences, the emotions, quirks of character, the nuances, joys, humiliations and sheer daftness of human behaviour. Add to these the idiosyncracies of national humour, which often travel worse than wine, and the need to provide some kind of updating in a way that may not be essential for tragedy. These are the regions of real flexibility, these are the aspects of human experience which are least affected by the gulf of years between now and then, between the playwrights, players and audiences of ancient Athens and those of our own century.

Each comic playwright of stature has a special drive and it is that drive for which the translator needs to find a corresponding context. A considerable disservice may be offered to a comic text on the page which, in the name of faithfulness to the original, loses its own comic impetus and thrust: qualities which Julius Caesar, some 250 years after Menander, described as *vis*, that quality of performance energy which he personally found in Menander but not in Terence.[35] The word *vis*, 'force', 'power', 'energy' is a handy one here, even if, as is possible, Caesar was not making an aesthetic judgement.[36] *Vis* is all those qualities of stage dynamic which cannot be translated simply by the substitution of a set of words in Greek or Latin or French or whatever, by their equivalent in English. David Constantine tackled this term by translating it as 'vitality':

The literary works we concern ourselves with as translators are ones that have survived or what we believe will survive. When they do, it is through a sort of reciprocity between the works and us. Value in the text itself engages with our discernment of and our need for that value. Though being vital will not ensure survival, we may, I think, say that no work will survive that isn't. The surviving works are vital: that is they have vitality and we need them. The question is how to translate vitality.[37]

A distinction has been made in the preceding pages between what might be considered legitimate for tragedy and what for comedy, the suggestion being that there is a leeway in Greek comedy to transfer, translocate, update or simply revamp comic ideas in a way that is not appropriate to Greek tragedy. In the final chapter there can be no shirking from tackling a resistance to this view which is proceeding like a forest fire and threatens to leave future generations with a far worse understanding of the tragedy of classical times than they've experienced since the dark ages. The plays have been torn between undramatic scholars and unscholarly practitioners. There has always been good theatre and bad, appropriation and perversion of basic texts. The defence, in the case of Shakespeare and the playwrights of other periods, has always been that the plays will still be there when current fashions are dead and buried. In the case of the Greeks this may not be true. With those who can understand ancient Greek rapidly becoming an endangered species, conservation of Aeschylus, Sophocles and Euripides resides with those translators whose first priority is to find how the plays were made, and then with directors who will give the translations that public *vis* and vitality without which the plays as plays will become a memory as distant as the dodo.

CHAPTER 10

When is a Translation Not a Translation?

If ever there were a phase of translation in which the principle of the moderniser was uncontestably to be preferred, it is in the rendering of the Greek play.

(Theodore Savory,
The Art of Translation, London, 1957)

In 1959 the poet Christopher Logue was invited by Donald Carne-Ross to translate part of Homer's *Iliad* for production on the BBC Third Programme. Logue knows no ancient Greek but Carne-Ross thought this unimportant and suggested that he look at other people's translations from Chapman onwards.[1] 'True translation is much more a commentary of the original than a substitute for it', wrote Carne-Ross later.[2]

In an interview with Rupert Christiansen published in *The Observer* in 1991, the English translator and director Jeremy Sams suggested that 'You can't perform something in English and the original at the same time; and frankly worrying that it doesn't sound sufficiently like the original is the least of my worries.' Christiansen in the same article revealed his concern at prevailing attitudes when he suggested that nowadays 'Respect for a playwright's precise meaning comes second to the hitting at a snappy approximation to it'.[3]

Brian Logan wrote an article for *The Guardian* in 2003 in which he considered the approaches of a number of translators to whom he had spoken, Christopher Hampton, Ranjit Bolt, Martin Crimp and Pam Gems among them. Bolt's approach was to take liberties. 'If I think, "There's a good laugh here and Molière hasn't got it", then I'll put in an extra couplet.' Most revealing was Philippe Le Moine who at the time ran Channels, the National Theatre's translation unit, in which he encouraged young playwrights to 'try their hand at translating'. The success of the unit, Logan concludes, 'is predicated on *the now established fact* [my italics] that translators don't have to speak the original language'.[4]

The number of stage translators who would accept that ignorance of the source language doesn't matter is, I suspect, rather lower than Logan believes, especially if it is taken to imply that knowledge of the original may be a positive handicap in preparing a foreign text for a production where, as Le Moine put it, 'theatres need to have something sellable'.

This is an issue that I knew could not be ducked but one I take up without enthusiasm: hence the security of borrowing a title from Susan Bassnett who, in one of her more recent forays into the field, revisited the relationship 'between what is termed "translation" and what is termed "original" '.[5] Though her main focus was literature her initial point was particularly apposite when applied to drama. For those who do not have the original, she suggested, the translation *is* the original. In the production of a play, it could be argued, the production is the original even if you *do* know the original, because no two productions can be the same, nor even consecutive performances for different audiences. A second visit to the same production of the same play in the same translation with the same cast may still be different for all manner of reasons from performance to reception. Here is Heraclitus' impossibility of stepping into the same river twice, capped by the paradox that you can't step into the same river once.

Bassnett moved the argument on to a consideration of the visibility of the translator, again something that is writ large in drama. As we have seen earlier, a play by Terence taken from Menander could still be claimed by Terence because Terence's language was Latin and his context Roman. Tom Stoppard may acknowledge Nestroy, Schnitzler or Pirandello as his source, but his play has been adjusted or renewed for a contemporary audience by a theatrical *nous* that engages with, amongst other cultural associations, the change in audience sophistication between source and target. The real question is whether Sophocles or Euripides can be *improved* at text level by an emphasis that makes the play more vibrant for today. In production it surely should be. The translation of a stage work as a piece of theatre rather than as a piece of literature needs to take into account that the finished article on the page is barely half way there. Butterfly eggs don't turn directly into new butterflies. They evolve through stages from larva to the torpid chrysalis before the new image can emerge. Is a dramatic translation anything more than the static but necessary pupa?

Bassnett's other essay in the same book, 'Still trapped in the labyrinth: further reflections on translation and theatre', is another message home from her long journey to try and pin down the factors that determine or define theatre translation.[6] All the points she raises, to do with sign systems, subtext, plurality, acculturation and performability – that term of which she is so wary (see p. 23) – are appropriate to the translation of the Greek play but only in general terms. Bluntly, most Greek drama in translation is either Greek, and happens to be drama, or it is drama, which happens to be from the Greek. The problem is trying to make it both.

Before entering the minefield of definitions for 'authenticity' and 'enhancement' it may help to try to offer some categories. Translation, being by general agreement a word that carries a greater burden of responsibility than its slender shoulders can bear, has been used of any and all of the following:

Jean Anouilh   *Antigone, Oedipe ou le roi boiteux, Médée, 'Tu étais si gentil quand tu étais petit!'*
Bertolt Brecht   *Die Antigone des Sophokles*
Lee Breuer   *The Gospel at Colonus*
Robert Browning   *The Agamemnon of Aeschylus*
Jean Cocteau   *Antigone, Oedipe-roi, La Machine infernale*
Rita Dove   *The Darker Face of the Earth*
T. S. Eliot   *The Family Reunion, The Cocktail Party, The Elder Statesman*
Dario Fo/Franca Rame   *Medea*
George Gascoigne and Francis Kinwelmershe   *Jocasta*
André Gide   *Oedipe*
Johann Wolfgang von Goethe   *Iphigenie auf Tauris*
Tony Harrison   *The Oresteia, Medea: A Sex War Opera, Hecuba*
Seamus Heaney   *The Cure at Troy, The Burial at Thebes*
Hugo von Hofmannsthal   *Elektra, König Ödipus*
Ted Hughes   *Alcestis, Oresteia*
Robinson Jeffers   *Medea*
Brendan Kennelly   *Antigone, Medea, The Trojan Women*
Liz Lochhead   *Medea*
Frank McGuinness   *Sophocles Electra, Hecuba*
Blake Morrison   *Antigone, Oedipus*
Heiner Müller   *Medeamaterial, Medeaspiel*
Eugene O'Neill   *Mourning Becomes Electra, Desire Under the Elms*
Tom Paulin   *The Riot Act, Seize the Fire*
Jean-Paul Sartre   *Les Mouches, Les Troyennes*
Wole Soyinka   *The Bacchae after Euripides, Oyedipo at Kolhuni*

John Todhunter   *Helena at Troas*
Timberlake Wertenbaker   *The Thebans*
William Butler Yeats   *Oedipus the King, Oedipus at Colonus*

They have not always been described as 'translations' by their authors
who have variously identified them as 'a version of', 'a new version of',
'after', 'based on', 'taken from', 'translated and adapted from': or simply
'a play by' recognising only the new author, with no more acknowledgement than would have been expected in any original play that
happens to choose a plotline already used by some other playwright or
playwrights. Nobody would have expected Euripides to have called his
Electra '*Electra, after Aeschylus*' (or even '*Electra, before Sophocles*'). But
then neither would anyone expect an English edition of the letters of
Cicero to include a jazzed up version of the more boring bits.

This book has attempted to address Greek tragedy and comedy in the
English language, not drama based on Greek myth. Plays by Seneca,
Racine, Corneille, Dryden, Talfourd, Todhunter and von Hofmannsthal
have been excluded: as have many of those listed above. There are
exceptions, plays by Harrison, Heaney, Hughes and Yeats amongst them.
To try and give some pattern to such choices I now offer a tentative series
of categories, if for no better reason than to justify what has been included
and what excluded:

1. Literals (cribs). Most of the earlier translations from the eighteenth and
   nineteenth centuries:
   Adams, Potter, the Bohn library, Kelly's Keys and the first Loeb
   editions.
2. Those with literary fidelity and the translator's stamp, but with no
   claims as performance texts:
   Browning, Lloyd-Jones, Aris and Phillips, Cambridge, later Loebs.
3. Faithful to the original but actable:
   Chicago, Oxford, Hern, Penguin.
4. Intended for, or deriving from, production, with occasional licence:
   Methuen, Everyman, MaCneice, Harrison, Bolt.
5. Adapted from, or based on, the original but from playwrights/writers
   without a direct knowledge of Greek:
   Sartre, Anouilh, Kennelly, Heaney, Hughes, McGuinness, Morrison.
6. Original plays inspired by specific classical tragedies:
   Seneca, Dryden, Racine, Todhunter, von Hofmannsthal, Jeffers,
   Cocteau, Brecht.

7. Translocations to another culture:
   O'Neill, Eliot, Friel, Soyinka, Williams, Breuer, Paulin, Dove, Carr, Kane, *ad infinitum*: and a large number of production texts by some of the world's most innovative directors from Asia, America and Europe.

Already the objections are piled high. Where do you put Murray or Müller? Bond or Berkoff? How possible is it to pigeonhole those who have remained both close to, and have veered away from, a more literal translation, according to the brief or the occasion? Would that there were as many words in English for 'translate' as there are in Latin, so that one could be allocated to each of the above categories or whatever better formula might be proposed.

A bigger question may be what need there is for any playwright to feel obliged to be faithful to the original, even were that possible? Much comes down to how far there is virtue in the preservation of ancient plays in a time where critical judgement homes in on the imaginative approach of directors to the externals of production. If the form of the original in performance is so adaptable, what is the point of making the text sacrosanct, even could some agreement be reached about what faithfulness to the original entails? A contemporary production is for a contemporary audience. But it is perhaps at this point that Gershon Shaked's remark that 'The past is a closed world unless we translate it into the present' (see p. 4) be subjected to closer scrutiny.

All translation may be adaptation but the categories identified above use the word 'translation' in different senses. Innumerable authors from the Renaissance onwards, aware that the importance of myth lies in its decoding, have returned to ancient Greek sources. Several of those who are writing today, concerned that their target audience would find a classical context obscure and alien, have responded by selecting one or more of the themes of an original Greek tragedy, usually a Sophocles or a Euripides, and recreating a Greek play in a cultural context that the new audience will recognise. African, Irish and Japanese examples have been particularly successful and demonstrated, as if demonstration were necessary, how pervasive the myths of ancient Greece remain.

Such plays, categories 6 and 7 above, have been considered so far as being outside the scope of the present study, being less translation than the recreating of an original in a different period or culture. They are all simply stage works which happen to adopt a classical context but sometimes as loosely as did Shakespeare or Offenbach. As the process of revitalising, in the present, stories from the deep past was precisely what

Aeschylus, Sophocles and Euripides did in every surviving Greek tragedy, probably including *Persians*, it would be impossible not to applaud both the writers and the myths themselves for proving such a rich vein of dramatic material. The list above is no more than a tiny selection of the world's repertoire which has found in Greek myth appropriate metaphors for its own time.

The argument is whether any dues need be paid to the past in a theatre which is necessarily concerned with the present. Is there any significant difference between Bolt inserting a gag into Molière when 'Molière hasn't got it' and a director inserting a piece of business as part of the *mise-en-scène*? Comedy may play by a different set of rules but what is the point at which a Greek tragedy, or the 'translation' of a play by Aeschylus, Sophocles or Euripides, seriously misrepresents the 'atmosphere' of the work? How often can an audience tell the difference between an import from a translator and one from a director?

In the February 1965 edition of *Bref*, the magazine of the Théâtre National Populaire, Bernard Pingaud invited Jean-Paul Sartre to give his reasons for adapting Euripides' *Trojan Women*, in a production by Michael Cacoyannis which had first been performed at the Palais de Chaillot in 1964. The interview was later reproduced in the published version of the text, where Pingaud introduced the subject as follows: 'Greek tragedy', he wrote, 'is a splendid ruin, to be visited respectfully with an erudite guide, but it would never occur to anyone to live in it.'[7] He proceeded to give his reasons for consigning Greek tragedy to the dustier realms of the archaeologist. Pastiche, the kindest term he could find for revival of tragedies by Aeschylus, Sophocles and Euripides, 'is not very credible. Ancient drama is remote from us because it is based on a religious outlook that is wholly alien to us'; and because of this, Pingaud believed, 'fails to convince'.[8] Pingaud may have been playing devil's advocate here, setting up Sartre to defend his choice of *Trojan Women*. This Sartre certainly did but in terms which are almost as uncompromising as Pingaud's own. For Sartre, Greek tragedy was 'primarily a ceremony whose purpose is certainly to impress the spectator, but not to engage his sympathies. Horror becomes majestic, cruelty ceremonious.' That sounds remarkably like the 'holy' theatre which three years later Peter Brook, in a series of lectures which eventually became *The Empty Space*, selected as one of his four categories, alongside 'deadly', 'rough' and 'immediate', into which he divided all theatrical work.[9] More recent perspectives suggest that Brook's divisions are far from exclusive, and that holy theatre can be as deadly as any other. As debatable is how many

Greek tragedies come down to 'majestic horror' and 'ceremonious cruelty'. Sartre did have a more substantial point, though, when he addressed the different resonance in Euripides from that of Aeschylus, and concluded that:

There is an implicit relation between Euripides' tragedy and fifth-century Athenian society which we today can only see from the outside. If I wish to express the sense of this relation, I cannot simply translate the play; I must adapt it.[10]

Michael Anderson had a number of intriguing points to make when he commented on the Sartre version which had been translated by Ronald Duncan and had now (1966) reached the Edinburgh Festival, as a 'pop' production by Frank Dunlop.[11] This was, then, at three removes from Euripides via Sartre, Duncan and Dunlop. The reaction of Anderson, himself a classicist, was favourable:

Euripides may have had something to say in *The Trojan Women* which is more significant for the nineteen-sixties than what we find in the better-known and more conventional Greek tragedies. If there is a *catharsis* in this play, it is one of horror and disgust rather than pity or fear. Over every scene there hangs an air of bitterness and disillusionment. Quite simply it is a play about the failure of civilisation.[12]

This was echoed by Helene P. Foley when she wrote:

As classicists, we may not be comfortable with the idea that modern performance will inevitably preserve the vitality of Greek dramas on the stage best by radically re-imagining and even at times defacing them, but I for one am beginning to move towards that position.[13]

Contemporary news coverage from any centre of war in any part of the world offers ample support for the view that a play about the 'failure of civilisation' is always going to be topical. Anderson's point, though, was how far additions to the text of Euripides serve to make inclusive the centuries between Euripides' post-Melian Athens and the wasteland of nearly two and a half thousand years in Europe. It also served to point that, however much Sartre appears to let Helen escape justice (*Le crime paie*), ultimately it is civilisation itself which is vulnerable:

Sartre ... is no doubt 'using' Euripides' play for his own purposes. But he is using it in precisely the manner in which Euripides 'used' the myth of the defeat of Troy – to force his audience to examine their conscience, to see the world in a new light, to consider the true nature of their actions.[14]

In the scheme of things Sartre's 'improvements' are not radical, but the implication of his statement about 'adaptation' is. Greek tragedy is so tied to the society from which it evolved and which it mirrored, he suggested, that the text as it stands cannot be played today. Recent years have seen a wealth of 'adaptations' and 'versions' of Greek classics which might argue in favour of Sartre's belief, and that of Savory and Foley, that a modern audience has to have a modernised text.

The series of public seminars initiated by Marianne McDonald in Dublin in 1999 on Irish versions of classical drama revealed every kind of approach to Greek myth, from the straight translation, whatever that may mean, of Desmond Egan; to the 'versions' of Yeats; to the 'new versions' of Brendan Kennelly, rooted in classical texts, but enlightened both by his own poetic response to the language, and by inserted passages to amplify the themes he wished to enhance; to an independent play defined around a Greek tragedy, or based on existing Greek tragedies, and recognisable as meditations on the original, such as Seamus Heaney's *The Cure at Troy*; to a wide variety of dramatic visions, some more stimulating than others, inspired by some story from myth, the most imaginative to be found in the work of such as Brian Friel and Marina Carr.[15]

To the purist the words 'a version' appended to what claims to be a classic work sends out warning signals. In one sense any translation is never more than a version of the original, and, but for translations, the entire non-anglophone repertoire would be lost to those who are comfortable only in English: and so on, according to the native language or languages of the reader. The point at which the original ideas of the playwright get submerged or overtaken by those of the translator is the point at which the word 'version' tends to be introduced as an apology or disclaimer; or even a 'claimer', where the translators (such as Sartre) admit that the original is all very well as a starting-point, but that theirs is more interesting. However cogent the argument it should not be overlooked that this is often the moment when version becomes perversion.[16] What is questionable is not the right of the author to write what he or she will but the claim to respectability by implying that Euripides is in any way reflected in such stuff.

There are honourable exceptions. No one could accuse Yeats of lack of respect for the classics. He called his *Oedipus the King* a 'version', and it is true that he cut certain passages and altered the emphasis of others.

Ultimately, though, what the play offered was Sophocles through the medium of Yeats. Some writers choose to flag the originality of their work by adjusting the title – Declan Donnellan's *Antigone* (1999) was billed as Donnellan's *Antigone*, rather than Sophocles'. Others – Brecht, Anouilh, Berkoff – have opted simply to write their own play: nothing wrong with that. In between, though, comes this group of writers who use enough of the original play to have to admit its provenance but are unable to resist their own muse. They have to be good to get away with it. The best can be superb. Brendan Kennelly, for example, made no claims on Sophocles and Euripides beyond an inspiration and a structure. Seamus Heaney entitled his meditations on Greek tragedy *Mycenae Lookout* (a poem inspired by the opening of Aeschylus' *Agamemnon*); *The Cure at Troy* (Sophocles' *Philoctetes*); and *The Burial at Thebes* (Sophocles' *Antigone*). Wole Soyinka's *The Bacchae of Euripides* has a similar castlist to Euripides, but the entire play has been rethought in terms of Yoruba culture and ceremonial, and the Yoruba god, Ogun. Soyinka acknowledged a debt to the translations of Gilbert Murray and William Arrowsmith from which he borrowed some lines, but the play was a genuine re-think as 'a communion rite'.[17]

Some others are simply cuckoos.

From the first serious consideration of the function of translation, and especially translation from the classics into English – Dryden through to Tytler, Goethe and Arnold – one of the central issues has been less the issue of verse and prose than the kind of language used. J. M. Cohen suggested that Browning 'invented his own Greek world and put Aeschylus in it'.[18] Virginia Woolf justified suggesting that reading Greek in translation was useless by pointing to the inevitable 'echoes and associations' of a target language and the 'vague equivalents' that are the best the translator can offer.[19] T. S. Eliot, in his tirade against Gilbert Murray, called for an effort 'to neutralize Professor Murray's influence upon Greek literature and English language in his translations by making better translations ... it is because Professor Murray has no creative instinct that he leaves Euripides quite dead'.[20] Cohen did not consider Murray much of an improvement on Browning because in the early years of the twentieth century he 'found an equivalent for the Greek verse in the measures of Swinburne' and fell into the same trap as Browning by translating Aeschylus into 'a clearer but none the less Victorian idiom'.[21]

This question of 'idiom' was addressed from a different direction by John McFarlane over fifty years ago when he quoted Newman's reply to Matthew Arnold on the failure of translators with the remark that 'The question is not, What translator is perfect? but, Who is the least imperfect?'[22] McFarlane used this as a launching pad for a definition of the difference between 'translation' and 'adaptation':

there must be some minimum essential quality that makes translation translation and not an adaptation, a variation on an original theme, a plagiarism or a completely independent composition.[23]

He then identified this 'minimum essential quality' as 'Accuracy'. But because Accuracy does not allow for elegance and vitality (Caesar's *vis* again) which he called 'Grace', he also acknowledged a need 'to play fast and loose with the original text'. Everything can be seen to come down to the balance between 'Accuracy' and 'Grace'. This may seem, fifty years on, to be an outmoded notion in the light of current experience of translating plays, but perhaps it is only the balance between the two that has changed. Grace being, as McFarlane suggested, the meaning (and McFarlane was not referring specifically to drama anyway), it is Accuracy that has to become protean, reflecting forward into the present as well as, or rather instead of, backwards into the past.

The immediate relevance of this distinction may be put into focus through the work of two major poets, Ted Hughes and Seamus Heaney, both of whom produced significant 'translations' in recent years, despite having to work for the most part from the translations of others. This is not a dishonourable position in itself. Indeed it may inspire a greater respect for the essence of the original; Yeats and Soyinka provide precedents. All are major writers with an awareness of what they are able to do: aware equally that what they can do may well be an advance on what is routinely done by those whose gift with language as language is not as great.

Poets who try their hand at Greek tragedy have been as successful as the personal taste of the reader will allow. No translator of the classics is going to satisfy everyone. Much comes down to what is omitted and what is added. Ted Hughes's *The Oresteia: A New Version* was published posthumously in 1999 and his *Alcestis: Translated and Adapted by Ted Hughes*, in the same year. *The Oresteia* was directed in 1999 by Katie Mitchell in the smallest of the National's three theatres, the Cottesloe. To return to a previous example (see pp. 55–61), in the second play, *Libation-Bearers* (*Choephori*), Orestes and his sister are reunited through the device of three recognition tokens. The first is the lock of hair which Orestes cuts off and lays on his father's tomb; the second, sets of footprints unwittingly left by Orestes and Pylades, and which Electra finds; the third, after Orestes steps from hiding to confront his sister and finally convinces her that he is her brother by showing a piece of cloth that she had woven for him in childhood. Tony Harrison had cut the second of these in the previous National Theatre production of *The Oresteia* by Peter Hall (1981).[24] Hughes extended the details of the lock of hair ('Colour, texture, everything about it / As I hold it – all so familiar') and included the footprints, but modified:

> Look! Fresh footprints.
> Though I have not stepped where they are, they are
> Familiar as my own.
> Do these footprints belong to the hair?
> As like my own as the hair is.
> Heel, instep, toes –
> My own prints magnified. Oh let me pray.
> My head throbs. I think my heart
> Is going to burst.[25]

Hughes left out the reference in Aeschylus to there being two sets of prints (those of Orestes and Pylades), but added in 'My own prints magnified' a suggestion that the footprints are not really the same but *like* Electra's, only bigger. In Mitchell's production the footprints were supplied, not by Orestes at all, but by the ghost of Agamemnon who patrolled the stage area, unseen by the living characters but determined to ensure that revenge on his behalf meet with no obstacle. The ghost purposely stepped in the water alongside the tomb to make the wet footprints, moments before Electra saw them and when they were already beginning to dry under the heat of the stage lights. They were not only unlike Electra's, but unlike those of Orestes too. So, where and what is the translation here?

Apart from this, Hughes's *Oresteia* is recognisable as Aeschylean in structure, but with reservations over treatment and language. His *Alcestis* is a very different matter.[26] Euripides' play, a brief 1163 lines in the Greek, is adjusted and stretched with the introduction of five new characters.[27] Two of them, Iolaus and Lichas, are servants of Heracles who 'enact' the twelve labours. There is also a vision of Prometheus and God who converse with Heracles before the arrival of a talking vulture. The Vulture has two lines, one of which is 'Ah', the other 'No, I am alive and you are not free', before it bursts into flames when Heracles shoots an arrow at it. These are not to be found in Euripides.

The most strenuous expression of dismay about Hughes came from Bernard Knox in an extended review of the published versions, under the title 'Uglification'.[28] Knox took issue with the descriptions as 'new translation' and 'translated and adapted', describing them as 'flying false colours'. So far are they from being translations, he suggested, as to be:

disfigured by the frequent and substantial interpolations of freely invented matter, by the omission of significant passages of the original, by bathetic sentimentalization, and – to borrow a term from a critic's description of a regular feature of Hughes's poetry – by uglification.[29]

Knox started with *The Oresteia* and proceeded to detail at least thirty words used by Hughes which have no equivalent in Aeschylus, including cockroaches, dysentery, maggots and putrescence (none of which can be much of a surprise to anyone familiar with the main body of Hughes's poetry). He made comparisons with Lattimore's translation which he found 'accurate' (interesting word) and 'sensitive', concluding that 'at a rough count, a good half of what the reader gets is nothing that Aeschylus ever wrote, but pure Hughes'. Knox was equally harsh over cuts, reserving some of his strongest criticism for a kind of cleansing of Athens as a peace-loving city: also for omitting Agamemnon's recognition of the army's right to demand the sacrifice of Iphigenia, and for sensationalising her death.

This is where the debate over translation becomes all-out war between those who might be said to represent the author and those who claim the author's authority for promoting their own slant on the drama. A diversion from Hughes and Knox leads to Blake Morrison's *Antigone*, written for Northern Broadsides, a company with the specific agenda to promote, as Edward Pearce noted:

not bloody-minded North of England, or anyway not just that. It is an insistence upon the plainness of classical English speech, its demotic clarity before court affectation and slatternliness got into the woodwork.[30]

In the published edition of *Oedipus* and *Antigone*, both plays are described as 'versions by Blake Morrison'.[31] It would be harder for a Knox to take issue here with Creon's assertion that 'We did the job. The terrorists are dead' or Antigone's blunt rehearsal of the ancient and immutable laws:

1: Don't kill your family. 2: Don't breed with them.
3: Honour your parents. 4: Bury the dead.[32]

Where an objection might be raised is not in the directness of the language but in the directiveness of the characterisation. When the angry Creon is asked by the Chorus how he intends to kill Antigone he replies, in Marianne McDonald's truer translation of Sophocles:

I'll take her to some remote place and bury her alive in a rocky hollow, giving her just enough food so the city will escape pollution for her death. She can pray to the gods of the underworld (they are the only ones she worships) and ask them to spare her life; she may finally learn that it is wasted time to revere a dead traitor. (ll. 773–80)[33]

This reveals much more than some technical quibble over responsibility for Antigone's death. It covers the anxiety over pollution which lay behind, not only the exposure of the body of Polyneices in the first place, but the unwitting fracture of natural law in Oedipus' murder of his father and marriage to his mother. It also points to Creon as an ambivalent figure, attempting to act the strong ruler without the instinct of when to bend before circumstance. The final part of the play devoted to the consequences of his compound misjudgement invites the possibility of sympathy as he finds himself culpable over the deaths of his own son and wife as well as of Antigone.

Morrison's version echoes the shape of the scene but has Creon respond to the Chorus' question about his plans for Antigone:

> I'll bring her out here and have her stoned
> till the ground's bloodier than a butcher's slab
> and her head's a smashed eggshell runny with slime.
> No, I've a better plan, I'll draw it out,
> there's a place on the moor no one ever goes,
> a stone outhouse, a windowless cell –
> I'll have her locked up there, walled in with bricks,
> but I won't let her suffocate, not quite,
> and I won't starve her to death either.
> I'll keep her alive – just– on morsels of bread,
> so no one can say my leadership's brutal.
> She can ask those gods of hers to save her.
> And when they don't she'll finally listen to what I've said:
> no one should place the living below the dead.[34]

Sophocles' Creon may be brutal but he is not this sadistic. Multiplying the torments he plans for Antigone interferes with the fine balance of the original play, disqualifying Creon from a sympathy that Sophocles makes possible. Were Morrison claiming this as a translation, this would be a major objection; in a 'version' it suggests no more than an alternative treatment.

The link between Hughes and Northern Broadsides is underlined both by Hughes' Yorkshire background and by this being the company who gave the first performance of the Hughes *Alcestis* in 2000. Knox found even more reason to defend Euripides over *Alcestis* than he had Aeschylus for the Hughes *Oresteia*. The damage done to the great Aeschylean trilogy is, wrote Knox:

> minor when compared to the shambles that he has made of one of the most elegant and subtle masterpieces of the Athenian theater, the *Alcestis* of Euripides.[35]

Of the first eight pages only just over half of one can be claimed as Euripides. This time Knox finds 150 intrusive words which include, amongst the more predictable physical functions, hypodermic syringes and asbestos. Knox ends with the statement that 'Hughes' version is a desecration, the literary equivalent of spray-painting a moustache on the *Mona Lisa*'.[36] This being the painting equivalent of what Jake and Dinos Chapman have subsequently done to Goya, we are in the territory of a much broader argument over independent artists and their relationship with the classics, a can of worms that needs no opening here. The only useful generalisation would appear to be that the relationship between author's text and dramatic production is as flexible as the taking up of cudgels on behalf of a dead playwright is risky. Some years ago there was an acrimonious dispute between Bernard Levin and a number of writers and directors over faithfulness to the text. The immediate context was Peter Barnes's revision of Ben Jonson's *The Devil is an Ass*. Barnes defended his work in a BBC Arena documentary in 1977 called *Hands off the Classics*, suggesting that:

> Adapting an old play is much like restoring an old painting. Time renders certain areas opaque and words, like protective varnish, go dead. These obsolete words have to be replaced by others of equal precision and force but whose meaning is clear.

Bernard Levin, then theatre critic for *The Sunday Times*, disagreed, accusing the Royal Shakespeare Company of inaugurating 'Ben Jonson bugger-the-text week'. Members of the theatrical profession were quick to leap to the defence of Barnes and the right of directors to innovation, amongst the most vociferous being Trevor Nunn – 'A theatre concerned with textual integrity at the expense of understanding is dead' – and Jonathan Miller – 'The emphasis on what is regarded as the core of the play, what is its topic and subject matter, will vary as the interests of the period will vary.'

What is sanctioned here is the right of a play, if a play can have rights, to a revision of emphasis in a new time and under different sensibilities and preoccupations. Yeats's decision to offer as Creon's excuse for not investigating the death of Laius that 'We were amid our troubles' may have been made in his first draft of 1912, but the line's inclusion in the first performance at the Abbey in 1926 can hardly have been made without an awareness that a Dublin audience of the day would make an association with 'the troubles' of their more immediate experience. If the same playtext may offer a new voice in a new age, then how much of an imposition can it be for a new translation to capitalise on that? There will always, in a stage production, be the possibility of an emotive meaning whose significance may have been unforeseeable a week, a day, an hour before the performance, never mind two and half thousand years earlier.

Seamus Heaney's two forays into the world of Sophocles offer a similar contrast in 'translation'. In *The Cure at Troy: A Version of Sophocles' Philoctetes*,[37] which he wrote for Field Day in 1990, he felt free to promote the play as a plea for reconciliation. Sophocles' *Philoctetes* is the only surviving Greek tragedy with an exclusively male list of characters. Heaney opted for a chorus of three women:

in order to give a sense that the action was being invigilated by the three Fates, the Weird Sisters or whoever . . . .There was also a dimension of gender politics in the anima (shall we call it?) impetus in Neoptolemus.[38]

Heaney created the play for performance during Mary Robinson's presidential campaign in Ireland in 1990. He is happy to acknowledge that his personal agenda in *The Cure at Troy* does little more than acknowledge the Sophocles as a framework for an original work.

The same is not true of *The Burial at Thebes* which is identified on the title page as 'translated by Seamus Heaney' and was commissioned by the Abbey Theatre for its centenary in 2004. *Antigone* has for many years been the 'Irish' Greek tragedy, being amongst the most malleable of all Greek plays in its direct confrontation between state and private conscience.[39] Tom Payne in a review of the published script pointed out how

Heaney subtly invited reader or audience to treat the play as contemporary without making direct parallels:

When Creon comes on stage, Heaney doesn't make him talk like George Bush, but he's opened our ears. Creon says of the man Antigone wants to bury, 'He terrorised us' and we get the point: a leader is about to make a terrible situation worse still by persisting with his dogmatic policies. But then that's the play Sophocles wrote, and once we accept that, we can start enjoying the Greek playwright and the Irish poet at their best.[40]

Michael Billington in *The Guardian* wrote that 'Heaney, as we know from his version of *Philoctetes* called *The Cure at Troy*, is a magnificent translator of Sophocles.'[41] Billington's loose use of the word 'translator' fails to distinguish between Heaney's 'version' of *Philoctetes* and his 'translation' of *Antigone*, though both bring the sensibility of one great artist engaging with another. *The Burial at Thebes* suggests that Heaney here has found a way fully to marry Sophocles to a modern idiom – trust the Irish to find a way to do this – rather than using Sophocles as a point of reference in an original play. Heaney's rendering of the passage about the punishment for Antigone (quoted above in the translation from the Greek by McDonald, and Morrison's 'new version') runs:

> Up in the rocks, up where nobody goes,
> There's a steep path that leads higher, to a cave.
> She'll be put in there and some food will be put in with her –
> To ward off any bloodguilt from the city.
> And once she's in, she can pray to her heart's content
> To her god of death. After all her Hades talk,
> It will be her chance to see if he can save her.[42]

Is a dead playwright damaged through misrepresentation by a translator or by a director? The original play, or rather the received text because the authenticity of the surviving manuscripts is frequently questioned, will survive. On the other hand I confess to a nagging concern on behalf of the integrity of any work of art. When Nahum Tate rewrote *King Lear* to give it a happy ending a generation of theatre-goers believed that Shakespeare was responsible for the kind of crassness to be found in the Hollywood *Billy Budd*, which ended with our hero rescued from the gallows by the timely arrival of a *deus ex machina*.

A legitimate engagement with the text as handed down, at least insofar as such engagement is possible: that is surely a responsibility of the translator. The re-creation, rooted in this original, but not wholly dependent on it, of something for a contemporary audience which takes account of the past but thrusts it firmly into the present: that is the responsibility of the director.

Translation may by definition be a hermeneutic act but what limits does the translator impose in 'reinterpreting'? Or is it up to the director to decide on the stage iconography? The generalising effect of modern dress sometimes works against the power of myth. One stage version of one story, the story of Hecuba, Andromache, Medea, Phaedra, is powerful because it is specific. The Trojan War may be every war. It may be the Peloponnesian War. It may be the First World War. It may be a war in the jungle or a war in the desert. The decoding lies with the audience according to the prompting of the production of which the translation is an integral but not the only part. Acts of revenge, acts of treachery, insane cruelty, sacrifice, resistance: any of these, and similar, form the spine of the Greek tragic canon. Any of them can be generalised, inviting the audience to home in on a single issue. Or they can be made specific, in a specific theatrical context, from which, again, the audience may draw the parallel they find most suitable. Greek plays are as amenable as any other classic playtexts to uprooting from the original context and relocating in a variety, not only of cultures, but also of periods. After all, the Thebes of *Antigone* or the Argos of *Orestes* are as far a cry from fifth-century Athens as are the Ephesus of *Comedy of Errors* or the Troy of *Troilus and Cressida* from Shakespeare's London.

The last hundred years have seen Greek drama rescued from the study where it had so long languished and restored to the stage. It still took time before the *noli-me-tangere* approach which limited productions gave way to a genuine appreciation that here were dramatic and theatrical texts whose openness offered a special kind of freedom. Greek drama now forges links that are unique for a theatre which is open to a wider variety of cultural and performance dimensions than at any time in its history. This is exciting and productive for designers, directors and actors; translation too needs to meet this challenge.

Of course, the plays are old. They come from a period some of whose terms of reference can be remote, if not unfathomable. A modern audience has to adjust to the Greek pantheon, the oracles and the prophets, the sacrifices and the curses. The hierarchy of authority, the balances in the family unit, the sense of terms like *aidōs, sōphrōn, hubris, xenos* (so inadequately translated as 'shame', 'prudent', 'insolence', 'friend/guest/ stranger') – all these affect what characters in Greek tragedy do and say. For the translator there are fundamental decisions to be made between identifying the nuances and rendering the text playable. The only real question in all this is what licence the translator may claim to nudge, tickle or just plain sabotage the original? Translators and directors may have today's actors, directors and audiences to answer to. A little voice does make itself heard in a corner of my mind, warning that the translators are also the keepers of the keys, the caretakers of the culture, the spirit voice of the long-dead dramatist. The seance may be stage-managed but the medium holds the message.

Why does any of this matter? It matters if the classics themselves matter: and if the theatre matters, for its past as well as for its present. At its best the strength of the theatre has been in its ability to remember its past; and having remembered it forget it again.

Appendix
A Comprehensive List of all Greek Plays
in English Translation

The following lists of translations of complete, or almost complete, ancient Greek tragedies and comedies (and including the eight 'mimes' of the third-century BC Herodas from Kos or Alexandria) are divided into three categories. Collections A includes, chronologically, the best-known and most established translations, from the earliest published to those still in print or in regular use today. Collections B contains less familiar collections where more than two plays have been included in the same volume. *The Oresteia* is treated for this purpose initially as a single play and is included first amongst the remaining entries for Aeschylus; followed by single editions of the three plays of the trilogy, and the remainder of Aeschylus by the most familiar title. The other playwrights are less complicated and simply follow the principle of Collections A, Collections B and individual plays which are otherwise listed alphabetically by main title.

Unless discussed within the book, only very few 'adaptations' and 'versions' have been included. Partial translations (apart from the Brumoy/Lennox), such as those by Gerard W. Smith which appeared sporadically and in diminishing-size portions in *The Monthly Packet* (edited by Charlotte Yonge) between 1881 and 1883, have also been ignored. Only significant reprints are recorded and it has not been possible to include all the compilations which have relied on earlier translations.

Some translations were published anonymously, others without a date or named publisher. Omitted are Dr J. A. Giles's 'Keys to the Classics' which included word-for-word renderings into English of Aeschylus and several of the plays of Euripides, with no pretensions to be anything other than schoolroom cribs; also single 'Thrift' editions published by Dover, currently in print, but in dated translations which are all mentioned elsewhere. It also proved impossible to run down a few of the American translations mentioned in Foster (New York, 1966) but not listed in the Library of Congress Catalogue.

Translations of the whole of Greek drama have been available periodically from Heinemann (Loeb Classical Library), Penguin (Penguin Classics), Methuen (Classical Greek Dramatists), Random House (The Complete Greek Drama, though these are all older translations), and the University of Pennsylvania (The

Penn Greek Drama Series), several of the latter more free than would normally be included here and claimed in 1998 (incorrectly) to be 'the only contemporary series of all the surviving work of Aeschylus, Sophocles and Euripides, Aristophanes and Menander'. The tragedies can be found in Chicago (The Complete Greek Tragedies) while the Oxford University Press series of the tragedies as single plays is comprehensive. Most of the serious publishers have moved on periodically to revised or new translations within the same series. Some single plays from Cambridge University Press and Aris and Phillips have been published too recently to be included. A variety of translations, many of them unpublished elsewhere, can also be found as part of the Bohn Library from the 1840s onwards, and in anthologies such as vol. 1 of *The Drama, its History, Literature and Influence* (published by The Athenian Society, London, 1903–4); *Fifteen Greek Plays Translated into English* (New York: Oxford University Press, 1943); *Greek Literature in Translation* (New York: Longman, Green, 1944); *Greek Plays in Modern Translations* (New York: Dial Press, 1947); *Six Greek Plays in Modern Translations* (New York: Dryden, 1955); *An Anthology of Greek Drama* (first series, New York: Rinehart, 1949; second series, 1954); *Ten Greek Plays* (Boston: Houghton Mifflin, 1957); and *Classical Tragedy: Greek and Roman* (New York: Applause Books, 1990).

Translations included in the Collections are not usually duplicated under individual titles which accounts for the apparent dearth of translations of certain plays (e.g. only three listed under Euripides' *Orestes* and *Rhesus*, two for his *Suppliants*).

AESCHYLUS

Collections A

[*The Greek Theatre of Father Brumoy*. Translated from Father Pierre Brumoy's *Le Théâtre des Grecs* (Paris, 1730) by MRS CHARLOTTE LENNOX in 3 vols. (London: Millar *et al.*, 1759), with résumés and partial translation of all the extant plays of Aeschylus, Sophocles and Euripides as well as the eleven plays of Aristophanes. Seven are translated in their entirety, but none of the seven is by Aeschylus.]

The Tragedies of Aeschylus. Translated into English verse by ROBERT POTTER, Norwich: printed by J. Crouse, 1777; reprinted 1779, 1808, corrected version 1819 (various publishers), 1831, 1886; New York: Harper, 1834.

The Seven Tragedies of Aeschylus. Literally translated into English prose, ANON. [possibly, by Charles James Blomfield], Oxford: D. A. Talboys, 1822; reprinted Henry Slatter, 1827, 1840.

Four Plays of Aeschylus [*The Suppliant Maidens, The Persians, The Seven Against Thebes, The Prometheus Bound*]. Translated by E. D. A. MORSHEAD, London: Kegan Paul and Co., 1881; revised edition, Simpkin and Marshall, 1889; Macmillan (The Golden Treasury Series), 1904 and 1908.

The Tragedies of Aeschylus. Translated into English prose by LEWIS CAMPBELL, London: Kegan Paul and Co., 1890; reprinted as *Aeschylus, The Seven Plays*, Oxford: Oxford University Press (The World's Classics), 1906.

Aeschylus in English Verse. Translated by ARTHUR S. WAY, London: Macmillan, 1906–08.

Aeschylus. Translated in 2 vols. by HERBERT WEIR SMYTH (Loeb Classical Library), London: Heinemann, and Cambridge, Mass.: 1922–6; reprinted 1946, 1957; reprinted with an appendix containing the more considerable fragments published since 1930 and a new text of Fragment 50, 1963.

Complete Plays. Translated into English rhyming verse with commentaries and notes by GILBERT MURRAY, London: Allen and Unwin, 1952; reprinted with the illustrations of John Flaxman, limited edn, Franklin Center, Pa.: Franklin Library, 1978.

Aeschylus I and II. Translated by SETH G. BENARDETE (*The Suppliant Maidens and The Persians*), DAVID GRENE (*Seven Against Thebes and Prometheus Bound*), and RICHMOND LATTIMORE (*The Oresteia*), Chicago: University of Chicago Press, 1953–6; reprinted regularly; *Oresteia* reprinted with etchings by Alaine Raphael and Don Bolognese in a limited edition, Franklin Center, Pa.: Franklin Library, 1980; included in *The Complete Greek Tragedies*, edited by David Grene and Richmond Lattimore, translated by WILLIAM ARROWSMITH, WITTER BYNNER, ROBERT FITZGERALD, RALPH GLADSTONE, DAVID GRENE, MICHAEL JAMESON, FRANK WILLIAM JONES, RICHMOND LATTIMORE, JOHN MOORE, JOHN FREDERICK NIMS, EMILY TOWNSEND VERMEULE, CHARLES R. WALKER, REX WARNER, RONALD FREDERICK WILLETTS, ELIZABETH WYCKOFF, Chicago: University of Chicago Press, 1959, 4 vols. [I Aeschylus].

The Oresteian Trilogy: Agamemnon, The Choephori, The Eumenides and *Prometheus and Other Plays* [*The Suppliants, Seven Against Thebes, The Persians*]. Translated by PHILIP VELLACOTT, Harmondsworth: Penguin Books, 1956 and 1961.

Aeschylus Plays: I [*Persians, Prometheus Bound, Suppliants* and *Seven Against Thebes*] and *Plays: II* [*The Oresteia*]. Translated by FREDERIC RAPHAEL and KENNETH MCLEISH, London: Methuen, 1991, reprinted 1998.

Aischylos Suppliants and other Dramas [*Persians, Seven Against Thebes,* Fragments, *Prometheus Bound*]. Translated by MICHAEL EWANS, London: Dent (Everyman), 1996.

Aeschylus: the Complete Plays. Translated by CARL R. MUELLER, Hanover, N.H.: Smith and Kraus, 2002.

Collections B

Aeschylus, the Tragedies. Translated by THEODORE ALOIS BUCKLEY, London: Henry G. Bohn, 1849 ('The translator gratefully acknowledges the help he has derived from the labours of his predecessors').

Greek Dramas [including *Agamemnon, Choephori, Eumenides, Prometheus Vinctus, Supplices*]. Adapted from the Versions of the Rev. ROBERT POTTER, by JOHN BENSON ROSE, London: printed by W. Clowes and sons for private circulation, 1867–72.

The Lyrical Dramas of Aeschylus in 2 vols. Translated into English verse by JOHN STUART BLACKIE, London: J. W. Parker, 1850; reprinted, London and New York: Dent (Everyman), 1906.

The Dramas of Aeschylus. Translated by ANNA SWANWICK, London: George Bell and Sons, 1873 (with the Flaxman illustrations), 1881 (Bohn's Classical Library), New York: 1890; revised edition, 1899.

Aeschylus. Translated in prose by F. A. PALEY, Cambridge: Deighton, Bell and Co., 1864; reprinted 1871.

The Tragedies of Æschylos. Translated by EDWARD HAYES PLUMPTRE, 2 vols., London: Strahan and Co., 1858; reprinted 1865, 1901 (Isbister and Co.); New York: Dutton, 1869, 1873, 1882.

Aeschylus. Translated by R. S. COPLESTON, Edinburgh: W. Blackwood and Sons (Ancient Classics for English Readers), 1870; Philadelphia: 1871.

The Suppliants, Persians and *Seven Against Thebes.* Translated by JOHN DUNNING COOPER, London: Simpkin and Marshall, undated [1889/90/91].

The Plays of Aeschylus [*The Persians* and *The Seven Against Thebes*]. Translated from a revised text of W. Headlam by C. E. S. HEADLAM, London: G. Bell and Sons (Bell's Classical Translations), 1900; the complete plays, Bell (Bohn's Classical Library); New York: Harcourt, 1909.

Three Greek Plays [including *Agamemnon, Prometheus Bound*]. Translated by EDITH HAMILTON, New York: W. W. Norton, 1937.

Four Plays of Aeschylus [*The Suppliant Maidens, The Persians, The Seven against Thebes, Prometheus Bound*]. Rendered into English verse by G. M. COOKSON, Oxford: Blackwell, 1922; *The Plays of Aeschylus*, reprinted Chicago: William Benton (for The Encyclopaedia Britannica), 1952; London: Dent, 1960.

Aeschylus 1 and *2*. In translations by GAIL HOLST-WARHAFT (*The Suppliants*), WILLIAM MATTHEWS (*Prometheus Bound*), STEPHEN SANDY (*Seven Against Thebes*) and DAVID R. SLAVITT (*The Persians* and *The Oresteia*), Philadelphia: University of Pennsylvania Press, 1998–9.

THE *ORESTEIA* (THE ORESTEIAN TRILOGY, THE HOUSE OF ATREUS)

First, in Potter, 1777.

The Agamemnon, Choephori, and Eumenides. Translated into English verse by ANNA SWANWICK, London: Bell and Daldy, 1865.

The Oresteia. Translated by Sir CORNELIUS NEALE DALTON K.C.M.G., London: J. R. Smith, 1868.

The House of Atreus: being the Agamemnon, Libation-Bearers, and Furies of Æschylus. Translated into English verse by E. D. A. MORSHEAD, London: Kegan Paul and Co., 1881, 1889; reprinted London: Macmillan, 1901, 1904 [*Studies from Attic Drama*], 1924, 1928; reprinted as *Oresteia*, New York: printed by A. Colish for the members of the Limited Editions Club, 1961.

The Orestean Trilogy (*The Oresteia of Aeschylus*). Translated and explained by GEORGE CHARLES WINTER WARR, with illustrations, London: George Allen (*The Athenian Drama* in 3 vols.), (1886), 1900.

The Agamemnon, Choephoræ, and Eumenides. Rendered into English verse by JOHN DUNNING COOPER (dedicated to Henry Irving), London: Simpkin, Marshall and Co., 1890.

The Oresteia of Æschylus. Translated into English prose by LEWIS CAMPBELL, London: Kegan Paul, 1890; reprinted in *Aeschylus, The Seven Plays*, 1906.

The Oresteia of Aeschylus. Agamemnon, Choephori, Eumenides. An English verse translation by R. C. TREVELYAN, Cambridge: Bowes and

Bowes, 1920; reprinted with the Greek text as arranged for performance at Cambridge, 1921; Liverpool: University of Liverpool Press; London: Hodder and Stoughton, 1922.

The Agamemnon, Choephoroi, Eumenides. Translated by G. M. COOKSON, London: Chapman and Hall, 1924.

The Oresteia. Translated into English rhyming verse by GILBERT MURRAY, London: G. Allen and Unwin, 1928; reprinted 1946, 1960.

The Oresteia of Aeschylus: the Agamemnon, the Choephoroi, the Eumenides. Translated from the Greek by CHARLES H. HITCHCOCK, Boston: B. Humphries Inc., 1932.

The Oresteia of Aeschylus. The Greek text as arranged for performance at Cambridge, 14th to 18th February 1933, with an English verse translation by J. T. SHEPPARD, Cambridge: Bowes and Bowes, 1933.

The Oresteia. Translated into English verse by the Earl of LONGFORD and CHRISTINE LONGFORD, Dublin: Hodges, Figgis and Co., 1933.

The Oresteia of Aeschylus. Edited with introduction and translation by GEORGE THOMSON, Cambridge: Cambridge University Press, 1938; reprinted in Auden (Wystan H.), *The Portable Greek Reader*, New York: Viking Press, 1948, pp. 249–373; revised edition, Prague, Academia, 1966.

The Oresteia. An acting version by ROBERT A. JOHNSTON, Boston: Christopher Pub. House, 1955.

The Orestes Plays of Aeschylus. The Agamemnon, The Libation Bearers, The Eumenides. A new translation by PAUL ROCHE, New York: New American Library, 1962.

The Oresteia. Translated and edited by PETER D. ARNOTT, New York: Appleton-Century-Crofts, 1964.

The Oresteia Trilogy: Agamemnon, The Choephoroe, The Eumenides; and Prometheus Bound. Translated by MICHAEL TOWNSEND, San Francisco: Chandler Publishing Co., 1966.

The House of Atreus. Adapted for the stage from *The Oresteia* by JOHN LEWIN, Minneapolis: University of Minnesota Press in association with the Minnesota Theatre Co., 1966.

The Oresteia, Aeschylus. Translated by HUGH LLOYD-JONES, Englewood Cliffs: Prentice-Hall, 1970; reprinted London: Duckworth, 1979; Berkeley: University of California Press, 1993.

The Oresteia, Aeschylus [*Agamemnon, The Libation-Bearers, The Eumenides*]. Translated into English verse from a scientifically conservative Greek text by DOUGLAS YOUNG, Norman: University of Oklahoma Press, 1974.

The Oresteia. Translated by ROBERT FAGLES, New York: Viking Press, 1975; reprinted London: Wildwood House, 1976; Harmondsworth: Penguin,

1977; introduction by Peter Levi, drawings by Lawrence Preece, London: Folio Society, 1984.

The Oresteian Trilogy. A theatre version adapted by RUSH REHM, Melbourne: Hawthorn Press, 1978.

The Oresteia of Aeschylus. Translated by ROBERT LOWELL, New York: Farrar, Straus, Giroux, 1978; reprinted London: Faber, 1979.

The Serpent Son. Translated by FREDERIC RAPHAEL and KENNETH McLEISH, Cambridge and New York: Cambridge University Press, 1979; revised in *Aeschylus Plays: II*, London: Methuen, 1991, 1998 (*see* Collections A above).

The Oresteia. Aeschylus. Translated by TONY HARRISON, London: Collings, 1981, new edition, Faber and Faber, 2002.

The Oresteia. A new translation for the theater by DAVID GRENE and WENDY DONIGER O'FLAHERTY, Chicago and London: University of Chicago Press, 1989.

Klytemnestra's Bairns. Being the full text of the major cycle of Aeschylus (*The Oresteia*) by BILL DUNLOP, as performed on Calton Hill, Edinburgh, Edinburgh: Diehard, 1993.

The Oresteia of Aeschylus [*Agamemnon, The Libation-Bearers, Eumenides*, Fragments]. Translated by EDWARD WRIGHT HAILE LANHAM, London: University Press of America, 1994.

Aischylos The Oresteia. Translated by MICHAEL EWANS, London: Dent (Everyman), 1995.

Aeschylus: Oresteia. Translated by PETER MEINECK, Indianapolis: Hackett Pub. Co., 1998.

The Oresteia by Aeschylus. In a version by TED HUGHES, London: Faber and Faber, 1999.

Aeschylus: Oresteia. Translated by CHRISTOPHER COLLARD, Oxford: Oxford University Press, 2002.

The Oresteia. Aeschylus. Translated by ALAN SHAPIRO and PETER BURIAN. Oxford: Oxford University Press, 2003.

AGAMEMNON

First in Potter, 1777.

The Agamemnon of Aeschylus. Translated by HUGH S. BOYD, Longman and Co.: London, 1823.

The Agamemnon. Translated by JOHN SYMMONS, London: Taylor and Hessey, 1824.

Agamemnon. English by JOHN S. HARFORD, London: John Murray, 1831.

Agamemnon. Translated into English verse by THOMAS MEDWIN, London: William Pickering, 1832.

'The Prometheus of Aeschylus' (with 'The Agamemnon'). Translated into English verse by GEORGE CROKER FOX, in George C. Fox, *The Death of Demosthenes*, London: 1839.

The Agamemnon. Translated literally and rhythmically by W. SEWELL, London: Longman and Co., 1846.

The Agamemnon of Aeschylus. Translator ANON., Boston: J. Munroe and Co., 1847.

The Agamemnon. The Greek text with a translation into English verse by JOHN CONINGTON, London: J. W. Parker, 1848.

The Prometheus and Agamemnon. Translated into English verse by HENRY WILLIAM HERBERT, Cambridge, Mass.: John Bartlett, 1849.

Agamemnon of Aeschylus. Translated by WILLIAM PETER, Philadelphia: Carey and Hart, 1852.

Agamemnon the King. Translated from the Greek of Aeschylus by WILLIAM JOHN BLEW, London: Longman and Co., 1855.

The Agamemnon of Æschylus and the Bacchanals of Euripides. With passages from the lyric and later poets of Greece, translated by HENRY HART MILMAN (with illustrations), London: John Murray, 1865.

The Agamemnon. Revised and translated by JOHN F. DAVIES, London: Williams and Norgate, 1868; reprinted 1874.

Agamemnon. A tragedy, taken from Æschylus by EDWARD FITZGERALD with MS. corrections by the translator, printed for private circulation, 1865; London: Bernard Quaritch, 1876.

The Agamemnon. Translated into English verse by E. D. A. MORSHEAD, London: H. S. King, 1877; revised version, see *The House of Atreus* (1881).

The Agamemnon of Æschylus. Translated by ROBERT BROWNING, London: Smith, Elder and Co., 1877; reprinted, in collected works, 1889.

The Agamemnon. With a metrical translation by BENJAMIN HALL KENNEDY, Cambridge: Cambridge University Press, 1878, reprinted 1882.

Agamemnon. Translated (in verse) by HENRY HOWARD MOLYNEUX, the Earl of Carnarvon, London: John Murray, 1879.

The Agamemnon. Translated into English prose by a First-Class Man of Balliol [THOMAS NASH], Oxford: J. Thornton, 1880.

The Agamemnon. Freely translated into English on the occasion of the performance of the play by students of the University of Sydney, Sydney: Gibbs and Shallard, 1886.

The Agamemnon. A translation by a Gold Medallist in Classics, Cambridge: University Correspondence College, 1888.

The Agamemnon of Aeschylus. With an introduction, commentary and translation by A. W. VERRALL, London: Macmillan and Co., 1889; reprinted 1904.

The Agamemnon. The Greek text with English verse translation parallel, by Upper Sixth Form boys of Bradfield College, London: Henry Frowde, 1900, reprinted for the College, 1934.

The Agamemnon. Translated into English verse by E. THRING, London: Constable and Co., 1904.

Agamemnon. With verse translation by WALTER HEADLAM, Cambridge: Cambridge University Press, 1904, 1910.

The Agamemnon. A revised text and a translation by WILLIAM WATSON GOODWIN, Boston: Ginn and Co, 1906.

The Agamemnon. Rendered into English verse by W. R. PATON, London: David Nutt, 1907.

The Agamemnon. Freely translated by ARTHUR PLATT, London: Grant Richards, 1911.

The Agamemnon. Translated (into verse) by RUSHWORTH KENNARD DAVIS, Oxford: Blackwell, 1919.

Agamemnon. After the Greek of Aeschylus by VIVIAN LOCKE ELLIS (in verse), London: Selwyn and Blount, 1920.

The Agamemnon. Translated into English rhyming verse with explanatory notes by GILBERT MURRAY, London: Allen and Unwin, 1920, reprinted 1924, 1927, 1932.

The Agamemnon of Aeschylus. Translated by MARION CLYDE WIER, Ann Arbor: C. W. Graham, 1920.

The Genius of the Greek Drama [including *Agamemnon*]. Rendered and adapted with an introduction, by CYRIL E. ROBINSON, New York: Humphrey Milford, 1921; Oxford: Clarendon Press, 1924; reprinted Freeport, N.Y., Books for Libraries Press, 1970.

The Agamemnon of Aeschylus. Translated by CHARLES H. HITCHCOCK, Walton, N.Y.: printed by the Reporter Company, 1927.

The Agamemnon. An English version by Sir HENRY SHARP (in verse), Oxford: Oxford University Press, 1928.

The Agamemnon of Aeschylus. A revised text, with introduction, verse translation, and critical notes by J. C. LAWSON, Cambridge: Cambridge University Press, 1932.

Agamemnon. Translated by HENRY T. SCHNITTKINI, Girard, Kan.: Haldeman-Julius and Co., 1934.

The Agamemnon of Aeschylus. Translated by T. G. TUCKER, Melbourne: Melbourne University Press; Oxford University Press, 1935.

The Agamemnon of Aeschylus. Translated by LOUIS MACNEICE, London: Faber and Faber, 1936, reprinted 1967.

Agamemnon. Translated by EDOUARD FRAENKEL in vol. 1 of his three-volume commentary, Oxford: Oxford University Press, 1950.

The Agamemnon of Aeschylus. The Greek text performed at Cambridge by members of the University, February 1953, with a verse translation by Sir JOHN SHEPPARD, Cambridge: Bowes and Bowes, 1952.

The Agamemnon of Aeschylus. Text edited by RAYMOND POSTGATE, with an introduction, a commentary and a translation into modern English prose, Cambridge: Rampant Lions Press, 1969.

Agamemnon. Translated and edited by ANTHONY HOLDEN, Cambridge: Cambridge University Press, 1969.

Agamemnon. Translated by HUGH LLOYD-JONES, Englewood Cliffs: Prentice-Hall, 1970; reprinted London: Duckworth, 1979.

The Greeks. Ten Greek plays adapted by JOHN BARTON and KENNETH CAVANDER, based on original translations by Kenneth Cavander [including *Agamemnon*], London: Heinemann, 1981.

Agamemnon by Aeschylus. An English version by WILLIAM R. LINK, Dublin, N.H.: William L. Bauhan, 1981.

The Agamemnon of Aeschylus. A radical interpretation, translation and commentary. D. W. MYATT, New York: Thormynd Press, 1993.

Agamemnon. A play by Aeschylus; translated from the Greek into English with introduction, notes, and synopsis by HOWARD RUBENSTEIN, El Cajon, Calif.: Granite Hills Press, 1998.

Aeschylus's Agamemnon in Scots. W. S. MILNE, London: Agenda Editions, 2002.

LIBATION-BEARERS (*CHOEPHOROI, CHOEPHORI*)

First in Potter, 1777.

'*The Choephori*'. Translated by THOMAS MEDWIN, in *Fraser's Town and Country*, 35, vol. VI part 2, Nov. 1832.

The Choephori. With an introduction, commentary and translation by A. W. VERRALL, London: Macmillan and Co., 1893.

The Choephori of Aeschylus. With a translation by T. G. TUCKER, Cambridge: Cambridge University Press, 1901.

The Plays of Aeschylus, the Choëphoroe. Translated by WALTER HEADLAM, London: George Bell, 1905; reprinted New York, 1909.

The Choëphoroe. Translated into English rhyming verse by GILBERT MURRAY, London: Allen and Unwin, 1923.

FURIES (EUMENIDES)

First in Potter, 1777.

Æschyli Eumenides. The Greek text, with an English verse translation by BERNARD DRAKE, Cambridge: Macmillan and Co., 1853.

The Eumenides of Æschylus. Translated into English verse by G. C. SWAYNE (with translations of poems by Schiller and Uhland), Edinburgh: W. Blackwood and Sons, 1855.

Eumenides. A critical edition, with metrical English translation by JOHN F. DAVIES, Dublin: Hodges Figgis and Co., 1885.

The Eumenides of Æschylus as arranged for performance at Cambridge. The text in Greek, with English translation by A. W. VERRALL, Cambridge: Cambridge University Press, 1885, 1906; with an introduction, commentary, and translation by A. W. VERRALL. London: Macmillan, 1908.

Æschylus: Eumenides. With a translation by F. G. PLAISTOWE, London: W. B. Clive (University Tutorial Press), 1901.

The Eumenides. Translated by GILBERT MURRAY, London: Allen and Unwin, 1925.

The Eumenides of Aischulos. Translated by CHARLES H. HITCHCOCK, Walton, N.Y.: printed by the Reporter Company, 1931.

Eumenides. Aeschylus. Edited with translation by ANTHONY J. PODLECKI, Warminster: Aris and Phillips, 1989.

PERSIANS (PERSAI, PERSAE)

First in Potter, 1777.

Aeschylus, The Persians. Translated by WILLIAM PALIN, London: Longman and Co., 1829.

'*The Persians*'. Translated by THOMAS MEDWIN, in *Fraser's Town and Country*, 37, vol. VII, Jan. 1833.

Persae. Translated by A Member of the University, Cambridge: Cambridge University Press, 1840.

The Persae. With English notes and a literal English translation by M. WOOD, Cambridge: E. Johnson, 1855.

The Persians. Translated into English verse by WILLIAM GURNEY, Cambridge: Deighton, Bell and Co., 1873.

The Persians. A popular version from the Greek. By JOHN STAUNTON with photographs of Flaxman's designs, Warwick: H. T. Cooke and Son, 1873.

Æschylus' Persæ. Literally translated by T. MEYER-WARLOW, London: J. Cornish and Sons, 1886.

The Persians. An English prose version by EDMUND SAMUEL CROOKE, Cambridge: J. Hall and Son, 1893.

Aeschylus: Persae. Greek and English, edited by J. H. HAYDON, London: W. B. Clive (University Tutorial Press), 1897.

The Persians of Aeschylus. Translated into English verse by C. B. ARMSTRONG, Dublin: Talbot Press, 1927; reprinted London: Allen and Unwin, 1928.

The Persians of Aeschylus. Translated by T. G. TUCKER, Melbourne: Melbourne University Press, 1935.

The Persians. Translated into English rhyming verse by GILBERT MURRAY, London: Allen and Unwin, 1939.

The Persians. A translation with commentary by ANTHONY J. PODLECKI, Englewood Cliffs, N.J.: Prentice-Hall, 1970; Bristol: Bristol Classical Press, 1991.

Persians. Aeschylus. Translated by JANET LEMBKE and C. J. HERINGTON, Oxford: Oxford University Press, 1981.

Aeschylus Persians. Edited with translation by EDITH HALL, Warminster: Aris and Phillips, 1996.

Six Greek Tragedies [including *Persians and Prometheus Bound*]. Translated by FREDERIC RAPHAEL and KENNETH MCLEISH, London: Methuen, 2002.

PROMETHEUS BOUND (PROMETHEUS DESMOTES, PROMETHEUS VINCTUS, PROMETHEUS IN CHAINS, PROMETHEUS CHAINED)

First, Thomas Morell 'Prometheus in Chains', in Thomas Stanley, Ed., Aeschylus: Single Works, Prometheus Vinctus (Polyglott), London: T. Longman, 1773.

Æschyli Prometheus Vinctus. To which is subjoined, a Greek ordo, a literal prose translation (Anon.), London: G. and W. B. Whittaker, 1822.

The Prometheus Chained. Literally translated into English prose by T. W. C. EDWARDS, London: Matthew Iley, 1823; reprinted New Haven, 1872–6.

Prometheus Vinctus. Translated by GEORGE BURGES, London: Longman and Co., 1831.

Prometheus Bound, a tragedy, from the Greek. Translated into English verse by THOMAS MEDWIN, Sienna: O. Porri, 1827; London: William Pickering, 1832.

Prometheus Bound. Translated from the Greek of Aeschylus and published with miscellaneous poems by the translator, ELIZABETH BARRETT (afterwards Barrett Browning), London: A. J. Valpy, 1833. Elizabeth Barrett Browning's second translation (*see below*, 1850) is very different from the first.

The Prometheus of Æschylus and the *Electra of Sophocles.* Translated by GEORGE CROKER FOX. London: Darton and Harvey, 1835.

'Prometheus Bound'. Translated by W. M. W. CALL in *Lyra Hellenica*, Cambridge: W. P. Grant, 1842.

'The Prometheus Bound'. Translated by HENRY DAVID THOREAU, in *The Dial*, 3, no. III, Boston, Mass., Jan. 1843.

The Prometheus Chained. Translated into English verse by Revd G. C. SWAYNE, Oxford: Francis Macpherson, 1846.

Prometheus Chained. Translated by ROSCOE MONGAN, Dublin: W. B. Kelly (Kelly's Keys to the Classics), 1848; reprinted London: James Cornish, 1858.

The Prometheus and *Agamemnon.* Translated into English verse by HENRY WILLIAM HERBERT, Cambridge, Mass.: John Bartlett, 1849.

'Prometheus Bound'. Translated by ELIZABETH BARRETT BROWNING, her second translation of the play (*see above*, 1833), in *Poems, Second edition*, vol. I, London: Chapman and Hall, 1850; reprinted with 1833 Preface in *The Poetical Works of Elizabeth Barrett Browning*, London: Henry Frowde, 1906.

Prometheus Chained. Translated into English verse by CHARLES CAVENDISH CLIFFORD, Oxford: J. H. Parker, 1852.

The Prometheus Bound of Æschylus. Literally translated into English verse by AUGUSTA WEBSTER, London and Cambridge: Macmillan and Co., 1866.

The Prometheus Bound. Translated in the original metres by C. B. CAYLEY, London: J. C. Hotten, 1867.

Prometheus Vinctus. Literally translated by JOHN PERKINS, Cambridge: J. Hall and Son, 1870.

Prometheus Vinctus. Translated into English verse by ERNEST LANG, London: Smart and Allen, 1870.

Prometheus Bound. Translated from the Greek by J. M. HUNT, London: published by the author, 1880.

Prometheus Bound. From the Greek of Æschylus, with original poems, by JOHN DUNNING COOPER, London: Simpkin, Marshall and Co., 1890.

The Prometheus Bound of Æschylus and the fragments of the Prometheus Unbound. Translated by F. D. ALLEN, Boston and London: Ginn and Co., 1891.

Aeschylus: Prometheus Vinctus. Edited with a translation by F. G. PLAISTOWE and W. F. MASOM, London: W. B. Clive and Co., 1892; revised translation by F. G. Plaistowe and T. R. Mills, London: W. B. Clive (University Tutorial Press), 1900.

Prometheus Bound. Translated by HENRY HOWARD MOLYNEUX, fourth Earl of Carnarvon, London: John Murray, 1892.

The Prometheus Vinctus. Translated by HERBERT HAILSTONE, Cambridge: E. Johnson, 1892.

'The Prometheus Bound'. In Edward H. Pember, *The Voyage of the Phocæans, ... with the Prometheus Bound done into English verse by E. H. Pember*, London: Chiswick Press for private distribution, 1895.

Prometheus Bound. Translated by the Rt. Hon. GEORGE DOWMAN (for private circulation), Cambridge: Cambridge University Press, 1896.

The Prometheus Bound of Aeschylus. Translated into English verse by E. D. A. MORSHEAD, London: Simpkin, Marshall and Co., 1899; reprinted London and New York: Macmillan and Co., 1908.

The Prometheus Bound of Æschylus. Translated with introduction and notes by PAUL ELMER MORE, Boston: Houghton, Mifflin, 1899.

The Prometheus Bound of Aeschylus. Rendered into English verse by EDWYN R. BEVAN, London: David Nutt, 1902.

Aeschylus. Prometheus Vinctus. Translated by E. S. BOUCHIER, Oxford: Blackwell, 1903.

The Prometheus Bound. Edited with introduction, translation and notes by JANET CASE, London: J. M. Dent and Co., 1905 (Temple Dramatists); New York: Dutton, 1905.

Prometheus Bound. Translated by ROBERT WHITELAW, Oxford: Clarendon Press, 1907.

Prometheus Bound. Translated by WALTER HEADLAM, London: G. Bell and Sons, 1908; reprinted New York, 1909.

The Prometheus Vinctus. Translated by MARION CLYDE WIER, New York: Century Co., 1916.

The Prometheus Bound of Aeschylus. Represented in English and explained by EDWARD GEORGE HARMAN, London: Edward Arnold, 1920.

Prometheus Bound. Translated into English verse by WILLIAM JAMES BYRAM, Brisbane: Simpson, Halligan and Co., 1922.

The Prometheus Bound of Aeschylus. Translated by CHARLES H. HITCHCOCK, Walton, N.Y.: printed by the Reporter Company, 1924.

A New Presentation of the Prometheus Bound of Aischylos: wherein is set forth the hidden meaning of the myth. By JAMES MORGAN PRYSE, Los Angeles: Wayside Press; London: J. M. Watkins, 1925.

Prometheus. 'Prometheus Bound' of Æschylus. A metrical version with 'Prometheus Unbound' (an original play in verse) by CLARENCE W. MENDELL, New Haven: Yale University Press, 1926.

'Prometheus Bound'. Translated by ARTHUR S. WAY in Henry H. Harper, ed., *Attic Tragedies*, Boston: Bibliophile Society, 1927.

Prometheus Bound. Translated into English rhyming verse by GILBERT MURRAY, London: Allen and Unwin, 1931.

The Prometheus Bound. Edited with an introduction, commentary and translation by GEORGE THOMSON, Cambridge: Cambridge University Press, 1932.

The Prometheus Bound of Aeschylus. Translated by T. G. TUCKER, Melbourne: Melbourne University Press, 1935.

The Binding of Prometheus. A translation in verse by LENNOX JAMES MORISON, Oxford: Blackwell, 1936.

Prometheus Bound. Translated by R. C. TREVELYAN, Cambridge: Cambridge University Press, 1939.

Three Greek Tragedies in Translation [including Aeschylus' *Prometheus Bound*]. By DAVID GRENE, Chicago: University of Chicago Press, 1942.

The Prometheus Bound of Aeschylus. A translation by REX WARNER, London: Bodley Head, 1947.

'Prometheus Bound'. In Havelock (Eric A.), *The Crucifixion of Intellectual Man*, Boston: Beacon Press, 1951, pp. 111–81; reprinted Seattle: University of Washington Press, 1968.

Prometheus Bound. By MARJORIE L. BURKE, illustrations by James McCray, Athens: 1961.

Prometheus Bound. Translated by WARREN D. ANDERSON, Indianapolis: Bobbs-Merril, 1963.

Prometheus Bound. A new translation by PAUL ROCHE, New York: New American Library, 1964.

Prometheus Bound, by Aeschylus. Translated by REX WARNER with *Prometheus Unbound*, by Percy Bysshe Shelley, New York: Heritage Press, 1966.

Seven against Thebes, and *Prometheus Bound.* Translated by PETER D. ARNOTT, London: Macmillan; New York: St Martin's Press, 1968.

Prometheus Bound. Derived from Aeschylus by ROBERT LOWELL, New York: Farrar, Straus and Giroux, 1969; London: Faber and Faber, 1970.

The Frogs, and Other Plays. Translated by KENNETH MCLEISH [including *Prometheus Bound*], London: Longman (Heritage of Literature series), 1970.

Prometheus Bound. Translated by JAMES SCULLY and C. J. HERINGTON, Oxford: Oxford University Press, 1975, 1989.

The Prometheus Trilogy. 'Prometheus Bound' (translated from the Greek of Aeschylus); 'Prometheus Unbound' (guided in part by the eleven extant fragments); 'Prometheus Firebearer' (an original play), by RUTH F. BIRNBAUM and HAROLD F. BIRNBAUM, Lawrence: Coronado Press, 1978.

'Prometheus Bound', Aeschylus. Translated by EMILY HILBURN in CHARLES Doria, ed., *The Tenth Muse*, Athens, Ohio, Chicago, London: The Ohio University Press, 1980.

Prometheus Bound. Edited with translation by ANTHONY J. PODLECKI, Warminster: Aris and Phillips, 2002, 2005.

Six Greek Tragedies including *Persians and Prometheus Bound.* Translated by FREDERIC RAPHAEL and KENNETH MCLEISH, London: Methuen, 2002.

SEVEN AGAINST THEBES (HEPTA EPI THEBAS, SEPTEM CONTRA THEBAS)

First in Potter, 1777.

Septem Contra Thebas. Translated by WILLIAM GURNEY, Cambridge: Deighton, Bell and Co., 1878.

Æschylus' Seven Chiefs against Thebes. Literally translated by ROSCOE MONGAN, London: J. Cornish and Sons (Kelly's Keys to the Classics), 1881.

The Seven against Thebes. With an introduction, commentary, and translation by A. W. VERRALL, London: Macmillan and Co., 1887.

Septem Contra Thebas. Translated by F. G. PLAISTOWE, London: W. B. Clive (University Tutorial Press), 1899.

The Seven against Thebes. Translated by T. G. TUCKER, Cambridge: Cambridge University Press, 1901.

The Seven against Thebes. Translated into English verse by E. D. A. MORSHEAD, London: Macmillan and Co., 1908.

The Seven against Thebes. Rendered into English verse by EDWYN R. BEVAN, London: Edward Arnold, 1912, 1931.

The Seven Against Thebes. Translated into English rhyming verse by GILBERT MURRAY, London: Allen and Unwin, 1935.

Seven against Thebes and *Prometheus Bound.* Translated by PETER D. ARNOTT. London: Macmillan; New York: St Martin's Press, 1968.

The Seven against Thebes. A translation with commentary by CHRISTOPHER M. DAWSON. Englewood Cliffs, N.J.: Prentice-Hall, 1970.

Seven against Thebes. Translated by ANTHONY HECHT and HELEN H. BACON, Oxford: Oxford University Press 1973, 1991.

Seven against Thebes. Translated by ROBERT EMMET MEAGHER, Wauconda, Ill.: Bolchazi-Carducci, 1996.

SUPPLIANT WOMEN (HIKETIDES, SUPPLICES, SUPPLIANTS)

First in Potter, 1777.

The Suppliants. Translated by ROSCOE MONGAN, Dublin: W. B. Kelly (Kelly's Keys to the Classics), 1856; reprinted London: James Cornish, 1858.

The Suppliant Maidens. Translated by E. D. A. MORSHEAD, London: Kegan Paul and Co., 1883.

The 'Supplices' of Aeschylus. A revised text, with introduction, critical notes, commentary and translation by T. G. TUCKER, London: Macmillan, 1889; reprinted New York, London: Garland, 1987.

The Suppliant Women. Translated into English rhyming verse, with introduction and notes, by GILBERT MURRAY, London: Allen and Unwin, 1930.

The Suppliants, vol. 1. The text, with introduction, critical apparatus and English translation by H. FRIIS JOHANSEN, Copenhagen: Gyldendalske Boghandel, 1970.

'The Suppliants, Aeschylus'. Translated by RICHARD CALDWELL in Charles Doria, ed., *The Tenth Muse,* Athens, Ohio, Chicago, London: The Ohio University Press, 1980.

The Suppliants. Translated by LINDLEY WILLIAMS HUBBELL, Hartford, Conn., 1980; Kobe: Ikuta Press, 1986.

Aeschylus: Suppliants. Translated by Janet Lembke, Oxford: Oxford University Press, 1975.

The Suppliants. Aeschylus. Translated by PETER BURIAN. Princeton, N.J.: Princeton University Press, 1991.

Suppliants of Aeschylus and *Ajax of Sophocles.* Translated by JAMES KERR, London: Oberon Books, 2001.

SOPHOCLES

Collections A

Sophocles Translated into English Prose by George Adams.   2 vols., London: C. Davis and S. Austen, 1729.

The Greek Theatre of Father Brumoy.   Translated from Father Pierre Brumoy's *Le Théâtre des Grecs* (Paris: 1730) by Mrs. CHARLOTTE LENNOX in 3 vols. (London: Millar *et al.*, 1759), with résumés and partial translation of all the extant plays of Aeschylus, Sophocles and Euripides as well as the eleven plays of Aristophanes. Seven are translated in their entirety, including in vol 1. Sophocles' *Electra, Oedipus* [*Tyrannus*] and *Philoctetes.*

The Tragedies of Sophocles.   A verse translation from the Greek by THOMAS FRANCKLIN, 2 vols., London: T. Davies, 1759, 1766, 1832; London: Routledge (Morley's Universal Library); New York: Dutton, 1886.

The Tragedies of Sophocles.   Translated in verse by ROBERT POTTER, London: Robinson, 1788; reprinted London: Bliss, 1820.

The Tragedies of Sophocles.   The Oxford translation (Anon.), Oxford: printed by D. A. Talboys, 1823; second impression, 1828; third impression, 1833. See Collections B for revised edition by Theodore Alois Buckley, London: H. G. Bohn, 1849.

Sophocles' Seven Plays in English Verse.   Translated by LEWIS CAMPBELL, London: Kegan and Paul, 1883; the three that he published ten years earlier (*see below*) are very much revised in this new edition; another revised edition for Oxford University Press (The World's Classics), 1906.

The Tragedies of Sophocles.   Translated by EDWARD P. COLERIDGE, London: George Bell, 1893, 1910.

Sophocles, the Plays and Fragments.   With critical notes, commentary and translation by RICHARD CLAVERHOUSE JEBB, in 3 vols., Cambridge: Cambridge University Press, 1883–96; reprinted as *The*

Tragedies of Sophocles (single volume), 1904, 1907, 1912; Amsterdam: Hakkert, 1962; New York: Bantam, 1967.

Sophocles in English Verse. By ARTHUR S. WAY, London, New York: Macmillan, 1909–14.

Sophocles: Plays. Translated by F. STORR, 2 vols., London, Cambridge, Mass.: Heinemann, Harvard University Press (Loeb Classical Library), 1912–13.

Three Greek Tragedies in Translation. [including *Oedipus the King*]. Translated by DAVID GRENE, Chicago, Ill.: The University of Chicago Press, 1942.

The Theban Plays. Translated by E. F. WATLING, Harmondsworth: Penguin, 1947.

Electra and Other Plays [*Ajax, Philoctetes* and *Women of Trachis*]. Translated by E. F. WATLING. Harmondsworth: Penguin, 1953.

Sophocles I and II. Translated by ROBERT FITZGERALD (*Oedipus at Colonus*), DAVID GRENE (*Oedipus the King, Electra and Philoctetes*), MICHAEL JAMESON (*The Women of Trachis*) and JOHN MOORE (*Ajax*) in *The Complete Greek Tragedies*, Chicago: University of Chicago Press, 1957, 4 vols. (II, Sophocles); regularly reprinted.

Three Tragedies [*Antigone, Oedipus the King* and *Electra*]. Translated into English verse by H. D. F. KITTO, Oxford: Oxford University Press, 1962; reprinted with an introduction and notes by Edith Hall, Oxford: Oxford University Press, 1994.

Electra, Antigone, Philoctetes. Translated by KENNETH MCLEISH, Cambridge: Cambridge University Press, 1979.

Sophocles the Three Theban Plays. Translated by ROBERT FAGLES, New York: Viking Press; London: Allen Lane, 1982; Harmondsworth: Penguin, 1984.

The Theban Plays. Translated by DON TAYLOR, London: Methuen, 1986; reprinted as vol. 1 in *Sophocles: Plays* (2 vols.), translated by ROBERT CANNON (*Ajax*), KENNETH MCLEISH (*Electra* and *Philoctetes*), DON TAYLOR (*Oedipus the King, Oedipus at Colonus and Antigone*) and J. MICHAEL WALTON (*Women of Trachis*), London: Methuen (Classical Greek Dramatists), 1990, 1998.

Sophocles. Edited and translated by HUGH LLOYD-JONES, Cambridge, Mass.: Harvard University Press, 1994.

Sophokles: Four Dramas of Maturity. Translated by MICHAEL EWANS (*Aias* and *Antigone*), GRAHAM LEY (*Young Women of Trachis*), GREGORY McCART (*Oidipous the King*), London: J. M. Dent (Everyman), 1999.

Sophokles: Three Dramas of Old Age. Translated by MICHAEL EWANS (*Elektra*), GRAHAM LEY (*Philoktetes*), GREGORY MCCART (*Oidipous at Kolonos*), London: J. M. Dent (Everyman), 2000.

Sophokles: The Complete Plays. Translated by CARL R. MUELLER and ANNA KRAJEWSKA-WIECZOREK, Hanover, N.H.: Smith and Kraus, 2000.

Sophocles: The Complete Plays. Translated by PAUL ROCHE, New York: Signet Classic, 2001.

Collections B

Sophocles: Works in English Verse. Translated by Revd THOMAS DALE, 2 vols., London: J. M. Richardson, 1824.

The Tragedies of Sophocles in English Prose. Trans. Anon., Cambridge: no listed publisher, 1844.

The Tragedies of Sophocles in English Verse. Translated by CHARLES DUKE YONGE, Cambridge: J. Hall, 1849.

The Tragedies of Sophocles. The Oxford translation revised by THEODORE ALOIS BUCKLEY, London: Henry G. Bohn, 1849; New York: Harper, 1855; *Oedipus Tyrannus, Electra, and Antigone of Sophocles*, Philadelphia: David McKay, 1897.

Sophocles Tragedies. Translated by EDWARD HAYES PLUMPTRE, London: A. Strahan, 1865, 1871, 1902, 1908; Boston and New York: D. C. Heath, 1866, 1872–6, 1908.

Greek Dramas [including *Ajax, Antigone, Oedipus at Colonus, Philoctetes*]. Adapted from the Version of the Revd Robert Potter, by JOHN BENSON ROSE, London: printed by W. Clowes and Sons for private circulation, 1867–72.

Three Plays of Sophocles: Antigone, Electra, Deianira or the Death of Hercules. Translated into English verse by LEWIS CAMPBELL, Edinburgh: W. Blackwood and Sons, 1873.

Sophocles Translated into English Verse. By ROBERT WHITELAW, London: Longman's, 1883, 1904.

The Dramas of Sophocles. Rendered in English verse dramatic and lyric by Sir GEORGE YOUNG, Cambridge: Deighton Bell, 1888; London: Constable and Company, 1899; J. M. Dent and Sons, 1906.

Œdipus Tyrannus, Œdipus up at Colonos, Antigone. Translated in verse and explained by JOHN S. PHILLIMORE, with illustrations (*The Athenian Drama*, vol. 2), London: George Allen, 1902.

Oedipus: Myth and Complex [*Antigone, Oedipus Rex, Oedipus at Colonus*]. Includes a translation by PATRICK MULLAHY, New York: Hermitage, 1948.

Three Theban Plays: Antigone, Oedipus the King, Oedipus at Colonus. Newly translated by THEODORE HOWARD BANKS, New York: Oxford University Press, 1956.

The Oedipus Plays of Sophocles. In a new translation by PAUL ROCHE, New York: New American Library (Mentor), 1958.

Four Greek Plays [including *Antigone* and *Oedipus the King*]. Translated and adapted by KENNETH MCLEISH, with illustrations, London: Longmans (Heritage of Literature Series), 1964.

Four Plays by Sophocles [*Ajax, Electra, Philoctetes* and *The Women of Trachis*]. Newly translated by THEODORE HOWARD BANKS, New York, Oxford University Press, 1966.

The Oedipus Trilogy. A version by STEPHEN SPENDER, London: Faber and Faber, 1985; New York: Random House, 1985.

The Three Theban Plays. Translated and introduced by C. A. TRYPANIS, Warminster: Aris and Phillips, 1986.

The Thebans. Translated by TIMBERLAKE WERTENBAKER, London: Faber and Faber, 1992.

The Theban Plays. Translated by DAVID GRENE, London: David Campbell, 1994.

Sophocles' the Oedipus Trilogy. Text by LAURIE KALMANSON, illustrations by Michael A. Kupka, Piscataway, NJ.: Research and Education Association, 1996.

Sophocles 1 and 2. In translations by KELLY CHERRY (*Antigone*), BRENDAN GALVIN (*Women of Trachis*), GEORGE GARRETT (*Oedipus at Colonus*), JASCHA FREDERICK KESSLER (*King Oedipus*), FREDERIC RAPHAEL and KENNETH MCLEISH (*Ajax*), ARMAND SCHWERNER (*Philoctetes*), HENRY TAYLOR (*Electra*), Philadelphia: Pennsylvania University Press, 1998.

The Oedipus Plays. Adapted from the plays by Sophocles by CAROLINE READER, London: Samuel French, 2002.

The Theban Plays. Translated by RUBY BLONDELL, Newburyport: Focus Classical Library, 2002.

The Theban Plays. Translated by PAUL WOODRUFF and PETER MEINECK, Indianapolis: Hackett Pub. Co., 2003.

The Oedipus Plays of Sophocles. Translated by ROBERT BAGG, Amherst: University of Massachusetts Press, 2004.

AJAX (*AIAS*)

First, Ajax of Sophocles. *Translated in verse from the Greek by Lewis Theobald, London: B. Lintott, 1714.*

The Ajax of Sophocles.   Literally translated by a First-Class Man of Balliol College [THOMAS NASH], Oxford: T. Shrimpton and Son, 1871.

Sophocles' Ajax. The Death and Burial of Aias.   Translated into English verse by LEWIS CAMPBELL, Edinburgh: W. Blackwood and Sons, 1876.

The Ajax of Sophocles.   Literally translated by ROSCOE MONGAN, Dublin: W. B. Kelly (Kelly's Keys to the Classics), 1881.

The Ajax of Sophocles.   As represented at Cambridge in 1882 with an English translation by R. C. JEBB, Cambridge: Macmillan and Bowes, 1882.

The Ajax and *Electra of Sophocles.*   Translated into English prose with an introduction by E. D. A. MORSHEAD, London: Methuen and Co., 1895.

Sophocles: Ajax.   A close translation, with test papers, by J. H. HAYDON, London: W. B. Clive (University Tutorial Press), 1896.

The Ajax of Sophocles.   Translated into literal English from the text of Jebb by J. CLUNES WILSON, Cambridge: J. Hall and Son, 1906.

The Ajax of Sophocles.   Translated by R. C. TREVELYAN, London: G. Allen and Unwin, 1919; reprinted Studio City, Calif.: Players Press, 1998.

Ajax and *The Women of Trachis.*   A translation in verse by LENNOX JAMES MORISON, Windsor: Savile Press, 1951.

Ajax. Edited with translation by A. F. GARVIE, Warminster: Aris and Phillips, 1998.

Aias (*Ajax*). Sophocles. Translated by HERBERT GOLDER and RICHARD PEVEAR, Oxford: Oxford University Press, 1999.

Suppliants of Aeschylus and *Ajax of Sophocles.*   Translated by JAMES KERR, London: Oberon Books, 2001.

Ajax.   A new translation and commentary by SHOMIT DUTTA, Cambridge: Cambridge University Press, 2001.

ANTIGONE

First, Adams, 1729.

Œdipus at Colonus and Antigone.   Literally translated by GEORGE DOWNES, Dublin: P. Byrne, 1823.

The Antigone.   Literally translated into English prose by T. W. C. EDWARDS, London: Matthew Iley, 1824, 1846.

The Antigone and Oedipus Colonaeus of Sophocles. A literal translation by DANIEL SPILLAN, Dublin: J. Cumming, 1831.

An Imitative Version of Sophocles' Tragedy Antigone. 'With its Melo-Dramatic dialogue and Choruses, as Written and Adapted to the Music of Dr. F. Mendelssohn-Bartholdy by WILLIAM BARTHOLOMEW', London: Joseph Bonsor, 1845. Bartholomew appears to have worked from Donner's German translation: 'although not a verbal translation, I trust it may render the general meaning of its ancient original apparent to the modern reader'.

The Antigone of Sophocles in Greek and English. Translated by J. W. DONALDSON, London: J. W. Parks, 1848.

The Antigone of Sophocles. Literally translated by J. G. BRINCKLÉ, in J. G. Brincklé, *Poems*, Philadelphia: Claxton, Remsen and Heffelfinger, 1872.

The Antigone. Literally translated by ROSCOE MONGAN. Dublin: W. B. Kelly (Kelly's Keys to the Classics), 1881.

The Antigone of Sophocles. The text closely rendered by REGINALD BROUGHTON, Oxford: A. T. Shrimpton and Son (The Oxford Translations of the Classics), 1887.

Sophocles' Antigone. With introduction, notes, vocabularies and translation by A. H. ALLCROFT and B. J. HAYES, London: W. B. Clive (University Tutorial Press), 1889.

The Antigone of Sophocles in Greek and English. Printed for the representation of the play by the students of University College, Toronto, 1894, translated by ELIZABETH BEALL GINTY, Boston: Ginn, 1894; New York, F. Ruilman, 1894.

Antigone. A close translation in metrical English by CHARLES EDWARD LAURENCE, in Marchant-Bell's Illustrated Classics series, London: Simpkin, Marshall and Co., 1898.

The Antigone of Sophocles. Translation by G. H. PALMER, Boston and New York: Houghton, Mifflin and Co., 1899.

Antigone. Translated by H. R. FAIRCLOUGH and A. T. MURRAY, San Francisco: P. Elder and M. Shepard, 1902.

'Antigone'. In ELSIE FOGERTY, *Standard Plays for Amateur Performance* [also Sophocles' *Electra* and Euripides' *Alkestis*], London: G. Allen and Unwin, 1903.

Antigone. An English version in rhymed verse by M. R. WELD, Bedford: F. Hockliffe, 1905.

The Antigone of Sophocles. Translated into English verse by JOSEPH EDWARD HARRY, Cincinnati: Robert Clarke Co., 1911.

The Antigone. Translated by JOHN HARROWER, Aberdeen: Aberdeen University Press, 1920.

The Genius of the Greek Drama [including *Antigone*]. Rendered and adapted with an introduction, by CYRIL E. ROBINSON, New York: Humphrey Milford, 1921; Oxford: Clarendon Press, 1924; reprinted Freeport, N.Y.: Books for Libraries Press, 1970.

The Antigone of Sophocles. Translated by R. C. TREVELYAN, Liverpool: Liverpool University Press, 1924; reprinted for the Cambridge Greek Play Committee, Cambridge: Bowes and Bowes, 1939, 1958.

Antigone. Translated from the Greek by ALEXANDER HARVEY, Girard, Kans.: Haldeman-Julius Co., 1924.

The Antigone. Translated in verse by HUGH MACNAGHTEN, Cambridge: Cambridge University Press, 1926.

The Antigone of Sophocles. Translated by MAURICE NEUFELD, Madison, Wis.: Experimental College Players, 1930.

Sophokles, Antigone. A new redaction in the American language, by SHAEMAS O'SHEEL, Brooklyn: privately printed, 1931; reprinted as Sophocles' 'Antigone' in *Ten Greek Plays in Contemporary Translations*, Boston: Houghton Mifflin, 1957.

The Antigone of Sophocles. Translated according to the metres of the original by OTHO LLOYD HOLLAND, London: Heath Cranton, 1931.

The Antigone of Sophocles. A translation in verse by LENNOX JAMES MORISON, London: Christophers, 1939.

The Antigone. An English version by DUDLEY FITTS and ROBERT FITZGERALD, New York and Oxford: Oxford University Press, 1939.

The Antigone. Translated into English rhyming verse with introduction and notes by GILBERT MURRAY, London: G. Allen and Unwin, 1941.

The Antigone of Sophocles. A dramatic translation by F. KINCHIN SMITH, London: Sidgwick and Jackson, 1950.

The Antigone of Sophocles. A verse-translation from the Greek by C. W. E. PECKETT, London and Glasgow: Blackie and Son, 1958.

The Antigone of Sophocles. Translated into English verse by CLARA WEAVER ROBINSON, New York: privately printed, 1959; Riedlinger and Riedlinger: 1970.

Oedipus the King and *Antigone.* Translated by PETER D. ARNOTT, New York: Appleton-Century-Crofts, 1960; reprinted Arlington Heights, Ill.: H. Davidson, 1987.

Antigone. Translated by MICHAEL TOWNSEND, San Francisco: Chandler Pub. Co., 1962.

Four Greek Plays [including *Antigone* and *Oedipus the King*]. Translated and adapted by KENNETH MCLEISH, London: Longman's (Heritage of Literature Series), 1964.

Antigone. A version, slightly abridged, made by DOUGLAS BROWN, Cambridge: Cambridge University Press, 1969.

Antigone. Translated by RICHARD EMIL BRAUN, New York and Oxford: Oxford University Press, 1974.

Antigone. Edited with translation by A. L. BROWN, Warminster: Aris and Phillips, 1987, 1991.

Antigone. A translation by D. W. MYATT, Shrewsbury: Thormynd Press, 1990.

Sophocles' Antigone. A new version by BRENDAN KENNELLY, Newcastle upon Tyne: Bloodaxe, 1996.

Antigone. In a new translation by NICHOLAS RUDALL, Chicago: Ivan R. Dee, 1998.

Antigone. Translated by MARIANNE MCDONALD, London: Nick Hern Books, 2000: reprinted in *Greek Tragedy*, 2005.

Antigone. Translated by PAUL WOODRUFF, Indianapolis: Hackett Pub. Co., 2001.

Antigone. A new translation and commentary by DAVID FRANKLIN and JOHN HARRISON, Cambridge: Cambridge University Press, 2003.

Oedipus and *Antigone by Sophocles.* Versions by BLAKE MORRISON, Halifax: Northern Broadsides, 2003.

Antigone. Translated by REGINALD GIBBONS and CHARLES SEGAL, Oxford: Oxford University Press, 2003.

The Burial at Thebes, Sophocles' Antigone. Translated by SEAMUS HEANEY, London: Faber and Faber, 2004.

ELECTRA (ELEKTRA)

First, Electra of Sophocles. *Translated in verse with an epilogue shewing the parallel in two poems, the Return and the Restauration by C[hristopher] W[ase], The Hague: S. Brown, 1649.*

Electra, a Tragedy. Translated from Sophocles, with notes by Mr [LEWIS] THEOBALD, London: B. Lintott, 1714; reprinted 1780, London: for Harrison and Co.; New York: AMS Press, 1979.

The Electra of Sophocles. Translated in verse by WILLIAM DRENNAN, Belfast: F. D. Finlay, 1817.

The Prometheus of Æschylus and *the Electra of Sophocles.* Translated by GEORGE CROKER FOX, London: Darton and Harvey, 1835.

The Elektra of Sophocles. Translated by J. G. BRINCKLÉ, Philadelphia: J. Campbell and Son, 1873.

Sophocles' Electra. Translated by NICHOLAS LONGWORTH, Cincinnati: R. Clarke, 1878.

Sophocles' Electra. Translated by EDWARD HAYES PLUMPTRE, Cambridge: The Tutorial Series ('to be had, by post only, direct from the College Office'), 1887; London: W. B. Clive, 1888.

Sophocles' Electra. Literally translated by W. J. HICKIE. Dublin: W. B. Kelly (Kelly's Keys to the Classics), 1892.

Sophocles: Electra. Edited with a translation by J. THOMPSON and BERNARD JOHN HAYES, London: W. B. Clive (University Tutorial Press), 1894.

The Ajax and *Electra of Sophocles.* Translated into English prose with an introduction by E. D. A. MORSHEAD, London: Methuen and Co., 1895.

'Electra'. In ELSIE FOGERTY, *Standard Plays for Amateur Performance* [also *Antigone* and Euripides' *Alkestis*], London: 1900.

The Electra of Sophocles. Together with the first part of the '*Peace*' of Aristophanes. The Greek texts, as performed at Cambridge 22–26 February, 1927, together with English verse translations by J. T. SHEPPARD, Cambridge: Bowes and Bowes, 1927.

Electra. A translation with commentary by WILLIAM SALE, Englewood Cliffs, N.J.: Prentice-Hall, 1973.

Oedipus at Colonus and Electra. Translated by PETER D. ARNOTT, Northbrook, Ill.: AHM Pub. Corp., 1975.

The Greeks. Ten Greek plays adapted by JOHN BARTON and KENNETH CAVANDER, based on original translations by Kenneth Cavander [including *Electra*], London: Heinemann, 1981.

Electra. Edited with translation by M. J. CROPP, Warminster: Aris and Phillips, 1988.

Sophocles Elektra. A version by EZRA POUND and RUDD FLEMING, Princeton: Princeton University Press, 1989; London: Faber and Faber, 1990.

Electra. In a new translation by NICHOLAS RUDALL. Chicago: Ivan R. Dee, 1993.

Electra. Translated by E. A. HEARY, Studio City, Calif.: Players Press, 1995.

Sophocles Elektra. Adapted by FRANK McGUINNESS, London: Faber and Faber, and Samuel French, 1997.

Electra. Edited with translation by JENNIFER R. MARCH, Warminster: Aris and Phillips, 1998, 2001.

Electra. Translated by ANNE CARSON, Oxford: Oxford University Press, 2001.

Electra of Sophocles. Translated by MARIANNE McDONALD and J. MICHAEL WALTON, London: Nick Hern Books, 2004.

OEDIPUS AT COLONUS (*OIDIPOUS EPI KOLONOI, OEDIPUS COLONEUS*)

First, Adams, 1729.

Œdipus at Colonus and *Antigone.* Literally translated by GEORGE DOWNES, Dublin: P. Byrne, 1823.

The Antigone and *Oedipus Colonaeus of Sophocles.* With a literal translation and critical notes, by DANIEL SPILLAN, Dublin: J. Cumming, 1831.

The Œdipus at Colonus of Sophocles. Translated (Anon.) into English prose (with *Medea*), by JOHN R. LEE, Oxford: Charles Richards; Oxford and London: Henry Washbourne, 1841.

An Abridged English Version of Sophocles' Oedipus at Colonos. Written and adapted for her most Gracious Majesty Queen Victoria, by W. BARTHOLOMEW to the music of F. Mendelssohn Bartholdy. London, 1848.

The Downfall and Death of King Œdipus. A drama in two parts, chiefly taken from the 'Oedipus Tyrannus' and 'Colonaeus' of Sophocles; the inter-act choruses are from Potter [the preface signed 'Littlegrange', i.e. Edward Fitzgerald], Guildford: Billing and Sons, 1880–81.

Oedipus at Colonus. Translated by R. C. JEBB, Cambridge: Cambridge University Press, 1886.

Oedipus at Colonus. Closely translated from the Greek, an experiment in metre by ARTHUR COMPTON AUCHMUTY, Hull: W. Andrews and Co., The Hull Press, 1894.

Oedipus Coloneus. A translation with test papers by W. H. BALGARNIE, London: W. B. Clive (University Tutorial Press), 1898.

'Œdipus at Colonos'. In *The Death-Song of Thamyris* with the 'Œdipus at Colonos' 'done into English verse' by EDWARD. H. PEMBER, London: Chiswick Press, 1899.

Oedipus Coloneus. Literally translated by J. A. PROUT, Dublin: W. B. Kelly (Kelly's Keys to the Classics), 1905.

Oedipus at Colonus. Translated from the original Greek by ALEX-
ANDER HARVEY, Girard, Kans.: Haldeman-Julius Co., 1925.

Sophocles' Oedipus at Colonus. A version for the modern stage in
W. B. YEATS, *Collected Plays,* London: Macmillan and Co., 1934.

Oedipus at Colonus. An English version by ROBERT FITZGERALD,
New York: Harcourt, Brace, 1941; reprinted Chicago: University of
Chicago Press, 1954.

Oedipus at Colonus. Translated by R. C. TREVELYAN, Cambridge:
Cambridge University Press, 1946.

Oedipus at Colonus. Translated into English rhyming verse with
introduction and notes by GILBERT MURRAY, London: Allen and
Unwin, 1948.

The Oedipus at Colonus. The Greek text performed at Cambridge by
members of the University, February 1950, together with the verse
translation by J. T. SHEPPARD, Cambridge: Bowes and Bowes: 1949.

The Oedipus at Colonus of Sophocles. Translated by FRANCIS A.
EVELYN, Malvern: privately printed, 1959.

Oedipus the King and *Oedipus at Colonus.* A new translation for
modern readers and theatergoers by CHARLES R. WALKER, New York:
Anchor Books, 1966.

Oedipus at Colonus and *Electra.* Translated and edited by PETER D.
ARNOTT, Northbrook, Ill.: AHM Pub. Corp., 1975.

Oedipus at Colonus. English version by LINDLEY WILLIAMS HUB-
BELL, Kobe, Japan: Ikuta Press, 1978.

Oedipus. Oedipus the King and *Oedipus at Colonus,* translated by
CHRISTOPHER STACE, Birmingham: Oberon Books, 1987.

King Oedipus and *Oedipus at Kolonos.* Translated by KENNETH
McLEISH, posthumously edited by Michael Sargent, London: Nick
Hern Books, 2001.

Oedipus at Colonus. In a new translation by NICHOLAS RUDALL,
Chicago: Ivan R. Dee, 2001.

Oedipus at Colonus. Translated by EAMON GRENNAN and RACHEL
KITZINGER, New York: Oxford University Press, 2004.

OEDIPUS TYRANNUS (OIDIPOUS TURANNOS, OEDIPUS REX, OEDIPUS THE KING, OEDIPUS KING OF THEBES)

First, Oedipus, King of Thebes: a Tragedy. *Translated in verse from
Sophocles by Mr [Lewis] Theobald, London: B. Lintott, 1715;
reprinted 1765 and New York: AMS Press, 1980.*

'A Free Translation (in verse) of the Oedipus Tyrannus'. By THOMAS MAURICE in Maurice (T.), *Poems and Miscellaneous Pieces*, London: printed for the author, 1779.

Oedipus, King of Thebes. A tragedy translated from the Greek of Sophocles into prose by GEORGE SOMERS CLARKE, Oxford: Clarendon Press, 1790.

Sophocles King Oedipus. Translated, by T. W. C. EDWARDS, London: Sherwood Jones and Co., 1823.

A Literal Translation of the Œdipus Tyrannus of Sophocles. By a Graduate of the University of Dublin, Dublin: J. Robertson and Co., 1837.

The Œdipus Tyrannus of Sophocles. With the Greek Scholia and an English prose version by the Rev. J. PRENDERGAST, etc., London: B. Fellowes, 1839.

Oedipus, King of Thebes. Translated from the Œdipus Tyrannus of Sophocles by Sir FRANCIS HASTINGS CHARLES DOYLE, London: J. H. Parker, 1849.

Sophoclis Œdipus Rex. With annotations, literally translated into English (Anon), London: Williams and Norgate, 1851.

Sophocles Œdipus Tyrannus. Literally translated by ROSCOE MONGAN, Dublin: W. B. Kelly (Kelly's Keys to the Classics), 1865.

The Œdipus Tyrannus of Sophocles. Literally translated, and explained in short notes on the translation, grammar, and parsing by a First-Class Man of Balliol College [THOMAS NASH], Oxford: T. and G. Shrimpton, 1870.

The King Œdipus and *Philoctetes of Sophocles.* Translated into English verse by LEWIS CAMPBELL, Edinburgh: W. Blackwood and Sons, 1874.

Oedipus, King of Thebes. Translated into English verse by G. VOLNEY DORSEY, Piqua, Ohio: Miami Publishing Co., 1880.

The Downfall and Death of King Œdipus. A drama in two parts, chiefly taken from the 'Oedipus Tyrannus' and 'Colonæus' of Sophocles; the inter-act choruses are from Potter [the preface signed 'Littlegrange', i.e. Edward Fitzgerald], Guildford: Billing and Sons, 1880–81.

King Oedipus. Translated by WILLIAM WELLS NEWELL, Cambridge, Mass.: printed for the translator, 1881.

The Œdipus Tyrannus. With translation by BENJAMIN HALL KENNEDY, Cambridge: Cambridge University Press, 1882; reprinted Deighton, Bell and Co., 1885.

Œdipus the King. Translated into English verse by E. D. A. MORSHEAD, London: Macmillan and Co., 1885.

The Œdipus Tyrannus. Literally translated by THOMAS NASH, revised by R. BROUGHTON, Oxford: A. T. Shrimpton and Son, 1887.

Oedipus the King. The dialogue metrically rendered by EDWARD CONYBEARE, with the songs of the chorus as written for the music of Dr. Stanford by A. W. VERRALL, London: Rivingtons, 1887.

The Oedipus Tyrannus of Sophocles. The Greek text performed at Cambridge, 22–6 November 1887, with a translation in prose by R. C. JEBB and a translation of the songs of the chorus in verse by A. W. VERRALL, Cambridge: Macmillan and Bowes, 1887; also performed Cambridge, 26–30 November 1912, reprinted Cambridge: Bowes and Bowes, 1912.

The Oedipus Tyrannus of Sophocles. Rendered in English verse, dramatic and lyric, by Sir GEORGE YOUNG, Cambridge: Deighton, Bell and Co., 1887; reprinted London: Dent, 1906.

Oedipus King of Thebes. Translated into English rhyming verse with explanatory notes by GILBERT MURRAY, London: George Allen and Sons, 1911.

The Œdipus Tyrannus. Translated and explained by J. T. SHEPPARD, Cambridge: Cambridge University Press, 1920.

Sophocles' King Oedipus. A version for the modern stage by W. B. YEATS, London: Macmillan, 1928.

The Oedipus Tyrannus. The Greek text as produced in the Bradfield College Greek Theatre, June 1937, with English translation by A. J. HUNT, Oxford: Oxford University Press, 1937.

'Oedipus Tyrannus'. Translated into English verse by CLARENCE W. MENDELL, in *Our Seneca*, New Haven: Yale University Press, 1941.

Oedipus, the King. A new translation by N. E. TRUMAN, New York: The Hobson Book Press, 1946.

Oedipus Rex. An English version by DUDLEY FITTS and ROBERT FITZGERALD, New York: Harcourt, Brace, 1949; reprinted London: Faber and Faber, 1951.

Oedipus the King. The Greek text translated into English verse by FRANCIS STORR, with an introduction by Thornton Wilder, illustrated with wood engravings by Demetrios Galanis, New York: printed for the members of the Limited Editions Club by J. Enschedé, 1955; reprinted New York: Heritage Press, 1956.

'Oedipus Rex'. Translated by ALBERT COOK in *Ten Greek Plays*, Boston: Houghton Mifflin, 1957.

Oedipus the King, and, *Antigone*. Translated by PETER D. ARNOTT, New York: Appleton-Century-Crofts, 1960; reprinted Arlington Heights, Ill.: H. Davidson, 1987.

Oedipus the King. Translated by KENNETH CAVANDER, with an introduction by Tom F. Driver, San Francisco: Chandler Pub. Co., 1961.

Four Greek Plays [including *Oedipus the King* and *Antigone*]. Translated and adapted by KENNETH MCLEISH, London: Longman's (Heritage of Literature Series), 1964.

Oedipus the King, and *Oedipus at Colonus*. A new translation for modern readers and theatergoers by CHARLES R. WALKER, New York: Anchor Books, 1966.

Oedipus Tyrannus. A new translation by FRANK K. WILSON, Bath: James Brodie (Kelly's Keys to the Classics), 1966.

Oedipus the King. Translated by PAUL ROCHE, New York: New American Library, 1968.

Oedipus the King. A translation with commentary by THOMAS GOULD, Englewood Cliffs, N.J.: Prentice-Hall, 1970.

Oedipus Tyrannus. A new translation by LUCI BERKOWITZ and THEODORE F. BRUNNER, New York: Norton, 1970.

Sophocles and Oedipus. A study of *Oedipus Tyrannus* with a new translation by PHILIP VELLACOTT, London: Macmillan, 1971.

Sophocles: Oedipus the King. Translated and adapted by ANTHONY BURGESS, Minneapolis: University of Minnesota Press in association with the Guthrie Theater, 1972.

Oedipus the King. Translated from the Greek by STEPHEN BERG and DISKIN CLAY, New York: Oxford University Press, 1978.

Oedipus the King. Translated by ROBERT BAGG, Amherst: University of Massachusetts Press, 1982.

Oedipus. 'Oedipus the King' and 'Oedipus at Colonus'. Translated by CHRISTOPHER STACE, Birmingham: Oberon Books, 1987.

Oedipus Tyrannus. A translation, interpretation and commentary by D. W. MYATT, Shrewsbury: Thormynd Press, 1991.

Oedipus the King. In a new translation by NICHOLAS RUDALL, Chicago: Ivan R. Dee, 2000.

Oedipus Tyrannus. Sophocles translated by PETER MEINECK and PAUL WOODRUFF, Indianapolis: Hackett Pub. Co., 2000.

King Oedipus and *Oedipus at Kolonos*. Translated by KENNETH MCLEISH, posthumously edited by Michael Sargent, London: Nick Hern Books, 2001.

Oedipus and Antigone by Sophocles.   Versions by BLAKE MORRISON, Halifax: Northern Broadsides, 2003.

Sophocles: Oedipus Tyrannus.   A new translation and commentary by IAN MCAUSLAN and JUDITH AFFLECK, Cambridge: Cambridge University Press, 2003.

PHILOCTETES (PHILOKTETES)

First, Sophocles Philoctetes. *Translated by Thomas Sheridan, Dublin:*
J. Hyde and E. Dobson for R. Owen, 1725; reprinted New York:
AMS Press, 1979.

The Philoctetes of Sophocles.   Literally translated into English prose by T. W. C. EDWARDS, London: W. Simpkin and R. Marshall, 1829.

Philoctetes.   From Hermann's edition, with a literal translation and critical notes by DANIEL SPILLAN, Dublin: J. Cumming, 1831.

The Philoctetes of Sophocles.   Literally translated, and explained in short notes on the grammar and construction by a First-Class Man of Balliol College [THOMAS NASH], Oxford: T. Shrimpton and Son, 1871.

The King Œdipus and *Philoctetes of Sophocles.*   Translated into English verse by LEWIS CAMPBELL, Edinburgh: W. Blackwood and Sons, 1874.

The Philoctetes of Sophocles.   Literally translated by ROSCOE MONGAN, Dublin: W. B. Kelly (Kelly's Keys to the Classics), 1881.

The Philoctetes of Sophocles.   Translated into English prose by M. T. TATHAM, London: Spottiswoode and Co., 1883.

Sophocles: Philoctetes.   Translated by R. C. JEBB, Cambridge: Cambridge University Press, 1890; second edition 1898.

Sophocles: Philoctetes.   A translation by F. G. PLAISTOWE, London: W. B. Clive (University Tutorial Press), 1892.

Two Greek Plays [The *Philoctetes* of Sophocles and the *Medea* of Euripides].   'Done into English' by JOHN JAY CHAPMAN, Boston and New York: Houghton Mifflin, 1928.

Medea and *Philoctetes.*   Translated by HORACE HOFFMAN, Yorktown, New York: privately printed, 1931.

'Philoctetes'.   Translated by JOHN ROWE WORKMAN in *An Anthology of Greek Drama: Second Series*, New York: Reinhart and Co. Inc., 1954.

Philoctetes. A new English translation by KENNETH CAVANDER, with an introduction by Edmund Wilson: San Francisco: Chandler Pub. Co., 1965.

The Women of Trachis and *Philoctetes.* A new translation in verse by ROBERT TORRANCE, Boston: Houghton Mifflin, 1966.

Philoctetes. A version, slightly abridged, made by DOUGLAS BROWN, Cambridge: Cambridge University Press, 1969.

'Philoctetes, Sophocles'. Translated by ARMAND SCHWERNER in Charles Doria, ed., *The Tenth Muse*, Athens, Ohio, Chicago, London: The Ohio University Press, 1980.

Philoktetes. Sophokles translated by GREGORY McNAMEE, Port Townsend, Wash.: Copper Canyon Press, 1986.

Philoctetes. Edited with translation by R. G. USSHER, Warminster: Aris and Phillips, 1990.

The Cure at Troy. A version of Sophocles' *Philoctetes* by SEAMUS HEANEY, Derry: Field Day; London: Faber and Faber in association with Field Day, 1990; New York: Farrar, Straus and Giroux, The Noonday Press, 1991.

Philoctetes. Translated by DESMOND EGAN, Newbridge, Co. Kildare: Goldsmith Press, 1998.

Philoctetes. In a new version by KEITH DEWHURST, London: Oberon Books, 2000.

Philoctetes. A new translation and commentary by JUDITH AFFLECK, Cambridge: Cambridge University Press, 2001.

Six Greek Tragedies [including *Philoctetes*]. Translated by KENNETH McLEISH, London: Methuen, 2002.

Philoktetes. Translated by SETH SCHEIN, Newburyport: Focus Classical Library, 2003.

WOMEN OF TRACHIS (*TRACHINIAI, TRACHINIAE, TRACHINIANS, TRACHINIAN WOMEN*)

First in Adams, 1729.

The Trachiniae. With critical notes, commentary, and translation in English prose, by R. C. JEBB, Cambridge: Cambridge University Press, 1892.

Sophocles' Trachiniae. Literally translated by J. A. PROUT, Dublin: W. B. Kelly (Kelly's Keys to the Classics), 1904.

The Trachinian Maidens. Translated into English verse by HUGO SHARPLEY, London: David Nutt, 1909.

The Trachiniae. Acting version for the performances given by Bedford College University of London, on 6, 7, and 8 July 1911, with the translation of the late Professor LEWIS CAMPBELL, Cambridge: Cambridge University Press, 1911.

The Trachiniae of Sophocles. Translated into English verse by ESTHER SOPHIA BARLOW, Manchester: Manchester University Press, 1938.

The Wife of Heracles. Being Sophocles' play *The Trachinian Women*, translated into English verse by GILBERT MURRAY, London: George Allen and Unwin, 1947.

Ajax and *The Women of Trachis.* A translation in verse by LENNOX JAMES MORISON, Windsor: Savile Press, 1951.

'Philoctetes'. Translated by ALSTON HURD CHASE in *Six Greek Plays in Modern Translations*, New York: The Dryden Press, 1955.

Women of Trachis. A version by EZRA POUND, London: Neville Spearman, 1956; reprinted New York: New Directions, 1957; London: Faber, 1969.

The Women of Trachis and *Philoctetes.* A new translation in verse by ROBERT TORRANCE, Boston: Houghton Mifflin, 1966.

Women of Trachis, Sophocles. Translated by C. K. WILLIAMS and GREGORY W. DICKERSON, New York: Oxford University Press, 1978.

Six Greek Tragedies [including *Women of Trachis*, translated by J. MICHAEL WALTON], London: Methuen, 2002.

EURIPIDES

Collections A

The Greek Theatre of Father Brumoy. Translated from Father Pierre Brumoy's *Le Théâtre des Grecs* (Paris: 1730) by Mrs CHARLOTTE LENNOX in 3 vols. (London: Millar *et al.*, 1759), with résumés and partial translation of all the extant plays of Aeschylus, Sophocles and Euripides as well as the eleven plays of Aristophanes. Seven are translated in their entirety, including in vol. 1 Euripides' *Alcestis, Hippolitus (sic), Iphigenia in Aulis* and *Iphigenia in Tauris.*

The Tragedies of Euripides. Translated by ROBERT POTTER in 2 vols. [*Bacchae, Ion, Alcestis, Medea, Hippolytus, The Phoenician Virgins, The Supplicants, Heracles, The Heraclidae* and *Iphigenia in Aulis, Rhesus, The Trojan Dames, Hecuba, Helena, Electra, Orestes, Iphigenia in Tauris* and

Andromache], London: J. Dodsley, 1781 and 1783; reprinted J. Mawman *et al.*, including Parker of Oxford, Bell and Deighton of Cambridge, 1807, and 1814; also 1827, 1835, 1872–76, 1887; New York: Harper and Brothers, 1834, 1848.

The Nineteen Plays and Fragments of Euripides. Translated by MICHAEL WODHULL, 4 vols., London: Printed for J. Walker and T. Payne, 1782; reprinted 1809, 1888, 1894.

Euripides, with an English translation. Translated by ARTHUR S. WAY, 3 vols., London: Macmillan, 1894–8; reprinted in 4 vols., Cambridge, Mass.: Harvard University Press and London: Heinemann (Loeb Classical Library), 1912–16; reprinted 1925, 1942–52, 1947, 1966; Henry H. Harper, *Attic Tragedies*, 3 vols., Boston: Bibliophile Society, 1927; London: J. M. Dent; New York: E. P. Dutton, 1956.

Three Plays [*Hippolytus, Alcestis* and *Iphigenia in Tauris*]. Translated by PHILIP VELLACOTT, Harmondsworth: Penguin, 1953; reissued with a revised text and new introduction, 1974.

The Bacchae, and Other Plays [*Helen, Ion* and *The Women of Troy*]. Translated by PHILIP VELLACOTT, Harmondsworth: Penguin, 1954; reprinted 1972.

Euripides I–V. Translated by WILLIAM ARROWSMITH (*The Cyclops, Heracles, Hecuba, Orestes* and *The Bacchae*), WITTER BYNNER (*Iphigenia in Tauris*), RALPH GLADSTONE (*The Heracleidae*), DAVID GRENE (*Hippolytus*), F. W. JONES (*The Suppliant Women*), RICHMOND LATTIMORE (*Alcestis, Helen, The Trojan Women* and *Rhesus*), JOHN FREDERICK NIMS (*Andromache*). EMILE TOWNSEND VERMEULE (*Electra*), CHARLES R. WALKER (*Iphigenia in Aulis*), REX WARNER (*The Medea*), RONALD FREDERICK WILLETTS (*Ion*), ELIZABETH WYCKOFF (*The Phoenician Women*), in *The Complete Greek Tragedies*, Chicago: University of Chicago Press, 1959, 4 vols. (I and III, Euripides, Chicago: University of Chicago Press, 1955–9; regularly reprinted).

Medea and Other Plays [*Electra, Hecabe* and *Heracles*]. Translated with an introduction by PHILIP VELLACOTT, Harmondsworth: Penguin, 1963.

Orestes, and Other Plays [*Andromache, The Children of Heracles, Iphigenia in Aulis, The Phoenician Women* and *The Suppliant Women*]. Translated with an introduction by PHILIP VELLACOTT, Harmondsworth: Penguin, 1972.

Euripides: Plays. One–Six. Translated by PETER D. ARNOTT (*Hecuba*), JEREMY BROOKS (*Medea*, replaced by J. MICHAEL WALTON, 2000), ROBERT CANNON (*Andromache*), KENNETH MCLEISH (*Helen, Ion, Elektra, Orestes, Iphigeneia in Tauris, Herakles' Children, Herakles and Suppliants*) and FREDERIC RAPHAEL and KENNETH MCLEISH (*Hippolytos*), DON TAYLOR (*The Women of Troy and Iphigenia at Aulis*),

DAVID THOMPSON (*The Phoenician Women*), and J. MICHAEL WALTON (*Bacchae, Cyclops, Alkestis, Rhesos* and, from 2000, *Medea*), London: Methuen (Classical Greek Dramatists), 1988–97; 1998, 2000.

Euripides. In 5 vols., translated by DAVID KOVACS, Cambridge, Mass., and London: Harvard University Press (Loeb), 1995–2002.

Medea and Other Plays [*Alcestis, Children of Heracles* and *Hippolytus*]. Translated by JOHN DAVIE, London: Penguin, 1996.

Medea, Hippolytus, Electra, Helen. Translated by JAMES MORWOOD, Oxford: Clarendon Press, 1997.

Electra and Other Plays [*Andromache, Hecuba, Suppliant Women* and *Trojan Women*]. Translated by JOHN DAVIE, London: Penguin, 1998.

Iphigenia among the Taurians, Bacchae, Iphigenia at Aulis, Rhesus. Translated with explanatory notes by JAMES MORWOOD, Oxford: Oxford University Press, 1999.

Hecuba, The Trojan Women, Andromache. Translated by JAMES MORWOOD, Oxford: Oxford University Press, 2000.

Ion, Orestes, Phoenician Women, Suppliant Women. Translated by ROBIN WATERFIELD, Oxford: Oxford University Press, 2001.

Helen, Phoenician Women, Orestes. Edited and translated by DAVID KOVACS, Cambridge, Mass., and London: Harvard University Press, 2002.

Euripides: Heracles and Other Plays [*Iphigenia Among the Taurians, Ion, Helen* and *Cyclops*]. Translated by JOHN DAVIE, London: Penguin, 2002.

Alcestis, Heracles, Children of Heracles, Cyclops. Translated by ROBIN WATERFIELD, Oxford: Oxford University Press, 2003.

Collections B

Select Tragedies of Euripides [*Phoenissae, Iphigenia in Aulis, Troades* and *Orestes*]. Translated from the original Greek in verse by JAMES BANNISTER, London: printed for N. Conant, 1780.

The Hecuba, Orestes, Phœnician Virgins, and Medea of Euripides. Literally translated into English prose by a Member of the University of Oxford, Oxford: D. A. Talboys, 1820; revised, London: Simpkin and Marshall, 1830.

The Hecuba, Medea, Phænissae, and Orestes. Literally translated into English by a Graduate in Honours of the University of Oxford, London: Henry Washbourne, 1846.

Euripides' Tragedies. Translated by THEODORE ALOIS BUCKLEY, in 2 vols., London: Henry G. Bohn, 1848. Buckley claims that 'The translations of the first six plays in the present volume [*Hecuba, Orestes, Phoenician Virgins, Medea, Hippolytus, Alcestis*] were published in Oxford some years since, and have been frequently reprinted', but such editions have proved elusive; reprinted as *The Tragedies of Euripides, Literally Translated*, New York: Harper and Bros., 1857; London: Bell and Daldy, 1866.

Translations from Euripides. Translated by JOHN CARTWRIGHT, London: D. Nutt and Co., 1866, 1868.

Greek Dramas [including *Alcestis, Hecuba*]. Adapted from the Version of the Revd Robert Potter, by JOHN BENSON ROSE, London: printed by W. Clowes and Sons for private circulation, 1867–72.

The Medea, Alcestis, and Hippolytus of Euripides. Translated into blank verse, with the Choruses in lyric and other metres, by H. WILLIAMS, London: Longman and Co., 1871.

Three Dramas of Euripides [*Alcestis, Hippolytus* and *Medea*]. Translated by WILLIAM CRANSTON LAWTON, Boston and New York: Houghton, Mifflin and Co., 1887.

The Bacchanals and Other Plays by Euripides. The Bacchanals. Translated by HENRY HART MILMAN (1865), the other plays translated by MICHAEL WODHULL, etc., Morley's Universal Library, Vol. 58, London: Routledge, 1888.

Euripides' Plays. Translated into English prose by EDWARD P. COLERIDGE, 2 vols., London: George Bell and Sons, New York: Harcourt, 1891; reprinted 1893, 1913, and in *Great Books of the Western World*, Chicago: William Benton (Encyclopaedia Britannica Inc.), 1952.

Euripides. Translated into English rhyming verse by GILBERT MURRAY, London: George Allen (*The Athenian Drama* in 3 vols.), 1900–02.

The Genius of the Greek Drama. Three plays, being the *Agamemnon* of Aeschylus, the *Antigone* of Sophocles, and the *Medea* of Euripides, rendered and adapted with an introduction, by CYRIL E. ROBINSON, Oxford: Clarendon Press; New York: Humphrey Milford, 1921; reprinted Freeport, N.Y., Books for Libraries Press, 1970.

Four Plays of Euripides [*Alcestis, Medea, Hippolytus* and *Iphigeneia Among the Taurians*]. Translated by AUGUSTUS TABER MURRAY, Stanford: Stanford University Press; New York, Oxford: Humphrey Milford, Oxford University Press, 1931.

The Plays of Euripides. Translated into English rhyming verse by GILBERT MURRAY, with wood-engravings from the Greek vase paintings by R. A. Maynard and H. W. Bray, Gregynog: Gregynog Press, 1931.

The Plays of Euripides [Including: *Alcestis, Medea, Hippolytus, Andro-mache, Ion, Trojan Women, Electra, Iphigenia among the Taurians, The Bacchants* and *Iphigenia at Aulis*]. 'Done into English' by MOSES HADAS and JOHN HARVEY MCLEAN, New York: The Dial Press, 1936; reprinted New York, Bantam Books, 1960.

Four Dramas of Euripides [*Hecuba, Heracles, Andromache* and *Orestes*]. Translated into English verse by HUGH OWEN MEREDITH, London: G. Allen and Unwin, 1936.

Three Great Plays of Euripides [*Medea, Hippolytus* and *Helen*]. Translated by REX WARNER, New York: New American Library, 1958.

Three Greek Plays for the Theatre [Including *Cyclops* and *Medea*]. Edited and translated by PETER D. ARNOTT, Bloomington: Indiana University Press, 1961.

The Bacchae, Hippolytus, Alcestis, Medea in Modern Translations. By SIMON GOLDFIELD, KENNETH CAVANDER, ALISTAIR ELLIOTT and MINOS VOLONAKIS, New York: Dell Pub. Co., 1965.

Medea. Hippolytus. The Bacchae. Newly translated by PHILIP VELLA-COTT, illustrated by Michael Ayrton, London: printed for the members of the Limited Editions Club at the Curwen Press, 1967.

Three Plays of Euripides: Alcestis, Medea, The Bacchae. Translated by PAUL ROCHE, New York: Norton, 1974.

The Trojan Women, Helen, The Bacchae. Translated by NEIL CURRY, Cambridge: Cambridge University Press, 1981.

The Greeks. Ten Greek plays adapted by JOHN BARTON and KENNETH CAVANDER [including *Iphigenia in Aulis, The Trojan Women, Hecuba, Helen, Andromache* and *Iphigenia in Tauris*], based on original translations by Kenneth Cavander, London: Heinemann, 1981.

The War Plays [*Helen, Iphigenia in Aulis* and *The Women of Troy*]. Translated and introduced by DON TAYLOR, London: Methuen, 1990.

After the Trojan War. Three plays by Euripides [*Hecuba, Helen* and *Women of Troy*], translated and introduced by KENNETH MCLEISH, London: Oberon Books, 1995.

Selected Fragmentary Plays. With introductions, translations and commentaries by C. COLLARD, M. J. CROPP and K. H. LEE, War-minster: Aris and Phillips, 1995.

Euripides. 4 vols. in translations by J. T. BARBARESE (*Children of Heracles*), PALMER BOVIE (*Cyclops*), FRED CHAPPELL (*Alcestis*), GREG DELANTY (*Orestes*), GEORG ECONOMOU (*Rhesus*), RICHARD ELMAN (*Phoenician Women*), DANIEL MARK EPSTEIN (*The Bacchae*), RACHEL

HADAS (*Helen*), DONALD JUNKINS (*Andromache*), CAROLYN KIZER (*Iphigenia in Tauris*), RICHARD MOORE (*Hippolytus*), ELIZABETH SEYDEL MORGAN (*Electra*), John F. NIMS (*Suppliant Women*), DEBORAH H. ROBERTS (*Ion*), MARK RUDMAN with KATHARINE WASHBURN (*Daughters of Troy*), ELAINE TERRANOVA (*Iphigenia at Aulis*), KATHARINE WASHBURN and DAVID CURZON (*The Madness of Heracles*), ELEANOR WILNER with INÉS AZAR (*Medea*), Philadelphia: University of Pennsylvania Press, 1997–9.

Euripides: Ten Plays [*Alcestis, The Bacchae, The Cyclops, Electra, Hippolytus, Ion, Iphigenia in Aulis, Iphigenia Among the Taurians, Medea, The Trojan Women*]. A new translation by PAUL ROCHE, New York: Signet Classic, 1998.

Women on the Edge: Four Plays by Euripides. Translated by RUBY BLONDELL (*Medea*), MARY-KAY GAMEL (*Iphigenia at Aulis*), NANCY SORKIN RABINOWITZ (*Alcestis*), BELLA ZWEIG (*Helen*), New York: Routledge, 1999.

ALCESTIS (ALKESTIS)

First, in Lennox (Brumoy), 1759.

Hippolytus and Alcestis. Translation Anon., Oxford: D. A. Talboys, 1822; second edition, corrected by D. A. Talboys, Oxford: 1834.

The Alcestis of Euripides. Literally translated into English prose by T. W. C. EDWARDS, London: Matthew Iley, 1824; reprinted 1838.

The Alcestis and Hippolytus of Euripides. Literally translated into English by a Graduate in Honours of the University of Oxford, London: Henry Washbourne, 1846.

Alcestis. Literally translated by ROSCOE MONGAN, Dublin: W. B. Kelly, 1848; reprinted 1879.

The Alcestis. Translated into English verse by Rev. JAMES BANKS (afterwards Davies), Prebendary of Hereford Cathedral, London: Longman, Brown, Green and Longmans, 1849.

The Alcestis of Euripides. Literally translated and explained in short notes on the translation, grammar, and parsing, by a First-Class Man of Balliol College [THOMAS NASH], Oxford: T. G. and G. Shrimpton, 1870.

The Alcestis of Euripides. Literally translated into English prose by HUGO SHARPLEY, Cambridge, J. Hall and Son, 1870.

The Alcestis of Euripides. Translated into English verse by W. FIELDING NEVINS, London: Longmans, Green and Co., 1870.

Balaustion's Adventure. Including a 'transcript' from Euripides' *Alcestis* in the form of a narrative poem 'imbedded in the dramatic romance called *Balaustion's Adventure*' (Mrs Sutherland Orr), lines 358–2651, by ROBERT BROWNING, London: Smith, Elder and Co., 1871; reprinted 1875, 1881.

The Alcestis of Euripides. Translated into English, now for the first time in its original metres, with preface, notes, and [highly fanciful] stage directions by H. B. L. [HENRY BARRETT LENNARD], London: Richard Bentley and Son, 1884.

The Alcestis of Euripides. Translated by the editors of the Analytical Series of Greek and Latin Classics (Greek–English Series of Classical Authors), London: Simpkin and Marshall, 1886.

The Alcestis of Euripides. Translated from the original text by MARGARET DUNLOP GIBSON, London: Williams and Norgate, 1886.

Euripides' Alcestis. With a literal interlineal translation by THOMAS J. ARNOLD, London: James Cornish (*Cornish's Interlinear Keys*), 1886.

The Alcestis of Euripides. Rendered into English verse by W. CUD-WORTH, privately printed, 1888 (with a note in the text 'not published').

The Alcestis of Euripides. Text, with translation by R. W. REYNOLDS, London: The Classical Translation Library, 1893.

Euripides Alcestis. Edited and a close translation by JOHN HAMPDEN HAYDON, London: W. B. Clive (University Tutorial Press), 1896.

Euripides Alcestis. Translated into English by HERBERT HAILSTONE, Cambridge: E. Johnson, 1896.

The Alkestis of Euripides. As performed by the boys of St. Gregory's, Downside, with a translation by the Revd A. L. KYNASTON, Weston-super-Mare: The Mendip Press, 1897.

The Book of the Alkestis of Euripides. Performed in Greek at the Edinburgh Academy with a translation by G. B. GREEN and R. J. MACKENZIE, Edinburgh: T. and A. Constable, 1898.

The Alcestis of Euripides. Literally translated according to the new Oxford text by ST G. STOCK, Oxford: Blackwell, 1902.

'Alkestis'. In ELSIE FOGERTY, *Standard Plays for Amateur Performance* [also Sophocles' *Electra* and *Antigone*], London: 1902.

The Alcestis of Euripides. The Oxford text with English verse translation by sixth form boys of Bradfield College, Oxford: James Parker and Co., 1904.

Alcestis. 'Done into English' by GERALD WARRE CORNISH, London: Arnold Fairbanks and Co., 1908.

Euripides' Alcestis. Translated by HERBERT KYNASTON, Oxford: Clarendon Press, 1906, 1923.

The Alcestis of Euripides. Translated into English rhyming verse by GILBERT MURRAY, London: Allen and Unwin, 1915, 1929, 1936, 1941, 1947.

Alcestis. Translated by RICHARD ALDINGTON, London: Chatto and Windus, 1930.

The Alcestis of Euripides. An English version by DUDLEY FITTS and ROBERT FITZGERALD, London: Faber and Faber; New York: Harcourt, Brace and Co., 1936.

The Alcestis of Euripides. Adapted for the stage and screen by G. E. O. KNIGHT, London: reproduced from typescript, 1947.

The Alcestis of Euripides. Translated into English prose by D. W. LUCAS, London: Cohen and West, 1951.

Alcestis. Translated by ALISTAIR ELLIOT, San Francisco: Chandler Publishing Co., 1962.

Alcestis. Translated by WILLIAM ARROWSMITH. Oxford: Oxford University Press, 1974.

Alcestis. A translation with commentary by CHARLES ROWAN BEYE, Englewood Cliffs, N.J.: Prentice-Hall, 1974.

Alcestis. Edited with translation by D. J. CONACHER, Warminster: Aris and Phillips, 1987, 1988.

Alcestis. In a new version by TED HUGHES, London: Faber and Faber, 1999.

The Alcestis of Euripides. Translation by JOHN E. THORBURN Jnr, Lampeter: Edwin Mellen Press, 2001.

Six Greek Comedies [Including *Alkestis* and *Cyclops* translated by J. MICHAEL WALTON]. London: Methuen, 2002.

Euripides of Athens: Medea and Alcestis. Translated into English verse by MICHAEL JAMES GOULD, Whitstable: Wave Crest Classics, 2003.

ANDROMACHE (ANDROMAKHE)

First, Wodhull, 1782.

The Andromache. Literally translated into English prose by a Member of the University, Cambridge: J. Hall, 1840.

Euripidis Andromache. Literally translated by W. J. HICKIE, Dublin: W. B. Kelly (Kelly's Keys to the Classics), 1887.

Euripides: Andromache.   Translated by H. CLARKE, London: W. B. Clive (University Tutorial Press), 1896.

'Andromache'.   Translated by VAN L. JOHNSON in *Six Greek Plays in Modern Translations*, New York: The Dryden Press, 1955.

'Andromache'.   Translated by L. R. LIND in *Ten Greek Plays*, Boston: Houghton Mifflin, 1957.

Andromache.   Edited with translation by MICHAEL LLOYD, Warminster: Aris and Phillips, 1994.

Euripides' Andromache.   Translated by SUSAN STEWART and WESLEY D. SMITH, Oxford: Oxford University Press, 2001.

Andromache.   Translated by MARIANNE McDONALD and J. MICHAEL WALTON, London: Nick Hern Books, 2001.

BACCHAE (BAKCHAI/BAKKHAI, THE BACCHANTS, THE BACCHANALS)

First, Potter, 1781.

The Bacchae and Heraclidae.   Translated into English prose (Anon.), Oxford: Henry Slatter, 1828.

The Bacchanals of Euripides.   Translated into English verse by Mons. GLOUTON, Brighton: printed for the translator, 1845.

The Bacchae and Heraclidae of Euripides.   Literally translated into English by a Graduate in Honours of the University of Oxford, London: Henry Washbourne, 1846.

The Agamemnon of Æschylus and the Bacchanals of Euripides.   With passages from the lyric and later poets of Greece, translated by HENRY HART MILMAN (with illustrations), London: John Murray, 1865.

The Bacchae.   Translated into English verse by JAMES EDWIN THOROLD ROGERS, Oxford: Parker, 1872.

Euripidis Bacchae.   Literally translated by W. J. HICKIE, Dublin: W. B. Kelly (Kelly's Keys to the Classics), 1886.

Euripides' Bacchae.   A new translation from the text of F. A. Paley by HERBERT HAILSTONE, Cambridge: J. Hall and Son, 1892.

The Bacchae.   Translation by W. H. BALGARNIE and B. J. HAYES, London: W. B. Clive (University Tutorial Press), 1896.

The Bacchae of Euripides.   The text and a translation in English verse by ALEXANDER KERR, Boston: Ginn and Co., 1899.

Euripides [The *Hippolytus* and *Bacchae* of Euripides, together with the *Frogs* of Aristophanes].   Translated into English rhyming verse by

GILBERT MURRAY, London: George Allen, 1902. *Bacchae* reprinted 1904, 1908, 1911, 1916, 1924, 1931, 1948.

A Translation of the Bacchae of Euripides. By FRANCIS A. EVELYN, in verse, London: Heath, Cranton and Ouseley, 1913.

The Bacchantes by Euripides. Translated by ALEXANDER HARVEY, Girard, Kans.: Haldeman-Julius, 1923.

The Bacchanals of Euripides. Rendered into English in the original metres by MARGARET KINMONT TENNANT, London: Methuen, 1926.

The Bacchae of Euripides. The Greek text as performed at Cambridge at the New Theatre, 4–8 March 1930, together with an English prose translation by D. W. LUCAS, Cambridge: Bowes and Bowes, 1930; reprinted London: Bowes and Bowes, 1955.

'Bacchae'. Translated by HENRY BIRKHEAD in *Ten Greek Plays*, Boston: Houghton Mifflin, 1957.

The Bacchae of Euripides. A new translation with a critical essay by DONALD SUTHERLAND, Lincoln: University of Nebraska Press, 1968.

The Bacchae. A translation with commentary by GEOFFREY S. KIRK. Englewood Cliffs, N.J.: Prentice-Hall, 1970.

The Bacchae: Dionysus the God. With color etchings by Michele Forgeois, unacknowledged translation, Kentfield, Calif.: Allen Press, 1972.

The Bakkhai. Translated by ROBERT BAGG, Amherst: University of Massachusetts Press, 1978.

The Bacchae. Euripides. In a new translation by NICHOLAS RUDALL, New York: New American Library, 1982; reprinted Chicago: Ivan R. Dee, 1996.

The Bacchae. Translated and edited by FRANCIS BLESSINGTON, Arlington Heights, Ill.: Harlan Davidson, 1993.

Bakkhai: Euripides. Translation by ROBERT EMMET MEAGHER, Wauconda, Ill.: Bolchazy-Carducci Publishers, 1995.

Bacchae. Edited with translation by RICHARD SEAFORD, Warminster: Aris and Phillips, 1996, 1997.

Bacchae. Translated by FREDERIC RAPHAEL and KENNETH McLEISH, London: Nick Hern Books, 1998.

Bacchae. Translated by PAUL WOODRUFF, Indianapolis: Hackett Pub. Co., 1998.

Bacchae. Translated by STEPHEN ESPOSITO, Newburyport: Focus Classical Library, 1998.

Bacchae. A new translation and commentary by DAVID FRANKLIN, Cambridge: Cambridge University Press, 2000.

Bakkhai. Translated by REGINALD GIBBONS, with introduction and notes by Charles Segal, Oxford: Oxford University Press, 2001.

The Bacchae. Translated by HERBERT GOLDER, New York: Applause Theatre and Cinema Books, 2001.

Euripides Bacchai. A new translation by COLIN TEEVAN, London: Oberon Books, 2002.

Six Greek Tragedies [including *Bacchae*, translated by J. MICHAEL WALTON]. London: Methuen, 2002.

CHILDREN OF HERACLES (HERAKLEIDAI, HERACLEIDAE)

First, Potter, 1781.

Euripides Heraclidae. Literally translated by W. J. HICKIE, Dublin: W. B. Kelly (Kelly's Keys to the Classics), 1886.

The Bacchae and Heraclidae of Euripides. Literally translated into English by a Graduate in Honours of the University of Oxford, London: Henry Washbourne, 1846.

Euripides' Heraclidae. A close translation by RICHARD M. THOMAS, London: W. B. Clive (University Tutorial Press), 1892.

Heracleidae. Translated by EDWARD P. COLERIDGE, London: George Bell and Sons (Bell's Classical Translations), 1892.

The Heraclidae of Euripides. Translated by HUGO SHARPLEY, Cambridge: J. Hall and Son, 1904.

The Heracleidae. Translated by RALPH GLADSTONE, Chicago: University of Chicago Press, 1955.

'The Bacchai'. Translated by CHARLES DORIA in Doria, ed., *The Tenth Muse*, Athens, Ohio, Chicago, London: The Ohio University Press, 1980.

The Children of Herakles. Translated by HENRY TAYLOR and ROBERT A. BROOKS, Oxford: Oxford University Press, 1981.

The Children of Heracles. Edited with translation by WILLIAM ALLAN, Warminster: Aris and Phillips, 2001.

CYCLOPS (KYKLOPS)

First in Wodhull, 1782.

Cyclops. Translated by P. B. SHELLEY, 1819, published by Mrs Shelley in *Posthumous Poems*, London: printed for John and Henry L. Hunt, 1824; reprinted in *The Poetical Works of Percy Bysshe Shelley*,

London: Reeves and Turner, 1882; also in *Miscellaneous Poetry, Prose, and Translations from the Bodleian*, London: Garland, 1995.

'The Cyclops'. Translated by GOLDWIN SMITH in *The Drama: Its History, Literature and Influence on Civilisation*, vol. I, London, New York: Smart and Stanley for The Athenian Society, 1903.

The Cyclops. Freely translated and adapted for performance in English by J. T. SHEPPARD, Cambridge: Cambridge University Press; New York: Macmillan, 1923.

'Euripides' Cyclops' in *Two Satyr Plays*. Translated with an introduction by ROGER LANCELYN GREEN, Harmondsworth: Penguin Books, 1957.

'The Cyclops, Euripides'. Translated GEORGE ECONOMOU in Charles Doria, ed., *The Tenth Muse*, Athens, Ohio, Chicago, London: The Ohio University Press, 1980.

Cyclops: Euripides. Translated by HEATHER McHUGH, Oxford: Oxford University Press, 2001.

Six Greek Comedies [Including *Cyclops* and *Alkestis*, translated by J. MICHAEL WALTON]. London: Methuen, 2002.

ELECTRA (ELEKTRA)

First in Wodhull, 1782.

The Electra of Euripides. Translated into English rhyming verse with explanatory notes by GILBERT MURRAY, London: George Allen, 1905, 1911, 1916, 1919, 1921, 1934, 1940, 1949.

Electra, Euripides. Translated from the original Greek by ALEXANDER HARVEY, Girard, Kans.: Haldeman-Julius Co., 1924.

Electra. Translated by MOSES HADAS, Indianapolis: Bobs-Merrill, 1950.

The Electra. Translated by D. W. LUCAS, London: Cohen and West, 1951.

Electra. Translated by DAVID THOMPSON, Old Woking: Newstage, Gresham Press, 1964.

Euripides: Electra. Edited with translation by M. J. CROPP, Warminster: Aris and Phillips, 1988.

Euripides: Electra. Translated by JANET LEMBKE and KENNETH J. RECKFORD, Oxford: Oxford University Press, 1993.

Electra by Euripides. Translated by MARIANNE McDONALD and J. MICHAEL WALTON, London: Nick Hern Books, 2004.

HECUBA (HEKABE, HECABE)

First, Hecuba. *A tragedy in five acts, and in verse; translated, with alterations, by Richard West, and performed at Drury Lane in 1726, London: printed for W. Wickens, 1726. 'I foresaw there would be some difficulty in making it agreeable, in its original purity, to the Taste of an* English *Audience. It was a failure because of 'a Rout of Vandals in the Galleries.'*

Hecuba. Translated from the Greek in five acts, and in verse, the dedication signed: T. M. [the Rev. Thomas Morell], London: for H. Manby *et al.*, 1749.

The Hecuba of Euripides. Literally translated into English prose, from the text of Porson: with the original Greek, the metres, the order, and English accentuation by T. W. C. Edwards, London: Matthew Iley, 1822.

The Hecuba of Euripides. Literally translated and explained, by the Revd Andrew Fausset, Dublin: M. W. Rooney, 1850.

Euripides' Hecuba. Translated into English prose by Daniel Spillan, Dublin: J. Cumming, 1861.

The Hecuba of Euripides. Literally translated by Roscoe Mongan, Dublin: W. B. Kelly (Kelly's Keys to the Classics), 1865.

Hecuba. In English verse, translated by Henry O'Donnell, Worcester: G. Williams, 1867.

The Hecuba of Euripides. The text closely rendered by a First-Class Man of Balliol College [Thomas Nash], Oxford: T. and G. Shrimpton, 1869.

The Hecuba of Euripides. Translated by the editors of Analytical Series of Greek and Latin Classics (Greek–English Series of Classical Authors), London: Simpkin and Marshall, 1875, 1880, 1886.

The Trojan Queen's Revenge. By A. H. Beesly, a translation in blank verse of the *Hecuba* of Euripides, London: Longmans, Green and Co., 1875.

Hecuba. Translated by Edward P. Coleridge, London: George Bell and Sons (Bell's Classical Texts), 1893.

Euripides: Hecuba. A translation by W. H. Balgarnie, London: W. B. Clive (University Correspondence College Press), 1899.

The Hecuba of Euripides. Literally translated according to the new Oxford text by St G. W. J. Stock, Oxford: Blackwell, 1902.

Hecuba. Partly in the original and partly in translation by J. T. Sheppard, Oxford: Clarendon Press, 1924; full translation, Oxford, 1925.

Hecuba. With illustrations and notes edited by MICHAEL EARLS for the performance of the play in the Greek Theatre, Holy Cross Stadium, Worcester, Mass.: Harrigan Press, 1926.

Hecuba, and The Madness of Heracles. Translated by PETER D. ARNOTT, London: Macmillan; New York: St Martin's Press, 1969.

Euripides: Hecuba. Translated by JANET LEMBKE and KENNETH J. RECKFORD, Oxford: Oxford University Press, 1991.

Euripides: Hecuba. Edited with translation by C. COLLARD, Warminster: Aris and Phillips, 1991.

Euripides' Hecuba. Translated by KIKI GOUNARIDOU and JOEL TANSEY, Lampeter: Edwin Mellen Press, 1995.

Euripides' Hecuba. In a new version by FRANK McGUINNESS, London: Faber and Faber, 2004.

Hecuba. Translated by TONY HARRISON, London: Faber, 2005.

Hecuba. Translated by JOHN HARRISON, Cambridge: Cambridge University Press, 2005.

Hecuba. Translated by MARIANNE McDONALD, London: Nick Hern Books, 2005.

HELEN (HELENE)

First, in Wodhull, 1782.

The Helen of Euripides. Translated by J. T. SHEPPARD, Cambridge: Cambridge University Press, 1925.

The Helen of Euripides. A translation by REX WARNER, London: Bodley Head, 1951; reprinted New York: New American Library, 1958.

Helen. Translated by JAMES MICHIE and COLIN LEACH, Oxford: Oxford University Press, 1981.

Euripides: Helen. Translated by ROBERT EMMET MEAGHER, Amherst: University of Massachusetts Press, 1986.

Euripides: Helen. Edited with translation by PETER BURIAN, Warminster: Aris and Phillips, 2005.

HERACLES (HERAKLES MAINOMENOS, HERCULES FURENS, THE MADNESS OF HERACLES, HERACLES MAD, HERACLES DISTRACTED)

First, in Potter, 1781.

Aristophanes' Apology. By ROBERT BROWNING, including a transcript from Euripides [a genuine translation of Euripides' *Hercules Furens*, as opposed to the narrative form adopted for his *Alcestis* in *Balaustion's Journey*, 1871], 'being the Last Journey of Balaustion', London: Smith, Elder and Co., 1875.

Euripides' Hercules Furens. Translated by a Graduate, Cambridge: J. Hall and Sons, 1876.

Euripides' Hercules Furens. Literally translated by THOMAS J. ARNOLD, Dublin: W. B. Kelly (Kelly's Keys to the Classics), 1884.

'Hercules Furens of Euripides'. Translated into literal English, by AUGUSTUS C. MAYBURY [better known for his Aids to Analytical Chemistry] in *How to Pass* 'written more especially for candidates preparing for the University of London examinations' [together with as bizarre and inaccurate a 'Life' of Euripides as it would be possible to find], London: published by the author, 1886.

Euripides: Hercules Furens. A literal translation by R. M. THOMAS, London: W. B. Clive (University Tutorial Press), 1894.

Hecuba and The Madness of Heracles. Translated by PETER D. ARNOTT, London: Macmillan; New York: St Martin's Press, 1969.

Herakles. Translated by MICHAEL HALLERAN, Newburyport: Focus Classical Library, 1988.

Euripides: Heracles. Edited with translation by SHIRLEY A. BARLOW, Warminster: Aris and Phillips, 1996.

Heracles. Translated by THOMAS SLEIGH, New York and Oxford: Oxford University Press, 2001.

HIPPOLYTOS (HIPPOLYTOS STEPHANEPHOROS, CROWNED HIPPOLYTOS)

First, in Lennox as Hippolitus *(Brumoy), 1759.*

A Literal Translation of Euripides' Hippolytus and Iphigenia [in Aulis]. By M. TUOMY, Dublin: printed by W. M'Kenzie, 1790.

Hippolytus and Alcestis. Translator Anon. (? Edwards), Oxford. D. A. Talboys, 1821; second edition, corrected by D. A. Talboys, Oxford, 1834.

The Hippolytus and Iphigenia in Aulis. With a literal translation by DANIEL SPILLAN, Dublin: printed for J. Cumming, 1830.

The Alcestis and Hippolytus of Euripides. Literally translated into English by a Graduate in Honours of the University of Oxford, London: Henry Washbourne, 1846.

The Hippolytus. Literally translated by ROSCOE MONGAN, Dublin: W. B. Kelly (Kelly's Keys to the Classics), 1866.

The Crowned Hippolytus of Euripides. Together with a selection from the pastoral and lyric poets of Greece, translated into English verse by MAURICE PURCELL FITZGERALD, London: Chapman and Hall, 1867.

The Hippolytus of Euripides. With notes and literal translation by F. A. S. FREELAND, Cambridge: H. W. Wallis, 1876.

The Crowned Hippolytus. Translated with new poems by AGNES MARY FRANCES ROBINSON (later Duclaux), London: Kegan Paul and Co., 1881.

Euripides' Hippolytus. Literally translated by a Graduate, Cambridge: J. Hall and Son, 1888.

The Hippolytus of Euripides. Translated into English by HERBERT HAILSTONE, Cambridge: E. Johnson, 1888.

The Hippolutos of Euripides. Now first translated into English, in its original and identical metres, with stage directions, suggesting how it may have been performed, also with preface and notes by H. B. L. (HENRY BARRETT LENNARD), London: Williams and Norgate, 1893.

Adrastus of Phrygia and other poems with the Hippolytus of Euripides, done into English verse. By E. H. PEMBER, London: printed at the Chiswick Press for private distribution, 1897.

The Hippolytus of Euripides. Translated into English rhyming verse by GILBERT MURRAY, London: George Allen, 1902, 1908, 1913, 1922, 1931, 1945.

The Medea and Hippolytus. With introduction, translations and notes by SYDNEY WATERLOW, London: J. M. Dent and Co. (The Temple Greek and Latin Classics), 1906.

Hippolytus. A tragedy by Euripides translated from the original Greek by ALEXANDER HARVEY, Girard, Kans.: Haldeman-Julius Co., 1924.

Three Greek Tragedies in Translation [including *Hippolytus*]. Translated by DAVID GRENE, Chicago: Chicago University Press, 1942.

The Hippolytus of Euripides. A translation by REX WARNER, London: The Bodley Head, 1949.

Hippolytus in Drama and Myth. 'The Hippolytus of Euripides', a new translation by DONALD SUTHERLAND, Lincoln, Nebr.: University of Nebraska Press, 1960.

Hippolytus. Translated by KENNETH CAVANDER, San Francisco: Chandler Publishing Co., 1962.

Hippolytus. Translated by ROBERT BAGG, illustrated by Leonard Baskin, Northampton, Mass.: Gehenna Press, 1969; reprinted New York: Oxford University Press, 1973, 1992.

Euripides: Hippolytus. A companion with translation by GILBERT and SARAH LAWALL, in *The Phaedra of Seneca*, Chicago: Bolchazi-Carducci, 1982; reprinted as a single play, Bristol: Bristol Classical Press, 1986.

Hippolytus. Euripides. Edited with translation by MICHAEL R. HALLERAN, Warminster: Aris and Phillips, 1995.

ION

First, in Potter, 1781.

The Ion. A new and accurate translation by EDMUND SAMUEL CROOKE, Cambridge: J. Hall and Son, 1866.

The Ion. New and literal translation by ROSCOE MONGAN, Dublin: W. B. Kelly (Kelly's Keys to the Classics), 1881.

The Ion of Euripides. Now first translated into English, in its original metres, and supplied with stage directions suggesting how it may have been performed on the Athenian stage, with preface and notes, by H. B. L. (HENRY BARRETT LENNARD), London: Williams and Norgate, 1889.

The Ion of Euripides. Translated into English by HERBERT HAILSTONE, Cambridge: J. Palmer, 1890.

Ion. With a translation into English verse by A. W. VERRALL, Cambridge: Cambridge University Press, 1890.

The Ion of Euripides. As performed at Cambridge, 25–9 November, 1890, with a translation in prose by M. A. BAYFIELD, Cambridge: Macmillan and Bowes, 1890.

The Ion of Euripides. Translated in verse by FRANCIS A. EVELYN, London: Heath, Cranton and Ouseley, 1921; reprinted as *An Acting Version of the Ion of Euripides*, 1932.

Euripides Ion. Translated with notes by H. D. [HILDA DOOLITTLE], London: Chatto and Windus, 1937.

The Ion of Euripides. Translated into English prose by D. W. LUCAS, London: Cohen and West, 1949; New York: R. F. Moore, 1950.

Ion. Translated into English rhyming verse with explanatory notes by GILBERT MURRAY, London: George Allen and Unwin, 1954.

Ion. A translation with commentary by ANNE PIPPIN BURNETT, Englewood Cliffs, N.J.: Prentice-Hall, 1970.

Euripides Ion. A new version by DAVID LAN, London: Methuen, 1994.

Ion. Translated by W. S. DI PIERO, Oxford: Oxford University Press, 1996.

Ion. Edited with translation by K. H. LEE, Warminster: Aris and Phillips, 1997.

IPHIGENIA/IPHIGENEIA IN AULIS (IPHIGENEIA HĒ EN AULIDI, IPHIGENIA/IPHIGENEIA AT AULIS)

First, Iphigenia at Aulis. *Translated by Lady Jane Lumley, c. 1555; reprinted from manuscript, London: Malone Society Reprints, 1909; reprinted in* Three Tragedies by Renaissance Women, *Harmondsworth: Penguin, 2000.*

A Literal Translation of Euripides's Hippolytus and Iphigenia [in Aulis] By M. TUOMY, Dublin: W. M'Kenzie, 1790.

The Hippolytus and Iphigenia in Aulis With a literal translation by DANIEL SPILLAN, Dublin: printed for J. Cumming, 1830.

Euripides' Iphigenia in Aulis. Literally translated by THOMAS. J. ARNOLD, Dublin: W. B. Kelly (Kelly's Keys to the Classics), 1884.

The Iphigeneia in Aulis of Euripides. Rendered into English verse by W. CUDWORTH, privately printed, 1889.

Iphigeneia at Aulis. Euripides, translated from the original Greek by ALEXANDER HARVEY, Girard, Kans.: Haldeman-Julius Co., 1925.

Iphigenia in Aulis. Translated by W. D. WARD, Los Angeles: printed by D. C. Welty, 1925.

Iphigenia in Aulis. Translated into English verse by F. MELIAN STAWELL, London: G. Bell and Sons, 1929; New York: Oxford University Press, 1929.

Iphigenia. Two plays, the *Iphigenia in Aulis* and the *Iphigenia in Tauris,* English by C. B. BONNER, London: Watts and Co., 1930.

Iphigenia in Aulis. 'Done into English verse' by Rev. S. CLAUDE TICKELL, London: University Research Society, 1950.

Iphigeneia at Aulis. A translation with commentary by KENNETH CAVANDER, Englewood Cliffs, N.J.: Prentice-Hall, 1973.

Iphigeneia at Aulis. Translated by W. S. MERWIN and GEORGE E. DIMOCK, Jnr, Oxford: Oxford University Press, 1978.

Iphigenia in Aulis. Euripides in a new translation by NICHOLAS RUDALL, Chicago: Ivan R. Dee, 1997.

IPHIGENIA/IPHIGENEIA AMONG THE TAURIANS/TAURI (IPHIGENEIA HĒ EN TAUROIS, IPHIGENEIA IN TAURIS)

First, Iphigenia in Tauris, *a tragedy in five acts and in verse, translated by Gilbert West, in Pindar,* Odes of Pindar, *with several other pieces in prose and verse, London: printed for R. Dodsley, 1749.*

Iphigenia in Tauris. Translated with notes by EDMUND SAMUEL CROOKE, Cambridge: J. Hall and Son, 1866.

The Iphigeneia among the Tauri. Translated into English by HERBERT HAILSTONE, Cambridge: E. Johnson, 1884.

Euripides' Iphigenia in Tauris. A literal translation, by G. F. H. SYKES and J. H. HAYDON, London: W. B. Clive (University Correspondence College Press), 1890.

Euripides: Iphigenia in Tauris. Literally translated by J. A. PROUT, Dublin: W. B. Kelly (Kelly's Keys to the Classics), 1892.

The Iphigenia in Tauris of Euripides. As performed at Cambridge, 30 Nov, 1–5 Dec 1894, with a translation in prose by A. W. VERRALL, Cambridge: Cambridge University Press, 1894.

The Iphigenia in Tauris of Euripides. Translated into English rhyming verse with explanatory notes by GILBERT MURRAY, London: George Allen and Sons: London, 1910, 1912, 1915, 1918, 1920, 1942.

Iphigenia in Tauris. An English version by WITTER BYNNER, New York: Mitchell Kennerley, 1915; reprinted in Chicago *The Complete Tragedies*, 1956.

Iphigenia. Two plays, the *Iphigenia in Aulis* and the *Iphigenia in Tauris*, English by C. B. BONNER, London: Watts and Co., 1930.

'The Tragic Maid'. Adapted from the *Iphigenia in Tauris* by G. E. O. KNIGHT, London: privately published, 1949.

Iphigeneia in Tauris. Translated by RICHMOND LATTIMORE, Oxford: Oxford University Press, 1973, 1992.

Iphigenia among the Taurians. Euripides in a new translation by NICHOLAS RUDALL, Chicago: Ivan R. Dee, 1997.

Iphigenia in Tauris. Edited with translation by M. J. CROPP, Warminster: Aris and Phillips, 2000.

MEDEA (MEDEIA)

First, in Potter, 1781.

The Medea of Euripides. Literally translated into English prose by T. W. C. EDWARDS, London: Matthew Iley, 1821.

Medea. Translated by JOHN R. LEE [with Sophocles' *Oedipus at Colonus*], Oxford: Charles Richards, 1841.

The Medea of Euripides. Literally translated and explained by the Rev. ANDREW R. FAUSSET, Dublin: M. W. Rooney, 1851.

Euripides' Medea. Translated into English prose by DANIEL SPILLAN, Dublin: J. Cumming, 1862.

Euripides: The Medea. Literally translated by ROSCOE MONGAN, Dublin: W. B. Kelly (Kelly's Keys to the Classics), 1865.

The Medea. Literally translated into English verse by AUGUSTA WEBSTER, London and Cambridge: Macmillan and Co., 1868.

The Medea. The Oxford edition literally translated by a First-Class Man of Balliol College [THOMAS NASH], Oxford: T. and G. Shrimpton, 1869.

Medea. Translated by WILLIAM JOHN BLEW in English verse from the tragedy of Euripides, with the choruses of Thomas Campbell from 'The Pleasure of Hope', London: Rivington's, 1887.

The Medea of Euripides. Translated from the Greek into English verse by JOHN PATTERSON, Louisville: J. P. Morton and Co., 1894.

The Medea and Hippolytus. With introduction, translations and notes by SYDNEY WATERLOW, London: J. M. Dent and Co. (The Temple Greek and Latin Classics), 1906.

Euripides Medea. With English notes and a literal translation by W. C. GREEN, Cambridge: J. Hall and Son, 1898, 1910.

The Medea of Euripides. Literally translated by THOMAS NASH, third edition, revised, with introduction, analysis and notes by R. Broughton, Oxford: A. T. Shrimpton and Son, 1898.

Euripides: Medea. A translation by J. F. STOUT, London: W. B. Clive (University Tutorial Press), 1901.

The Medea of Euripides. Translated into English rhyming verse, with explanatory notes, by GILBERT MURRAY, London: George Allen, 1906, 1913, 1921, 1923, 1933, 1941, 1946.

The Genius of the Greek Drama [including *Medea*]. Rendered and adapted with an introduction, by CYRIL E. ROBINSON, New York: Humphrey Milford, 1921; Oxford: Clarendon Press, 1924; reprinted Freeport, N.Y., Books for Libraries Press, 1970.

Medea. Translated from the Greek by Alexander Harvey, Girard, Kans.: Haldeman-Julius Co., 1924.

The Medea of Euripides. Translated into English prose, with introduction and notes, by D. W. LUCAS, Oxford: Clarendon Press, 1924.

Medea. Translated by W. D. WARD, Los Angeles: printed by D. C. Welty, 1927.

Two Greek Plays [the *Philoctetes* of Sophocles and the *Medea* of Euripides). 'Done into English' by JOHN JAY CHAPMAN, Boston and New York: Houghton Mifflin, 1928.

The Medea of Euripides. A translation and introduction by HORACE A. HOFFMAN, Rahway, N.J.: privately printed, 1931.

Medea. Translated by R. C. TREVELYAN, Cambridge: Cambridge University Press, 1939.

Medea. Translated by FRED PROKOSCH in Dudley Fitts, ed., *Greek Plays in Modern Translations*, New York: the Dial Press, 1941.

The Medea of Euripides. A translation by REX WARNER, London: John Lane, 1944.

The Medea of Euripides. Translated by WALTER R. AGARD in *Classics in Translation*, vol. 1, Madison, Wis.: University of Wisconsin Press, 1952.

Medea. Translated by MICHAEL TOWNSEND, San Francisco: Chandler Publishing Co., 1966.

'Medea', in *The Frogs and Other Greek Plays.* Translated by KENNETH McLEISH, London: Longman's (Heritage of Literature Series), 1970.

Euripides' Medea. A new version by BRENDAN KENNELLY, Newcastle upon Tyne: Bloodaxe, 1991.

Medea. Translated by DESMOND EGAN, Laurinburg, N.C.: St Andrews Press; Newbridge, Co. Kildare: Kavanagh Press, 1991.

Medea. Translated by ALISTAIR ELLIOT, illustrations by Andrej Klimowski, London: Oberon Books, 1993.

Medea by Euripides. Translated and introduced by FREDERIC RAPHAEL and KENNETH McLEISH, London: Nick Hern Books, 1994.

Medea. Translated by ANTHONY PODLECKI, Newburyport: Focus Classical Library, 1998.

Medea. A new translation and commentary by JOHN HARRISON, Cambridge: Cambridge University Press, 2000.

Medea. In a new translation by NICHOLAS RUDALL, Chicago: Ivan R. Dee, 2000.

Medea. Translated by J. MICHAEL WALTON, London: Methuen (Methuen Student Edition), 2002.

Medea: Euripides. Translated by DONALD J. MASTRONARDE, Cambridge: Cambridge University Press, 2002.

Medea and Alcestis. Translated into English verse by MICHAEL JAMES GOULD, Whitstable: Wave Crest Classics, 2003.

ORESTES

First, in Bannister, 1780.

The Orestes of Euripides. Literally translated into English prose with the original Greek, the metres, the order, and English accentuation by T. W. C. EDWARDS, London: Simpkin, Marshall and Co., 1823.

Orestes. Edited with translation by M. L. WEST, Warminster: Aris and Phillips, 1987.

Orestes. Translated by JOHN PECK and FRANK NISETICH, Oxford: Oxford University Press, 1995.

PHOENICIAN WOMEN (*PHOENISSAI, PHOENISSAE, THE PHOENICIAN MAIDENS/VIRGINS*)

First, in Bannister, 1780.

Jocasta by George Gascoigne and Francis Kinwelmershe (presented at Gray's Inn in 1566 and published in Gascoigne's *Poesies* in 1572), is based on Euripides' *Phoenissae* and claimed by many sources as the first translation of a Greek play into English. But, as Brüggemann quotes from Warton's *History of English Poetry*, 'this is by no means a just or exact translation of the *Jocasta*, that is the *Phoenissae* of Euripides. It is partly a paraphrase, and partly an abridgement, of the tragedy. There are many omissions, retrenchments and transpositions.' Lumley's *Iphigenia* is not only earlier than the Gascoigne and Kinwelmershe, but has claims to being a translation in a way that the *Jocasta* is not. Nevertheless, the details are included below:

'Phœnissæ, English, Jocasta: a Tragedie written in Greke by Euripides, translated and digested into Actes by G. Gascoygne, and F. Kinwelmershe', in Gascoigne (G.), *A hundreth sundrie Flowres bounde up in one small Poesie*, etc. [1572.] Also in C. F. J., *Four Old Plays*, etc. 1848.

The Phœnician Virgins of Euripides. Literally translated into English prose with the original Greek; the metres; the order; and English accentuation by T. W. C. EDWARDS, London: Matthew Iley, 1823.

Euripides: the Phoenician Virgins. Literally translated by ROSCOE MONGAN, Dublin: W. B. Kelly (Kelly's Keys to the Classics), 1865.

The Phoenician Women. Euripides. Translated by PETER BURIAN and BRIAN SWANN, Oxford: Oxford University Press, 1981.

Phoenician Women. Edited with translation by ELIZABETH CRAIK, Warminster: Aris and Phillips, 1988.

RHESUS (RHESOS)

First, in Wodhull, 1782.

The Rhesus of Euripides. Translated into English rhyming verse with explanatory notes by GILBERT MURRAY, London: George Allen, 1913, reprinted 1924, 1946.

The Rhesus of Euripides. The Greek text with English translation by members of Bradfield College, as produced in the Bradfield College Greek Theatre, June 1928. Oxford: Oxford University Press, 1928.

Rhesos. Translated by RICHARD EMIL BRAUN, Oxford and New York: Oxford University Press, 1978, 1992.

SUPPLIANT WOMEN (HIKETIDES, SUPPLICES, SUPPLIANTS)

First, in Potter, 1781.

'Suppliants'. Translated by L. R. LIND in *Ten Greek Plays*, Boston: Houghton Mifflin, 1957.

Suppliant Women. Translated by ROSANNA WARREN and STEPHEN SCULLY, Oxford: Oxford University Press, 1995.

THE TROJAN WOMEN (TROADES, WOMEN OF TROY, DAUGHTERS OF TROY)

First, in Bannister, 1780.

The Troades of Euripides. Translated into literal English by H. J. C. KNIGHT, Cambridge: J. Hall and Son, 1882.

Euripides' The Troades. Literally translated by THOMAS J. ARNOLD, Dublin: W. B. Kelly (Kelly's Keys to the Classics), 1884.

The Trojan Women. A translation into English verse by W. D. STANDFAST, London: J. Heywood, 1887.

The Trojan Women of Euripides. Translated into English rhyming verse by GILBERT MURRAY, London: George Allen, 1905, 1910, 1915, 1919, 1925, 1934.

The Women of Troy. Translated in verse by FRANCIS A. EVELYN, London: Heath, Cranton and Ouseley, 1920.

Three Greek Plays [including *The Trojan Women*]. Translated with introduction by EDITH HAMILTON, New York: W. W. Norton, 1937.

The Trojan Women of Euripides. A new dramatic translation by F. KINCHIN SMITH, London: Sidgwick and Jackson, 1951.

'The Trojan Women'. Translated by ISABELLE K. and ANTONY E. RAUBITSCHEK in *An Anthology of Greek Drama: second series*, New York: Reinhart and Co. Inc., 1954.

The Trojan Women. Adapted by NEIL CURRY, Old Woking: Newslage, Gresham Press, 1964; reprinted Methuen, 1966; Cambridge: Cambridge University Press, 1981.

Trojan Women. Edited with translation by SHIRLEY A. BARLOW, Warminster: Aris and Phillips, 1986.

Euripides' The Trojan Women. A new version by BRENDAN KENNELLY, Newcastle upon Tyne: Bloodaxe Books, 1993.

The Trojan Women. In a new translation by NICHOLAS RUDALL, Chicago: Ivan R. Dee, 1999.

Six Greek Tragedies. [Including *Trojan Women*, translated by MARIANNE McDONALD], London: Methuen, 2002.

Women of Troy. Translated by KENNETH McLEISH, London: Nick Hern Books, 2004.

Trojan Women. Translated by DISKIN CLAY, Newburyport: Focus Classical Library, 2005.

ARISTOPHANES

Collections A

Comedies. Translated into English (*Clouds* translated by RICHARD CUMBERLAND, 1786/1797), *Plutus* by HENRY FIELDING and WILLIAM YOUNG (1742), *Frogs* by CHARLES DUNSTER (1785), *Birds* by 'a Member of One of the Universities', London: A. J. Valpy for Lackington, Allen and Co., 1812.

The Comedies of Aristophanes. Translated by THOMAS MITCHELL [*Acharnians, Knights*], [*Wasps* with a reprint of *Clouds* translated by Richard Cumberland], 2 vols., London: John Murray, 1820–22; reprinted in Sanford, *The Works of the British Poets*, vols. 43, 44, 1822.

The Comedies of Aristophanes. All eleven plays translated into familiar blank verse by C. A. WHEELWRIGHT, 2 vols., Oxford: D. A. Talboys, 1837.

Aristophanes Frogs, Acharnians, Knights, Birds. Translated by JOHN HOOKHAM FRERE, Malta: The Government Press, 1839; *Acharnians, Knights and Birds*, London: William Pickering, 1840; in *The Works of John Hookham Frere*, vol. III [with *Frogs* and *Peace*], London: Pickering, 1872; the four plays [ex *Peace*], Oxford: Oxford University Press (The World's Classics), 1907. See also *Birds* below.

Comedies. Edited, translated and explained by BENJAMIN BICKLEY ROGERS, 4 vols., London: Bell, 1902, 1910–13, 1916; reprinted *Dr. Rogers' Translations from Aristophanes* (5 vols.), London: G. Bell and Sons,

1919–23; reprinted, 3 vols., London: Heinemann (Loeb Classical Library), 1924, 1938, 1950, 1960; *Five Comedies*, New York: Doubleday, 1955.

Aristophanes in English Verse. Translated by ARTHUR S. WAY, 2 vols., London: Macmillan and Co., 1927, 1934.

Aristophanes, Four Comedies [*Lysistrata, The Frogs, The Birds* and *Ladies' Day*]. New English versions by DUDLEY FITTS, New York: Harcourt, Brace and World, 1959, 1962.

The Frogs, and Other Plays [*The Wasps* and *The Poet and the Women*]. Translated by DAVID BARRETT, Harmondsworth: Penguin, 1964; as *The Wasps, The Poet and the Women, The Frogs*, 2003.

Four Comedies by Aristophanes. Translated by DOUGLASS PARKER [*Lysistrata, The Acharnians* and *The Congresswomen*], *Frogs* translated by RICHMOND LATTIMORE, Ann Arbor: University of Michigan Press, 1969.

Three Comedies by Aristophanes. Translated by WILLIAM ARROWSMITH [*The Birds* and *The Clouds*], *The Wasps* translated by DOUGLASS PARKER, Ann Arbor: University of Michigan Press, 1969.

The Acharnians, The Clouds, Lysistrata. Translated with an introduction by ALAN H. SOMMERSTEIN, Harmondsworth: Penguin, 1973; revised as *Lysistrata and Other Plays*, 2002.

Aristophanes. Translated by ALAN H. SOMMERSTEIN [*The Knights, Peace* and *Wealth*] and DAVID BARRETT (*The Birds* and *The Assembly Women*). Harmondsworth: Penguin, 1978, 1982.

Clouds, Women in Power, Knights. Translated by KENNETH McLEISH, Cambridge: Cambridge University Press, 1979.

Aristophanes: Plays. 2 vols. Translated by KENNETH McLEISH, London: Methuen (Methuen Classical Dramatists), 1993, 1998.

Aristophanes and Menander: New Comedy. [Including *Wealth* and *Women in Power* translated by KENNETH McLEISH] London: Methuen, 1994, 1998.

Three Plays by Aristophanes: Staging Women [*Lysistrata, Women at the Thesmophoria* and *Assemblywomen*]. Translated and edited by JEFFREY HENDERSON, New York: Routledge, 1996.

Birds and Other Plays [*Lysistrata, Assembly-Women* and *Wealth*]. Translated by STEPHEN HALLIWELL, Oxford: Oxford University Press (Oxford World Classics), 1997.

Aristophanes: Plays. 4 vols. Translated by JEFFREY HENDERSON, Cambridge, Mass.: Harvard University Press (Loeb), 1998–2002; *Birds, Lysistrata* and *Women at the Thesmophoria*, reprinted, 2000.

Four Plays by Aristophanes [*Lysistrata, The Frogs, A Parliament of Women* and *Plutus* (*Wealth*)]. The new translations by PAUL ROCHE, New York: Signet Classic, 2004.

The Complete Plays: Aristophanes. Translated by PAUL ROCHE, New York: New American Library, 2005.

Collections B

The Acharnians, Knights, Wasps, and Birds of Aristophanes. Translated into English prose by a Graduate of the University of Oxford [JOHN W. WARTER], Oxford: Henry Slatter, 1830.

Three Plays [*Acharnians, Knights* and *Clouds*]. Translated by BENJAMIN DANN WALSH, vol. I [vols. II and III never published], London: A. H. Bailey, 1837, 1848.

The Comedies of Aristophanes. A new and literal translation, by WILLIAM JAMES HICKIE, 2 vols., London: Henry G. Bohn, 1848, 1853; reprinted London: George Bell and Sons, 1874–5, 1882–3, 1901; New York, 1872–6.

Eight Comedies [all except *Lysistrata, Thesmophoriazousae* and *Ekklesiazousae*]. Translated into rhymed meters by LEONARD HAMPSON RUDD, London: Longmans Green and Co., 1867.

Aristophanes, Comedies. Translated by WILLIAM LUCAS COLLINS, Edinburgh: W. Blackwood and Sons, 1872; Philadelphia: 1872.

Aristophanes [*The Acharnians, The Knights* and *The Clouds*]. Literally and completely translated from the Greek by HORACE LIVERIGHT, London: privately printed for the Athenian Society, 1898.

Aristophanes. The Eleven Comedies. Now for the first time literally and completely translated from the Greek tongue into English by HORACE LIVERIGHT, London: privately printed for the Athenian Society, 1912.

The Complete Greek Drama. All the extant tragedies of Aeschylus, Sophocles and Euripides, and the comedies of Aristophanes and Menander, in a variety of translations [Aeschylus – Morshead, Potter and More; Sophocles – Trevelyan, Jebb and Francklin; Euripides – Coleridge, Potter, Murray and Stawell]; Aristophanes – ten listed as 'Anon.' but by Liveright, together with Murray's *Frogs*; Menander – Post; all edited by Whitney J. Oates and Eugene O'Neill, Jnr, New York: Random House, 1938.

Aristophanes against War [*The Acharnians, Lysistrata* and *Peace*]. Translated by PATRIC DICKINSON, Oxford: Oxford University Press, 1957.

Complete Plays of Aristophanes. Translated by MOSES HADAS, New York: Bantam, 1962.

Aristophanes Plays 1 and 2. Translated into English verse by PATRIC DICKINSON, Oxford: Oxford University Press, 1970.

Four Plays of Aristophanes [*The Birds, The Clouds, Frogs* and *Lysistrata*]. Translated by JAMES H. MANTINBAND. Washington, D.C.: University Press of America, 1983.

Aristophanes. 3 vols. in translations by FRED BEAKE (*Peace*), PALMER BOVIE (*Wealth*), ALFRED DEWART CORN (*Frogs*), GREG DELANTY (*The Suits* [*Knights*]), R. H. W. DILLARD (*The Sexual Congress* [*Ecclesiazousae*]), JACK FLAVIN (*Acharnians*), X. J. KENNEDY (*Lysistrata*), CAMPBELL MCGRATH (*Wasps*), PAUL MULDOON with RICHARD MARTIN (*Birds*), CAROL POSTER (*Clouds*) and DAVID R. SLAVITT (*Celebrating Ladies* [*Thesmophoriazousae*]), Philadelphia: University of Pennsylvania Press, 1998.

Aristophanes I [*Clouds, Wasps* and *Birds*]. Translated by PETER MEINECK, Indianapolis: Hackett Pub. Co., 1998.

Six Greek Comedies [Including *Birds, Frogs* and *Women in Power*]. Translated by KENNETH MCLEISH, London: Methuen, 2002.

ACHARNIANS (ACHARNES)

First, Mitchell, 1820.

Acharnians. Translated into English verse, by CHARLES J. BILLSON, London: Kegan, Paul and Co., 1882.

Acharnians. Translated into English verse by ROBERT YELVERTON TYRRELL, Dublin: Hodges Figgis, and London: Longman's, 1883, 1890; New York, Oxford: Humphrey Milford, Oxford University Press, 1914.

Acharnians of Aristophanes. Literally translated by a First-Class Man of Balliol College [THOMAS NASH] for interleaving with the Clarendon Press edition, Oxford: A. J. Shrimpton and Son, 1883.

Aristophanes' Acharnians. Translated with an introduction and memoir by W. H. COVINGTON, London: G. Bell and Sons, 1894.

The Acharnians of Aristophanes. English prose translation by the Rt. Hon. WILLIAM JOSEPH STARKIE, London: Macmillan, 1909; reprinted

New York, 1910; Amsterdam: A. M. Hakkert, 1968; New York: Arno Press, 1979.

The Acharnians. Translated from the original Greek by ALEXANDER HARVEY, Girard, Kans.: Haldeman-Julius Co., 1925.

The Acharnians. Translated by DOUGLASS PARKER, with sketches by Geraldine Sakall, Ann Arbor: University of Michigan Press, 1961, 1969.

Four Greek Plays [Including *The Acharnians* and *Peace*]. Translated and adapted by KENNETH McLEISH, London: Longman's (Heritage of Literature Series), 1964.

Acharnians. Edited with translation by ALAN H. SOMMERSTEIN, Warminster: Aris and Phillips, 1980.

BIRDS (ORNITHES, AVES)

First, 'A Member of One of the Universities', 1812.

The Birds of Aristophanes. Translated by the Rev. HENRY FRANCIS CARY, London: Taylor and Hessey, 1824.

The 'Birds' of Aristophanes. A dramatic experiment in one act, 'Being an Humble Attempt to Adapt the said "Birds" to this Climate, by giving them New Names, New Feathers, New Songs, and New Tales' by JAMES ROBINSON PLANCHÉ, London: G. S. Fairbrother and W. Strange, 1846; reprinted in James Robinson, *Lacy's Acting Edition*, vol. xx, London, 1864; *The Extravaganzas*, vol. III, London: Samuel French, 1879.

The Birds of Aristophanes. Translated by JOHN HOOKHAM FRERE (first published with others in Malta, 1839; see Collections A above), revised to coincide with the production of *Birds* as the 1883 Cambridge Greek Play, Cambridge: Macmillan and Bowes, 1883. 'In this edition the text of Mr Frere has been arranged in conformity with the acting edition of the Greek text': 'The Translation of the Parabasis by Mr Swinburne which appeared in the Athenaeum, 30th October, 1880...has been printed at the end of Mr Frere's version.'

The Birds of Aristophanes. Translated into English verse, by BENJAMIN HALL KENNEDY, London: Macmillan and Co., 1874; also reprinted to coincide with the production of *Birds* as the Cambridge Greek Play of 1883, Cambridge: Macmillan and Bowes, 1883. 'Mr Frere's clever translation of the Parabasis represented his own witty conception, but not the mind of Aristophanes' (B. H. Kennedy).

The Birds of Aristophanes in English Rhyme for English Readers.
Translated by GEORGE SAMUEL HODGES, London: Houlston and Sons,
1896.

The Birds. As presented at Vassar College, translated by ELSA
HILLYER, New York: The Willetts Press, 1902.

The Birds. Translated by BENJAMIN BICKLEY ROGERS, London: G.
Bell and Sons, 1906.

The Birds of Aristophanes. As arranged for performance at Cambridge
26 Feb to 1 March 1924, with a translation by J. T. SHEPPARD and an
English version of the songs by the late A. W. VERRALL, Cambridge:
Bowes and Bowes, 1924.

The Birds. Translated from the original Greek by ALEXANDER
HARVEY, Girard, Kans.: Haldeman-Julius Co., 1924.

The Birds and The Frogs. Translated into rhymed English verse by
MARSHALL MACGREGOR, London: E. Arnold and Co., 1927.

The Birds. Translated into English verse with introduction and
notes by GILBERT MURRAY, London: George Allen and Unwin,
1950.

The Birds. An acting edition prepared by WALTER KERR,
Washington: Catholic University of America Press, 1952; reprinted San
Francisco: Chandler Pub. Co., 1968.

'The Birds'. A 'composite translation' in *Six Greek Plays in Modern
Translations*, New York: The Dryden Press, 1955.

The Birds. An English version by DUDLEY FITTS, New York:
Harcourt, Brace, 1957; reprinted Faber and Faber: London, 1958; New
York: Heritage Press, 1959; with a new series of illustrations by Quentin
Blake, London: Lion and Unicorn Press, 1971.

Two Classical Comedies [*The Birds* and *The Brothers Menaechmus*
(Plautus)]. Translated by PETER D. ARNOTT, New York: Appleton-
Century-Crofts, 1958.

The Burdies. A comedy in Scots verse by DOUGLAS YOUNG, from
the Greek of Aristophanes, Tayport: published by the author, 1959.

The Birds. Translated by WILLIAM ARROWSMITH, Ann Arbor:
University of Michigan Press, 1961.

The Frogs, and Other Greek Plays [Including *The Birds*]. Translated
by KENNETH McLEISH, London: Longman's (Heritage of Literature
Series), 1970.

Birds. Edited with translation by ALAN H. SOMMERSTEIN,
Warminster: Aris and Phillips, 1987.

The Birds. A modern adaptation of Aristophanes' comedy by GWENDOLYN MACEWEN, Toronto: Exile Editions, 1993.

The Birds. Translated from Aristophanes by PAUL MULDOON with RICHARD MARTIN, Oldcastle: County Meath, Ireland Gallery Press, 1999.

The Birds by Aristophanes. A verse version by SEAN O'BRIEN, London: Methuen, 2002.

CLOUDS (NEPHELAI, NUBES)

First, translated by Thomas Stanley, in his The History of Philosophy, *part iii, London: printed for Humphrey Mosley and Thomas Dring, 1655, pp. 67–93; reprinted 1701 and in facsimile, Hildesheim and New York: Georg Olms. Verlag, 1975, pp. 103–13.*

The Clouds. A comedy translated from the Greek of Aristophanes by LEWIS THEOBALD, London: Jonas Brown, 1715.

The Clouds: a comedy. Written by Aristophanes, the wittiest man of his age, against Socrates, who was the wisest, and best... Now first intirely translated by JAMES WHITE, London: printed for Thomas Payne, 1759.

The Clouds of Aristophanes. Translated by RICHARD CUMBERLAND, London, 1786; also in Cumberland (Richard) LL.D., Dramatist, *The Observer*, 6, 1798; see also *Comedies*, 1812, and *The Comedies of Aristophanes*, 1820 (above).

The Clouds, and *Peace*, of Aristophanes. Translated into English prose, by a Graduate of the University of Oxford [JOHN W. WARTER], Oxford: Henry Slatter, 1840.

A Literal Translation of the Clouds of Aristophanes, with the Greek Text and English Notes. By CHARLES P. GERARD, London: G. Biggs, 1842.

The Clouds of Aristophanes. Literally translated by THOMAS J. ARNOLD, London: James Cornish (Kelly's Keys to the Classics), 1876.

The Clouds of Aristophanes. Literally translated by WILLIAM C. GREEN, Cambridge: J. Hall and Son, 1880.

A Literal Translation of Aristophanes: The Clouds. Arranged for interleaving with the text of the Clarendon Press edition, by a First-Class Man of Balliol College [THOMAS NASH], London: A. T. Shrimpton and Son: London, 1883.

The Clouds of Aristophanes. Translated into English by HERBERT HAILSTONE, Cambridge: E. Johnson, 1888.

The Clouds and *Plutus*. A prose translation by B. PERRIN, New York: Appleton, 1904.

The Clouds of Aristophanes. Adapted for performance by the Oxford University Dramatic Society, 1905, with an English version by A. D. GODLEY and C. BAILEY, Oxford: Horace Hart, 1905; Oxford: Clarendon Press, 1928.

The Clouds of Aristophanes. With English prose translation by the Rt. Hon. WILLIAM JOSEPH MYLES STARKIE, London: Macmillan and Co., 1911; reprinted, Amsterdam: Hakkert, 1966.

The Clouds of Aristophanes. Newly translated by PETER RUDOLPH and illustrated by Andre Durenceau, Mount Vernon, New York: The Peter Pauper Press, 1941.

The Clouds. Translated by JAMES CURTIN, Melbourne: Collegiate Press, 1947.

Clouds of Aristophanes. Newly translated from the Greek by ROBERT HENNING WEBB, Charlottesville, Va.: University of Virginia Press, 1960.

The Clouds. The Greek text performed at Cambridge in February 1962, with an English translation by H. J. EASTERLING and P. E. EASTERLING, Cambridge: published for the Greek Play Committee by W. Heffer and Sons, 1961.

The Clouds. Translated by WILLIAM ARROWSMITH, with sketches by Thomas McClure, Ann Arbor: University of Michigan Press, 1962.

The Clouds. A new translation by FRANK K. WILSON, Bath: James Brodie (Kelly's Keys to the Classics), 1966.

Two Classical Comedies [*The Clouds* and *The Pot of Gold* (Plautus)]. Translated by PETER D. ARNOTT, New York: Appleton-Century-Crofts, 1967.

Clouds. Edited with translation by ALAN H. SOMMERSTEIN, Warminster: Aris and Phillips, 1982.

'Clouds' in *Four Texts on Socrates* [Plato's *Euthyphro*, *Apology* and *Crito* and Aristophanes' *Clouds*]. Translated with notes by THOMAS G. WEST and GRACE STARRY WEST, Ithaca: Cornell University Press: 1984; revised, 1998.

The Clouds. An annotated translation by MARIE C. MARIANETTI, Lanham, Md.: University Press of America, 1997.

FROGS (BATRACHOI, RANAE)

First, Frogs, a Comedy. Translated by Charles Dunster, Oxford: J. and J. Fletcher, 1785.

Plutus and Frogs. Translated into English prose (Anon.), Oxford: D. A. Talboys, 1822.

The Frogs. A translation into English verse by JOHN HOOKHAM FRERE, London: W. Nicol, 1839.

The Frogs of Aristophanes. Translated by CHARLES CAVENDISH CLIFFORD, Oxford and London: J. H. Parker, 1848.

The Frogs of Aristophanes. Translated by WILLIAM C. GREEN, Cambridge: Cambridge University Press, 1879.

A Literal Translation of Aristophanes: The Frogs. By a First-Class Man of Balliol College [THOMAS NASH], Oxford, A. J. Shrimpton and Son, 1883; reprinted, revised by Edward L. Hawkins, 1895.

The Frogs of Aristophanes. Adapted for performance by the Oxford University Dramatic Society, 1892, with an English version partly adapted from that of J. HOOKHAM FRERE and partly written for the occasion by D. G. HOGARTH and A. D. GODLEY, Oxford: H. Frowde, 1892.

Aristophanes' Ranae, Frogs. Literally translated by J. A. PROUT, London: J. Cornish and Sons, 1896.

Aristophanes: Ranae. A close translation by F. G. PLAISTOWE, London: W. B. Clive (University Tutorial Press), 1896.

The Frogs. Acting edition prepared for performance at St Gregory's, Downside College, with a translation by the Rev. A. L. KYNASTON, Weston-super-Mare: The Mendip Press, 1899.

The Frogs of Aristophanes. Translated by E. W. HUNTINGFORD, London: Methuen and Co., 1900.

The Frogs. Translated by BENJAMIN BICKLEY ROGERS, London: G. Bell and Sons, 1902.

The Frogs of Aristophanes. Translated into English rhyming verse by GILBERT MURRAY, London: Allen and Unwin (*The Athenian Drama*, vol. III), 1902; reprinted 1908, New York: 1915, 1920, 1946, 1959.

The Frogs of Aristophanes. Translated into kindred metres by ALFRED DAVIES COPE, Oxford: Blackwell, 1911.

The Frogs. Translated from the Greek by ALEXANDER HARVEY, Girard, Kans.: Haldeman-Julius Co., 1925.

The Birds and *The Frogs.* Translated into rhymed English verse by MARSHALL MACGREGOR, London: E. Arnold and Co., 1927.

The Frogs of Aristophanes. The Greek text as arranged for performance at Cambridge, March, 1936, with an English translation by D. W. LUCAS and F. J. A. CRUSO, Cambridge: Bowes and Bowes, 1936; reprinted as a 'schools edition', 1946.

'The Frogs of Aristophanes'.   Translated by JOHN G. HAWTHORNE in *Classics in Translation*, vol. 1, Madison, Wis.: University of Wisconsin Press, 1952.

The Frogs. An English version by DUDLEY FITTS, New York: Harcourt, Brace, 1955; London: Faber and Faber, 1957.

The Puddocks.   A verse play in Scots, by DOUGLAS YOUNG, 'Frae the auld Greek o Aristophanes', Tayport: published by the author, 1957.

Three Greek Plays for the Theatre [Including *Frogs*].   Edited and translated by PETER ARNOTT, Bloomington: Indiana University Press, 1961.

The Frogs.   Translated by RICHMOND LATTIMORE, with sketches by Richard Sears, Ann Arbor: University of Michigan Press, 1962.

The Frogs and Other Greek Plays.   Translated by KENNETH McLEISH, London: Longman's (Heritage of Literature Series), 1970.

The Frogs.   Translated and edited by FRANCIS BLESSINGTON, Arlington Heights, Ill.: Harlan Davidson, 1993.

Frogs.   Edited with translation by ALAN H. SOMMERSTEIN, Warminster: Aris and Phillips, 1994, 1996.

KNIGHTS (HIPPEIS, EQUITES)

First, Mitchell, 1820.

The Knights of Aristophanes.   Literally translated into English prose by F. H. WILLIAMS, Dublin: B. Geraghty, 1844; reprinted, London: William Allan, 1854.

The Knights of Aristophanes.   Adapted for performance by the Oxford University Dramatic Society, 1897, with an English version adapted from that of J. Hookham Frere by LEOPOLD EDWARD BERMAN, Oxford: Horace Hart, printer to the University; London: Henry Frowde, 1897.

Equites. Literally translated by J. A. PROUT, Dublin: W. B. Kelly (Kelly's Keys to the Classics), 1899; reprinted London: J. Cornish and Sons, 1901.

The Knights.   Translated from the original Greek by ALEXANDER HARVEY, Girard, Kans.: Haldeman-Julius Co., 1925.

The Knights.   Translated into English rhyming verse with introduction and notes by GILBERT MURRAY, London: George Allen and Unwin, 1956.

Knights.   Edited with translation by ALAN H. SOMMERSTEIN, Warminster: Aris and Phillips, 1981.

LYSISTRATA (LYSISTRATE, THE REVOLT OF THE WOMEN)

First, Wheelwright, 1837.

The Revolt of the Women. A free translation of the *Lysistrata* of Aristophanes by BENJAMIN BICKLEY ROGERS, London: G. Bell and Sons, 1878; reprinted New York, 1902.

The Lysistrata of Aristophanes. Now first wholly translated into English by SAMUEL SMITH and illustrated by Aubrey Beardsley, London: Smithers, 1896; reprinted New York: Odyssey Publications, 1968.

Lysistrata. A modern paraphrase from the Greek of Aristophanes by LAURENCE HOUSMAN, London: Women's Press, 1911.

Lysistrata. Adapted and arranged by WINIFRED AYRES HOPE, New York: Samuel French, 1915.

Lysistrata. 'Done into English verse' by JACK LINDSAY, with illustrations and decorations by Norman Lindsay, New York: Three Sirens Press, 1925; London and Sydney: Fanfrolico Press, 1926; reprinted Cleveland: The World Publishing Company, 1943.

Aristophanes' Lysistrata. A new version by GILBERT SELDES, New York: Farrar and Rinehart 1930; reprinted New York: The Limited Editions Club, 1934.

Lysistrata, or The Peacemaker (The Sit-Down Strike). With a scene from the comedy *Thesmorphorasusae [sic].* Translated by HENRY BERTRAM LISTER (limited edition of 55 mimeographed copies), San Francisco: La Bohemia Club, 1938.

'Lysistrata'. Translated by CHARLES THEOPHILUS MURPHY, in Whitney J. Oates and Charles Theophilus Murphy, eds., *Greek Literature in Translation*, New York: David McKay Co., 1944; reprinted in *Ten Greek Plays*, Boston: Houghton Mifflin, 1957.

'Lysistrata' in *Aristophanes: Two Plays.* A new translation by DOROS ALASTOS [Eudoros Ionannides], London: Zeno, 1953.

Lysistrata. An English version by DUDLEY FITTS, London: Faber and Faber, 1955; new version in Robert Saffron, *Great Farces*, London: Collier-Macmillan; New York: Collier, 1966.

Lysistrata. Translated and with an introduction by DONALD SUTHERLAND, Scranton, Penn.: Chandler, 1961.

Lysistrata. Newly translated by ROBERT HENNING WEBB, Charlottesville: University of Virginia Press, 1963.

Lysistrata. Translated by DOUGLASS PARKER, with sketches by Ellen Raskin, Ann Arbor: University of Michigan Press, 1964; reprinted New York: Signet Classic, 2001.

Aristophanes Lysistrata. English version by JACK BRUSSEL, with the Aubrey Beardsley illustrations, New York: Land's End Press, 1968.

Lysistrata. Translated by JAY FREYMAN and WALTER SHERWIN, Columbus, Ohio: D. L. Hedrick, 1974.

Lysistrata. Edited with translation by ALAN H. SOMMERSTEIN, Warminster: Aris and Phillips, 1990, 1992.

Lysistrata. In a new translation by NICHOLAS RUDALL, Chicago: Ivan R. Dee, 1991.

The Common Chorus. A version of Aristophanes' *Lysistrata* by TONY HARRISON, London: Faber and Faber, 1992 (originally published in The Agni Review, 1988).

Lysistrata. A new translation for performance and study by MATT NEUBURG, Arlington Heights, Ill.: H. Davidson, 1992.

Lysistrata. Translated by SARAH RUDEN, Indianapolis: Hackett Pub. Co., 2003.

PEACE (*EIRENE, PAX*)

First, Wheelwright, *1837.*

The Clouds, and *Peace*, of Aristophanes. Translated into English prose, by a Graduate of the University of Oxford [JOHN W. WARTER], Oxford: Henry Slatter, 1840.

The Peace. Translated by BENJAMIN BICKLEY ROGERS, London: Bell and Daldy, 1866; reprinted New York, 1912.

Aristophanes: Peace. Literal translation from Glasgow 'Translations to the Classics', Glasgow: W. S. Sime, 1893.

Peace. Translated from the original Greek by ALEXANDER HARVEY, Girard, Kans.: Haldeman-Julius Co., 1925.

'Peace' in *Aristophanes: Two Plays.* A new translation by DOROS ALASTOS [Eudoros Ionannides], London: Zeno, 1953.

Four Greek Plays [including *Peace and The Acharnians*]. Translated and adapted by KENNETH McLEISH, London: Longmans (Heritage of Literature Series), 1964.

Peace of Aristophanes. Newly translated by ROBERT HENNING WEBB, Charlottesville: University Press of Virginia Press, 1964.

'Peace', Aristophanes. Translated by TIM REYNOLDS in Charles Doria, ed., *The Tenth Muse*, Athens, Ohio, Chicago, London: The Ohio University Press, 1980.

Peace. Edited with translation by ALAN H. SOMMERSTEIN, Warminster: Aris and Phillips, 1985.

WASPS (SPHĒKES, VESPAE)

First, Mitchell, 1822.

The Wasps. Translated by BENJAMIN BICKLEY ROGERS, London: G. Bell and Sons, 1875; reprinted Cambridge: Macmillan and Bowes, 1897, 1916; New York, 1916.

Vespae. Translated by FRANCIS G. PLAISTOWE, London: W. B. Clive (University Tutorial Press), 1893.

Aristophanes, Vespae. Translated into English by HERBERT HAILSTONE, Cambridge: E. Johnson, 1896.

Aristophanes' Vespae. Wasps. Literally translated by J. A. PROUT, London: J. Cornish and Sons (Kelly's Keys to the Classics), 1896.

The Wasps of Aristophanes. Literally translated, with notes and test papers, by J. W. RUNDALL, Cambridge: J. Hall and Son, 1896.

The Wasps of Aristophanes. With prose translation by the Rt. Hon. WILLIAM JOSEPH MYLES STARKIE, London: Macmillan and Co., 1897; reprinted, Amsterdam: Hakkert, 1968.

The Wasps. Translated from the original Greek by ALEXANDER HARVEY, Girard, Kans.: Haldeman-Julius Co., 1925.

Wasps. Edited with translation by ALAN H. SOMMERSTEIN, Warminster: Aris and Phillips, 1983.

WEALTH (PLOUTOS, PLUTUS)

First, A pleasant comedie, entituled [sic] Hey for Honesty, Down with Knavery. 'Translated out of Aristophanes his Plutus, by Tho. Randolph, augmented and published by F. J.' [F. Jaques], London: printed in the Year 1651.

The World's Idol. Plutus, a comedy written in Greek by Aristophanes, translated by H. H. B. [HENRY BURNELL], together with his notes, and a short discourse upon it, London: sold by Richard Skelton, 1659.

Plutus: or, the Worlds Idol. A comedy translated from the Greek of Aristophanes by LEWIS THEOBALD, London: Jonas Brown, 1715.

Plutus, the God of Riches. A comedy translated from the original Greek of Aristophanes by HENRY FIELDING and the Revd WILLIAM YOUNG, London: T. Waller, 1742.

Plutus and Frogs. Translated into English prose (Anon.), Oxford: D. A. Talboys, 1822.

Plutus, or, the God of Riches. A comedy of Aristophanes translated by EDMUND F. J. CARRINGTON, London: Wheatley and Adlard, 1825.

The Plutus of Aristophanes. Translated into English verse by CHARLES P. GERARD, London: Robinson, 1847.

The Plutus of Aristophanes. Translated by HERBERT HAILSTONE, Cambridge: E. Johnson, 1887.

The Clouds and *Plutus.* A prose translation by B. PERRIN, New York: Appleton, 1904.

Plutus, to which is added a specimen of the new comedy, a translation of the Menaechmi of Plautus. Translated by BENJAMIN BICKLEY ROGERS, London: G. Bell and Sons, 1907.

The Plutus of Aristophanes. Translated by WILLIAM CHARLES GREEN, Cambridge: J. Hall and Son, 1887; reprinted Cambridge: Cambridge University Press, 1913.

The Plutus of Aristophanes. With introduction and notes, by MICHAEL T. QUINN, with an English translation, London: W. B. Clive (University Tutorial Press), 1889; reprinted London: G. Bell and Sons, 1896.

Aristophanes: The Plutus. Literally translated by J. A. PROUT, London: J. Cornish and Sons (Kelly's Keys to the Classics), 1901.

The Plutus of Aristophanes. Translated into English verse by the Rt. Hon. Sir WILLIAM RANN KENNEDY, London: John Murray, 1912.

The Plutus of Aristophanes. Translated from the text by C. H. PRICHARD (in the Pitt Press Series), Cambridge: E. Johnson, 1912.

Wealth. Edited with translation by ALAN H. SOMMERSTEIN, Warminster: Aris and Phillips, 2001.

WOMEN IN ASSEMBLY (EKKLESIAZOUSAI, ECCLESIAZUSAE, CONGRESSWOMEN, WOMEN IN PARLIAMENT, A PARLIAMENT OF WOMEN WOMEN IN CHARGE, WOMEN IN POWER, ASSEMBLY OF WOMEN)

First, The Ecclesiazousae or Female Parliament. *Translated by Revd Rowland Smith, Oxford, J. H. Parker, 1833.*

Women in Parliament by Aristophanes. 'Done into English' by JACK LINDSAY, with illustrations by Norman Lindsay and a foreword by Edgell Rickword, London: Fanfrolico Press, 1929.

The Congresswomen (Ecclesiazusae). Translated by DOUGLASS PARKER, with sketches by Leo and Diane Dillon, Ann Arbor: University of Michigan Press, 1967.

Assembly of Women. Translated by ROBERT MAYHEW, Amherst, New York: Prometheus Books, 1997.

Ecclesiazusae. Edited with translation by ALAN H. SOMMERSTEIN, Warminster: Aris and Phillips, 1998, 1999.

WOMEN AT THE THESMOPHORIA
(THESMOPHORIAZOUSAI, THESMOPHORIAZOUSAE, FESTIVAL TIME, THE POET AND THE WOMEN, LADIES' DAY)

First, Wheelwright, 1837.

Thesmophoriazusae. Translated by BENJAMIN BICKLEY ROGERS, London: G. Bell and Sons, 1904; revised version, Bell, 1920.

Thesmophoriazusae. Edited with translation by ALAN H. SOMMERSTEIN, Warminster: Aris and Phillips, 1994.

Ladies' Day. An English version by DUDLEY FITTS, New York: Harcourt, Brace and Co., 1959; London: Faber, 1960.

MENANDER
Collections

'The Fragments of Menander Translated into English Verse'. In FRANCIS FAWKES, *Original Poems and Translations*, London, 1761.

The Lately Discovered Fragments of Menander. Edited with an English version by Unus Multorum [J. S. POMEROY, Viscount Harberton], London: James Parker and Co., 1909.

Menander, The Principal Fragments. Translated by FRANCIS GREENLEAF ALLINSON, London: Heinemann (Loeb Classical Library), 1921; rev. edn, 1930.

Three Plays [*The Girl from Samos, The Arbitration, The Shearing of Glycera*]. Translated and interpreted by LEVI ARNOLD POST, London: Routledge; New York: Dutton and Co., 1929.

Menander: Plays and Fragments, Theophrastus: The Characters. Translated by PHILIP VELLACOTT, Harmondsworth: Penguin, 1967, 1973.

The Plays of Menander.   Edited and translated by LIONEL CASSON, New York: New York University Press, 1971.

Menander. In 3 vols.   Translated by W. G. ARNOTT, Cambridge, Mass. and London: Heinemann (Loeb), 1979–2000.

Menander, Plays and Fragments.   Translated by NORMA MILLER, Harmondsworth: Penguin, 1987.

Menander. In translations by SHEILA D'ATRI (*The Grouch*), RICHARD ELMAN (*The Girl from Samos*) and three fragmentary plays 'reconstructed', Philadelphia: University of Pennsylvania Press, 1998.

Aristophanes and Menander: New Comedy [Including *The Malcontent* and *The Woman from Samos*].   Translated by J. MICHAEL WALTON, London: Methuen (Methuen Classical Dramatists), 1994; revised edition, 1998.

The Plays and Fragments.   Menander translated with explanatory notes by MAURICE BALME, Oxford: Oxford University Press, 2001.

THE BAD-TEMPERED MAN (DYSKOLOS, THE MALCONTENT, THE GROUCH, THE CROSS OLD DEVIL, OLD CANTANKEROUS, THE MAN WHO DIDN'T LIKE PEOPLE, THE PEEVISH MAN, THE FEAST OF PAN)

First, Le Dyscolos. *Publié, with a facsimile of the manuscript and translations in French and German, English translation by Gordon Graham, Cologny-Genève: Victor Martin, 1958.*

Menander's Dyskolos; or, The Man Who Didn't Like People. Translated into English prose by W. G. ARNOTT, London: Athlone Press, 1960.

The Bad-Tempered Man, or, the Misanthrope.   Translated by PHILIP VELLACOTT, Oxford: Oxford University Press, 1960.

Three Classical Comedies. [Including *The Cross Old Devil* with Plautus' *Prisoners of War* and *Thirty Bob Day*].   Translated by H. C. FAY, Leeds: E. J. Arnold, 1967.

Feast of Pan.   A translation of the *Dyscolus* of Menander by R. N. BENTON, Louth: published by the author, 1977.

The Dyskolos by Menander.   Translated with an introduction and notes by CARROLL MOULTON, New York: New American Library, 1977.

The Bad-Tempered Man. Dyskolos.   Edited with translation by STANLEY IRELAND, Warminster: Aris and Phillips, 1995.

THE WOMAN FROM SAMOS (SAMIA, THE GIRL FROM SAMOS, THE SAMIAN GIRL)

First complete, The Girl from Samos, or The In-laws. *Translated into English blank verse by Eric G. Turner. London: Athlone Press, 1972.*

The Samia of Menander. An augmented text, with notes and a verse translation by J. M. EDMONDS, Cambridge: Deighton, Bell and Co., 1951.

Samia. Edited with translation by D. M. BAIN, Warminster: Aris and Phillips, 1983.

Six Greek Comedies [Including *The Woman from Samos*]. Translated by J. MICHAEL WALTON, London: Methuen, 2002.

HERODAS (HERODES, HERONDAS)

Translated by J. A. SYMONDS in *Studies of the Greek Poets*, vol. II, New York: Harper and Brothers, 1880.

Herondas. A translation of the third mime by E. H. BLAKENEY, 4 page pamphlet housed in the British Library, 1892.

A Realist in the Aegean: being a verse translation of the Mimes of Herodas. Translated by HUGO SHARPLEY, London: David Nutt, 1906.

The Characters of Theophrastus, The Mimes of Herodas, the Tablet of Kebes. Translated by ROBERT THOMSON CLARK, London: Routledge and New York: E. P. Dutton, 1909.

The Mimes of Herondas. Translated by M. S. BUCK, New York: privately printed, 1921.

Herodas, the Mimes and Fragments. Translated by ALFRED DILLWYN KNOX in the revised annotated version of Walter Headlam, Cambridge: Cambridge University Press, 1922.

The Mimiambs of Herondas. Translated (in verse) by JACK LINDSAY, decorated by Alan Odle, London: Fanfrolico Press, 1926.

Herodes, Cereidas and the Greek Choliambic Poets. Revised translation by ALFRED DILLWYN KNOX, London: Heinemann and New York: G. P. Putnam (Loeb Classical Library), 1929.

The Mimes of Herondas. Translated by GUY DAVENPORT, San Francisco: Grey Fox Press, c.1981.

Herodas Mimes. Translated by IAN C. CUNNINGHAM in *Theophrastus Characters, Herodas Mimes*, Cambridge, Mass. and London: Harvard University Press (Loeb Classical Library), 1993; third edition adding *Sophron and Other Mime Fragments*, 2002.

Notes

INTRODUCTION

1 Alfred Jarry, *Ubu Rex*, in *The Ubu Plays*, trans. Cyril Connolly and Simon Watson Taylor (London, 1958), Act V, scene 1.
2 At this range in time Gilbert Murray may not seem improved by the use in his *Agamemnon* and *Choephori* of such coinages as 'encharioted', 'man-entangler', 'far-gleameth' and 'out-blotteth'. Tony Harrison is far more extreme, with over seventy neologisms which he lists in the Introduction to the newest edition of his *Oresteia* (London, 2002) including 'thronestones', 'bloodgrudge', 'spearspoil' and Agamemnon described by Clytemnestra as 'Shaggermemnon'.
3 The Bartholomew *Antigone* with Helen Faucit was a landmark in the history of the Greek revival. Lewis Campbell's first version of *Trachiniae* was produced in Scotland in 1877 under the title of *Deianira or The Death of Heracles*.
4 George Steiner, *After Babel* (Oxford: Oxford University Press, 1975).
5 Gershon Shaked, 'The play: gateway to cultural dialogue', trans. Jeffrey Green in Hanna Scolnicov and Peter Holland, eds., *The Play out of Context: Transferring Plays from Culture to Culture* (Cambridge, 1989), p. 13.
6 Klaudyna Rozhin, 'Translating the Untranslatable', in Carole-Anne Upton, ed., *Moving Target* (Manchester, 2000), p. 139.

CHAPTER I

1 Sirkku Aaltonen, *Time-Sharing on Stage: Drama Translation in Theatre and Society* (Clevedon, 2000).
2 Peter Green, 'Some version of aeschylus: A study of tradition and method in translating classical poetry', in Green, *Essays in Antiquity* (London, 1960), p. 185.
3 When, for example, Louis Kelly suggested that a 'complete' theory of translation 'has three components: specification of function and goal; description and analysis of operations; and critical comment on relationships between goal and operations', any one of which may at any time be

prioritised, the second and third are not so much inapplicable as unappliable. L. G. Kelly, *The True Interpreter: A History of Translation Theory and Practice in the West* (Oxford, 1979) quoted in *The Translation Studies Reader*, ed. Lawrence Venuti (London, 2000), p. 4.

4 Aaltonen, *Time-Sharing*, p. 29.

5 These issues have been interrogated with particular cogency by Erika Fischer-Lichter (E. Fischer-Lichte, J. Riley and M. Gissenwehrer, eds., *The Dramatic Touch of Difference*, Tübingen, 1990), pp. 11–19 and 277–87; in P. Pavis, ed., *The Intercultural Performance Reader* (London and New York, 1996), pp. 27–40; and in R. Schulte and J. Biguenet, eds., *Theories of Translation: An Anthology of Essays from Dryden to Derrida* (which includes translation essays by Dryden, Goethe, Humboldt, Nietzsche, Benjamin, Pound, Nabokov and Derrida) (Chicago and London, 1992); D. Johnston, ed., *Stages of Translation: Essays and Interviews on Translating for the Stage* (Bath, 1996); C.-A. Upton, ed., *Moving Target: Theatre Translation and Cultural Relocation* (Manchester, 2000); and J. Barsby, ed., *Greek and Roman Drama: Translation and Performance*, dedicated issue of *Drama: Beiträge zum antiken Drama und seiner Rezeption*, Band 12 (Stuttgart, 2002), as well as by specific critics discussed below.

6 See, in particular, Susan Bassnett, 'Preface to the revised edition' of *Translation Studies* (London, 1991), pp. xi–xix.

7 Cicero, *On Ends*, 1.5.

8 Terence, *Eunuch*, 7–8.

9 See also George Steiner, *After Babel* (Oxford, 1975), pp. 236–40, where he outlines the 'four periods' of translation, beginning with Cicero.

10 John Ogleby, translator of Homer and Virgil.

11 In *John Dryden: Of Dramatic Poesy: And Other Critical Essays*, vol. II, ed. George Watson (London, 1962), pp. 18 ff.

12 Watson, *John Dryden*, pp. 214–15.

13 Alexander Fraser Tytler, Lord Woodhouselee, *Essay on the Principles of Translation* (Edinburgh, 1790, repr. J. M. Dent for the Everyman's Library, ed. Ernest Rhys, n.d.).

14 Tytler, *Essay*, p. 9.

15 Laurence Echard, whose translation of Plautus' *Amphitryon, Epidicus* and *Rudens* was published in 1694, and of Terence's *Andria* the same year listed as *Comedies Made English* by several hands (L. Eachard [*sic*], etc.): Tytler, *Essay*, p. 77.

16 Tytler, *Essay*, p. 77.

17 Tytler, *Essay*, pp. 140–1.

18 Lawrence Venuti, *The Translation Studies Reader* (London, 2000), p. 121.

19 Edith Hamilton, 'On Translating', in *Three Greek Plays* (New York, 1937), p. 10.

20 William Arrowsmith and Roger Shattuck, eds., *The Craft and Context of Translation* (Austin, 1961).

21 D. S. Carne-Ross, 'Translation and transposition', in Arrowsmith and Shattuck, *Craft and Context*, p. 6.

22 Arrowsmith, in Arrowsmith and Shattuck, *Craft and Context*, p. 125. Such questions are considered in some detail by, amongst others, John McFarlane, in 'Modes of translation', *Durham University Journal*, 45.3, 1953, pp. 77–93; Theodore Savory, *The Art of Translation* (London, 1957); Peter Green, 'Some versions of Aeschylus', *Essays in Antiquity* (London, 1960), pp. 185–215; Walter Benjamin, 'The task of the translator', trans. H. Zohn, *Illuminations* (London, 1970), pp. 69–82; Reuben Brower, *Mirror on Mirror: Translation, Imitation, Parody* (Cambridge, Mass., 1974); and in Barsby, *Greek and Roman Drama*.

23 Steiner, *After Babel*, pp. 296–303, repr. as 'The hermeneutic motion', in Venuti, pp. 186–91.

24 Steiner, *After Babel*.

25 Steiner, *After Babel*, pp. 414–70. See also his *Antigones* (Oxford, 1981).

26 Steiner, *After Babel*, p. 22.

27 Steiner, *After Babel*, p. 257.

28 Umberto Eco, *Mouse or Rat? Translation as Negotiation* (London, 2003).

29 Eco, *Mouse or Rat?*, p. 88.

30 The three 'Electra' plays are the only extant examples of direct overlap of plot between the three major tragedians. There is, however, an intriguing essay by Dio Chrysostom (first–second century AD) comparing the three playwrights' versions of *Philoctetes*, of which only the Sophocles has come down to us.

31 Eco, *Mouse or Rat?*, p. 126.

32 Ortrun Zuber, *The Languages of Theatre* (Oxford, 1980).

33 Link, in Zuber, *Languages of Theatre*, p. 35.

34 Sir Arthur Pickard-Cambridge, *The Dramatic Festivals of Athens*, 2nd edn, rev. John Gould and D. M. Lewis (Oxford, 1968), pp. 264 ff.

35 Zuber, *Languages of Theatre*, pp. 132–45.

36 Zuber, *Languages of Theatre*, pp. 153–61.

37 Zuber, *Languages of Theatre*, p. 159.

38 Zuber, *Languages of Theatre*, p. 159.

39 Zuber (as Zuber-Skerritt) offers a summary of the historical background to translation theory and drama translation in 'Translation and science and drama translation', in *Page to Stage: Theatre as Translation*, ed. Ortrun Zuber-Skerritt (Amsterdam, 1984), pp. 2–11.

40 Susan Bassnett, *Translation Studies* (London, 1980, rev. edn, London, 1991).

41 Bassnett, *Translation Studies*, p. 72.

42 Bassnett, *Translation Studies*, p. 70.

43 André Lefevere and Susan Bassnett, 'Where are we in translation studies?', in Bassnett and Lefevere, eds., *Constructing Cultures: Essays on Literary Translation* (Clevedon, 1998), pp. 1–11.

44 Bassnett and Lefevere, *Constructing Cultures*, pp. 90–108.

45 Bassnett and Lefevere, *Constructing Cultures*, p. xxi.

46 Bassnett and Lefevere, *Constructing Cultures*, p. 107.

47 Bassnett and Lefevere, *Constructing Cultures*, pp. 95–8. But see also Eva Espasa, 'Performability in translation: speakability? playability? Or just saleability?', in Upton, *Moving Target*, pp. 49–61.

48 See also Aaltonen, *Time-Sharing*, pp. 41–4; Bassnett and Lefevere, *Constructing Cultures*, p. 95.

49 Rustam Bharucha, *Theatre and the World: Performance and the Politics of Culture* (London, 1993).

50 Bharucha, *Theatre and the World*, p. 3 on *The Mahabharata*, trans. Peter Brook, based on the Indian epic, from the French *Le Mahabharata* of Jean-Claude Carrière (London, 1987).

51 Shaw played the McLeish translations of Sophocles' *Electra* and Euripides' *Medea*, in productions by Deborah Warner, in London, Dublin and New York.

52 Patrice Pavis, 'Problems of translation for the stage: interculturalism and post-modern theatre', trans. Loren Kruger in Scolnicov and Holland, *Play out of Context*, pp. 25–44.

53 Pavis, 'Problems of translation', p. 27.

54 Pavis, 'Problems of translation', p. 25.

55 See also Pavis, *Theatre at the Crossroads of Culture* (London, 1992).

CHAPTER 2

1 Virginia Woolf, 'On not knowing Greek', repr. in Andrew McNeillie, ed., *The Essays of Virginia Woolf*, vol. IV: *1925 to 1929* (London, 1994), pp. 39–53.

2 Woolf, 'On not knowing Greek', p. 45.

3 J. Michael Walton, *Living Greek Theatre: A Handbook of Classical Performance and Modern Production* (Westport, 1987), p. 330.

4 A. R. Braumuller and Michael Hattaway, eds., *The Cambridge Companion to Renaissance Drama* (Cambridge, 1990), p. 397.

5 Henrietta Palmer, *List of English Editions and Translations of the Classics Printed before 1641* (London, 1911); Henry Burrowes Lathrop, *Translations from the Classics into English from Caxton to Chapman 1477–1620* (Madison, 1933); William J. Harris, *The First Printed Translations into English of the Great Foreign Classics* (London, 1909); F. M. K. Foster, *English Translations from the Greek* (New York, 1918) refers to *Iocasta: A Tragedy written in Greek by Euripides, translated and digested into Actes by George Gascoigne and Francis Kinvvelmershe of Grayes Inne, and there presented by them, 1566.*

6 British Museum, MS. Reg 15. A. ix; first published as *Iphigenia at Aulis Translated by Lady Lumley*, ed. Harold H. Child for The Malone Society (Chiswick, The Malone Society Reprints, 1909).

7 *Three Tragedies by Renaissance Women*, ed. Diane Purkiss, with an introduction and notes (Harmondsworth, 1998), pp. xi–xliii. Lady Lumley's spelling is erratic. Purkiss uses Iphigeneia, as appears in Lady Lumley's own hand on the title page but Iphigenia, Iphigeneya, and, indeed, Ephigeneya and Iphigeneya are all found in her manuscript.

8 Lewis William Brüggemann, *A View of the English Editions, Translations and Illustrations of the Ancient Greek and Latin Authors, with Remarks*, vol. I

(Stettin, 1797). Brüggemann was, amongst his other titles, Counsellor for the Consistory at Stettin in Pomerania and Chaplain in Ordinary to his Prussian Majesty.

9 David H. Grene, 'Lady Lumley and Greek tragedy', *Classical Journal*, 36.9, 1941, pp. 537–47; Frank D. Crane, 'Euripides, Erasmus, and Lady Lumley', *Classical Journal*, 39, 1944, pp. 223–8.

10 Jane Lumley's translation of Euripides' *Iphigeinia at Aulis*, performed by The Brass Farthingale Company, Clifton Drama Studio, University of Sunderland, January, 1997.

11 Edith Milner, *Records of the Lumleys of Lumley Castle* (London, 1904), pp. 50–1. See also R. Warnicke, *Women of the English Renaissance and Reformation* (Westport, 1983), ch. 6, for details of the family background.

12 See Purkiss, ed., *Three Tragedies*.

13 'A play of Euripides translated into Latin, by Elizabeth, Queen of England is mentioned by Mr Walpole in his Catalogue of the Royal and Noble Authors of England, with Lists of their Works. The second Edition' (London, 1759), 8. vol. I, p. 31, in Brüggemann, *View of English Editions*, p. 91.

14 The *Latina versio metrica Iphigeniae in Aulide*, according to Palmer, published in London in 1519.

15 *Nusquam, enim mihi magis ineptissime videtur antiquitas, quam in huiusmodi choris, ubi dum nimium affectat nove loqui, vitiavit eloquentiam: dumque verborum miracula venatur, in rerum judicio cessavit*, Erasmus, *Opera Omnia* (Amsterdam, 1703), 1.1154.

16 Lumley, *Tragedie of Euripides*, pp. 204–5, and pp. 206–7.

17 Lumley, *Tragedie of Euripides*, pp. 1319–27.

18 Grene, 'Lumley and Greek tragedy', p. 542; Crane, 'Euripides, Erasmus', p. 228.

19 Euripides, *Iphigeneia at Aulis* (Oxford, 1992), ll. 1891–5 (translator's numbering; Oxford Text, ll. 1400–03).

20 Lumley, *Tragedie of Euripides*, ll. 1173 ff.

21 Lumley, *Tragedie of Euripides*, ll. 1270–3.

22 In trochaics not iambics: Lumley, *Tragedie of Euripides*, ll. 786–90.

23 *Euripides I*, trans. A. S. Way (Loeb edn, 1912), p. 83, *Iphigeneia at Aulis*, l. 874.

24 Lumley, *Tragedie of Euripides*, ll. 149–51 (original, 105–6) and 898–900 (original, 1033–4).

25 Lumley, *Tragedie of Euripides*, ll. 1394–7 (original, 1615–18).

26 *The Complete Works of George Gascoigne*, vol. I (Cambridge, 1907), p. 283.

27 Gascoigne, *Works*, p. 293.

28 Gascoigne, *Works*, p. 248.

29 Euripides' *Phoenissae*, trans. David Thompson in *Euripides' Plays: One* (London, 1988, 1998 and 2000), ll. 1758–63.

30 Gascoigne, *Works*, p. 324.

31 T. E. Bach, *Oedipus: Three Cantoes* (London, 1615) to which is appended a note by both Foster and Palmer '? translation or adaptation'. See *The Works of John Dryden*, ed. Alan Roper (Berkeley, 1984), p. 453.

32 C(hristopher) W(ase), *Electra of Sophocles* (At the Hague for Sam Brown, 1649). For a fuller account, see Edith Hall and Fiona Macintosh, *Greek Tragedy and the British Theatre, 1660–1914* (Oxford, 2005), pp. 163–5.

33 Foster, *English Translations*, p. 21.

34 See Peter Burian, 'Tragedy adapted for stage and screen', in P. E. Easterling, ed., *The Cambridge Companion to Greek Tragedy* (Cambridge, 1997), pp. 228–83.

35 At a revival in 1790 'the audience were unable to support it to an end; the boxes being all emptied before the third act was concluded', quoted in Jebb's Introduction to *Oedipus Tyrannus* (Cambridge, 1887), p. xlviii.

36 Richard West's *Hecuba,* performed at Drury Lane in 1726, had an exposition scene with a gloating Polymnestor [*sic*] instead of the Ghost prologue from Polydorus, and a new character, Iphis, instead of the Chorus. Otherwise it was close to the Euripides. For its hostile reception and West's reaction, see p. 242.

37 George Adams, *The Tragedies of Sophocles*, in two volumes (London, for C. Davis of Paternoster Row, 1729).

38 Lennox was the daughter of the lieutenant-general of New York and had come to live in England at the age of fifteen.

39 There is a reference to a publication of the same name in Amsterdam in 1722.

40 *Greek Theatre of Father Brumoy*, translated by Mrs Charlotte Lennox in three volumes (London, printed by Mess(rs) Millar, Vailland, Baldwin, Crowder, Johnston, Dodsley and Wilson and Durham, 1759). Lennox largely maintains the structure and detail of Brumoy's original, but the volumes are slightly differently organised to make the English volumes of more equal length. Brumoy's page numbering is sometimes erratic. Lennox also makes some adjustment in the text for English as opposed to French readership. She follows Brumoy's view that the earliest play of Aeschylus (Eschyle) was *Prometheus*, the last *Persians*. Perhaps for reasons of decorum she has the passages from Euripides' *Cyclops* and from Aristophanes translated by various different hands. *The Discourse on the Greek Comedy* and the *General Conclusion*, both in vol. III, are credited to 'the celebrated author of the *Rambler*' [Samuel Johnson].

41 Lennox, *Greek Theatre*, Preface, p. v.

42 Lennox, *Greek Theatre*, p. vii.

43 Published by D. A. Talboys, 1889.

44 Lennox, *Greek Theatre*, p. vii.

45 Lennox, *Greek Theatre*, p. xiv.

46 *The Monthly Review* was a touch patronising, 'The translation itself, considering the difficulty of the undertaking, has great merit ... It is but just to say that some imperfections and inaccuracies in Mr Potter's version, are more than balanced by its excellencies, and that there are many passages rendered with peculiar felicity', Oct. 1778, pp. 186 and 297. See also David Stoker, 'Greek tragedy with a happy ending: the publication of Robert Potter's translations of Aeschylus, Euripides and Sophocles', *Studies in Bibliography*, 46, 1993, pp. 282–302.

47 Robert Potter, *The Tragedies of Euripides translated in Two Volumes*, printed for J. Dodsley, Pall-Mall (London, 1781 and 1783).

48 Despite his declaration that 'I would give the English Reader all that remains of the Tragic Muse of Greece' (Preface to *The Tragedies of Sophocles* by R. Potter (London, 1788), new edn printed by and for N. Bliss, 1820, p. vii. Potter's *Sophocles* suffered by comparison with earlier translations of the seven plays by George Adams (1729), Thomas Francklin (1759) and several translations of individual plays by Lewis Theobald in 1714 and 1715. On Potter, 'When we give this translation the praise of fidelity, it is all that we can afford', *Monthly Review* for Oct. 1789, p. 382. See also Stoker; 'Greek tragedy with a happy ending', pp. 298–301; Hall and Macintosh, *Greek Tragedy*, pp. 220–1.

49 Potter's first volume of Euripides (1781) contained, in order: *The Bacchae, Ion, Alcestis, Medea, Hippolytus. The Phoenician Virgins, The Supplicants, Heracles* and *The Heraclidae*. There is a more than peevish tone to be found Wodhull's *The Nineteen Tragedies and Fragments of Euripides* (which includes *Cyclops* as one of the nineteen) the following year. In an introduction to vol. 1 Wodhull claims that he first announced his intention to publish all of Euripides in translation in 1774 but that the task proved too arduous. Discovering then that 'it was given out by some ... that I had totally abandoned this undertaking' he is publishing now to refute the 'suspicion that I kept myself in reserve, merely to undertake advantages in availing myself of the labors of my competitors'. Amongst these competitors is the 'quarto volume with which the Reverend Mr Potter of Scarning in Norfolk, last summer, favored his Subscribers' (Preface to vol. 1, London, sold by Thomas Payne and Son, 1782, p. xv). Nor does Wodhull think much of the order of the plays favoured by Potter, preferring to open with *Hecuba* and *Orestes*. Potter's second volume of Euripides was published in 1783, omitting from the canon only *Cyclops* which he found perhaps unworthy of his time or calling. Both Potter and Wodhull refer regularly to Brumoy in their introductions and notes to individual plays.

50 James Boswell, *Life of Johnson* (Oxford, new edn, reset 1953), pp. 920–1.

51 J. M. Cohen, *English Translators and Translations* (London, 1962), pp. 9–10.

CHAPTER 3

1 Terence Rattigan, *The Browning Version*, in *The Deep Blue Sea and Other Plays* (London, 1955), pp. 219 and 230.

2 Aeschylus, *Agamemnon*, ed. J. D. Denniston and D. Page (Oxford, 1957), pp. 224–40.

3 *The Tragedies of Aeschylus*, trans. Revd R. Potter (Norwich, 1777), reprinted with an essay on the Grecian Drama in *Family Classical Library: No. XLV, Aeschylus* (London, 1833).

4 Aeschylus, *The Agamemnon*, trans. Gilbert Murray (London, 1920).

5 Private letter of 22 Oct 1940, quoted in *Gilbert Murray: An Unfinished Autobiography* (London, 1960), p. 135.

6 *The Works of Robert Browning*, with introduction by Sir F. G. Kenyon (London, 1967). It is only fair to record that reviews from, amongst others, F. A. Paley, himself a translator of Aeschylus, in *The Athenaeum* (27 Oct 1877), were more enthusiastic. See B. Litzenberg and O. Smalley, *Browning: The Critical Heritage* (London, 1970).

7 *Works of Browning*, ed. Kenyon, p. 299, ll. 4–19.

8 John Conington, *The Agamemnon of Aeschylus; The Greek Text with a Translation into English Verse* (London, 1848), Preface, p. vi.

9 Kenyon, *Works of Browning*, ed., p. x.

10 Kenyon, *Works of Browning*, ed., p. xii.

11 An interesting comparison of specific aspects of the translations of Potter, Murray and others, may be found in Reuben Brower, 'Seven Agamemnons', in *Mirror on Mirror: Translation, Imitation, Parody* (Cambridge, Mass., 1974), pp. 159–80.

12 *The Oresteia: The Trilogy by Aeschylus in a Version by Tony Harrison* (London, 1981; repr. 2002).

13 *Aeschylus the Oresteia: A New Version by Ted Hughes* (London, 1999).

14 Peter Green, 'Some versions of Aeschylus: a study of tradition and method in translating Greek poetry', in *Essays in Antiquity* (London, 1960), pp. 185–215.

15 T. S. Eliot, 'Euripides and Professor Murray', in *Selected Essays, 1917–1932* (London, 1932), p. 64.

16 Green, 'Versions of Aeschylus', pp. 197–8.

17 Green, 'Versions of Aeschylus', p. 185.

18 Virginia Woolf, 'On not knowing Greek', in *The Essays of Virginia Woolf*, vol. IV, *1925–1928*, ed. Andrew McNeillie (London, 1994).

19 A version of this chapter appears in Fiona Macintosh, Pantelis Michelakis, Edith Hall and Oliver Taplin, eds., *'Agamemnon' in Performance 458 BC–AD 2004* (Oxford, 2005), pp. 189–206, under the title of 'Translation or transubstantiation'.

20 Murray, *Agamemnon*, pp. 2–3.

21 Murray may have been influenced by the Reinhardt production of *Oedipus King of Thebes* (1912) for which his translation was commissioned, and which demonstrated a typically Reinhardtian enthusiasm for the spectacular.

22 David Grene and Wendy Doniger O'Flaherty, *The Oresteia by Aeschylus* (Chicago, 1989).

23 Aeschylus, *The Oresteia*, trans. Michael Ewans (London, 1995), after ll. 901 and 1071.

24 Louis MacNeice, *The Agamemnon of Aeschylus* (London, 1936), p. 8.

25 Michael Sidnell, 'Another "death of tragedy": Louis MacNeice's translation of *Agamemnon* in the context of his work in the theatre', in *Greek Tragedy and its Legacy: Essays Presented to D. J. Conacher*, ed. Martin Cropp, Elaine Fantham and S. E. Scully (Calgary, 1986), pp. 323–35.

26 Sidnell, 'Another "death of tragedy"', p. 327.

27 Robert Lowell, *The Oresteia of Aeschylus* (London, 1978), frontispiece. Kenneth Dover was especially severe on Lowell: 'What goes wrong in this genre of pseudo-translation is not just ignorance of the literature and the culture to which the original work belongs, but narrowness of vision and indifference to character, plot and the intelligence and imagination of the original author', in 'The speakable and the unspeakable', corrected version in K. J. Dover, *Greek and the Greeks* (Oxford, 1987), p. 177.

28 Harrison omits this recognition token. See also Chapter 10.

29 Harrison, *The Oresteia*, pp. 27–9 (Oxford Classical Text ll. 905–13 and 944–57).

30 Hughes, *Oresteia*, pp. 43–7.

31 This was a production which Stein subsequently revised in Moscow with a Russian cast in the aftermath of the fall of communism, seeing in the *Oresteia* a parallel between the Athens of 458 BC and Russia in 1994, both striving to come to terms with the unfamiliar concept of democratic government.

32 Video recordings of stage productions are notoriously deceptive, especially when they have been prepared with an eye to film or television presentation, replete with camera tricks. What they can do is serve as a memory trigger for those who have seen the production while giving some impression of the production priorities for those who haven't. The Royal National Theatre archive in London contains a basic record filmed of all three parts of the Mitchell production.

33 Oliver Taplin, *The Stagecraft of Aeschylus* (Oxford, 1977), pp. 308–16.

34 Strangely Ariane Mnouchkine chose *not* to stage Agamemnon's walk on the tapestries in her *Les Atrides* (1991). See Marianne McDonald, 'The atrocities of *Les Atrides*: Mnouchkine's tragic vision', *Theatre Forum*, 1, Spring 1992, pp. 12–19.

35 Uncertain though we remain as to the pronunciation of ancient Greek in the time of Aeschylus, there must at least have been some echo between *heimasi* ('with garments') and *haimasi* (the plural of 'with blood').

36 See John Chioles, 'The *Oresteia* and the avant-garde: three decades of discourse', *The Performing Arts Journal*, 45, 1993, pp. 5–14. Chioles also considers Stein and Mnouchkine in the same article.

37 *The Oresteia* in *Aeschylus Plays: Two* (London, 1991).

CHAPTER 4

1 Eco, *Mouse or Rat?*, p. 5.

2 Hilaire Belloc, 'On translation', *London Mercury*, 10 (London, 1924), pp. 10 ff.; repr. in *A Conversation with an Angel and Other Essays* (London, 1929) and *On Translation: The Taylorian Lecture* (Oxford, 1931).

3 Theodore Savory, *The Art of Translation* (London, 1957), pp. 60 and 63.

4 Aristotle, *The Poetics*, 1450. a. 33.

5 R. C. Jebb, *The Electra of Sophocles* (Cambridge, 1905), p. 53.

6 Whether the lock of hair is picked up by Electra or, later, by Orestes, to offer to his sister, is a production issue which does not affect the development of the scene.

7 A. Shapiro and P. Burian, *Aeschylus: The Oresteia* (Oxford, 2003).

8 J. R. Green, *Theatre in Ancient Greek Society* (London, 1994); David Wiles, *Tragedy in Athens* (Cambridge, 1997); Rush Rehm, *The Play of Space* (Princeton, 2002).

9 Aeschylus, *Furies*, between ll. 116 and 130.

10 The Davenant version of *Macbeth* concluded with the dying regicide proclaiming 'Farewell vain world, and what's most vain in it, Ambition'.

11 *Electra, a Tragedy*, translated from Sophocles by Mr Theobald (London, 1714); incorrectly in plays from the 1779–80 repertoire of the Theatres Royal, Drury Lane and Covent Garden (London, 1780; repr. New York, 1979).

12 The prompt-book for *Iphigenia in Tauris* is disappointingly thin on staging details from Barker, confining itself for the most part to a small number of moves relating to grouping and stage positions, and some lighting cues written in a different hand.

13 Sophocles, *Antigone*, trans. Richard Emil Braun (Oxford, 1974), p. ix.

14 This is the reading preferred by Diggle in the Oxford text, l. 585, following Wilamowitz for '*seie*' and Murray for '*ennosi*' rather than '*enosi*' as in the Laurentian and Palatine manuscripts.

15 Edith Hall, *Introduction* to *Euripides' Bacchai*, translated by Colin Teevan (London, 2002), p. 14.

16 Mueller and Krajewska-Wieczorek, *Sophokles: The Complete Plays*, pp. 442 and 443, 446 and 447. The translations have no line numbering.

17 *The Ion of Euripides* by H. B. L. (London, 1889), p. 33 to follow l. 508. The translator's case for reconstruction is not helped by a remark preceding his notes that 'Smollett, in his tour of the Continent, observes that it is remarkable how slightly customs and superstitions have varied there, since periods of remote antiquity' (p. 91).

18 Ulysses, i.e. Odysseus.

19 *The Nineteen Tragedies of Euripides* translated by Michael Wodhull, reprinted in three volumes, vol. II (London, 1809), pp. 274–5. Wodhull, for all his annoyance at Bannister and Potter pre-publishing him, does bring a sense of drama that is lacking in both the others, though well understood by the earlier Lewis Theobald. Theobald was an original playwright who was misleadingly credited with the translation of *Electra* from Voltaire staged at Drury Lane in 1774 (with Smith as Orestes), several years after his death in poverty (see Hall and Macintosh, *Greek Tragedy*). Wodhull, however, tends to identify scenes in the light of eighteenth-century theatre convention: e.g. in *The Trojan Captives*, 'The Scene opens, and discovers Hecuba on a Couch'. In *Rhesus* (note 4) he states 'Though Dolon now makes his first appearance as a speaker, he has evidently been on the stage during the whole of the conference between Hector and Aeneas; he must therefore, either have entered with the latter, or as I am rather inclin'd to think, is one of the watch

who form the Chorus, and remains undistinguish'd among the body, till he comes forward, to accept the employment offer'd by Hector'. This is the sort of consideration which would never occur to most translators before the late nineteenth century – and, indeed, many after.

20 Anne Carson, 'Screaming in translation: the *Elektra* of Sophokles', in *Drama: Beiträge zum antiken Drama und seiner Rezeption*, Band 4 (1996), pp. 5–11.

21 *Oedipus Rex* directed by Michel St Denis at the Old Vic, in the Yeats translation, July 1945.

22 Laurence Olivier, *Confessions of an Actor* (London, 1984), p. 154.

23 Reprinted in Kenneth Tynan, *A View of the English Stage* (London, 1984), p. 27.

24 In *The Bacchae and other Plays*, trans. Philip Vellacott (Harmondsworth, 1954), pp. 237–44.

25 See also A. Lefevere, 'Changing the code: Soyinka's ironic aetiology', in Ortrun Zuber, ed., *The Languages of the Theatre: Problems in the Translation and Transposition of Drama* (Oxford, 1980), pp. 132–45.

26 Lefevere, 'Changing the code', p. 141 discusses Wole Soyinka's device of having Dionysus hold out a cup at this point in his *The Bacchae of Euripides*.

CHAPTER 5

1 H. D. F. Kitto, *Oedipus the King* (Oxford, 1994; reissued as an Oxford World's Classic paperback, edited with an introduction and notes by Edith Hall, 1998), pp. 577–92.

2 The nature of ambition was taken by Jean Anouilh as the central part of Creon's defence in his *Oedipe ou le roi boiteux* when he has Creon say, 'You could never have been satisfied to live at one remove from power. But I could and can. Because I do not have ambition .... That power for which you fight each other like dogs over a bone, I have looked closely at it, and know it for what it is worth' (unpublished translation, McDonald and Walton).

3 George Adams, *The Tragedies of Sophocles, translated from the Greek with Notes, Historical, Moral and Critical*, vol. 1 (London, 1729), Act III, scene 2.

4 Sophocles, *Oedipus the King, a translation with commentary by Thomas Gould* (Englewood Cliffs, 1970), p. 79.

5 *The Greek Theatre of Father Brumoy*, translated from Father Pierre Brumoy's *Le Théâtre des Grecs* (Paris, 1730) by Mrs. Charlotte Lennox in 3 vols. (London, 1759), vol. 1, p. 28. For a recent evaluation of the Lennox translation and others, see Hall and Macintosh, *Greek Tragedy*, esp. pp. 217–24.

6 See Bernard Knox, *Oedipus at Thebes* (Yale, 1957, rev. edn, New York, 1971), pp. 53–60 and 212 (where two of his references are incorrect).

7 R. C. Jebb, *Sophocles, the Plays and Fragments, Part I. The Oedipus Tyrannus* (Cambridge, 1887).

8 Plato, *Politics*, 301 C and *Republic*, 573 B.

9 Lewis Theobald, *Oedipus, King of Thebes: a Tragedy. Translated from Sophocles with Notes by Mr Theobald* (London, 1715), Act III, scene 5, ll. 391 ff.

10 Adams, *Sophocles*, Act III, scene 4.

11 *palaismata* (plural) is the word used of Creon's struggle in Euripides' *Medea* (l. 1214) trying to detach himself from the poisoned dress which has already consumed his daughter.

12 *The Tragedies of Sophocles*. A verse translation from the Greek by Thomas Francklin, 2 vols. (London, 1759), Act III, scene 5.

13 Lennox, *Greek Theatre*, pp. 38–9.

14 The Revd Thomas Maurice, *Poems and Miscellaneous Pieces with a Free Translation of the Oedipus Tyrannus of Sophocles* (privately printed, London, 1779), p. 200.

15 The Revd Robert Potter, *The Tragedies of Sophocles* (London, 1788, new edn, 1820), p. 39.

16 George Somers Clarke, *Oedipus Tyrannus* (Oxford, 1790).

17 Robert Fagles, *Sophocles: The Theban Plays* (London, 1982; Harmondsworth, 1984), ll. 84.

18 It was Betterton who had played in Davenant's version of Shakespeare's *Macbeth* in 1667.

19 Richard Jenkyns, *The Victorians and Ancient Greece* (Oxford, 1981).

20 Jenkyns, *Victorians and Greece*, p. 91, quoting the Preface to *Merope*.

21 Jenkyns, *Victorians and Greece*, p. 81.

22 Sir Francis Doyle, *Oedipus, King of Thebes, translated from the Oedipus Tyrannus of Sophocles* (London, 1849).

23 Doyle, *Oedipus*, Notice to the text, p. v.

24 He seems to have taken the business seriously, as evidenced by his reference to a Dutch translation as *Edipus Treursdel* by J. V. Vondels (Amstordam [*sic*], 1705).

25 *Agamemnon the King*, anonymous notice in *The Saturday Review*, 2 Feb 1856, p. 258.

26 *The Saturday Review*, 16 March 1872, pp. 347–8.

27 See Fiona Macintosh, 'Tragedy in performance: nineteenth and twentieth century productions', in Easterling, *Cambridge Companion to Greek Tragedy*, p. 289: also Hall and Macintosh, *Greek Tragedy*, pp. 521–6.

28 Macintosh, 'Tragedy in performance', pp. 284–321. See also her 'Alcestis on the British stage' in *Cahiers du GITA*, 14, 2001, pp. 281–308.

29 Robert Whitelaw, whose translation was one of those used by Yeats, came up with the elegant 'Rooted in pride the tyrant grows', a neat juxtaposition of the two nouns.

30 Sir Charles Oman, *Memories of Victorian Oxford* (London, 1941), pp. 69–70, on his schooldays at Winchester recalls that 'E. D. A. Morshead – commonly called Mush … translated the *Agamemnon* and some other things into English verse, in a style which was rather diffuse, because he tried to get into his English every shadow of a shade of meaning in the original Greek. Hence the translation had far more lines than the original. Morshead had a vocabulary of his own, so peculiar that some clever boys of the generation next below my own compiled, and actually printed, a small Mushri-English dictionary.

31 The choruses were adapted to the music of Charles Villiers Stanford by the iconoclastic scholar A. W. Verrall whose innovative, if eccentric, approach to the plays of Euripides was to make a significant impact on the notion of Greek tragedy as available for interpretation.

32 Aristotle, *Poetics*, 1453a (my translation).

33 See E. R. Dodds, 'On misunderstanding the *Oedipus Rex*', in *Oxford Readings in Greek Tragedy*, ed. Erich Segal (Oxford, 1987), pp. 187–8.

34 It was emended by Brunck in his edition of 1786.

35 Bernard Knox, *Oedipus at Thebes* (New York, 1971), pp. 7–8.

36 Gould, *Oedipus the King* (1970), p. 60.

37 Jebb, *Sophocles*, Intro., p. xxvii.

38 Darwin's *On the Origin of Species* was published in 1859; *The Descent of Man* in 1871; Nietzsche's new edition of *The Birth of Tragedy* in 1886; Freud's *The Interpretation of Dreams*, in which he first rehearsed the idea of the Oedipus complex in any depth, in 1900.

39 Friedrich Nietzsche, *The Birth of Tragedy*, trans. Walter Kaufman (New York, 1967), p. 73.

40 From Sigmund Freud, *The Interpretation of Dreams*: see Bernard Knox, 'Introduction' to *Oedipus the King* in *Sophocles: Three Theban Plays*, trans. Fagles, pp. 131–53.

41 See, in particular, Jean-Pierre Vernant and Pierre Vidal-Naquet, *Tragedy and Myth in Ancient Greece*, trans. Janet Lloyd (London, 1981), pp. 63–80.

42 Though the Herdsman at l. 1176 does say that there was a prophecy that the child of Laius and Jocasta would kill his parents (plural).

43 Judith Affleck in a note in *Sophocles: Oedipus Tyrannus*, translated by Ian McAuslan with notes by Judith Affleck (Cambridge, 2003), p. 58 properly draws attention to Oedipus' cry at line 738 '*ō Zeu, ti mou drasai bebouleusai peri?*' 'O Zeus, what are you planning for me?'

44 Second Loeb, vol. 1 (Heinemann, 1994), ll. 1197–207. In the Introduction to his *Oresteia* (Englewood Cliffs, 1970) Hugh Lloyd-Jones wrote of his translation 'The present version makes no attempt to be poetic, or even literary; it tries to render the sense faithfully and to reproduce the impact made by the idiom of the original more faithfully than a translation with any literary ambitions could afford to do' (Introduction, p. 10). This honest declaration of intent is carried over in the two volumes of Lloyd-Jones' Loeb *Sophocles*.

45 Gould, *Oedipus the King* (1970), pp. 17–18.

46 l. 874 in Potter, *Tragedies*.

47 l. 1382 in Potter, *Tragedies*.

48 In Michael Ewans, ed., *Four Dramas of Maturity* (London, 1999).

49 See David R. Clark and James B. McGuire, *W. B. Yeats: The Writing of Sophocles' King Oedipus* (Philadelphia, 1989) for a comprehensive study of the circumstances surrounding Yeats's interest in the play, p. 9.

50 In *The Collected Plays of W. B. Yeats* (London, 1928).

51 *Oedipus, King of Thebes*, trans. Gilbert Murray (London, 1911), p. vii.

52 Quoted from *Essays in Honour of Gilbert Murray* (London, 1936) in *Gilbert Murray: An Unfinished Autobiography* (London, 1960), pp. 152–3.

CHAPTER 6

1 Steiner, *After Babel*, p. 28.
2 The most obvious examples here are the endings of Aeschylus' *Seven Against Thebes* and Euripides' *Iphigenia at Aulis*, and the whole of Aeschylus' *Prometheus Bound* and Euripides' *Rhesus*, all of which are treated with suspicion.
3 Aristophanes, *The Frogs*, trans. David Barrett (Harmondsworth, 1964), ll. 837–9.
4 Barrett, *Frogs*, ll. 924–6.
5 Barrett, *Frogs*, ll. 1301–3.
6 Robert Frost's well-known aphorism, in Louis Untermeyer, *Robert Frost* (Washington, 1964), p. 18, is acknowledged in the title of Sofia Coppola's 2003 film *Lost in Translation*.
7 William Frost, *Dryden and the Art of Translation* (Yale, 1955), repr. in *Dryden's Dramatic Poesy and Other Essays*, introduced by William Henry Hudson (London, undated), p. 47.
8 Tytler, *Essays on the Principles of Translation*, p. 111.
9 Thomas Morell, *Aischulou Promētheus Desmōtēs ... ac anglicanam interpretationem* (London, 1773).
10 The 1850 translation is the one more usually found in editions of Elizabeth Barrett Browning's work. The 1833 translation is more interesting in the present context for the approach to the choruses, a deal more versatile than most before this time. It was published by A. J. Valpy in Elizabeth Barrett Browning, *Prometheus Bound and Other Poems* (London, 1833). See also C. Drummond, *Two Translations of* 'Prometheus Bound' *by Elizabeth Barrett Browning*, Boston University Ph.D., 2004.
11 In Elizabeth Barrett Browning, *Poems, Second Edition*, vol. 1 (London, 1850). In a preface she writes disarmingly of the 1833 translation 'One early failure, which, though happily free from the current of publication, may be remembered against me by a few of my personal friends, I have replaced by an entirely new version made for them and for my conscience.'
12 Sir F. G. Kenyon in the Introduction to *The Works of Robert Browning* (London, 1912), pp. xi–xii.
13 Belloc, 'On translation', p. 37.
14 D. S. Carne-Ross, 'Translation and transposition', in Arrowsmith and Shattuck, *Craft and Context*, p. 7.
15 Arrowsmith, 'The lively conventions of translation', in Arrowsmith and Shattuck, *Craft and Context*, p. 137.
16 Arrowsmith, 'Lively conventions', p. 123.
17 The first, Vellacott (1953); the second, Raphael and McLeish (1997).

18 Christina Babou-Pagoureli, from an unpublished talk entitled 'Translating Shakespeare in Greek', delivered in Thessaloniki in 2000.
19 Michael Alexander, 'Homer, sweet Homer', *The Times Higher Education Supplement*, 16 Sept 1988, p. 15.
20 The commissioning of a 'literal', has long been the undesirable policy of a number of theatres, including the National Theatre in London.
21 With a few exceptions, the Trojan slave in Euripides' *Orestes* being the most obvious, tragedy appears not to exploit regional differences. There is no indication, for example, that Trojan heroes speak anything different from Attic Greek.
22 The section which Theobald chose to cut, by more than half.
23 David Seale, *Vision and Stagecraft in Sophocles* (London, 1982), p. 30.
24 This is not the first translation of *Philoctetes*. Thomas Sheridan's *Philoctetes* was published in Dublin four years earlier in 1725. The latinised Ulysses for the Greek Odysseus is common in early translations.
25 Potter, *The Tragedies of Sophocles* (1788).
26 The Greek *episkopos* translated as 'spy'.
27 In an article published in *Theatre Quarterly*, vol. X, 40, autumn–winter, 1981, (pp. 37–49) Susan Bassnett-McGuire recorded the outcome of a survey taken amongst a group of practising translators at the Riverside Studios in which she found that nobody claimed to translate solely for publication. This is certainly not reflected historically. For better or worse there have been far more translations from Greek and Latin published than have ever been produced.
28 Tabard, 'At last Greek for the ordinary punter', *The Stage*, 16 March 1995.
29 *The Observer*, 12 March 1995.
30 Murray's translation of *Bacchae* was first produced by William Poel in 1908 with Lillah McCarthy in the role of Pentheus.

CHAPTER 7

1 Edith Hall, Fiona Macintosh and Oliver Taplin, eds., *Medea in Performance, 1500–2000* (Oxford, 2000). See also Marianne McDonald, *Euripides in Cinema: The Heart Made Visible* (Philadelphia, 1982); *Ancient Sun, Modern Light: Greek Drama on the Modern Stage* (New York, 1992); *The Living Art of Greek Tragedy* (Bloomington, 2003); also James J. Claus and Sarah Iles Johnston, eds., *Medea* (Princeton, 1997).
2 See also Edith Hall, 'Medea and British legislation before the second world war', *Greece and Rome*, NS 46, pp. 42–77; Lorna Hardwick, 'Theatres of the mind: Greek tragedy and women's writing in the nineteenth century', in L. Hardwick, P. E. Easterling, S. Ireland, N. Lowe and F. Macintosh, eds., *Theatre: Ancient and Modern* (Milton Keynes, 2000); and L. Hardwick, *Translating Words, Translating Cultures* (London, 2000).
3 In Hardwick, 'Theatres of the mind', pp. 68–81.

4 Marianne McDonald, *Sing Sorrow: Classics, History, and Heroines in Opera* (Westport, 2001). A burlesque by Mark Lemon, the founder of *Punch*, entitled *Medea; A Libel on the Lady of Colchis* (with a male Medea), opened on the same day as *Medea; or, the Best of Mothers with a Brute of a Husband* by Robert Brough, in London in 1856. Henry Treece, *Jason* (London, 1961); Christa Wolf, *Medea* (London, 1998); Robert Holdstock, *Celtika* (London, 2001).

5 *Euripides' Medea: A New Version by Brendan Kennelly* (Newcastle, 1991), p. 44.

6 Liz Lochhead, *Medea after Euripides* (London, 2000), p. 22.

7 'Tragedy, even the work of an "advanced" playwright like Euripides, remained circumspect almost to prudishness in its language and subject-matter, though euphemistic metaphor (then as always) was a great standby: a serious Greek poet was not allowed to call a cunt a cunt, but he could, and did, talk about "the split meadow of Aphrodite." ' Peter Green, *Classical Bearings: Interpreting Ancient History and Culture* (Berkeley, 1998), p. 139.

8 This is quite something for the single word *pagkakiste* but pales into insignificance compared with the sheer fury of Brendan Kennelly's 'new version':

> Stink of the grave, rot of a corpse's flesh,
> slime of this putrid world,
> unburied carcase of a dog in the street,
> the black-yellow-greeny spit of a drunk at midnight –
> these are my words for you.
>
> (Kennelly, p. 36)

9 Both translations in Walton, ed., *Four Roman Comedies* (London, 2003).

10 Brian Logan in 'Whose play is it anyway', *The Guardian*, 3 March 2003, p. 17, concurred with the belief of Philippe Le Moine who runs the National Theatre Studio's 'translation arm' that professional translators 'are not in contact with what they need to do: to translate for particular types of performance and staging'. How hard have they tried? See also Chapter 10 (p. 179).

11 The verb *kēdeuein* also means 'to attend to a corpse' or 'bury'.

12 Lennox, *Greek Theatre*, vol. II, p. 414.

13 Alcestis as a subject for drama goes back at least as far as Phrynichus, the contemporary of Aeschylus, though no more than a fragment of his play survives.

14 There is a body of belief that Shakespeare may have known *Alcestis* through a Latin translation at the time of writing *The Winter's Tale*. It is not only in the resurrection of the 'dead' queen that echoes can be found. One translation (Methuen, 1997), consciously invokes Shakespeare on a couple of occasions before 'quoting' Leontes direct at the unveiling of Alcestis.

15 Helene Foley in *Female Acts in Greek Tragedy* (Princeton, 2000), p. 315, identifies the intriguing central contradiction in the play that 'Alcestis' selfless sacrifice ironically puts Admetus' reputation in jeopardy, as the hero himself realizes in the aftermath of his humiliating argument with his father Pheres'.

16 The others by Euripides being *Hippolytus, Iphigenia in Tauris* and *Iphigenia in Aulis.*
17 Lennox, *Greek Theatre*, vol. II, pp. 69–70.
18 Lennox, *Greek Theatre*, vol. II, p. 118.
19 And especially shocking, one might conclude, to the Age of Reason.
20 Death's argument that he gets more *kudos* the younger the victim is certainly curious when Admetus could as easily have nominated one of his aged parents had they been agreeable.
21 Lennox, *Greek Theatre*, vol. II, pp. 81–2.
22 *Euripides' Alcestis*, trans. Richard Aldington (London, 1930), pp. 19–20.
23 Vellacott (1953), p. 130.
24 Lennox, *Greek Theatre*, pp. 81–2.
25 'Alkestis, the late wife', Methuen (1997).
26 Vellacott (1974), pp. 130–1.
27 See in particular Anne Pippin Burnett, 'The virtues of Admetus', *Classical Philology* 60, 1965, pp. 240–55. Hall and Macintosh, *Greek Tragedy*, chs. 14–15 consider in detail nineteenth-century attitudes to various 'versions' of both Medea and Alcestis.
28 Kovacs also follows Diggle's Oxford text in reordering the dialogue so that this appears as line 149 rather than 145.
29 In *Alcestis*, translated and adapted by Ted Hughes (London, 1999), published posthumously, there seems to be an example of the poet proposing a number of alternatives from which he was prevented by his death from providing a preferred solution. He gives the equivalent of line 145 not to the Maid but to the Chorus:

> I am afraid
> Admetos does not know
> What his loss will mean.
> He has not identified it.
> He does not know what loss is.
> Nothing has ever hurt him.
> But when she has gone he will know it.
> When everything is too late
> Then he will know it.
> When he has to live in what has happened.

CHAPTER 8

1 *Poetical and Dramatic Works of Thomas Randolph*, vol. II, ed. W. Carew Hazlitt (London and New York, 1875), p. 375.
2 Act II, scene 6.
3 Act III, scene 1.
4 F. W. Hall and W. M. Geldhart, *Aristophanis Comoediae, Tomus 1* (Oxford, 1990).

5 K. J. Dover, *Aristophanic Comedy* (London, 1972), esp. chs. 11 and 13 and pp. 230–7; and William Arrowsmith, Introduction to a reprint of his translation of *The Birds* in *Three Comedies of Aristophanes* (Ann Arbor, 1969), p. 4.

6 This is one of the simplest and most definitive of translations from Greek, *nephelokokkygia* meaning precisely 'Cloudcuckooland'.

7 The anonymous translation of *Birds*, at one time believed to be by Mitchell, was published in 1812. Mitchell's verse translations of *Acharnians* and *Knights* (1820) were reviewed in the *Critical Quarterly* of July 1820 by John Hookham Frere writing as 'W' – Frere used the pseudonym of 'Whistlecraft' for some of his satirical writing. Frere's essay, reprinted as an Introduction to the Everyman edition of Aristophanes in 1911, is significant for the distinction he makes between translators he identifies as 'Spirited' and those he describes as 'Faithful'.

8 Inaccurately translated by Walter Shewring in *The Odyssey* (Oxford, 1980), IX.92, as 'no matter for laughter nor yet forbearance'.

9 In Edith Hamilton, *The Greek Way to Western Civilisation* (New York, 1930; repr. New York, 1948), p. 88.

10 Plato, *Republic* III. 394–5. My translation.

11 Plato, *Symposium*, 223d.

12 Amongst them *Dionysus as Alexander*, *The Odysseus Comedy* and *Nemesis* by Cratinus, *Daedalus*, *Phoenician Women* and *Danaides* by Aristophanes.

13 Tony Harrison, *The Trackers of Oxyrhynchus* (London, 1990). It was first played for a single performance in the Stadium at Delphi in 1988 under the auspices of the European Cultural Centre of Delphi, subsequently in repertoire at the National Theatre in London (Olivier Theatre).

14 It may be worth recording that during my own schooling we read Greek and Latin classics in expurgated versions, spotlit by the line numbering becoming seductively elliptical. Though this might have been understandable in the case of Juvenal and Martial, the blue pencil was even wielded across mild sexual references in Homer.

15 *Euripides II*, with an English translation by Arthur Way (London, 1912), 577.

16 J. T. Sheppard, *The Cyclops: freely translated and adapted for Performance in English from the satyric drama of Euripides*, (Cambridge, 1923).

17 Dr Grainger in Charlotte Lennox from Brumoy, *Greek Theatre*, vol. III, p. 472.

18 *Cyclops*, in *The Nineteen Tragedies and Fragments of Euripides* in four volumes, translated by Michael Wodhull (1782), reprinted in *Hecuba and Other Plays by Euripides*, vol. IV (London, 1888).

19 Shelley's translation reprinted in *The Plays of Euripides in English*, vol. I (London, 1906), p. 17.

20 *Two Satyr Plays*, a new translation by Roger Lancelyn Green (Harmondsworth, 1957), p. 13.

21 Both translations are to be found in Walton, ed., *Six Greek Comedies* (London, 2002).

22 These latter two, the Fielding and Young *Plutus*, and White's *Clouds*, are the first two which Foster acknowledges as being respectively 'Translated with notes' and 'Translated with a [*sic*] principal scholia'.

23 *Comedies of Aristophanes. viz. The Clouds, Plutus, The Frogs, The Birds; translated into English* (London, 1812), p. vii.

24 Richard Cumberland was himself a Cambridge graduate who wrote some fifty plays, most of which were produced at either Drury Lane or Covent Garden between 1761 and 1811 when he died. They include *The Brothers* which shares only a title with the Terence play; *The Widow of Delphi*; and *The West Indian* on which his reputation principally rests.

25 'The editors do indeed thank Dunster for allowing them to republish his *Frogs* which has been long before the public', Advertisement, *Comedies of Aristophanes*, p. xii.

26 *Comedies of Aristophanes*, p. 408.

27 J. R. Planché's, '*The Birds*' of Aristophanes, reprinted in Planché, *The Extravaganzas*, vol. III (London, 1879).

28 Unpublished commissioning letter.

CHAPTER 9

1 Arrowsmith and Shattuck, *Craft and Context*, pp. 122–40.

2 Arrowsmith and Shattuck, *Craft and Context*, pp. 123 and 135.

3 Jeffrey Henderson, translator of the new editions of the Loeb Aristophanes, charted the range and function of Aristophanic obscene invention in *The Maculate Muse: Obscene Language in Attic Comedy* (New Haven and London, 1975). Peter Jones in *Classics in Translation* (London, 1998) managed to render thirty-eight Aristophanic euphemisms for penis into English and forty-five for the vagina. Now, that is translation!

4 Dover; *Aristophanic Comedy* (London, 1972), p. 230.

5 *Aristophanes Plays: One; Aristophanes Plays: Two*; and *Aristophanes and Menander: New Comedy* (London, 1991–8).

6 Arrowsmith and Shattuck, *Craft and Context*, p. 126.

7 Arrowsmith and Shattuck, *Craft and Context*, p. 126.

8 Nicholas de Jongh in *The Evening Standard* (29 July 2002).

9 Aristophanes has Peisetairos recommend starving the gods into submission 'like the Melians'. The people of Melos had refused to join the Athenian side against Sparta in the Peloponnesian War, preferring neutrality. The Athenian response was to blockade the city. When the Melians finally gave way in 416, two years before *Birds*, the entire male population was put to death, and the women and children were sold into slavery. It was an atrocity that shocked and shamed many Athenians, provoking Euripides, it is widely believed, to write *Trojan Women*.

10 Another political reference. At the time of the first production of *Birds* the Athenian fleet had just set out on what was to prove a disastrous military

expedition to Sicily. O'Brien includes a reference to the expedition in his text but as though it had already happened, a decision inspired, presumably, as an invitation to today's audience to make parallels with the invasion of Iraq.

11 Karolos Koun's productions in Greece, as Gonda Van Steen has pointed out in *Venom in Verse: Aristophanes in Modern Greece* (Princeton, 2000), p. 8, gave licence to promote current causes, principally through his *Birds* in demotic Greek in 1959. Koun's productions were notable, for the most part, for a faithfulness to the text rather than a freedom from it, but that text was itself translated from ancient Greek into modern.

12 O. Taplin, *Comic Angels* (Oxford, 1993).

13 Plutarch, *Moralia*, 10.853, my translation, reprinted from J. Michael Walton and Peter D. Arnott, *Menander and the Making of Comedy* (Westport, 1996).

14 Foster, *English Translations* p. 85.

15 *Menander*, trans. F. G. Allinson (London and Harvard, 1930).

16 *The Arbitration: the Epitrepontes of Menander, the fragments translated and the gaps conjecturally filled in by Gilbert Murray* (London, 1945, second impression, 1951), p. 7.

17 Walton and Arnott, *Menander*. See also Walton, Introduction to *Aristophanes and Menander: New Comedy* and *Six Greek Comedies* (London, 1994 and 2002).

18 This is the scene which is illustrated in one of the Mytilene mosaics, with the characters identified by name as Demeas, Chrysis and Mageiros (Cook) who seems to be black and to have his hair in dreadlocks.

19 In Philip Vellacott, *Menander: Plays and Fragments* (Harmondsworth, 1967), p. 182.

20 *Menander*, vol. III, ed. and trans. W. G. Arnott (Harvard, 2000), pp. 90–1.

21 Menander, *Samia*, ed. and trans. D. M. Bain (Warminster, 1983).

22 Norma Miller, *Menander, Plays and Fragments* (Harmondsworth, 1987).

23 Lewis Casson, *The Plays of Menander* (New York, 1971), in *Aristophanes and Menander* (1994 and 1998), revised translation in *Six Greek Comedies* (London, 2002); Richard Elman, *The Girl from Samos*, in *Menander* (Philadelphia, 1998).

24 In Michael Hackett's 1994 production, with the late Tressa Sharbough in the title role at the J. Paul Getty Museum in Malibu, this brief exchange took more than thirty seconds.

25 Netta Zagagi, *The Comedy of Menander* (London, 1994).

26 Zagagi, *Comedy of Menander*, p. 52.

27 See J. Michael Walton, 'Realising Menander: get-in at the Getty', *Drama: Beiträge zum antiken Drama und seiner Rezeption*, Band 5 (1997), pp. 171–91.

28 David Constantine, 'Finding the words: translation and the survival of the human', an edited version of the 1998 British Centre for Translation's annual St Jerome lecture, published in *The Times Literary Supplement*, 21 May 1999, pp. 14–15.

29 *Dyskolos* has been variously translated in England and America as, amongst other titles, *The Bad-Tempered Man* (Aris and Phillips), *Old Cantankerous*

(Penguin), *The Peevish Fellow* (Loeb), *The Malcontent* (Methuen), and *The Grouch* (New York University and the University of Pennsylvania). Everyone except Vellacott avoided the obvious '*The Misanthrope*', direct echoes of Molière being misleading.

30 Eco, *Mouse or Rat?*, p. 126.
31 Aris and Phillips, p. 148.
32 See Richard C. Beacham, *The Roman Theatre and its Audience* (London, 1991).
33 Terence, *Brothers*, 14, in *Four Roman Comedies*, ed. and trans. J. Michael Walton (London, 2003).
34 Terence, *Eunuch*, 7–8.
35 Recorded in Suetonius, *Life of Terence*, 5.
36 See Sander Goldberg, *Understanding Terence* (Princeton, 1986).
37 Constantine, 'Finding the words', p. 14.

CHAPTER 10

1 Review by Christopher Wood, 'Iliad with sex, and a plucked chicken', *Times Higher Educational Supplement*, 21/28 Dec 2001, p. 29.
2 D. S. Carne-Ross, 'Translation and transposition', in Arrowsmith and Shattuck, *Craft and Context*, p. 6.
3 Rupert Christiansen, 'The difficulties of staying faithful', *The Observer*, 10 Nov. 1991, p. 55.
4 Brian Logan, 'Whose play is it anyway?', *The Guardian*, 12 March 2003, pp. 16–17.
5 Susan Bassnett, 'When is a translation not a translation' in Susan Bassnett and André Lefevere, eds., *Constructing Cultures: Essays on Literary Translation* (Clevedon, 1997), pp. 25–40.
6 In Bassnett and Lefevere, *Constructing Cultures*, pp. 90–108.
7 M. Contat and J. M. Rybalka, eds., *Sartre on Theater* (New York, 1976), pp. 309–15.
8 Contat and Rybalka, *Sartre on Theater*, pp. 309–10.
9 Peter Brook, *The Empty Space* (London, 1968).
10 Contat and Rybalka, *Sartre on Theater*, p. 311.
11 Michael Anderson, 'Translating Euripides', *New Theatre Magazine*, 7, no. 1, autumn 1966, pp. 26–32.
12 Anderson, 'Translating Euripides', p. 26.
13 Helene Foley, 'Twentieth century performance and adaptation of Euripides', *Illinois Classical Studies* (1999–2000), pp. 24–5. See also J. Michael Walton, 'Page or stage: a response to Helene Foley', *ICS* 26 (2001), pp. 77–80.
14 Anderson, 'Translating Euripides', p. 31.
15 See Marianne McDonald and J. Michael Walton, eds., *Amid Our Troubles: Irish Versions of Greek Tragedy* (London, 2002).

16 One *Euripides' Bacchae: A Version*, for instance (unpublished) extended the first speech of Dionysus from Euripides' 73 lines to 163; his final speech from 14 lines to 207. Zeus was described as 'Superfuck' who 'spurted seed up the cleft'. Pentheus inviting Dionysus to 'feel my cock'; or saying of the women of Thebes that 'when a hysterical woman starts hitting the bottle it's cock she's after' brings to mind less Euripides than a giggly adolescent scrawling rude words in a library book. Not many of them turn into a Joe Orton.

17 See Lefevere, 'Changing the code: Soyinka's ironic aetiology', in Ortrun Zuber, ed., *The Languages of Theatre* (Oxford, 1980), pp. 132–45.

18 J. M. Cohen, *English Translators and Translations* (London, 1962), p. 27.

19 Woolf, 'On not knowing Greek', pp. 39–53.

20 Eliot, 'Euripides and Professor Murray', pp. 59–64.

21 Cohen, *English Translators*, p. 27.

22 J. McFarlane, 'Modes of translation', *Durham University Journal*, 45.3, 1953, pp. 77–93.

23 McFarlane, 'Modes of translation', p. 78.

24 Harrison's decision to omit the second of these three recognition tokens, the footprints, both in Peter Hall's production (1981) and in the published edition, was presumably based on the implausibility of a brother's footprint matching those of his sister. The scene was well enough remembered in Athens after Aeschylus' death for Euripides, some fifty years later in his *Electra*, to parody it, when an old man tries to convince Electra that Orestes has returned and she dismisses his 'evidence' as absurd – hair ('Why should our hair match? / He of high birth, groomed in the wrestling-ring, / I, a woman with fine-combed hair?'); footprints ('He's a man with bigger feet'); and a piece of woven cloth ('It wouldn't have grown bigger as he grew').

25 Hughes, *Oresteia*, p. 99.

26 *Euripides, Alcestis: Translated and Adapted by Ted Hughes* (London, 1999).

27 The inclusion of additional characters is a prominent feature of stage adaptations of the Greeks from Seneca onwards, but especially in the seventeenth to nineteenth centuries, with an array of extraneous individuals supplying subplots and unexpected diversions to the stories of Oedipus, Medea, Orestes and Andromache, amongst others.

28 Bernard Knox, 'Uglification', *The New Republic*, April 17 and 24, 2000, pp. 79–85.

29 Knox, 'Uglification', p. 79.

30 Edward Pearce in the programme for Northern Broadsides' *Oedipus and The Cracked Pot* (2001).

31 Blake Morrison, *Oedipus and Antigone by Sophocles: Versions by Blake Morrison* (Halifax, 2003).

32 Morrison, *Oedipus and Antigone*, pp. 72 and 82.

33 Trans. Marianne McDonald, *Sophocles Antigone* (London, 2000), p. 32.

34 Morrison, *Antigone*, p. 95.

35 Knox, 'Uglification', p. 82.

36 Knox, 'Uglification', p. 85.

37 Seamus Heaney, *The Cure at Troy: A Version of Sophocles' Philoctetes* (London, 1990).

38 Seamus Heaney, '*The Cure at Troy*: production notes in no particular order', in McDonald and Walton, *Amid our Troubles*, p. 172. A pragmatic reason for the female chorus was that there were three otherwise unemployed actresses in the company.

39 See the essays by McDonald, Paulin and Arkins in McDonald and Walton, *Amid our Troubles*.

40 *The Daily Telegraph*, 10 April 2004. A note of dissent was sounded by Thomas Sutcliffe in *The Independent* (23 April 2004) who questioned whether 'the copper coinage of daily speech' might not make Sophocles 'simplistic'.

41 *The Guardian*, 7 April 2004.

42 Seamus Heaney, *The Burial at Thebes* (London, 2004), p. 36.

Select Bibliography

Aaltonen, S., *Acculturation of the Other*, Joensuu, 1996.
  'Translating plays or baking apple pies: a functional approach to the study of drama translation', in M. Snell-Hornby, Z. Jettmarová and K. Kaindl, eds., *Translation as Intercultural Communication – Selected Papers from the EST Congress – Prague 1995*, Amsterdam and Philadelphia, 1997, pp. 89–98.
  Time-Sharing on Stage, Clevedon, 2000.
Adams, R. M., *Proteus: His Lies, His Truth: Discussions of Literary Translation*, New York, 1973.
Ahl, F., *Introduction to* Seneca: Three Tragedies, Ithaca and London, 1986.
Alexander, M., 'Homer, sweet Homer . . .', *The Times Higher Education Supplement*, 16 Sept 1988, p. 15.
Alvarez, R. and M. Vidal, eds., *Translation, Power, Subversion*, Clevedon, 1996.
Amos, F. R., *Early Theories of Translation*, New York, 1920.
Anderman, G., 'Drama translation', in M. Baker, ed., *The Routledge Encyclopedia of Translation Studies*, London, 1998, pp. 71–4.
Anderson, M., 'Translating Euripides', *New Theatre Magazine* 7, autumn 1966, pp. 26–32.
Anon., 'Agamemnon the king' [on William Blew's translation], *The Saturday Review*, 2 Feb 1856, pp. 258–9.
Arnold, M., 'On translating Homer', London, 1861; repr. in *Essays Literary and Critical*, introduction and notes by W. H. D. Rouse, London, 1906; *Essays by Matthew Arnold*, London, 1914.
Arrowsmith, W. and R. Shattuck, eds., *The Craft and Context of Translation*, Austin, 1961.
Auden, W. H., 'Translation and tradition: a review of Ezra Pound's translations', *Encounter*, 1, 1953, pp. 75–8.
  'The Greeks and us', in *Forewords and Afterwords*, New York, 1943; London, 1973, pp. 3–32.
Baker, M., ed., *The Routledge Encyclopedia of Translation Studies*, London, 1998.
Banu, G., ed., 'Traduire', *Théâtre/Public*, 44, 1982.
Barba, E., 'Eurasian theatre', in P. Pavis, ed., *The Intercultural Performance Reader*, London and New York, 1996, pp. 217–22.
Barnstone, W., 'ABCs of translation', *Translation Review*, 2, 1978, pp. 35–66.

Barsby, J., ed., *Greek and Roman Drama: Translation and Performance*, dedicated issue of *Drama: Beiträge zum antiken Drama und seiner Rezeption*, Band 12, Stuttgart, 2002.

Barthes, R., 'The death of the author' and 'From work to text', trans. S. Heath, *Image, Music, Text*, New York, 1977.

Bassnett, S., 'An introduction to theatre semiotics', *Theatre Quarterly*, vol. x, 38, 1980, pp. 47–55.

'Translating dramatic texts', in *Translation Studies*, London, 1980, pp. 120–32; rev. edn, 1988, 1991, repr. 1996.

'Ways through the labyrinth: strategies and methods for translating theatre texts', in T. Hermans, ed., *The Manipulation of Literature*, New York, 1985, pp. 87–102.

'Byron and translation', *The Byron Journal*, 14, 1986, pp. 22–32.

'Beyond translation', *New Comparisons*, 8, autumn, 1989.

'Translating for the theatre: textual complexities', *Essays in Poetics*, 15, 1990, pp. 71–84.

'Translating for the theatre: the case against performability', *TTR: Traduction, Terminologie, Rédaction*, 4.1, 1991, pp. 99–111.

'When is a translation not a translation', in S. Bassnett and A. Lefevere, eds., *Constructing Cultures: Essays on Literary Translation*, Clevedon, 1998, pp. 25–40.

'Still trapped in the labyrinth: further reflections on translation and theatre', in S. Bassnett and A. Lefevere, eds., *Constructing Cultures*, Clevedon, 1998, pp. 90–108.

'Theatre and opera', in P. France, ed., *The Oxford Guide to Literature in English Translation*, Oxford, 2000, pp. 96–103.

and A. Lefevere, eds., *Translation, History and Culture*, London, 1990; London and New York, 1995.

and A. Lefevere, eds., *Constructing Cultures*, Clevedon, 1998.

and H. Trivedi, *Post-Colonial Translation*, London, 1998.

as Bassnett-McGuire, S., *Translation Studies*, London, 1980; rev. edn, London, 1991.

'The translator in the theatre', *Theatre Quarterly*, vol. x, 40, 1981, pp. 37–48.

Bates, E. S., *Modern Translation*, London, 1936.

Beaugrande, R. de, *Factors in a Theory of Poetic Translating*, Amsterdam and Assen, 1978.

Bellitt, B., *Adam's Dream: A Preface to Translation*, New York, 1978.

Belloc, H., 'On translation', *London Mercury*, 10, London, 1924, pp. 10 ff.; repr. in *A Conversation with an Angel and Other Essays*, London, 1929 and *On Translation: The Taylorian Lecture*, Oxford, 1931.

Benjamin, W., 'Die Aufgabe des Übersetzers', in *Baudelaire: Tableaux parisiens*, Heidelberg, 1923; repr. in T. Adorno *et al.*, eds., *Schriften*, Frankfurt, 1955, pp. 40–54.

'The task of the translator', trans. H. Zohn, *Illuminations*, London, 1970, pp. 69–82.

Bharucha, R., *Theatre and the World – Performance and the Politics of Culture*, London and New York, 1990; repr. 1993.

Biddis, M. and M. Wyke, *The Uses and Abuses of Antiquity*, Bern and New York, 1999.

Biguenet, J. and R. Schulte, eds., *The Craft of Translation*, Chicago, 1989.

Billington, M., 'Oresteia: Barbican, London', *The Guardian*, 14 Oct, 1998, p. 12.

Bloom, H., 'A meditation upon priority, and a synopsis', in S. Burke, ed., *Authorship: From Plato to the Postmodern Reader*, Edinburgh, 1995, pp. 131–9.

Bolgar, R. R., *The Classical Heritage and Its Beneficiaries*, Cambridge, 1954.

Booth, A. D. *et al.*, eds., *Aspects of Translation: Studies in Communication*, 2, London, 1958.

Brislin, R. W., ed., *Translation: Application and Research*, New York, 1976.

Brower, R. A., 'Seven Agamemnons', in R. A. Brower, ed., *On Translation*, Cambridge, Mass., 1959, pp. 173–95; *Harvard Studies in Comparative Literature*, 23, Cambridge, Mass., 1974, pp. 159–80.

Mirror on Mirror: Translation, Imitation, Parody, Cambridge, Mass., 1974.

ed., *On Translation*, Cambridge, Mass., 1959.

Brüggemann, L. W., *English Editions, Translations and Illustrations of the Ancient Greek and Latin Authors*, vol. 1, Stettin, 1797; repr. New York, 1965.

Brumoy, Pierre, *Le Théâtre des Grecs*, Paris, 1730.

Burger, B., ed., *Traduire et le Théâtre II*, Lausanne, 1994.

Burian, P., 'Translation yesterday and today', in P. E. Easterling, ed., *The Cambridge Companion to Greek Tragedy*, Cambridge, 1997, pp. 271–4.

Butler, R., 'The Oresteia', *The Independent*, 5 Dec 1999.

Cairns, D. and S. Richards, *Writing Ireland: Colonialism, Nationalism and Culture*, Manchester, 1988.

Carlson, H., 'Problems in play translation', *Educational Theatre Journal*, 16, 1965.

Carrière, J.-C., *The Mahabharata*, trans. Peter Brook, London, 1987.

Carson, A., 'Screaming in translation: the *Elektra* of Sophokles', *Drama: Beiträge zum antiken Drama unde seiner Rezeption*, Band 4, Stuttgart, 1996, pp. 5–11.

Cartledge, P., *Aristophanes and his Theatre of the Absurd*, London, 1990.

Cary, E., and R. W. Jumpfelt, *Quality in Translation: Proceedings of the IIIrd Congress of the International Federation of Translators*, Bad Godesberg, 1959; New York, 1963.

Centre for Performance Studies, *Working Papers No. 1, Translation and Performance*, Sydney, 1995.

Choate, E. T., 'The Greek world revisited: Carl R. Mueller translates Aeschylus', *Performing Arts Journal*, 74, 2003, pp. 118–26.

Christiansen, R., 'The difficulties of staying faithful', *The Observer*, 10 Nov 1991, p. 55.

Chukovski, K., *A High Art; the Art of Translation*, trans. L. G. Leighton, Knoxville, Tenn., 1984.

Clapp, S., '*Oresteia* development: the Trojan War comes to Bosnia in a new version of Aeschylus's revenge tragedy by Ted Hughes', *The Observer*, 5 Dec 1999, p. 9.

Clark, D. R. and J. B. McGuire, *W. B. Yeats: The Writing of Sophocles' King Oedipus*, Philadelphia, 1989.

Clarke, M. L., *Greek Studies in England, 1700–1830*, Cambridge, 1945.

Classical Education in Britain 1500–1900, Cambridge, 1959.

Cobin, M., 'Text, subtext, antitext: the relation of verbal and nonverbal communication in the production of Shakespeare', *Maske und Kothurn*, 29, 1983, pp. 153–60.

Cohen, J. M., *English Translators and Translations*, London, 1962.

Conley, C. H., *The First English Translators of the Classics*, New Haven, 1927.

Constantine, D., 'Finding the words: translation and the survival of the human', *Times Literary Supplement*, 21 May 1999, pp. 14–15.

Contat, M. and J. M. Rybalka, eds., *Sartre on Theater*, New York, 1976.

Corcoran, N., 'The state we're in' [on Heaney's *The Burial at Thebes*], *The Guardian*, 1 Jan 2004, p. 24.

Corrigan, R., 'Translating for actors', in W. Arrowsmith and R. Shattuck, eds., *The Craft of Translation*, Austin, 1961, pp. 95–106.

Coulthard, M. and P. A. Odeber de Baubeta, eds., *The Knowledges of the Translator*, Lewiston, Queenston and Lampeter, 1996.

Cowper, W., Preface to his translation of *The Iliad of Homer*, London, 1791.

Crane, F. D., 'Euripides, Erasmus, and Lady Lumley', in *The Classical Journal*, 39, 1944, pp. 223–8.

Cropp, M. E. Fantham and S. E. Scully, eds., *Greek Tragedy and Its Legacy: Essays Presented to D. J. Conacher*, Calgary, 1986.

D'Alembert, J. L. and D. Diderot, 'La traduction', *Encyclopédie ou dictionnaire raisonné des sciences, des arts, et des métiers*, Paris and Neufchatel, 1751–65, vol. XVI, pp. 510–12.

Davie, D., *Poetry in Translation*, Milton Keynes, 1975.

Day-Lewis, C., *On Translating Poetry: The Jackson Knight Memorial Lecture, University of Exeter 1969*, Abingdon-on-Thames, 1970.

Delgado, M. and D. Fancy, 'The theatre of Bernard-Marie Koltès and the "other" spaces of translation', *New Theatre Quarterly*, vol. XVII, 66, pt 2, May 2001, pp. 141–60.

Delisle, J. and J. Woodsworth, eds., *Translators through History*, Amsterdam and Philadelphia, 1995.

Déprats, J.-M., ed., *Antoine Vitez – le devoir de traduire*, Montpelier, 1996.

Derrida, J., 'Les tours de Babel', trans. J. F. Graham, in J. F. Graham, ed., *Difference in Translation*, Ithaca and London, 1985, pp. 165–208.

Dingwaney, A. and G. Maier, eds., *Between Languages and Cultures: Translation and Cross-Cultural Texts*, Pittsburgh and London, 1995.

Dodds, E. R., 'On misunderstanding the *Oedipus Rex*', in E. Segal, ed., *Greek Tragedy: Modern Essays in Criticism*, New York, 1983, pp. 177–88.

Donaldson, I., ed., *Transformations in Modern European Drama*, London and Canberra, 1983.

Dorn, K., 'Stage production and the Greek theatre movement: W. B. Yeatss play *The Resurrection* and his version of *King Oedipus at Colonus*', *Theatre Research International*, 1(3) 1976, pp. 182–204.

'Dossier: traduction théâtrale', *Jeu*, 56, 1990.

Dover, K. J., *Introduction* to Aristophanes' *Clouds*, Oxford, 1968.

Aristophanic Comedy, London, 1972.

'The speakable and the unspeakable', reprinted (with one revision) from *Essays in Criticism* 30 (1980) in *Greek and the Greeks*, Oxford, 1987, pp. 176–81.

Drummond, C., 'Two Translations of "*Prometheus Bound*" by Elizabeth Barrett Browning', Boston University Ph.D., 2004; see Dissertation Abstracts International, vol. 65–03A, p. 941.

Dryden, J., 'Of dramatic poesy: an essay' (1668), in G. Watson, ed., *Dryden: Of Dramatic Poesy*, vol. 1, London, 1962, pp. 10–92.

'A defence of *An Essay of Dramatic Poesy*' (1668), in Watson, ed., *Dryden*, pp. 110–30.

'Preface to *Ovid's Epistles* (1680)', in Watson, ed., *Dryden*, pp. 262–73.

'To the earl of Roscommon, on his essay on translated verse' (1684), in Watson, ed., *Dryden*, vol. 11, pp. 14–17.

'Preface to *Sylvae: or, the Second Part of Poetical Miscellanies*' (1685), in Watson, ed., *Dryden*, vol. 11, pp. 18–33.

'To Lord Radcliffe', prefixed to *Examen Poeticum: being the Third Part of Miscellany of Poems* (1693), in Watson, ed., *Dryden*, vol. 11, pp. 156–68.

Preface to *Fables, Ancient and Modern, Translated into Verse* (1700), in Watson, ed., *Dryden*, vol. 11, pp. 269–94.

Duckworth, G. E., *The Nature of Roman Comedy*, Princeton, 1952.

Eagleton, T., 'Translation and transformation', *Stand*, 19 (3), 1977, pp. 72–7.

Easterling, P. E., 'Greek plays at Cambridge', in *Le Théâtre Antique des Nos Jours: Symposium International à Delphes 18–22 Août 1981*, Athens, 1984, pp. 89–94.

'Anachronism in Greek tragedy', *Journal of Hellenic Studies*, 105, 1985, pp. 1–10.

ed., *The Cambridge Companion to Greek Tragedy*, Cambridge, 1997.

'The early years of the Cambridge Greek Play, 1882–1912', in C. A. Stray, ed., *Classics in 19th and 20th Century Cambridge: Curriculum, Culture and Community*, Cambridge, 1999, pp. 27–48.

and L. Hardwick, S. Ireland, N. Lowe, and F. Macintosh, eds., *Selected Proceedings – Conference on 'Theatre Ancient and Modern'*, available at http://www.open.ac.uk/Arts/CC99/ccfrontpage.htm

Eco, U., *Mouse or Rat? Translation as Negotiation*, London, 2003.

Elam, K., *Semiotics of Theatre and Drama*, London, 1980.

Eliot, T. S., 'Euripides and Professor Murray', in *Selected Essays: 1917–1932*, London, 1932; 2nd edn, London, 1951, pp. 59–64.

'Seneca in Elizabethan translation', in *Selected Essays*, pp. 65–77.

'Poetry and drama', in *On Poetry and Poets*, London, 1957, pp. 72–88.

'Tradition and individual talent', in F. Kermode, ed., *Selected Prose of T. S. Eliot*, New York, 1988, pp. 37–44.

Esslin, M., *The Field of Drama*, London, 1994.

Even-Zohar, I., 'Polysystem studies', *Poetics Today*, 11.1, spring, 1990.

Ewans, M., *Introduction* to Aischylos *The Oresteia*, London, 1995, pp. xxxiv–xxxvii.

Ezard, J., 'Fact vies with fiction in pursuit of the classic English poisoner', *The Guardian*, 26 Feb 2000, p. 3.

Fagles, R., Foreword to Aeschylus' *Oresteia*, Harmondsworth, 1966, p. 7.

Farrel, J., 'Servant of many masters', in D. Johnston, ed., *Stages of Translation*, Bath, 1996, pp. 45–55.

Fischer-Lichte, E. *et al.*, eds., *Soziale und theatralische Konventionen als Problem der Dramenübersetzung*, Tübingen, 1988.

Fischer-Lichte, E., 'Intercultural aspects in post-modern theatre: a Japanese version of Chekhov's *Three Sisters*', in H. Scolnicov and P. Holland, eds., *The Play Out of Context*, Cambridge, 1989, pp. 173–85.

'Theatre, own and foreign: the intercultural trend in contemporary theatre', in E. Fischer-Lichte, J. Riley and M. Gissenwehrer, eds., *The Dramatic Touch of Difference*, Tübingen, 1990, pp. 11–19.

'Staging the foreign as cultural transformation', in Fischer-Lichte *et al.*, *The Dramatic Touch of Difference*, pp. 277–87.

'Interculturalism in contemporary theatre', in P. Pavis, ed., *The Intercultural Performance Reader*, London and New York, 1996, pp. 27–40.

Foley, H., 'Twentieth-century performance and adaptation of Euripides', *Illinois Classical Studies*, 24–5, 1999–2000, pp. 1–13.

Foster, F. M. K., *English Translations from the Greek*, New York, 1918; repr. 1966.

Frajnd, M., 'The translation of dramatic works as a means of cultural communication', in *Proceedings of the International Comparative Literature Association*, Innsbruck, 1980.

France, P., ed., *Oxford Guide to Literature in English Translation*, Oxford, 2001.

Frawley, W., ed., *Translation: Literary, Linguistic and Philosophical Perspectives*, Newark, 1984.

Frayn, M., 'Interview with Jill Dunning', *ITI Bulletin*, Jan–Feb 2003, pp. 11–14.

Frere, J. H., *see* Whistlecraft.

Friedrich, H., 'On the art of translation', in R. Schulte and J. Biguenet, eds., *Theories of Translation: An Anthology of Essays from Dryden to Derrida*, Chicago and London, 1992, pp. 11–16.

Frost, W., *Dryden and the Art of Translation*, New Haven, 1955.

Gaddis-Rose, M., ed., *Translation Spectrum: Essays in Theory and Practice*, Albany, 1981.

Gardner, L., '*Suppliants*', *The Guardian*, 25 Nov 1998, p. 12.

Garland, R., *Surviving Greek Tragedy*, London, 2004.

Gibbons, R., 'Poetic form and the translator', *Critical Inquiry*, 11(4), 1985, pp. 654–71.

Gilula, D., 'Greek drama in Rome: some aspects of cultural transposition', in H. Scolnicov and P. Holland, eds., *The Play Out of Context: Transferring Plays from Culture to Culture*, Cambridge, 1989, pp. 99–109.

Goethe, J.W. von, 'Übersetzungen', in 'Noten und Abhandlungen zum besserem Verständniss des West-östlichen Divans', *West-Östlichen Divan*, Stuttgart, 1819.

Goldberg, S., *Understanding Terence*, Princeton, 1986.

Goldhill, S., *Reading Greek Tragedy*, Cambridge, 1988.

Gooch, S., 'Fatal attraction', in D. Johnston, ed., *Stages of Translation*, Bath, 1996, pp. 13–21.

Goody, J., 'Literacy and achievement in the ancient world', in F. Coulmas and K. Ehlich, eds., *Writing in Focus*, Berlin, Amsterdam and New York, 1983 (Trends in Linguistics. Studies and Monographs, 24), pp. 83–98.

Graham, J., ed., *Difference in Translation*, Ithaca, 1985.

Green, J. R., *Theatre in Ancient Greek Society*, London, 1994.

Green, P. M., 'Some versions of Aeschylus', *Essays in Antiquity*, London, 1960, pp. 185–215.

Grene, D. H., 'Lady Lumley and Greek tragedy', in *The Classical Journal*, 36, no. 9, June 1941, pp. 537–47.

Griffiths, M., 'Presence and presentation: dilemmas in translating for the theatre', in T. Hermans, ed., *Second Hand: Papers on the Theory and Historical Study of Literary Translation*, *ALW-Cahier*, 3, 1985, pp. 161–82.

Gross, J., 'How to put the tragic into tragedy', *Sunday Telegraph*, 5 Dec 1999, p. 12.

Hall, E., *Inventing the Barbarian: Greek Definition Through Tragedy*, Oxford, 1991.

'Sophocles' Electra in Britain', in J. Griffin, ed., *Sophocles Revisited: Essays Presented to Sir Hugh Lloyd-Jones*, Oxford, 1999.

'Medea and British legislation before the First World War', *Greece and Rome*, 46, 1999, pp. 42–77.

F. Macintosh and O. Taplin, eds., *Medea in Performance 1500–2000*, Oxford, 2000.

and F. Macintosh, *Greek Tragedy and the British Theatre, 1660–1914*, Oxford, 2005.

Halleran, M. R., *Stagecraft in Euripides*, Totowa, N. J., 1985.

Hamilton, E., 'On translating', in *Three Greek Plays*, New York, 1937.

Handley, E. W., 'Menander and Plautus: a study in comparison', Inaugural lecture, London, 1968.

'Plautus and his public: some thoughts on New Comedy in Latin', *Dionisio*, 46, 1975, pp. 117–32.

Hardwick, L., *Translating Words, Translating Cultures*, London, 2000.

'Women, translation and empowerment', in J. Bellamy, A. Laurence and G. Perry, eds., *Women, Scholarship and Criticism – Gender and Knowledge c.1790–1900*, Manchester, 2000, pp. 180–203.

Harris, W. J., *The First Printed Translations into English of the Great Foreign Classics*, London, 1909.

Harrison, T., 'Facing up to the Muses', *Proceedings of the Classical Association*, 85, 1988, pp. 7–29.

Hartigan, K. V., *Greek Tragedy on the American Stage: Ancient Drama in the Commercial Theatre, 1882–1994*, Westport, 1995.

Hawkes, D., 'The translator, the mirror, and the dream: some observations on a new theory', *Renditions*, 13, 1980, pp. 5–20.

Heaney, S., ' "Me as metre": on translating *Antigone*', in J. Dillon, and S. E. Wilmer, *Rebel Women: Staging Ancient Greek Drama Today*, London, 2005, pp. 169–73.

Henderson, J., *The Maculate Muse: Obscene Language in Attic Comedy*, New Haven, 1975; repr. with addenda, New York, 1991.

    'Translating Aristophanes for performance', in *Drama: Beiträge zum Antiken Drama und seiner Rezeption*, Band 2, Stuttgart, 1993, pp. 81–91.

Heylen, R., *Translation, Poetics, and the Stage – Six French 'Hamlets'*, London and New York, 1993.

Hines, S. P., 'English translations of Aristophanes' comedies, 1655–1742', Ph.D. diss. University of North Carolina at Chapel Hill, 1966.

Hofmannsthal, H. von, 'On characters in novels and plays', trans. M. Hottinger and J. and T. Stern, *Selected Prose*, New York, 1952.

Holmes, J. S., ed., *The Nature of Translation: Essays on the Theory and Practice of Literary Translation*, The Hague, 1970.

    J. Lambert, and A. Lefevere, eds., *Literature and Translation*, Louvain, 1978.

    Translated! Papers in Literary Translation and Translation Studies, Amsterdam, 1988; repr. 1994.

Hugo, V., 'Préface pour la nouvelle traduction de Shakespeare', 1864; repr. in F. Bouvet, ed., *Oeuvres critiques complètes*, Paris, 1963.

Humboldt, W. von, 'Einleitung zu *Agamemnon*', *Aeschylos Agamemnon metrisch übersetzt*, Leipzig, 1816, trans. by S. Sloan as 'Wilhelm von Humboldt: from the introduction to his translation of *Agamemnon*', in R. Schulte and J. Biguenet, eds., *Theories of Translation: An Anthology of Essays from Dryden to Derrida*, Chicago, 1992, pp. 55–9.

Ivir, V., 'Procedures and strategies for the translation of culture', *Indian Journal of Applied Linguistics*, 12, 1987, pp. 35–46.

Jacobsen, E., *Translation: A Traditional Craft*, Copenhagen, 1958.

Jenkyns, R., *The Victorians and Ancient Greece*, Oxford, 1981.

Johnson, J. A., 'Sophocles' *Philoctetes*: deictic language and the claims of Odysseus', *Eranos*, 86, 1988, pp. 117–21.

Johnston, D., ed., *Stages of Translation: Essays and Interviews on Translating for the Stage*, Bath, 1996.

    'Text and ideotext: translation and adaptation for the stage', in M. Coulthard and P. A. Odeber de Baubeta, eds., *The Knowledges of the Translator*, Lewiston, Queenston and Lampeter, 1996, pp. 243–58.

Jones, F., 'Translation: fun or folly?', *Georgia Review*, 35(3), 1981, pp. 557–70.

Jones, P., *Classics in Translation: From Homer to Juvenal*, London, 1998.

Joshi, S., ed., *Rethinking English: Essays in Literature, Language, History*, New Delhi, 1991.

Kaimio, M., *Physical Contact in Greek Tragedy: A Study of Stage Conventions* (*Annales Academiae Scientiarum Fennicoe*, Ser. B, 244), Helsinki, 1988.

Katrak, K. H., *Wole Soyinka and Modern Tragedy, Contributions in Afro-American and African Studies*, 96, New York, 1986.

Kelly, L. G., *The True Interpreter: A History of Translation Theory and Practice in the West*, Oxford, 1978.

'Bibliography of the translation of literature', *Comparative Criticism*, 6, 1984, pp. 347–59.

Ker, W. P., ed., *Essays of John Dryden*, 2 vols., 1900; repr. Oxford, 1926, New York, 1961.

Kewes, P., *Authorship and Appropriation: Writing for the Stage in England, 1660–1710*, Oxford, 1988.

Knight, D., *Pope and the Heroic Tradition: A Critical Study of his Iliad*, New Haven, 1951.

Knox, B. M. W., *Word and Action: Essays on Ancient Theatre*, Baltimore and London, 1979.

'Uglification', *The New Republic*, 17 and 24 April 2000, pp. 79–85.

Knox, R. A., *On English Translation: The Romanes Lecture Delivered in the Sheldonian Theatre 11 June 1957*, Oxford, 1957.

Kowzan, T., 'From written text to performance – from performance to written text', in E. Fischer-Lichte *et al.*, eds., *Das drama und seine inszenierung. Vorträge des internationalen Literatur- und kultursemiotischen Kolloquiums. Frankfurt am Main, 1983*, Tübingen, 1985, pp. 1–11.

Kruger, L., 'Translating (for) the theatre: the appropriation, *mise-en-scène* and reception of theater texts', Ann Arbor, Microfilms International, 1986.

Larose, R., *Théories contemporaines de la traduction*, Quebec, 1987.

Lathrop, H. B., *Translations from the Classics into English from Caxton to Chapman 1477–1620*, Madison, 1933.

Lattimore, R., *The Poetry of Greek Tragedy*, Baltimore, 1958.

Lefevere, A., *Translating Poetry: Seven Strategies and a Blueprint*, Amsterdam and Assen, 1975.

ed., *Translating Literature: The German Tradition from Luther to Rosenzweig*, Amsterdam and Assen, 1977.

'Changing the code: Soyinka's ironic aetiology', in O. Zuber, ed., *The Languages of Theatre*, Oxford, 1980, pp. 132–45.

'Mother Courage's cucumbers: text, system and refraction in a theory of literature', *Modern Language Studies*, 12, 4 (fall), 1982, pp. 3–20.

Western Translation Theory: A Reader, London, 1991.

Translation, Rewriting and the Manipulation of Literary Fame, London, 1992.

Translating Literature: Practice and Theory in a Comparative Literature Context, New York, 1992.

ed., *Translation/History/Culture: A Sourcebook*, London, 1992.

Lenschen, W., ed., *Traduire le théâtre: Je perce l'énigme mais je garde le mystère*, Lausanne, 1993.

Litzenberg, B. and D. Smalley, *Browning: The Critical Heritage*, London, 1970.

Lloyd, G., 'Ancient ways to peace of mind', *The Times Higher*, 21–8 Dec 2001, p. 28.

Lloyd-Jones, H., *Blood for Ghosts: Classical Influences in the Nineteenth and Twentieth Centuries*, London, 1982.

Logan, B., 'Whose play is it anyway?', *The Guardian*, 3 Dec 2003, pp. 16–17.

McDonald, M., *Euripides in Cinema: The Heart Made Visible*, Philadelphia, 1983.

Ancient Sun, Modern Light: Greek Drama on the Modern Stage, New York, 1992.

'The atrocities of *Les Atrides*: Mnouchkine's tragic vision', *Theatre Forum*, 1, spring 1992, pp. 12–19.

'A bomb at the door: Kennelly's *Medea*, 1988', *Éire-Ireland*, 28.2, 1993, pp. 129–37.

'Seamus Heaney's *Cure at Troy*: politics and poetry', *Classics Ireland*, 3 May 1996, pp. 129–40.

'When despair and history rhyme: colonialism and Greek tragedy', *New Hibernia Review*, 1.2, summer 1997, pp. 57–70.

'Recent Irish translations of Greek tragedy: Derek Mahon's *Bacchai*', in E. Patrikiou, ed., *Translation of Ancient Greek Drama in All the Languages of the World*, Athens, 1998, pp. 190–200.

'Mapping Dionysus in new global spaces: multiculturalism and ancient Greek tragedy', in S. Patsalidis and E. Sakellaridou, eds., *(Dis)Placing Classical Greek Theatre*, Thessaloniki, 1999, pp. 145–67.

'*Agamemnon* in England: vital Greek tragedy', *The Hellenic Chronicle*, 1 Dec 1999.

Classics as Celtic firebrand: Greek tragedy, Irish playwrights, and colonialism', in E. Jordan, ed., *Theatre Stuff: Critical Essays on Contemporary Irish Theatre*, Dublin, 2000, pp. 16–26.

Sing Sorrow: Classics, History and Heroines in Opera, Westport, 2001.

The Living Art of Greek Tragedy, Bloomington, 2003.

and J. M. Walton, eds., *Amid our Troubles: Irish Versions of Greek Tragedy*, London, 2002.

McFarlane, J., 'Modes of translation', *Durham University Journal*, 45.3, 1953, pp. 77–93.

Macintosh, F., 'Tragedy in performance: nineteenth- and twentieth-century productions', in P. E. Easterling, ed., *The Cambridge Companion to Greek Tragedy*, Cambridge, 1997, pp. 284–323.

'Alcestis in Britain', *Cahiers du GITA*, 14, 2001, pp. 281–308.

Macintosh, F., P. Michelakis, E. Hall and O. Taplin (eds.) *Agamemon in Performance 458 BC to AD 2004*, Oxford, 2004.

McLeish, K., 'Translating comedy', unpublished keynote address given at the Performance Translation Centre, University of Hull, 1997.

McNeillie, A., *The Essays of Virginia Woolf,* vol. IV, 1925–1928, London, 1996.

Manguel, A., 'The translator as reader', in A. Manguel, *A History of Reading,* London, 1996.

Manton, G. R., 'Identification of speakers in Greek drama', *Antichthon,* 16, 1982, pp. 1–16.

Marowitz, C., 'Translators are not creators', *New Statesman,* 24 Oct 1980, pp. 29–30.

Mason, H. A., *To Homer Through Pope: An Introduction to Homer's Iliad and Pope's Translation,* New York, 1972.

Mateo, M., 'Translation strategies and the reception of drama performances: a mutual influence', in M. Snell-Hornby, Z. Jettmarová, and K. Kaindl, eds., *Translation as Intercultural Communication – Selected Papers from the EST Congress – Prague 1995,* Amsterdam and Philadelphia, 1997.

Matthiesson, F. O., *Translation: An Elizabethan Art,* Cambridge, Mass., 1931; repr. New York, 1965.

Mayes, I., 'Sacred rights: the reader's editor on … the pitfall of direct translation', *The Guardian,* 7 April 2001, p. 7.

Melrose, S., *A Semiotics of the Dramatic Text,* Basingstoke, 1994.

Meredith, H. O., Introduction to *Four Plays of Euripides,* London, 1936, pp. 13–33.

Meyer, M., 'On translating plays', *Twentieth Century Studies,* 11, Sept 1974, pp. 44–51.

'Bluff your way in Marivaux', *The Times Literary Supplement,* Nov 1996, p. 35.

Milner, E., *Records of the Lumleys of Lumley Castle,* London, 1904.

Modern Drama, 41(1) [on translation], spring, 1998.

Moroney, M., '*Iphigenia at* Aulis', *The Guardian,* 30 March 2001, p. 18.

Morris, M., 'The "Eumenides" at Cambridge', *MacMillan's,* 53 Nov 1885–April 1886, pp. 205–12.

Morrison, B., 'Femme fatale', *The Guardian,* 4 Oct 2003, pp. 16–17.

Muecke, F., 'Playing with the play: theatrical self-consciousness in Aristophanes', *Antichthon,* 11, 1977, pp. 52–67.

Mullen, P., 'Wassail – whassat?', *The Oldie,* Dec 1999, p. 36.

Murray, G., 'Part I', in J. Smith and A. Toynbee, eds., *Gilbert Murray: An Unfinished Autobiography,* London, 1960.

Nabokov, V., 'The art of translation', *New Republic,* 105, 1941, pp. 160–2.

Newman, F. W., *Homeric Translation in Theory and Practice: A Reply to Matthew Arnold,* London, 1861; repr. in *Essays by Matthew Arnold,* London, 1965.

Newmark, P., 'Twenty-three restricted rules of translation', *The Incorporated Linguistic,* 12(1), 1973, pp. 9–15.

Approaches to Translation, Oxford, 1981.

A Textbook of Translation, New York, 1988.

Nida, E. A., *Toward a Science of Translating with Special Reference to Principles and Procedures Involved in Bible Translating,* Leiden, 1964.

and C. Taber, *The Theory and Practice of Translation,* Leiden, 1969.

Nietzsche, F., 'Zum problem des Übersetzens', *Jenseits von Gut und Böse*, Leipzig, 1886; repr. in *Werke in drei Bändern*, Munich, 1962, Band 20, section 28, pp. 593 ff.

Ober, J. and B. Strauss, 'Political rhetoric, and the discourse of Athenian democracy', in J. J. Winkler and F. I. Zeitlin, eds., *Nothing to do with Dionysos? Athenian Drama in Its Social Context*, Princeton, 1989, pp. 237–70.

Oliphant, M., 'Aristophanes' apology', *Blackwood's Magazine*, 118, Dec 1875, pp. 90–3.

O'Regan, D. E., *Rhetoric, Comedy, and the Violence of Language in Aristophanes' Clouds*, New York, 1992.

Osborn, M., 'Translation, translocation and the native context of Caedmon's Hymn', *New Comparison*, 8, 1989, pp. 12–23.

Page, D. L., *Actors' Interpolations in Greek Tragedy*, Oxford, 1934.

Palmer, H. R., *List of English Editions and Translations of Greek and Latin Classics Printed Before 1641*, London, 1911.

Pappenheim, M., 'Cloud-Cuckoo land unveiled', *BBC Music Magazine*, June 2001.

Parker, L. P. E., 'Alcestis: Euripides to Ted Hughes', *Greece and Rome*, vol. 50, 2003, pp. 1–30.

Parker, R. B., 'The National Theatre's *Oresteia*, 1981–1982', in M. Cropp, E. Fantham, and S. E. Scully, eds., *Greek Tragedy and its Legacy: Essays Presented to D. J. Conacher*, Calgary, 1986, pp. 237–57.

Patrikiou, E., *Translation of Ancient Greek Drama in All the Languages of the World*, Athens, 1998.

Pavis, P., 'Production et réception au théâtre', in *Voix et images de la scène*, Lille, 1985.

'The classical heritage of modern drama: the case of postmodern theatre', trans. L. Kruger, *Modern Drama*, 29, March 1986, pp. 1–22.

'Problems of translation for the stage: interculturalism and post-modern theatre', trans. L. Kruger, in H. Scolnicov and P. Holland, eds., *The Play Out of Context*, Cambridge, 1989, pp. 25–44.

Theatre at the Crossroads of Culture, trans. L. Kruger, London, 1992; repr. 1995.

ed., *The Intercultural Performance Reader*, London and New York, 1996.

Pfeiffer, C., ed., *History of Classical Scholarship*, Oxford, 1968.

Phillimore, J. S., 'Some remarks on translation and translators', *The English Association Pamphlet*, 3, no. 42, Oxford, 1919.

Picken, C., *The Translator's Handbook*, 2nd edn, London, 1983 and 1989.

Platform Papers 1. Translation, London National Theatre (Michael Frayn, Christopher Hampton and Timberlake Wertenbaker in a conversation chaired by Colin Chambers), London, 1989.

Pope, A., Preface to his translation of *Homer's Iliad*, London, 1715.

Postgate, J. P., *Translation and Translations: Theory and Practice*, London, 1922.

Pound, E., 'Notes on Elizabethan classicists', *Egoist*, 4, nos. 8–11, 1917, and 5, no. 1, 1918.

'Translators of Greek: early translators of Homer', *Instigations*, 1920; repr. in T. S. Eliot, ed., *Literary Essays of Ezra Pound*, Norfolk, Conn., 1954 [composed of parts originally published in the *Egoist*, 1917].

Literary Essays, London, 1954.

Rabassa, G., ed., *The World of Translation*, New York, 1971.

Radice, W. and B. Reynolds, *The Translator's Art: Essays in Honour of Betty Radice*, Middlesex, 1987.

Raffel, B., *The Forked Tongue: A Study of the Translation Process*, The Hague, 1971.

Rehm, R., *The Play of Space*, Princeton, 2002.

Reynolds, M., 'Browning and translationese', in *Essays in Criticism LIII*, Oxford, 2003, pp. 70–8.

Rieu, E. V., 'Classics in translation', in W. E. Williams, ed., *The Reader's Guide*, Harmondsworth, 1960.

Roscommon, the Earl of, *An Essay on Translated Verse*, London, 1684; repr. and enlarged, 1685.

Rose, M. G., ed., *Translation: Agent of Communication*, Hamilton, NZ, 1980.

Rosenberg, J., 'Constant factors in translation', in G. F. Merkel, ed., *On Romanticism and the Art of Translation: Studies in Honor of Edwin Hermann Zeydel*, Princeton, 1956.

Russell, D. A., *Criticism in Antiquity*, London, 1981.

and M. Winterbottom, eds., *Ancient Literary Criticism: The Principal Texts in New Translations*, Oxford, 1972.

Said, E. W., *Orientalism*, London and Henley, 1978.

Savory, T., *The Art of Translation*, London, 1957; repr. Boston, 1968.

Schechner, R., *The End of Humanism*, New York, 1982.

Scholz, H., *The Art of Translation*, Philadelphia, 1918.

Schulte, R., 'Translation and reading', *Translation Review*, 18, 1985, pp. 1–2.

'Multiple translations: an interpretive perspective', *Translation Review*, 28, 1988, pp. 1–2.

'The study of translation: re-creative dynamics in literature and humanities', *Mid-American Review*, 9(20), 1989, pp. 69–80.

and J. Biguenet, eds., *Theories of Translation: An Anthology of Essays from Dryden to Derrida* (includes in translation essays by Nossack, Goethe, Humboldt, Nietzsche, Benjamin, Valety, Nabokov, Derrida), Chicago and London, 1992.

Schultze, B., 'In search of a theory of drama translation: problems of translating literature (reading) and theatre (implied performance)', in *Proceedings of the First Congress of the Associação Portuguesa de Literatura Comparada in 1989*, Lisbon, 1990, pp. 267–74.

Scolnicov, H. and P. Holland, eds., *The Play Out of Context: Transferring Plays from Culture to Culture*, Cambridge, 1989.

Segal, E., *Roman Laughter: The Comedy of Plautus*, Cambridge, Mass., 1968; 2nd edn, Oxford, 1987.

Selver, P., *The Art of Translating Poetry*, Boston and London, 1966.

Shaked, G., 'The play: gateway to cultural dialogue', trans. J. Green, in H. Scolnicov and P. Holland, eds., *The Play Out of Context: Transferring Plays from Culture to Culture*, Cambridge, 1989, pp. 7–24.

Sidnell, M., 'Another "death of tragedy": Louis MacNeice's translation of *Agamemnon* in the context of his work in the theatre', in M. Cropp, E. Fantham and S. E. Scully, eds., *Greek Tragedy and its Legacy: Essays Presented to D. J. Conacher*, Calgary, 1986, pp. 323–35.

Slater, N. W., *Plautus in Performance*, Princeton, 1985.

Smith, F. S., *The Classics in Translation: An Annotated Guide to the Best Translations of the Greek and Latin Classics into English*, London, 1930.

Snell, B., *The Discovery of the Mind: The Greek Origins of European Thought*, trans. T. G. Rosenmeyer, Oxford, 1953.

Snell-Hornby, M., *Translation Studies: An Integrated Approach*, Philadelphia, 1988.

    'Linguistic transcoding and cultural transfer? A critique of translation theory in Germany', in S. Bassnett and A. Lefevere, eds., *Translation, History and Culture*, London and New York, 1995, pp. 79–86.

    Z. Jettmarová and K. Kaindl, eds., *Translation as Intercultural Communication: Selected Papers from the EST Congress – Prague 1995*, Amsterdam and Philadelphia, 1997.

Sommerstein, A. H., 'On translating Aristophanes: ends and means', *Greece and Rome*, 20, 1973, pp. 140–54.

Spencer, C., 'Euripides goes to Brookside as Warner and Shaw bring out the worst in each other', *The Daily Telegraph*, 1 Feb 2001, p. 10.

Spitzbarth, A., *Untersuchungen zur Spieltechnik der griechischen Tragödie*, Zurich, 1946.

Stanford, W. B., *Greek Tragedy and the Emotions*, London, 1983.

Steiner, G., *The Death of Tragedy*, New York, 1961.

    After Babel: Aspects of Language and Translation, London, 1975; 2nd edn, Oxford, 1992.

    Antigones, Oxford, 1984.

Steiner, T. R., *English Translation Theory: 1650–1800*, Amsterdam and Assen, 1975.

Stoker, D., 'Greek tragedy with a happy ending: the publication of Robert Potter's translations of Aeschylus, Euripides and Sophocles', *Studies in Bibliography*, 46, 1993, pp. 282–302.

Stray, C. A., ed., *Classics in 19th and 20th Century Cambridge: Curriculum, Culture and Community*, Cambridge, 1999.

    Classics Transformed: Schools, Universities and Society in England, 1830–1960, Oxford, 1998.

Tabard, 'At last, Greek for the ordinary punter', *The Stage*, 16 March 1995, p. 12.

Tate, A., *The Translation of Poetry: A Lecture*, Washington, D.C., 1972.

Thaxter, J., 'Tragedy given urgent impact', *The Stage*, 19 Dec 1999, p. 12.

Thomas, G. E., 'A glancing eloquence: Heather Neill talks to Michael Frayn about his translation of Chekhov's "*Uncle Vanya*"', *The Times Educational Supplement*, 13 May 1988, p. 9.

Thorndike, S., 'The theatre and Gilbert Murray', in J. Smith and A. Toynbee, eds., *Gilbert Murray: An Unfinished Autobiography*, London, 1960.

Tolman, H. C., *The Art of Translating*, Boston, 1901.

Toury, G., *In Search of a Theory of Translation*, Tel Aviv, 1980.

Törnqvist, E., *Transposing Drama: Studies in Representations*, Basingstoke, 1991.

Trivedi, H., 'The politics of post-colonial translation', in A. K. Singh, ed., *Translation: Its Theory and Practice*, New Delhi, 1996.

and M. Mukherjee, eds., *Interrogating Post-colonialism: Theory, Text and Context*, Shimla, 1996.

Tytler, A. F., *Essay on the Principles of Translation*, Edinburgh, 1790; repr. Edinburgh, 1813.

Ubersfeld, A., *Lire le théâtre*, Paris, 1978.

Upton, C.-A., ed., *Moving Target: Theatre Translation and Cultural Relocation*, Manchester, 2000.

Vellacott, P., *Sophocles and Oedipus*, Ann Arbor, 1971.

Venuti, L., 'The translator's invisibility', *Criticism*, 28(2), 1986, pp. 179–211.

'Simpatico', *Sub-Stance*, 65, 1991, pp. 3–20.

The Translator's Invisibility: A History of Translation, London and New York, 1995.

Vitez, A., 'Le devoir du traduire', *Théâtre/public*, 44, 1982.

Vivis, A., 'The stages of translation', in D. Johnston, ed., *Stages of Translation*, Bath, 1996, pp. 35–44.

Waley, A., 'Notes on translation', *Delos*, 3, 1969, pp. 159–69.

Walsh, D. D., 'Poets betrayed by poets', in *Fact and Opinion*, 1974, pp. 140–4.

Walton, J. M., 'Revival: England', in Walton, *Living Greek Theatre: A Handbook of Classical Performance and Modern Production*, Westport, 1987, pp. 329–54.

The Greek Sense of Theatre: Tragedy Reviewed, 2nd edn, Amsterdam, 1996.

and P. D., Arnott, *Menander and the Making of Comedy*, Westport, 1996.

'Realising Menander: Get-in at the Getty', *Drama: Beiträge zum antiken Drama und seiner Rezeption*, Band 5, 1997, pp. 171–91.

'Ancient drama today: translation for translocation', *Fifth International Symposium on Ancient Greek Drama*, Nicosia, 1999, pp. 256–62.

' "Playing in the Dark": masks and Euripides' *Rhesus*', *Helios*, 27, no. 2, fall 2000, pp. 137–47.

'Page or stage: a response to Helene Foley', *Illinois Classical Studies*, 26, 2001, pp. 77–80.

'Hit or myth: the Greeks and Irish drama', in M. McDonald and J. M. Walton, eds., *Amid Our Troubles: Irish Versions of Greek Tragedy*, London, 2002, pp. 3–36.

Warren, R., *The Art of Translation: Voices from the Field*, Boston, 1989.

Weissbort, D., ed., *Translating Poetry: The Double Labyrinth*, Iowa City, 1989.

Welsh, A. M., 'Play's poetic punch grows weak', *Union-Tribune*, 15 Feb 2000, E-3.

Whistlecraft (John Hookham Frere), A review by 'W' of the first volume of the Mitchell translations of Aristophanes in *The Quarterly Review*, 23 July 1820;

repr. under Frere's name as the Introduction to *The Plays of Aristophanes*, London and New York (Everyman Library), 1911, pp. vii–xlii.

Wiles, D., 'Reading Greek tragedy', *Greece and Rome*, 34, 1987, pp. 136–51.

Greek Theatre Performance: An Introduction, Cambridge, 2000.

Willett, J., 'Creation myth', *New Statesman*, 24 Oct 1980, pp. 27–8.

Williams, W. E., ed., *The Reader's Guide*, Harmondsworth, 1960.

Winnington-Ingram, R. P., *Sophocles: An Interpretation*, Cambridge, 1980.

Wood, C., '*Iliad* with sex, and a plucked chicken', *The Times Higher*, 21–8 Dec 2001, p. 29.

Woolf, V., 'On not knowing Greek', in A. McNeillie, ed., *The Essays of Virginia Woolf*, vol. IV, *1925–1928*, London, 1994.

Worthen, W. B., 'Homeless words: Field Day and the politics of translation', *Modern Drama*, 38(1), spring 1995, pp. 22–41.

Wroe, N., 'Michael Frayn: a serious kind of joker', *The Guardian*, 14 Aug 1999, pp. 6–7.

Ydstie, J. T., ed., *Translating for the Theatre: In Honour of Nigel Chaffey*, Oslo, 1988.

Zagagi, N., *The Comedy of Menander*, London, 1994.

Zuber, O., ed., *The Languages of the Theatre: Problems in the Translation and Transposition of Drama*, Oxford, 1980.

'The translation of non-verbal signs in drama', in M. G. Rose, ed., *Translation: Agent of Communication*, Hamilton, NZ, 1980, pp. 61–74.

as Zuber-Skerritt, O., 'Translation science and drama translation', in Zuber-Skerritt, ed., *Page to Stage – Theatre as Translation*, Amsterdam, 1984, pp. 3–11.

Index of Translators

Translators listed in the Appendix are indexed here, rather than in the General index, for all references as well as for examples of their work within the main text.

General Index

Though plays are listed below individually by playwright, those looking for translations of a particular play should also consult the Appendix, both at Collections A and B and under the play's own title.